Arsenic in Drinking Water

Subcommittee on Arsenic in Drinking Water

Committee on Toxicology

Board on Environmental Studies and Toxicology

Commission on Life Sciences

National Research Council

NATIONAL ACADEMY PRESS
Washington, DC

ISBN: 1609101

NATIONAL ACADEMY PRESS • 2101 Constitution Ave., N.W. • Washington, D.C. 20418

NOTICE: The project that is the subject of this report was approved by the Governing Board of the National Research Council, whose members are drawn from the councils of the National Academy of Sciences, the National Academy of Engineering, and the Institute of Medicine. The members of the committee responsible for the report were chosen for their special competences and with regard for appropriate balance.

The National Academy of Sciences is a private, nonprofit, self-perpetuating society of distinguished scholars engaged in scientific and engineering research, dedicated to the furtherance of science and technology and to their use for the general welfare. Upon the authority of the charter granted to it by the Congress in 1863, the Academy has a mandate that requires it to advise the federal government on scientific and technical matters. Dr. Bruce Alberts is president of the National Academy of Sciences.

The National Academy of Engineering was established in 1964, under the charter of the National Academy of Sciences, as a parallel organization of outstanding engineers. It is autonomous in its administration and in the selection of its members, sharing with the National Academy of Sciences the responsibility for advising the federal government. The National Academy of Engineering also sponsors engineering programs aimed at meeting national needs, encourages education and research, and recognizes the superior achievements of engineers. Dr. William A. Wulf is president of the National Academy of Engineering.

The Institute of Medicine was established in 1970 by the National Academy of Sciences to secure the services of eminent members of appropriate professions in the examination of policy matters pertaining to the health of the public. The Institute acts under the responsibility given to the National Academy of Sciences by its congressional charter to be an adviser to the federal government and, upon its own initiative, to identify issues of medical care, research, and education. Dr. Kenneth I. Shine is president of the Institute of Medicine.

The National Research Council was organized by the National Academy of Sciences in 1916 to associate the broad community of science and technology with the Academy's purposes of furthering knowledge and advising the federal government. Functioning in accordance with general policies determined by the Academy, the Council has become the principal operating agency of both the National Academy of Sciences and the National Academy of Engineering in providing services to the government, the public, and the scientific and engineering communities. The Council is administered jointly by both Academies and the Institute of Medicine. Dr. Bruce M. Alberts and Dr. William A. Wulf are chairman and vice chairman, respectively, of the National Research Council.

This project was supported by Cooperative Agreement No. CX825107-01-0 between the National Academy of Sciences and the U.S. Environmental Protection Agency. Any opinions, findings, conclusions, or recommendations expressed in this publication are those of the author(s) and do not necessarily reflect the view of the organizations or agencies that provided support for this project.

Library of Congress Catalog Card Number 99-62141
International Standard Book Number 0-309-06333-7

Additional copies of this report are available from:

National Academy Press
2101 Constitution Ave., NW
Box 285
Washington, DC 20055
800-624-6242
202-334-3313 (in the Washington metropolitan area)
http://www.nap.edu

RA
1231
.A7
N38
1999

Printed in the United States of America
First Printing, June 1999
Second Printing, June 2000

SUBCOMMITTEE ON ARSENIC IN DRINKING WATER

ROBERT A. GOYER, *Chair*, (emeritus) University of Western Ontario, London, Ont., Canada

H. VASKEN APOSHIAN, University of Arizona, Tucson, Ariz.

KENNETH G. BROWN, Kenneth G. Brown, Inc., Chapel Hill, N.C.

KENNETH P. CANTOR, National Cancer Institute, Bethesda, Md.

GARY P. CARLSON, Purdue University, West Lafayette, Ind.

WILLIAM R. CULLEN, University of British Columbia, Vancouver, B.C., Canada

GEORGE P. DASTON, The Procter & Gamble Company, Cincinnati, Ohio

BRUCE A. FOWLER, University of Maryland Medical School, Baltimore, Md.

CURTIS D. KLAASSEN, University of Kansas Medical Center, Kansas City, Kans.

MICHAEL J. KOSNETT, University of Colorado Health Sciences Center, Denver, Colo.

WALTER MERTZ, (retired) Director of Beltsville Human Nutrition Research Center, Rockville, Md.

R. JULIAN PRESTON, Chemical Industry Institute of Toxicology, Research Triangle Park, N.C.

LOUISE M. RYAN, Harvard School of Public Health and Dana Farber Cancer Institute, Boston, Mass.

ALLAN H. SMITH, University of California, Berkeley, Calif.

MARIE E. VAHTER, Karolinska Institute, Stockholm, Sweden

JOHN K. WIENCKE, University of California, San Francisco, Calif.

Staff
CAROL A. MACZKA, Director, Toxicology and Risk Assessment Program
KULBIR S. BAKSHI, Program Director for the Committee on Toxicology
MARGARET E. MCVEY, Project Director (prior to January 1998)
RUTH E. CROSSGROVE, Editor
MIRSADA KARALIC-LONCAREVIC, Information Specialist
CATHERINE M. KUBIK, Senior Program Assistant
LUCY V. FUSCO, Project Assistant

Sponsor: U.S. Environmental Protection Agency

Other Reports of the
Board on Environmental Studies and Toxicology

Research Priorities for Airborne Particulate Matter: I. Immediate Priorities and a Long-Range Research Portfolio (1998)

Brucellosis in the Greater Yellowstone Area (1998)

The National Research Council's Committee on Toxicology: The First 50 Years (1997)

Toxicologic Assessment of the Army's Zinc Cadmium Sulfide Dispersion Tests (1997)

Carcinogens and Anticarcinogens in the Human Diet (1996)

Upstream: Salmon and Society in the Pacific Northwest (1996)

Science and the Endangered Species Act (1995)

Wetlands: Characteristics and Boundaries (1995)

Biologic Markers [Urinary Toxicology (1995), Immunotoxicology (1992), Neurotoxicology (1992), Pulmonary Toxicology (1989), Reproductive Toxicology (1989)]

Review of EPA's Environmental Monitoring and Assessment Program (3 reports, 1994-1995)

Science and Judgment in Risk Assessment (1994)

Ranking Hazardous Waste Sites for Remedial Action (1994)

Pesticides in the Diets of Infants and Children (1993)

Issues in Risk Assessment (1993)

Setting Priorities for Land Conservation (1993)

Protecting Visibility in National Parks and Wilderness Areas (1993)

Dolphins and the Tuna Industry (1992)

Hazardous Materials on the Public Lands (1992)

Science and the National Parks (1992)

Animals as Sentinels of Environmental Health Hazards (1991)

Assessment of the U.S. Outer Continental Shelf Environmental Studies Program, Volumes I-IV (1991-1993)

Human Exposure Assessment for Airborne Pollutants (1991)

Monitoring Human Tissues for Toxic Substances (1991)

Rethinking the Ozone Problem in Urban and Regional Air Pollution (1991)

Decline of the Sea Turtles (1990)

Copies of these reports may be ordered from
the National Academy Press
(800) 624-6242   (202) 334-3313
www.nap.edu

Preface

IN 1976 under the Safe Drinking Water Act, the U.S. Environmental Protection Agency (EPA) proposed an interim maximum contaminant level (MCL) for arsenic in drinking water of 50 micrograms per liter (μg/L) as part of the National Interim Primary Drinking Water Standards. That standard will apply until EPA adopts a new MCL. As part of a periodic review process, EPA has been reviewing data on arsenic exposure and toxicity to determine the adequacy of the 50-μg/L MCL for protecting public health. To ensure a solid and unbiased scientific basis for its arsenic standard for drinking water and surface waters, EPA requested that the National Research Council (NRC) review and comment on the arsenic toxicity data base and evaluate the scientific validity of EPA's 1988 risk assessment for arsenic in drinking water.

For this report, the Subcommittee on Arsenic in Drinking Water of the NRC's Committee on Toxicology reviewed EPA's characterization of existing human health risks from ingestion of arsenic found in drinking water and food; determined the adequacy of the current EPA MCL for protecting human health in the context of stated EPA policy; and identified priorities for research to fill data gaps. The subcommittee evaluated the Taiwanese epidemiological data for carcinogenic and noncarcinogenic health effects of arsenic exposure; compared effects of arsenic exposure demonstrated in other countries, including the United States, with those documented for Taiwanese populations; and reviewed data on toxicokinetics, metabolism, and mechanism and mode of action of arsenic to ascertain how these data could assist in assessing human health risks from arsenic exposures. In areas where the subcommittee concluded that EPA could improve the toxicity analysis and risk characterization, specific changes are recommended, and the implications of the changes for EPA's current MCL for arsenic are described in this report.

This report has been reviewed in draft form by individuals chosen for their diverse perspectives and technical expertise in accordance with procedures approved by the NRC's Report Review Committee for reviewing NRC and Institute of Medicine reports. The purpose of this independent review is to provide candid and critical comments that will assist the NRC in making the published report as sound as possible and to ensure that the report meets institutional standards for objectivity, evidence, and responsiveness to the study charge. The review comments and draft manuscript remain confidential to protect the integrity of the deliberative process. We wish to thank the following individuals, who are neither officials nor employees of the NRC, for their participation in the review of this report: Dean E. Carter, University of Arizona; Gerald F. Combs, Cornell University; K.S. Crump, Jr., Fred Hutchinson Cancer Research Center; John L. Emmerson of Portland, Oregon; Janet L. Greger, University of Wisconsin–Madison; Edward Harris, Texas A&M University; Ronald D. Hood, The University of Alabama; David A. Kalman, University of Washington; Karl T. Kelsey, Harvard School of Public Health; Harold H. Sandstead, University of Texas Medical Branch; Joyce S. Tsuji, Exponent; John E. Vanderveen of Rockville, Maryland; and Michael P. Waalkes, National Institute of Environmental Health Sciences.

The individuals listed above have provided many constructive comments and suggestions. It must be emphasized, however, that responsibility for the final content of this report rests entirely with the authoring subcommittee and the NRC.

The subcommittee gratefully acknowledges Charles Abernathy, Jeanette Wiltse, Herman Gibb, Denise Lewis, and David Thomas, all of the U.S. Environmental Protection Agency; Michael Bolger, U.S. Food and Drug Administration; Ruth Hund, American Water Works Association Research Foundation; Erik Olson and David Wallinga, Natural Resources Defense Council; Robert Fensterheim, Environmental Arsenic Council; Janice Yager, Electric Power Research Institute; Warner North, Decision Focus, Inc.; Raymond Grissom, Agency for Toxic Substances and Disease Registry; and Chien-Jen Chen, National Taiwan University; for providing background information or for making presentations to the subcommittee. In addition, Chris Le, University of Alberta, at the request of the subcommittee, contributed information on the collection and storage of urine samples for arsenic speciation. That information became an integral section of the report.

We are grateful for the assistance of the NRC staff for preparing the report. Staff members who contributed to this effort are Paul Gilman, former executive director of the Commission on Life Sciences; James J. Reisa, director of the Board on Environmental Studies and Toxicology; Carol A. Maczka, the project director, who coordinated and contributed to the preparation of the subcommittee's report; Margaret M. McVey, former project director; Ruth E. Crossgrove, editor; Mirsada Karalic-Loncarevic, information specialist; Lucy V. Fusco, project assistant; and Catherine M. Kubik, senior program assistant.

Finally, I would like to thank all the members of the subcommittee for their dedicated efforts throughout the development of this report.

Robert A. Goyer, M.D.
Chair, Subcommittee on
Arsenic in Drinking Water

Contents

EXECUTIVE SUMMARY   *1*

1 INTRODUCTION   *10*
   Background, *11*
   Scientific Controversies, *12*
   Organization of this Report, *13*
   References, *14*

2 THE U.S. ENVIRONMENTAL PROTECTION AGENCY'S 1988 RISK
   ASSESSMENT FOR ARSENIC   *16*
   Overview of the EPA 1988 Special Report, *16*
   EPA's 1988 Risk Assessment: 10 Years Later, *21*
   Summary, *24*
   References, *25*

3 CHEMISTRY AND ANALYSIS OF ARSENIC SPECIES IN WATER AND
   BIOLOGICAL MATERIALS   *27*
   Summary of Arsenic Compounds in Water and Food, *27*
   Relevant Chemical Considerations, *30*
   Analysis of Arsenic Compounds, *35*
   Arsenic in Water, *41*
   Arsenic in Food, *46*
   Arsenic in Urine, Blood, Hair, and Nails, *56*
   Summary and Conclusions, *66*
   Recommendations, *68*
   References, *68*

4 HEALTH EFFECTS OF ARSENIC   *83*

Cancer Effects, *83*
Noncancer Effects, *101*
Summary and Conclusions, *130*
Recommendations, *133*
References, *133*

5 DISPOSITION OF INORGANIC ARSENIC   *150*
Absorption, *150*
Biotransformation, *151*
Transportation, Distribution, and Elimination, *159*
Kinetic Model, *164*
Summary and Conclusions, *165*
Recommendations, *167*
References, *167*

6 BIOMARKERS OF ARSENIC EXPOSURE   *177*
Arsenic in Urine, *177*
Arsenic in Blood, *180*
Arsenic in Hair and Nails, *182*
Summary and Conclusions, *184*
Recommendations, *185*
References, *186*

7 MECHANISMS OF TOXICITY   *193*
Cancer Effects, *193*
Noncancer Effects, *207*
Summary and Conclusions, *213*
Recommendations, *214*
References, *215*

8 VARIATION IN HUMAN SENSITIVITY   *229*
Variation in Arsenic Metabolism, *229*
Nutritional Status, *235*
Summary and Conclusions, *243*
Recommendations, *244*
References, *244*

9 ESSENTIALITY AND THERAPEUTIC USES   *251*
Definition of Essentiality, *251*
Evidence for Essentiality, *252*
Therapeutic Uses of Arsenic, *257*
Summary and Conclusions, *259*

Recommendations, *260*
References, *260*

10 STATISTICAL ISSUES   *264*
A Review of Dose-Response Modeling and Risk
    Assessment, *265*
The EPA 1988 Analysis, *267*
Problems with Risk Assessment Based on Ecological
    Data, *269*
Internal-Cancer Data from Taiwan, *273*
Other Issues, *284*
Discussion, *290*
Summary and Conclusions, *293*
Recommendations, *295*
References, *296*

11 RISK CHARACTERIZATION   *299*
References, *301*

ADDENDUM TO CHAPTER 9   *302*

ADDENDUM TO CHAPTER 10   *307*

Arsenic in Drinking Water

Executive Summary

THE Safe Drinking Water Act (SDWA) directs the U.S. Environmental Protection Agency (EPA) to establish national standards for contaminants in public drinking-water supplies. Enforceable standards are to be set at concentrations at which no adverse health effects in humans are expected to occur and for which there are adequate margins of safety. Enforceable standards are standards that can be achieved with the use of the best technology available.

Arsenic is a naturally occurring element present in the environment in both inorganic and organic forms. Inorganic arsenic is considered to be the most toxic form of the element and is found in groundwater and surface water, as well as in many foods. A wide variety of adverse health effects, including skin and internal cancers and cardiovascular and neurological effects, have been attributed to chronic arsenic exposure, primarily from drinking water. EPA's interim maximum contaminant level (MCL) for arsenic in drinking water is 50 micrograms per liter (μg/L). Under the 1996 SDWA amendments, EPA is required to propose a standard (an MCL) for arsenic in drinking water by January 2000 and finalize it by January 2001.

THE CHARGE TO THE SUBCOMMITTEE

In 1996, EPA's Office of Water requested that the National Research Council (NRC) independently review the arsenic toxicity data base and evaluate the scientific validity of EPA's 1988 risk assessment for arsenic in drinking water. The NRC assigned this project to the Committee on Toxicology (COT), which convened the Subcommittee on Arsenic in Drinking Water, whose membership includes experts in toxicology, pharmacology, pathology, chemistry, nutrition, medicine, epidemiology, risk assessment, and biostatistics. The subcommittee was charged with the following tasks: (1) review

1

EPA's characterization of human health risks from ingestion of arsenic compounds found in food and drinking water and the uncertainties associated with that characterization; (2) review available data on cancer and noncancer health effects from exposure to arsenic compounds in drinking water and the implications of these effects on the assessment of the human health risks from arsenic exposure; (3) review data on the toxicokinetics, metabolism, and mechanism or mode of action of arsenic and ascertain how these data could assist in assessing human health risks from drinking-water exposures; and (4) identify research priorities to fill data gaps. EPA did not request, nor did the subcommittee endeavor to provide, a formal risk assessment for arsenic in drinking water.

THE SUBCOMMITTEE'S APPROACH TO ITS CHARGE

The subcommittee evaluated data relating to key elements of the risk-assessment process—hazard identification, dose response, and risk characterization—that addresses the protective nature of the current MCL. Specifically, the subcommittee reviewed information on the health effects of arsenic exposure and data on the disposition and the mechanism or mode of action of arsenic. The subcommittee also evaluated other information that could affect the risk assessment, such as variations in human susceptibility, and current capabilities to measure arsenic in various media, including biological tissues. The major conclusions and recommendations of the subcommittee in each of those areas are discussed in the remainder of this summary. The implications of these findings on the assessment of human health risk is provided below in the section on risk characterization.

THE SUBCOMMITTEE'S EVALUATION

Health Effects

The subcommittee concludes that there is sufficient evidence from human epidemiological studies in Taiwan, Chile, and Argentina that chronic ingestion of inorganic arsenic causes bladder and lung cancer, as well as skin cancer. With minor exceptions, epidemiological studies for cancer are based on populations exposed to arsenic concentrations in drinking water of at least several hundred micrograms per liter. Few data address the degree of cancer risk at lower concentrations of ingested arsenic. Noncancer effects resulting from chronic ingestion of inorganic arsenic have been detected at doses of 0.01 milligram per kilogram (mg/kg) and higher per day. Of the noncancer effects, cutaneous manifestations of exposure have been studied most widely. Developmental and reproductive effects resulting from chronic ingestion of inorganic arsenic have not been demonstrated in humans, although arsenic is known to pass through the placenta. Parenteral administration of inorganic and organic forms of arsenic are known to be teratogenic in a number of mammalian species, and oral administration affects fetal growth and prenatal viability. Arsenic has not been tested for essentiality in humans, nor has it been found to be required for any essential biochemical processes. Arsenic supplementation at very high concentrations (e.g., 350-4,500 nanograms per gram (ng/g)) in the diet has been shown to affect growth and reproduction in minipigs, chicks, goats, and rats.

Recommendations

Additional epidemiological evaluations are needed to characterize the dose-response relationship for arsenic-associated cancer and noncancer end points, especially at low doses. Such studies are of critical importance for improving the scientific validity of risk assessment. With respect to cancer, studies are recommended to refine the dose-response relationship between arsenic ingestion and cancer of the skin, bladder, and lung, and to investigate the effect of arsenic on cancer at other sites. With respect to noncancer effects, particular emphasis should be placed on epidemiological study of arsenic-associated cutaneous effects, cardiovascular and cerebrovascular disease, diabetes mellitus, and adverse reproductive outcomes.

Future studies on the beneficial effects of arsenic in experimental animals should carefully monitor the amount and speciation of arsenic in diets and water, use biomarkers to assess arsenic exposure and bioavailability, and use techniques that assess the toxicity and benefits of arsenic in a more specific manner than is possible through measurement of growth and reproductive success. In humans, the concentration of arsenic in total parenteral nutrition (TPN) should be determined by validated analytical methods and related to the health status of patients on long-term TPN.

Disposition (Absorption, Distribution, Metabolism, and Excretion)

In humans, inorganic arsenic is readily absorbed from the gastrointestinal tract and is primarily transported in the blood bound to sulfhydryl groups in proteins and low-molecular-weight compounds, such as amino acids and peptides. The half-life of arsenic in the body is about 4 days, and it is primarily excreted in the urine. Humans and some animals methylate inorganic arsenic to forms that are less acutely toxic and more readily excreted. However, the methylation process varies among animal species, making most animal models less suitable for studying the disposition of arsenic in humans. The methylation of ingested arsenic is not inhibited or overloaded, unless acute toxic doses are ingested. Substantial variations in the fractions of methylated forms of arsenic in urine are also known to occur among different populations and individuals within the same exposed population. Such variations might be indicative of genetic differences in the enzymes responsible for the methylation of arsenic. Methylation of arsenic might also be influenced by such factors as the arsenic species absorbed, high acute doses, nutrition, and disease. The extent to which variation in arsenic methylation affects its toxicity, including carcinogenicity, is not known.

Recommendations

Because of interspecies differences in the disposition of arsenic, more human studies are needed, including research using human tissues. Factors influencing the methylation, tissue retention, and excretion of arsenic in humans also need to be investigated.

Mechanism or Mode of Action

The mechanism or mode of action by which inorganic arsenic causes toxicity, including cancer, is not well established. In vivo studies in rats and mice to determine the ability of inorganic arsenic to act as a cocarcinogen or as a promoter have produced conflicting results. Studies on the arsenic metabolite, dimethylarsinate (DMA), suggest that it is not an initiator but might act as a promoter. However, those studies used very high doses, making interpretation of the results difficult, especially if DMA is formed in situ following the administration of inorganic arsenic.

The most accepted explanation for the mode of action for arsenic carcinogenicity is that it induces chromosomal abnormalities without interacting directly with DNA. These markers of tumor response would lead to a dose-response curve that exhibits sublinear characteristics at some undetermined region in the low-dose range, although linearity cannot be ruled out.

The mechanism of action by which arsenic induces noncancer effects is centered on its inhibitory effects on cellular respiration at the level of the mitochondrion. Hepatotoxicity is a major health effect related to decreased cellular respiration. Oxidative stress might also have an important role in both cancer and noncancer effects.

Recommendations

Identification of proximate markers of arsenic-induced cancers and their application in carefully designed epidemiological studies might better define the cancer dose-response curves at low concentrations. Molecular and cellular characterization of neoplasms from arsenic exposed populations and appropriate controls might aid in identifying the mechanism by which arsenic induces tumors. Chronic low-dose studies in a suitable animal model (mouse, hamster, or rabbit) might increase our understanding of the mode of action of arsenic carcinogenicity, particularly the potential role of chromosomal alterations.

A greater understanding is needed of the inter-relationships between arsenic's effects on cellular respiration and its effects on biochemical processes, including methylation, formation of reactive oxygen species, oxidative stress, and protein stress response.

Variation in Human Sensitivity

Human sensitivity to the toxic effects of inorganic arsenic exposure is likely to vary based on genetics, metabolism, diet, health status, sex, and other possible factors. These factors can have important implications in the assessment of risk from exposure to arsenic. A wider margin of safety might be needed when conducting risk assessments of arsenic because of variations in metabolism and sensitivity among individuals or groups. For example, people with reduced ability to methylate arsenic retain more arsenic in their bodies and may be more at risk for toxic effects. One study suggests that children have a lower arsenic-methylation efficiency than adults. Similarly, poor nutritional status might decrease the ability of an individual to methylate arsenic, resulting in increased arsenic concentrations in tissues and the development of toxic effects. There is some evidence from animal studies that low concentrations of S-adenosylmethionine, choline, or protein decrease arsenic methylation.

Recommendations

Factors that influence sensitivity to or expression of arsenic-associated cancer and noncancer effects need to be better characterized. Particular attention should be given to the extent of human variability and the reasons for it with respect to arsenic metabolism, tissue accumulation, and excretion (including total and relative amounts of urinary arsenic metabolites) under various conditions of exposure. Gene products responsible for metabolism, diet, and other environmental factors that might influence the susceptibility to or expression of arsenic-associated toxicity also need to be characterized in human studies and in suitable animal models. Potential differences between young children and adults in arsenic-methylation efficiency need to be validated and considered in any risk assessment of arsenic. Finally, quality-control data are needed to ensure that reported variations are not due to the analytical methods or procedures used. Standard reference materials are needed to analyze arsenic species in urine.

Other Considerations

Assessment of arsenic exposure via drinking water is often based on the measurements of arsenic concentrations in drinking water and assumptions regarding the amount of water consumed. Such data are estimates, the uncertainty of which will depend on the method used. The subcommittee evaluated various biomarkers (e.g., arsenic in urine, blood, hair, and nails) to measure the absorbed dose of inorganic arsenic and concluded that blood, hair, and nails are much less sensitive than urine as biomarkers of exposure. Specifically, the subcommittee concluded that the total concentration of inorganic arsenic and its metabolites in urine is a useful biomarker for both recent (previous day) and ongoing exposure. The concentration of urinary inorganic arsenic and its metabolites is less influenced by the consumption of seafood than is the total concentration of urinary arsenic. The concentration of arsenic in blood is a less-useful biomarker of continuous exposure because the half-life of arsenic in blood is short (approximately 1 hr), the concentration might be markedly affected by recent consumption of seafood, and it is difficult to speciate arsenic in blood. Measurements of arsenic in hair and nails have little use as biomarkers of absorbed dose, largely because of the difficulty in distinguishing between arsenic absorbed from ingestion and arsenic uptake in hair and nails from washing with contaminated water.

At present, the practical quantitation limit (PQL) for arsenic in water in most commercial and water utility laboratories is 4 μg/L. Measurement of total concentration of arsenic in drinking water is adequate for regulatory purposes.

Recommendations

More data are needed that tie biomarkers of absorbed arsenic dose (especially urinary concentrations of arsenic metabolites) to arsenic exposure concentrations, tissue concentrations, and the clinical evidence of arsenic toxicity. Data are particularly lacking for people living in different parts of the United States. Possible relationships between arsenic concentrations in urine, blood, hair, and nails need to be evaluated. In particular, the degree of external binding of arsenic to hair and nails should be examined.

There is a need for further development of analytical techniques to determine the chemical species of arsenic in various media—water, food, urine, and biological tissues. Quality-control data and certified standards for arsenic speciation are also needed.

RISK CHARACTERIZATION

In the context of its task, the subcommittee was asked to consider whether cancer or noncancer effects are likely to occur at the current MCL. No human studies of sufficient statistical power or scope have examined whether consumption of arsenic in drinking water at the current MCL results in an increased incidence of cancer or noncancer effects. Therefore, the subcommittee's characterization of risks at the current MCL is based on observed epidemiological findings, experimental data on the mode of action of arsenic, and available information on the variations in human susceptibility.

In the absence of a well-designed and well-conducted epidemiological study that includes individual exposure assessments, the subcommittee concluded that ecological studies from the arsenic endemic area of Taiwan provide the best available empirical human data for assessing the risks of arsenic-induced cancer. The cultural homogeneity of this region reduces concern about unmeasured confounders, although the potential for bias still exists due to considerable uncertainty about the exposure concentrations assigned to each village. Ecological studies in Chile and Argentina have observed risks of lung and bladder cancer of the same magnitude as those reported in the studies in Taiwan at comparable levels of exposure.

Information on the mode of action of arsenic and other available data that can help to determine the shape of the dose-response curve in the range of extrapolation are inconclusive and do not meet EPA's 1996 stated criteria for departure from the default assumption of linearity. Of the several modes of action that are considered most plausible, a sublinear dose-response curve in the low-dose range is predicted, although linearity cannot be ruled out. In vitro studies of the genotoxic effects of arsenic indicate that changes in cellular function related to plausible modes of carcinogenesis can occur at arsenic concentrations similar to the current MCL. However, the subcommittee believes that those data and the confidence with which they can be linked to arsenic-induced neoplasia are insufficient to determine the shape of the dose-response curve in the low-dose range (point of departure). The subcommittee also finds that existing scientific knowledge regarding the pattern of arsenic metabolism and disposition across this dose range does not establish the mechanisms that mitigate neoplastic effects.

Human susceptibility to adverse effects resulting from chronic exposure to inorganic arsenic is likely to vary based on genetics, nutrition, sex, and other possible factors. Some factors, such as poor nutrition and arsenic intake from food might affect assessment of risk in Taiwan or extrapolation of results in the United States.

The subcommittee also concludes that the choice of model for statistical analysis can have a major impact on estimated cancer risks at low-dose exposures, especially when the model accounts for age as well as concentration. Applying different statistical models to the Taiwanese male bladder-cancer data revealed that a more stable and reliable fit is provided by Poisson regression models that characterized the log relative risk as a linear function of exposure. The estimation of risk at low doses using those models is substantially higher than that using the multistage Weibull model. As an alternative to model-based estimates of risk, the subcommittee finds that the point-of-departure methods discussed in the 1996 draft EPA guidelines for cancer risk assessment give much more consistent low-dose estimates across a wide range of dose-response models. For male bladder cancer, a straight-line extrapolation from the 1% point of departure yielded a risk at the MCL of 1 to 1.5 per 1,000. Because some studies have shown that excess lung cancer deaths attributed to arsenic are 2-5 fold greater than the excess bladder cancer deaths, a similar approach for all cancers could easily result in a combined cancer risk on the order of 1 in 100.[1] It is also instructive to note that daily arsenic ingestion at the MCL provides a margin of exposure less than 10 from the point of departure for bladder cancer alone. The public health significance of daily ingestion of a given amount of arsenic in drinking water will be influenced by the background levels of arsenic consumed in food

Recommendations

On the basis of its review of epidemiological findings, experimental data on the mode of action of arsenic, and available information on the variations in human susceptibility, it is the subcommittee's consensus that the current

---

[1] Two of the 16 members of the subcommittee did not agree with the 1 in 100 estimate pending further analysis of the risk of lung cancer, as done for bladder cancer in Chapter 10.

EPA MCL for arsenic in drinking water of 50 µg/L does not achieve EPA's goal for public-health protection and, therefore, requires downward revision as promptly as possible.

To improve future risk characterizations, the following are recommended: Sensitivity analyses should be conducted to determine whether the results, including the way exposure concentrations are grouped together, are sensitive to the choice of model. The potential effect of measurement error and confounding on the dose-response curve and associated confidence limits should be further addressed.

To assist in the application of cancer data observed in different populations to cancer risks predicted for the United States, information on nutritional factors in study populations that pertains to susceptibility to arsenic-induced cancer should be investigated.

Modeling of epidemiological data should not be limited to the multistage Weibull model. Other models, including those which incorporate information from an appropriate control population, should be considered. The final risk value should be supported by a range of analyses over a broad range of feasible assumptions.

1

Introduction

THE U.S. Environmental Protection Agency (EPA) Office of Water is reviewing the interim maximum contaminant level (MCL) for arsenic in drinking water and is considering lowering the current level of 50 micrograms per liter (μg/L). The Safe Drinking Water Act (SDWA) Amendments of 1996 (PL 104-182) require that EPA propose a standard for arsenic by January 2000, and promulgate a final standard by January 2001. To meet those requirements, EPA's Office of Water requested that the National Research Council (NRC) review the arsenic toxicity data base and evaluate the scientific validity of EPA's 1988 risk assessment for arsenic in drinking water.

In response to EPA's request, the NRC assigned the project to the Committee on Toxicology (COT), which convened the Subcommittee on Arsenic in Drinking Water. Members of the subcommittee selected to serve have expertise in toxicology, pharmacology, pathology, chemistry, nutrition, medicine, epidemiology, risk assessment, and biostatistics. The specific tasks of the subcommittee were as follows: (1) review EPA's characterization of existing human health risks from ingestion of different compounds of arsenic found in drinking water and food and identify areas of major uncertainty in that characterization; (2) review the quantitative and qualitative evidence of human cancer and noncancer health effects from exposure to various forms of arsenic in drinking water and identify how that information would be relevant to a reassessment of human health risks from arsenic in drinking water; (3) review the data on the toxicokinetics, metabolism, and mechanism or mode of action of arsenic to ascertain how those data could assist in assessing human health risks from arsenic exposures; and (4) identify priorities for research to fill data gaps.

In this report, the subcommittee identifies the evidence that it considers relevant for determining the cancer risks to humans from exposure to arsenic and what inferences can be drawn from the evidence, including low-dose

10

extrapolation. The report also contains the subcommittee's review and critique of epidemiological studies on skin and internal cancers and other health effects in Taiwanese populations and in other studies in which exposure to arsenic in drinking water has been documented in other parts of the world. Although EPA's Office of Water considers inorganic arsenic the form of concern in drinking water, the subcommittee decided to evaluate whether organic arsenic compounds in drinking water also contribute substantially to health risks. The report contains the subcommittee's review of data on the metabolism, toxicokinetics, and mechanism of action of arsenic in humans and animals and evaluation of the implications of those data for estimating exposure-response relationships below the range of detectable responses in human epidemiological studies. The subcommittee also evaluates the implications of its findings for risks that might be associated with exposure to varying concentrations of arsenic in drinking water and states its assumptions about arsenic intake from food.

The remainder of this chapter is divided into three sections. The first provides a brief background of the current MCL for arsenic, the second outlines the scientific controversies associated with the arsenic MCL, and the third describes the organization of this report.

BACKGROUND

The current MCL of 50 µg/L has been the standard for arsenic in drinking water in the United States since 1942. In response to the 1974 SDWA, EPA adopted 50 µg/L as the interim standard for total arsenic in drinking water in 1975. Although the SDWA Amendments of 1986 required EPA to finalize its maximum contaminant level goal (MCLG) and enforceable MCL for arsenic by 1989, EPA has not yet finalized the MCLG or MCL for arsenic in part because of the scientific uncertainties and controversies associated with the chronic toxicity of arsenic.

The SDWA Amendments of 1996 required EPA to develop an arsenic research strategy within 180 days of enactment of the amendments. The EPA (1996a,b) strategy was reviewed by its Board of Scientific Counselors (EPA 1997), which encouraged EPA to propose an MCL by the year 2000 that "balances current scientific information on health risks with costs and other risk management factors," and then "establish a more definitive MCL by the year 2010, or earlier if feasible, based on results available from long-term studies."

SCIENTIFIC CONTROVERSIES

The scientific controversies surrounding the current MCL for arsenic primarily involve the carcinogenic potency of arsenic, which has been evaluated by several EPA or EPA-sponsored groups over the past 20 years, and to a lesser extent whether arsenic might be an essential nutrient. In 1968, Tseng and co-workers reported an association of arsenic in drinking water and skin cancer in a Taiwanese population. Based on those data, in 1984, EPA's Office of Research and Development estimated the potency of arsenic as a skin carcinogen in its health assessment document (HAD) for arsenic. The upper-bound estimate of potency suggested that the risk of skin cancer for individuals consuming 2 L of water with arsenic at 50 μg/L would be 2% (or 2/100). In 1988, EPA's Risk Assessment Forum published a special report reviewing the carcinogenicity of arsenic and the data suggesting that it might be an essential nutrient in birds and mammals. Using the same Taiwanese data, the forum estimated the risk of skin cancer associated with drinking 2 L of water containing arsenic at 50 μg/L on a daily basis over a lifetime to be 0.25% (or 2.5/1,000). Using the same risk-assessment assumptions to lower the estimated risk to 1/10,000, which is the upper bound of what EPA typically considers to be an "acceptable" risk, the forum concluded that the concentration of arsenic in drinking water would need to be lowered to 2 μg/L. In 1989, EPA's Scientific Advisory Board (SAB) recommended that the agency revise its arsenic risk assessment to consider possible detoxification mechanisms that might substantially reduce cancer risks at low exposure levels (EPA 1989). SAB also concluded that available data are inadequate to conclude that arsenic is an essential nutrient for humans.

Over the past two decades, there have been repeated calls by EPA (1988, 1991, 1992, 1996b), the NRC (1977, 1980, 1983, 1986), the Agency for Toxic Substances and Disease Registry (ATSDR 1993), and interest groups, such as the American Water Works Association Research Foundation (AWWARF 1995), for additional research on the health effects of exposure to arsenic. In 1983, the NRC Committee on Drinking Water and Health concluded in Volume 5 of its report that (1) "epidemiological studies on U.S. populations have failed to confirm the association between arsenic in drinking water and the incidence of cancer observed in Taiwan"; (2) 50 μg/L provides "a sufficient margin of safety," but that "further experimental research and epidemiological evaluations of the association of elevated levels of arsenic in drinking water and skin cancer be undertaken"; and (3) in the absence of new data, arsenic should be presumed an "essential" nutrient for humans on the basis of mammalian animal studies. In Volume 6, published in 1986, the committee stated that EPA should consider metabolism and pharmacokinetics in assessing the risks of carcinogenic substances in drinking water. Although epidemiological and experimental research on arsenic toxicity has continued, studies have largely identified the same data gaps.

Clearly, any reassessment of the potential health risks of arsenic in drinking water before the completion of the long-term studies proposed by EPA (or others) should focus on two developments over the past decade: (1) the epidemiological studies published during that time, and (2) data on arsenic metabolism and mechanisms of genotoxicity and carcinogenicity.

ORGANIZATION OF THIS REPORT

The remainder of this report is organized in 11 chapters and two addendums. Chapter 2 provides an overview of EPA's current risk assessment for arsenic in drinking water (EPA 1988); it identifies the major areas of uncertainty in the assessment and raises questions that the subcommittee will address in the remaining chapters. Chapter 3 provides the background on analytical methods for measuring arsenic in water, food, urine, blood, hair, and nails needed to evaluate the epidemiological and experimental studies of arsenic toxicity. In Chapter 4, the subcommittee reviews the known cancer and noncancer health effects of oral exposures to arsenic and evaluates the reliability of exposure estimates of the most sensitive effects. Chapter 5 provides an overview of what is known about the disposition of arsenic in humans and nonhuman mammals and the implications of that information for estimating health effects associated with low-level exposures. In Chapter 6, the subcommittee evaluates various biomarkers as meaningful measures of the absorbed dose of inorganic arsenic. Several proposed mechanisms or modes of action by which ingestion of arsenic might cause skin cancer, other cancers, and other noncancer health effects are reviewed in Chapter 7. Chapter 8 presents a discussion on the factors that influence variation in human sensitivity to arsenic, including genetic and nutritional factors and interactions with other micronutrients and environmental exposures. Chapter 9 reviews the evidence for the essentiality of arsenic as a nutrient for animals and humans and its therapeutic uses. Chapter 10 describes statistical issues that are important for interpretation of epidemiological studies and for any reassessment of human health risks from arsenic exposure. Chapter 11 discusses the adequacy of the current EPA MCLs and ambient-water-quality-criteria values for protecting human health. It should be noted that, with the exception of the term sublinear, the definitions for the terms linear, point of departure, nonlinear, and margin of exposure used throughout this report are consistent with EPA proposed guidelines (EPA 1996c). The term sublinear is used in this report but is not defined in the EPA proposed guidelines. For sublinear responses, the risk per unit dose increases with increasing dose. At exposures below the point of departure, the risk is lower when based on a sublinear curve rather than a linear curve.

REFERENCES

ATSDR (Agency for Toxic Substances and Disease Registry). 1993. Toxico-
    logical Profile for Arsenic. Rep. TP-92.02. U.S. Department of Health and
    Human Services, Agency for Toxic Substances and Disease Registry,
    Atlanta, Ga.
AWWARF (American Water Works Association Research Foundation). 1995.
    Research Needs Report: Arsenic in Drinking Water. Draft Report. Interna-
    tional Expert Workshop, T.D. Chinn, rapporteur; May 31–June 2, Ellicott
    City, Md.
EPA (U.S. Environmental Protection Agency). 1984. Health Assessment
    Document for Inorganic Arsenic. Final Report. EPA 600/8-83/021F. U.S.
    Environmental Protection Agency, Office of Health and Environmental
    Assessment, Environmental Criteria and Assessment Office, Cincinnati,
    Ohio.
EPA (U.S. Environmental Protection Agency). 1988. Special Report on
    Ingested Inorganic Arsenic: Skin Cancer; Nutritional Essentiality. EPA
    625/3-87/013. U.S. Environmental Protection Agency, Risk Assessment
    Forum, Washington, D.C.
EPA (U.S. Environmental Protection Agency). 1989. Science Advisory
    Board's Review of the Arsenic Issues Relating to the Phase II Proposed
    Regulations from the Office of Drinking Water. EPA-SAB-EHC-89-038.
    U.S. Environmental Protection Agency, Science Advisory Board, Washing-
    ton, D.C.
EPA (U.S. Environmental Protection Agency). 1991. Arsenic Research
    Recommendations — Report of the Ad Hoc Arsenic Research Recommen-
    dation Workgroup. U.S. Environmental Protection Agency, Health Effects
    Research Laboratory, Research Triangle Park, N.C.
EPA (U.S. Environmental Protection Agency). 1992. Review of Arsenic
    Research Recommendations — Review by the Drinking Water Committee
    of the Office of Research and Development's Arsenic Research Recom-
    mendations. EPA-SAB-DWC-92-018. U.S. Environmental Protection
    Agency, Science Advisory Board, Office of Drinking Water, Washington,
    D.C.
EPA (U.S. Environmental Protection Agency). 1996a. Research Plan for
    Arsenic in Drinking Water: Board of Scientific Counselors (BOSC)

Review Draft. U.S. Environmental Protection Agency, Office of Research and Development, Washington, D.C.

EPA (U.S. Environmental Protection Agency). 1996b. Workshop on Developing an Epidemiology Research Strategy for Arsenic in Drinking Water. U.S. Environmental Protection Agency, National Health and Environmental Effects Research Laboratory, Research Triangle Park, N.C.

EPA (U.S. Environmental Protection Agency). 1996c. Proposed guidelines for carcinogen risk assessment. Notice. Fed. Regist. 61(79):17959-18011.

EPA (U.S. Environmental Protection Agency). 1997. Peer review of EPA's Research Plan for Arsenic in Drinking Water. Draft Report. Ad Hoc Subcommittee on Arsenic Research, Board of Scientific Counselors (BOSC), Office of Research and Development, Washington, D.C.

NRC (National Research Council). 1977. Drinking Water and Health, Vol. 1. Washington, D.C.: National Academy Press.

NRC (National Research Council). 1980. Drinking Water and Health, Vol. 3. Washington, D.C.: National Academy Press.

NRC (National Research Council). 1983. Drinking Water and Health, Vol. 5. Washington, D.C.: National Academy Press.

NRC (National Research Council). 1986. Drinking Water and Health, Vol. 6. Washington, D.C.: National Academy Press.

Tseng, W.P., H.M. Chu, S.W. How, J.M. Fong, C.S. Lin, and S. Yeh. 1968. Prevalence of skin cancer in an endemic area of chronic arsenicism in Taiwan. J. Natl. Cancer Inst. 40:453-463.

2

The U.S. Environmental Protection Agency's 1988 Risk Assessment for Arsenic

THIS chapter provides an overview of the U.S. Environmental Protection Agency's (EPA's) 1988 risk assessment for arsenic and a discussion of what was done, how it was done, what issues were considered important, and how those issues were addressed. The risk assessment is then discussed in light of the events and information from the past 10 years that might affect its interpretation and utility.

OVERVIEW OF THE EPA 1988 SPECIAL REPORT

EPA's 1988 risk assessment for arsenic is a special report of the EPA Risk Assessment Forum. Its development was motivated by major scientific controversies within EPA surrounding the health effects of ingested arsenic. A Technical Panel on Arsenic was charged with preparing a report on the health effects of arsenic for agencywide concurrence and use. A draft of the report was peer reviewed externally at a workshop of experts, and many reviewer comments were incorporated into the final report. The designation "special report" was used to distinguish this report, which is limited to issues of skin cancer and nutritional essentiality, from the agency's comprehensive hazard-assessment documents. As described in the report, the forum "addresses many of the hazard identification, dose-response assessment, and risk characterization parameters called for in the cancer guidelines, but it does not fully assess or characterize arsenic risks for skin cancer nor does it analyze the other cancers associated with exposure to this element" (EPA 1988, p. 1).

There is general agreement that inhalation of inorganic arsenic is associated with increased lung-cancer risk and that available data are adequate to estimate the magnitude of the risk. The forum identified three sources of uncertainty and controversy, however, with respect to the assessment of risk from ingestion of arsenic (EPA 1988, p. 3): (1) Evidence of human carcinogenicity is primarily from epidemiological studies conducted in other countries, and its applicability to the U.S. population is uncertain. (2) The primary tumor response in those studies is skin cancer, which is more likely to be detected and successfully treated than many other forms of cancer. (3) Limited animal evidence suggests that arsenic might be an essential nutrient, raising the possibility that reducing the level of arsenic below some critical level (as yet unspecified) might result in a decrement of health in some way (as yet unknown).

The forum concluded that the epidemiological studies conducted in Taiwan on arsenic in drinking water (Tseng et al. 1968) and confirmatory studies (Albores et al. 1979; Cebrian et al. 1983) demonstrate that inorganic arsenic is a human carcinogen by the oral route (group A by EPA's classification scheme) (EPA 1988, p.3). The forum also concluded that the Taiwanese studies provide a reasonable basis for quantitative risk assessment of skin cancer in the United States, despite many uncertainties. Those two conclusions affirm the adequacy of the evidence to address the first two steps (i.e., hazard identification and dose-response assessment) of the four-step risk-assessment paradigm developed by the National Research Council (NRC 1983). EPA's group A classification for hazard identification does not refer to potency but to the strength of the evidence for human carcinogenicity. The result of the dose-response assessment is an estimated increase of U.S. lifetime skin-cancer risk of 3-7 x 10^{-5} $(\mu g/L)^{-1}$ (i.e., 3-7 additional cases of skin cancer per 100,000 persons for each microgram of inorganic arsenic per liter in the drinking water). The "3" and "7" are not statistical bounds, but the outcomes from data on females and males, respectively. A value of 5 x 10^{-5} $(\mu g/L)^{-1}$ has been used to estimate skin-cancer risk for both sexes in the United States. An implicit assumption in those values, which are a consequence of the methodology of EPA's risk-assessment guidelines, is that at low arsenic concentrations the risk of skin cancer increases linearly with the arsenic concentration in drinking water. The forum noted that assumption as a source of uncertainty, stating that the dose-response curve might be less than linear and might not pass through the origin. The forum pointed out, but did not explore in depth, epidemiological evidence of an association between inorganic arsenic and internal cancers (EPA 1988, Appendix C) and concluded that more studies are needed to determine if arsenic is a nutritional requirement in humans (EPA 1988, p. 40).

The remainder of this section examines each chapter of the special report to highlight what was done and how it was done, issues that were or were not resolved, and the remaining sources of uncertainty and possible data gaps.

The objective is to provide a baseline for considering the contributions of research in the past 10 years to current understanding of issues related to exposure and health effects of ingested inorganic arsenic. The discussion to follow is organized according to hazard identification, dose-response assessment, and nutritional essentiality of arsenic.

Hazard Identification

The EPA forum based its 1988 risk assessment on skin cancer as the health-effects end point. Evidence of an association between arsenic and cancer at internal sites (e.g., liver, kidney, lung, and bladder) had begun to appear in the literature, but the data needed to quantify risk were not yet available to EPA (1988, p. 11). Three studies were found suitable for quantification of skin-cancer risk. The primary study (called the "Tseng study") is a large cross-sectional prevalence survey conducted in a region of southwest Taiwan endemic to blackfoot disease (Tseng et al. 1968). The two supporting studies are a prevalence study conducted in the Region Lagunera of Mexico (Albores et al. 1979; Cebrian et al. 1983) and a retrospective study of clinical patients treated with a 1:1 dilution of Fowler's solution containing 3.8 grams (g) of arsenic per liter (Fierz 1965).

Strengths of the Tseng study noted in the report (EPA 1988, p. 16) are (1) the large size (40,421 exposed and 7,500 controls), (2) a statistically significant increase in skin cancer in the exposed population many years after first exposure, (3) a pronounced skin-cancer response by arsenic exposure level, (4) comparability of the exposed and control populations, aside from arsenic exposure, and (5) a high rate of pathological confirmation of observed skin cancer (over 70%). Important uncertainties identified in the Tseng study are (1) the possibility of confounding by other chemicals in the drinking water, (2) the lack of blinding of the examiners, and (3) the possibility that diet might be a risk modifier.

The forum studied the genotoxicity, metabolism, and pathology of arsenic in relation to the possible mechanism by which arsenic might induce carcinogenic effects but concluded that current knowledge was inadequate to be factored "with confidence" into the risk-assessment process (EPA 1988, p. 7). The interrelationships between various lesions of chronic arsenic poisoning and the progression of lesions were studied for their potential use in dose-response assessment, but the information was insufficient to develop a mechanistic model. Hyperpigmentation, a pathological hallmark of chronic arsenic exposure, was not considered an end point for dose-response assessment because it is not a malignant condition and does not appear to be a premalignant condition (EPA 1988, p. 19).

The weight of evidence from tests for mutagenicity is summarized in the report (p. 22), and possible genotoxicity mechanisms, such as interference with DNA synthesis or repair, are postulated. However, the genotoxicity mechanisms of arsenic were not sufficiently understood to incorporate them into a dose-response model formulation, although their importance was noted. Genotoxicity at low doses is an important indicator of irreversible change in genetic function. Such changes are a critical feature of many postulated mechanisms for chemical carcinogenesis and the basis for ascribing low-dose linearity to carcinogenic processes. Although the lack of genotoxic response does not preclude linearity at low doses, it is potentially important as a consideration in selecting a model for extrapolation of carcinogenic risk (EPA 1988, p. 23).

Metabolism and distribution are described (EPA 1988, p. 24) as important factors in evaluating the carcinogenic properties of arsenic, but the information was inadequate for use in dose-response assessment. The forum noted that methylation appears to be a means of detoxifying inorganic arsenic forms; compounds become less acutely toxic as methyl groups are added. At low intakes of arsenic, intake and excretion seem to be balanced, but at sufficiently high intakes, urinary excretion might be compromised, leading to increased tissue concentrations. There is also evidence that the methylating capacity of the body changes as a function of exposure, and maximal levels of excretion of methylated arsenicals are reached after weeks of exposure to the compound. Similarly, the ability to excrete the methylated arsenicals seems to be lost as a function of time after removal of arsenical exposure (EPA 1988, p. 25). In addition, diet might influence methylating capacity and, if so, might affect the reliability of results extrapolated from the Tseng study to the U.S. population. Thus, metabolism and distribution data are considered important for evaluating the carcinogenic properties of arsenic, but further study is needed (EPA 1988, p. 26).

Dose-Response Assessment

Lacking definitive data on genotoxicity, pathology, metabolism, and pharmacokinetics to help determine the shape of the dose-response curve, particularly at low doses, EPA used the multistage model to fit the data of the Tseng study and included a factor for duration of exposure. (That model is called the "generalized multistage model" in the report and is also commonly known as the "multistage Weibull model.") Using that model, the forum found that the estimated risk of skin cancer at low doses increased linearly with dose and stated that the estimate should be considered an "upper-bound estimate" because multiple hits or threshold considerations might apply. "The risk at low doses may be much lower than the current estimates, as low as zero, due to such factors as the metabolism or pharmacokinetics of arsenic" (EPA 1988, p. 28).

To test the model fit, it was used to predict the prevalence of skin cancer in Region Lagunera in Mexico (Cebrian et al. 1983). The prediction was judged consistent with the observed number, which was four. Similarly, model estimates were calculated for the patients given Fowler's solution in Germany, as reported by Fierz (1965). The number of observed skin cancers was judged "not inconsistent" with the model prediction (EPA 1988, p. 30).

The forum attempted to quantify two uncertainties in the dose-response evaluation: use of prevalence data in place of cumulative incidence data in the model, and the intake of arsenic from sources other than drinking water (e.g., food). An implicit assumption in the use of prevalence data is that mortality is the same in persons with skin cancer as in those without. Skin cancer can cause death, but mortality is not high. Of greater concern is the correlation of skin cancer with other diseases, such as blackfoot disease, that affect mortality. The net effect of the association of skin cancer with blackfoot disease and possibly other causes of death is an underestimation of the risk of skin cancer. Persons with blackfoot disease and skin cancer have a shorter life expectancy than do persons with skin cancer alone and thus were less likely to be included in the Tseng study. Under a reasonable set of assumptions, it was calculated that the dose-response relationship would be underestimated by up to 50% (EPA 1988, p. 31).

Information on the concentrations of inorganic arsenic in food was lacking, so the dietary intake from that source could not be calculated. The concern is that food items, principally rice and yams grown in arsenic-contaminated water and fish, might also have been a source of inorganic arsenic. It is noted that arsenic intake from sources other than the drinking water would overestimate the unit arsenic risk calculated from the Taiwan study (EPA 1988, p. 86). Some illustrative calculations are included on how the arsenic intake from food consumption could affect the risk estimate, using rice and sweet potatoes as an example.

In its summary discussion of the uncertainties, the forum repeated a precaution: "absent animal data or reliable human data under conditions of low exposure, the shape of the dose-response, if any, at low doses is uncertain" (EPA 1988, p. 31).

Nutritional Essentiality

Evidence of nutritional essentiality of trace amounts of inorganic arsenic would affect any interpretation of the health risks at low exposure levels. The report addressed two questions of uncertainty with respect to nutritional essentiality, one qualitative and the other quantitative. The qualitative question concerns whether inorganic arsenic is nutritionally essential in humans. Experimental studies with rats, chicks, minipigs, and goats have suggested the "plausibility" of essentiality (EPA 1988, p. 38). However, the published information was insufficient to determine the reproducibility of arsenic deficiency syndrome in those species, and a physiological role of arsenic or mechanism of action had not been identified. If arsenic is required in animals, the forum noted, then it is highly probable that it is also required in humans. Although somewhat academic if the essentiality of arsenic has not been established, the quantitative question concerns how essentiality would be incorporated into a risk assessment. Essentiality suggests that below a certain threshold, arsenic is not harmful but needed, and a quantitative value would be needed for implementation in dose-response assessment.

EPA'S 1988 RISK ASSESSMENT: 10 YEARS LATER

At the time of the 1988 EPA risk assessment and the preceding arsenic risk assessment (EPA 1984), the only source of dose-response data on skin cancer was from the Tseng study. EPA was aware of a mortality study on cancer at multiple internal sites conducted in the same region of Taiwan as the Tseng study (EPA 1988, p. 90), but dose-response data from that study were not published until 1988 (Chen et al. 1988). Currently, more detailed data are available for cancer at multiple internal sites in the "Chen study" than for skin cancer in the Tseng study. Thus, some choices, albeit limited, of data sets and end points are available for use in dose-response assessment, and additional studies might soon provide more choices. Subsequent to the 1988 EPA risk assessment, more detailed information has become available on the distribution of arsenic concentrations in well water used as a measurement of exposure in the Tseng study and the Chen study. Moreover, much more epidemiological and clinical evidence has been reported from other countries, and some advances have been made in understanding arsenic metabolism and the mode of action of arsenic carcinogenicity. These subjects are discussed in more detail in the following chapters. The remainder of this chapter focuses on the 1988 EPA risk assessment and the developments since 1988 that might affect its interpretation and current usefulness.

Data Limitations

As stated previously, the EPA forum based its risk assessment on the Tseng study. That study involved a house-to-house survey of 40,421 inhabitants of a southwestern region of Taiwan where artesian wells with a high arsenic concentration had been in use for at least 45 years. The study clearly established a dose-response relationship between arsenic in drinking water and the prevalence of skin cancer and, along with other confirmatory sources, provided ample evidence for EPA's classification of inorganic arsenic as a group A human carcinogen. EPA's dose-response assessment, however, which was also based on the Tseng data, deserves closer scrutiny.

The data limitations of the Tseng study for application to dose-response assessment are due to insufficient detail, at least as reported. The Tseng study, which contains only a summary of the study data, remains the single data source. Only the sex-specific and age-specific (20-year intervals) prevalence rates were reported for skin cancer (Tseng et al. 1968, Table 1). To associate those outcomes with arsenic exposure, other information in the article had to be used to estimate how the total number of persons at risk and the number of skin-cancer cases (by sex and age) were distributed over three broad exposure categories (low, 0-300 μg/L; medium, >300-600 μg/L; and high, $\geq$600 μg/L) plus an "undetermined category" as described below. The median value of arsenic well-water tests in each exposure range was then used by Tseng et al. (1968) as the representative arsenic concentration for dose-response assessment. (The effect of grouping data on dose-response assessment is addressed for bladder cancer in Chapter 10.)

Epidemiological data are desirable because they provide observations on humans instead of animals, but human exposures are seldom known precisely. Assumptions about exposure to arsenic are generally indicated in the forum's risk assessment. Briefly, each individual's rate of exposure to arsenic was treated as constant since birth. (Some temporal variability might occur in arsenic concentrations in wells (Tseng et al. 1968), in sources of drinking water or rates of consumption, or in dietary sources of arsenic.) Except for an unspecified number of villages assigned to an "undetermined" category, villages were assigned to a low-, medium-, or high- exposure category on the basis of the outcomes of tests for arsenic in village wells. (As described in Tseng et al. (1968), the undetermined category included those villages where either the artesian wells with arsenic-polluted water were not in use or the difference in the arsenic content in water from various artesian wells in the same village was so great that it was impossible to put them into the low, medium, or high category.) The health-effects data were then summarized across villages in each of the low-, medium-, and high-exposure categories; the undetermined category contained about 40% of the cancer cases. Thus, although over 40,000 people were personally examined in the field, the observations on health effects could only be associated with broad exposure categories.

For the dose-response assessment, the EPA forum assumed that the skin-cancer rates for the three exposure categories applied to median arsenic concentrations of 170 μg/L, 470 μg/L, and 800 μg/L, concentrations based on a histogram of all arsenic tests of well water for all villages combined. The actual well-water measurements were not reported for each of the villages.

Estimating Risk in the United States

The objective of the dose-response assessment was to estimate the risk of skin cancer at low concentrations of arsenic in drinking water in the United States. That was done in two steps: (1) estimation of risk at low arsenic concentrations in the observed Taiwanese population, and (2) extrapolation of that risk to the U.S. population by rescaling dose to account for differences between Taiwan and the United States in average body weight and average rate of consumption of drinking water. The first step was accomplished by fitting the multistage Weibull model to the Tseng data by maximum likelihood and then evaluating the fitted curve at a specified age and arsenic dose for an estimate of the prevalence of skin cancer at that age and dose. For the second step, the dose was rescaled to an equivalent arsenic intake (per unit of body weight per day) for a U.S. reference person (weighs 70 kilograms (kg) and drinks 2 L of water per day). U.S. Life Tables from the National Center for Health Statistics were used to convert prevalence estimates to estimates of lifetime risk of skin cancer.

The determinants of the outcome of the first step are the data and the choice of model fit to the data. As discussed above, the response data are highly summarized with limited knowledge of the correct representative doses. Aside from concern about data validity, however, data summarization can bias the shape of the estimated dose-response curve (see Chapter 10). The other determinant of the outcome of the first step, the choice of model, provides further reason for caution. The correct formulation of the model to fit to the data is unknown. It is not uncommon for several hypothesized models to fit observed data about equally well but to produce substantially different risk estimates at a low-dose exposure. As noted previously, the EPA dose-response assessment (using the data summarized in the low-, medium-, and high-exposure categories) predicts linearity at low dose—i.e., that excess risk of skin cancer increases proportional to rate of arsenic intake for a fixed number of years of exposure. More recently, an expert committee has reviewed the evidence on the mode or modes of action for arsenic and the implications for linearity or nonlinearity (see Chapter 7). Further studies on the metabolism of arsenic have found no evidence of a threshold (see Chapter 5).

With regard to the second step (extrapolation of risk from Taiwan to the United States), after rescaling for difference in body weight and consumption of water in Taiwan and the United States, EPA applied the dose-response assessment of arsenic in drinking water in Taiwan to estimate the risk of arsenic in drinking water in the United States. The contribution to arsenic intake from dietary sources could not be factored into the dose-response assessment for Taiwan or the extrapolation to the United States because of insufficient information on arsenic in food. Limited data on dietary arsenic intake in the blackfoot-disease region now available suggest that arsenic intake from food is higher in Taiwan than in the United States, although more data and improved quantification are needed for confirmation (see discussion of arsenic in food in Chapter 3 and evidence for essentiality and beneficial effects in Chapter 9). Ideally, the health effects from arsenic should be attributable to total intake from both food and drinking water, rather than drinking water alone. Consideration of arsenic in food might affect both the dose-response relationship for arsenic in drinking water in the study population of Taiwan and the implications for risk from arsenic in drinking water in the United States where dietary arsenic might differ from that in the study population in Taiwan (Brown and Abernathy 1997).

SUMMARY

EPA's 1988 risk assessment of ingestion of inorganic arsenic is described in this chapter. This special report of the EPA Risk Assessment Forum was limited to the issues of skin cancer and nutritional essentiality. Quantification of skin-cancer risk for hazard identification and dose-response assessment was based on three studies in humans. The primary study was the large prevalence study conducted in southwestern Taiwan (the Tseng study), where people were exposed to high concentrations of arsenic in drinking water. The two supporting studies were a prevalence study of persons exposed to arsenic in groundwater in Mexico and a study of clinical patients treated with arsenicals in Germany. The EPA 1988 report concluded that arsenic is a carcinogen by the oral route and estimated an increase of lifetime skin-cancer risk of 3-7 cases per 100,000 population for each microgram of inorganic arsenic per liter of drinking water. The report cautioned, however, that the risk at low doses could be much lower because of the pharmacokinetics of arsenic.

Since the EPA 1988 report, additional evidence has been found that reinforces the forum's conclusion that ingestion of inorganic arsenic causes skin cancer. Sufficient evidence has also been published to confirm that arsenic ingestion causes cancers more fatal than skin cancer, in particular, lung cancer and bladder cancer. The risk of those cancers warrant consideration and would add to risk of skin cancer. New information related to EPA's estimate of lifetime risk of skin cancer from arsenic, however, has added additional uncertainty to the sources used in the EPA report. In particular, it has been learned that arsenic exposure among persons and villages grouped together in the data reported in the Tseng study is more variable than previously realized. This variability might be largely accounted for by Tseng's creation of an undetermined category, but the specifics are unclear. Another concern is the need to consider arsenic intake from both food and water. Although recognized as a source of arsenic in the forum's report, dietary intake of arsenic in Taiwan and the United States was not sufficiently documented to be included in the 1988 risk assessment. Only sparse data are currently available, but estimates of lifetime risk of skin cancer from consumption of arsenic in drinking water show that estimates could be sensitive to differences in dietary intake of arsenic.

REFERENCES

Albores, A., M.E. Cebrian, I. Tellez, and B. Valdez. 1979. Comparative study of chronic hydroarsenicism in two rural communities in the Region Lagunra of Mexico. Bol. Oficina Sanit. Panam. 86:196-205.

Brown, K.G., and C.O. Abernathy. 1997. The Taiwan skin cancer risk analysis of inorganic arsenic ingestion: Effects of water consumption rates and food arsenic levels. Pp. 260-271 in Arsenic: Exposure and Health Effects, C.O. Abernathy, R.L. Calderon, and W.R. Chappell, eds. London: Chapman & Hall.

Brown, K.G., H.R. Guo, T.L. Kuo, and H.L. Greene. 1997. Skin cancer and inorganic arsenic: Uncertainty-status of risk. Risk Anal. 17:37-42.

Cebrian, M.E., A. Albores, M. Aguilar, and E. Blakely. 1983. Chronic arsenic poisoning in the north of Mexico. Hum. Toxicol. 2:121-133.

Chen, C.J., T.L. Kuo, and M..M. Wu. 1988. Arsenic and cancers [letter]. Lancet i(8582):414-415.

EPA (U.S. Environmental Protection Agency). 1984. Health Assessment Document for Inorganic Arsenic. Final Report. EPA 600/8-83-021F. U.S. Environmental Protection Agency, Office of Health and Environmental Assessment, Environmental Criteria and Assessment Office, Cincinnati, Ohio.

EPA (U.S. Environmental Protection Agency). 1988. Special Report on Ingested Inorganic Arsenic: Skin Cancer; Nutritional Essentiality. EPA 625/3-87/013. U.S. Environmental Protection Agency, Risk Assessment

Forum, Washington, D.C.

Fierz, U. 1965. Catamnestic investigations of the side effects of therapy of skin diseases with inorganic arsenic. Dermatologica 131:41-58.

NRC (National Research Council). 1983. Risk Assessment in the Federal Government: Managing the Process. Washington D.C.: National Academy Press.

Tseng, W.P., H.M. Chu, S.W. How, J.M. Fong, C.S. Lin, and S. Yeh. 1968. Prevalence of skin cancer in an endemic area of chronic arsenicism in Taiwan. J. Natl. Cancer Inst. 40:453-63.

3

Chemistry and Analysis of Arsenic Species in Water, Food, Urine, Blood, Hair, and Nails

IN this chapter, the subcommittee describes the chemistry of arsenic and its analysis in water and biological materials. The chapter is divided into four sections. The first section, Arsenic Compounds in Water and Food, provides the reader with general information on the various arsenic species that are now known to be present in food and water and that could be of concern in assessing normal human exposure (i.e., nonoccupational exposure) to arsenic. However, it should be emphasized that many unidentified arsenic species are probably present in the environment, including many in living organisms. It is not an easy task to detect and identify low concentrations of arsenicals, and methods to do so have been developed only in recent years.

The second section, Relevant Chemical Considerations, provides a brief account of arsenic's chemistry that is relevant to considerations of toxicity and carcinogenicity. In the third section, Analysis of Arsenic Compounds, general methods that have been used to analyze arsenic and its species are outlined. The results of applying these methods to the analysis of water and food, respectively, are presented in the sections Arsenic in Water and Arsenic in Food. A separate section discusses the application of these methods to the analysis of arsenic in urine, blood, hair, and nails.

SUMMARY OF ARSENIC COMPOUNDS IN WATER AND FOOD

Table 3-1 lists the most important arsenic compounds and species known to be present in water and food consumed by humans. The identified compounds that are not listed are (1) the volatile arsines Me_xAsH_{3-x}

TABLE 3-1 Some Arsenic Compounds and Species Known to be Present in Water and Food Consumed by Humans

Name	Abbreviation	Chemical Formula
Arsenous acid	As(III)	H_3AsO_3
Arsenic acid	As(V)	H_3AsO_4
Oxythioarsenic acid		H_3AsO_3S
Monomethylarsonic acid	MMA	$CH_3AsO(OH)_2$
Methylarsonous acid	MMA(III)	$CH_3As(OH)_2[CH_3AsO]_n$
Dimethylarsinic acid	DMA	$(CH_3)_2AsO(OH)$
Dimethylarsinous acid	DMA(III)	$(CH_3)_2AsOH[((CH_3)_2As)_2O]$
Trimethylarsine	TMA	$(CH_3)_3As$
Trimethylarsine oxide	TMAO	$(CH_3)_3AsO$
Tetramethylarsonium ion	Me_4As^+	$(CH_3)_4As^+$
Arsenocholine	AsC	$(CH_3)_3As^+CH_2CH_2OH$
Arsenobetaine	AsB	$(CH_3)_3As^+CH_2COO^-$
Arsenic-containing ribo-sides	Arsenosugar X-XV[a] Arsenolipid[b]	

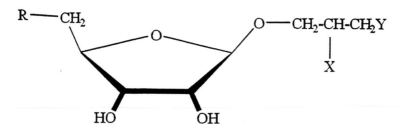

[a]Arsenosugar

	R	X	Y
X	$(CH_3)_2As(O)-$	-OH	-OH
XI	$(CH_3)_2As(O)-$	-OH	$-OPO_3HCH_2CH(OH)CH_2OH$
XII	$(CH_3)_2As(O)-$	-OH	$-SO_3H$
XIII	$(CH_3)_2As(O)-$	-OH	$-OSO_3H$
XIV	$(CH_3)_2As(O)-$	$-NH_2$	$-SO_3H$
XV	$(CH_3)_3As^+-$	-OH	$-OSO_3H$

[b]Arsenolipid

	R	X	Y
	$(CH_3)_2AsO-$	-OH	$-OPO_3HCH_2CH(OPalm)CH_2OPalm$

(Me=CH$_3$, x = 0-3) produced naturally by the action of microorganisms on available arsenicals (Cullen and Reimer 1989); (2) the ethylmethylarsines Et$_x$AsMe$_{3-x}$ (Et=C$_2$H$_5$, x = 1-3) found in natural gas (Irgolic et al. 1991); (3) phenylarsonic acid, C$_6$H$_5$AsO(OH)$_2$, found in shale oil and retort water (Fish et al. 1982); and (4) the undoubtedly numerous arsenicals not yet discovered.

The structures of the arylarsenicals that are approved as animal-food additives are shown in Figure 3-1. 4-Hydroxy-3-nitrophenylarsonic acid (3-NHPAA) and p-arsanilic acid (p-ASA) are approved for poultry and swine. 4-Nitrophenylarsonic acid (4-NPAA) and p-ureidophenylarsonic acid (p-UPAA) are approved only for controlling blackhead disease in turkeys (Ledet and Buck 1978; Adams et al. 1994). Melarsoprol, a related arylarsenical, is still the drug of choice for treating secondary trypanosomiasis in humans in rural Africa (Berger and Fairlamb 1994).

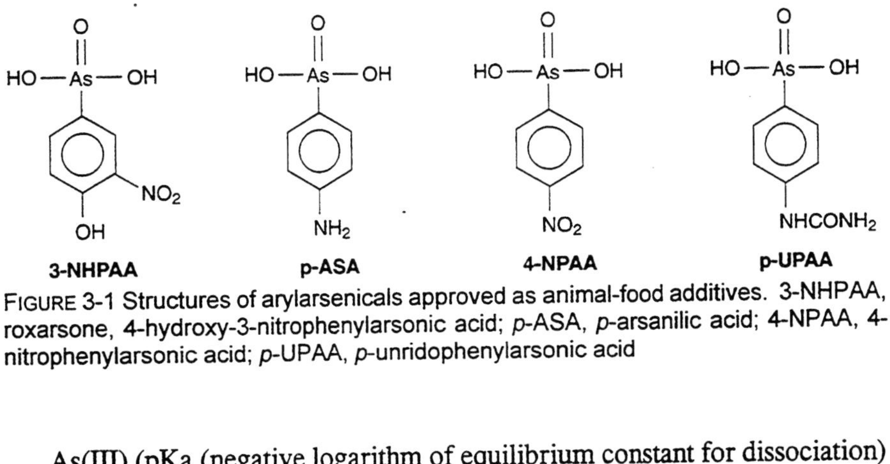

FIGURE 3-1 Structures of arylarsenicals approved as animal-food additives. 3-NHPAA, roxarsone, 4-hydroxy-3-nitrophenylarsonic acid; p-ASA, p-arsanilic acid; 4-NPAA, 4-nitrophenylarsonic acid; p-UPAA, p-unridophenylarsonic acid

As(III) (pKa (negative logarithm of equilibrium constant for dissociation) = 9.23, 12.13, 13.4), As(V) (pKa = 2.22, 6.98, 11.53), MMA (pKa = 4.1, 8.7), DMA (pKa = 6.2), TMA, and TMAO are usually associated with the terrestrial environment, As(III) and As(V) being dominant in water. Unidentified species ("hidden species" not detected by using hydride generation; see section Hidden Arsenic Species), however, can reach up to 22% of total arsenic in river water (Sturgeon et al. 1989), and methylarsenicals can reach up to 59% of total arsenic in lake water (Anderson and Burland 1991). The recent discoveries of AsB, AsC, and Me$_4$As$^+$ in mushrooms (Byrne et al. 1995; Kuehnelt et al. 1997a,b); arsenosugar X in algae (Lai et al. 1997); and oxythioarsenic acid and methylarsenic(III) species MMA(III) and DMA(III) in water (Bright et al. 1994; Hasegawa 1996, 1997; Schwedt and Reickoff 1996a,b) extend the range of identified species.

In the marine environment, all the compounds shown in Table 3-1, except

the oxythioarsenate, have been identified. The most important arsenic compounds in seawater are the inorganic species As(III) and As(V). Those species
are usually associated with much lower concentrations of DMA and MMA.
In fish, the principal arsenic species is AsB, which is regarded as being
ubiquitous. The telost fish Silver Drummer, however, does not contain any
AsB, and its principal arsenic species is TMAO (Edmonds et al. 1997). Small
amounts of AsC, DMA, MMA, As(V), TMAO, Me_4As^+, and arsenosugars
also are found in marine animals (e.g., Larsen et al. 1993a), although the last
two arsenic species can be important in some bivalves. High concentrations
of unknown arsenicals have been identified in the abalone (Edmonds et al.
1997). Marine algae contain arsenosugars, principally X-XIII, and 15 arsenosugars have been identified to date. In addition, marine algae contain small
amounts of inorganic arsenic and DMA (Francesconi and Edmonds 1997).
High concentrations of inorganic arsenic (38-61% of total arsenic) are found
in some marine algae, notably *Sargassum muticum* and *Hizikia fusiforme*
(Morita and Shibata 1990; Francesconi and Edmonds 1997). The arsenolipid
(Table 3-1) is a minor component of the brown alga *Undaria pinnatifida*, an
edible seaweed known as Wakame (Shibata et al. 1992), but lipid-soluble
arsenicals can reach high concentrations in some species.

RELEVANT CHEMICAL CONSIDERATIONS

Is Arsenic Similar to Phosphorus?

Arsenic is situated in the Periodic Table in Group 15 (old Group V) below
nitrogen and phosphorus. The oxidation state of arsenic in compounds found
in the environment is either III or V (Table 3-1), and much of the chemistry
of those compounds results from the easy conversion between those two states.
The two-electron reduction of arsenate As(V) to arsenite As(III) is favored in
acidic solution (E° (standard reduction potential) = 0.56 volts), whereas the
reverse is true in basic solution (E° = -0.67 volts) (Latimer and Hildebrand
1951). In contrast, phosphorus(V) compounds are difficult to reduce.

Another major difference between arsenic and phosphorus is the stability
of the esters of phosphoric acid to hydrolysis, allowing the existence of, for
example, DNA and adenosine 5'-triphosphate (ATP). Esters of As(V) acids
are easily hydrolyzed; the half-life in neutral pH is about 30 min. If As(V)-
OR has a good leaving group such as -P(V) or C(O)R', the half-life falls to
seconds. Enzymes can accept arsenate to incorporate into other compounds,
such as ATP, but the analogues formed hydrolyze immediately. Thus, arsenate uncouples oxidative metabolism from ATP biosynthesis. That phenome-

non is believed to account for some of the toxicity of arsenate (Dixon 1997; see Chapter 7).

Many As(III) compounds are formulated as RAsX or $(R_2As)_2X$ (X = 0, S). In the solid state, some of those compounds can be polymeric (e.g., $(CH_3AsO)_3$ and $(CH_3AsS)_3$), but $CH_3As(OH)_2$ and $(CH_3)_2AsOH$ seem to exist in dilute aqueous solution (Hasegawa 1996, 1997).

Affinity of Arsenic for Sulfur

The affinity of arsenic for sulfur is revealed in any list of natural arsenic-containing minerals. Many are sulfides and include As_4S_4 (realgar), As_4S_6 (orpiment), and FeAsS (arsenical pyrites, mispickel). That affinity also has been invoked to account for the toxicity of As(III) compounds through the interaction with protein thiols, as shown in Equation 3-1 in Figure 3-2 (see also Chapter 7). Such binding to proteins might inhibit the function of such enzymes as pyruvate dehydrogenase and 2-oxoglutarate dehydrogenase (Knowles and Benson 1983a,b; Dixon 1997).

Equation 3-1

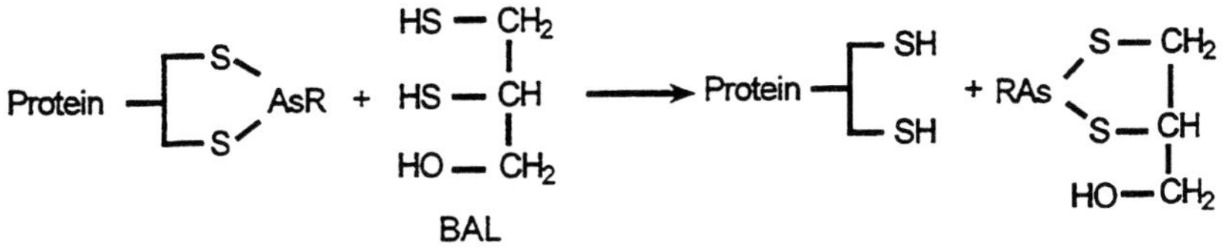

Equation 3-2

FIGURE 3-2 Affinity of arsenic for sulfur. BAL, British Anti-Lewisite (dimercaprol).

The action of dimercaprol, British Anti-Lewisite (BAL), in aiding the elimination of arsenic species from humans, is believed to result from the displacement of bound arsenic from a protein because of the formation of a more stable complex (Equation 3-2). However that action does not necessarily mean that the initial postulate of Equation 3-1 is correct. Binding of the arsenic to BAL could restore the function of an enzyme regardless of how the arsenic was originally bound. Li and Pickart (1995) pointed out that little evidence supports the proposal that the binding of As(III) compounds to enzymes is solely or even predominantly that represented in Equation 3-1. Li and Pickart (1995) found that the binding of phenylarsenoxide, $(C_6H_5AsO)_n$, (which is possibly $C_6H_5As(OH)_2$ in dilute aqueous solution) to Arg [Arginine]-tRNA protein transferase does not involve vicinal thiols. However, Cys [Cysteine]-31 and Cys-184 seem to be implicated in lecithin-cholesterolacyl transferase (Jauhiainen et al. 1988).

The reduction of As(V) compounds by thiols has been well documented (Cullen et al. 1984), but sulfhydryl groups in enzymes do not always affect the reduction (Dixon 1997), presumably because this reductive interaction with sulfhydryl groups requires that more than one sulfhydryl group reach the same arsenic atom (i.e., reduction is a two-electron process).

The As(III)-sulfur bond is much more resistant to hydrolysis than the As(III)-oxygen moiety (Sagan et al. 1972; Zingaro and Thomson 1973).

Biomethylation of Arsenic

Endogenous thiols probably play a critical role in the metabolic conversion of As(III) and As(V) species. It is likely that glutathione (GSH) acts as a reducing agent for As(V) species; the resulting As(III) species can then accept a methyl group from S-adenosylmethionine (SAM) to produce the methyl-arsenic(V) species in an oxidative-addition reaction, as illustrated in Figure 3-3 (Cullen and Reimer 1989). This cycle of reduction followed by oxidative addition of a methyl group can be continued, and the end product seems to depend on the organism. This cycle is based on the pioneering studies of Challenger (1951). The end products can be trimethylarsine oxide or tri-methylarsine for fungi, the tetramethylarsonium ion for clams, and probably DMA for humans (Cullen and Reimer 1989; Cullen et al. 1994) (see Chapter 5).

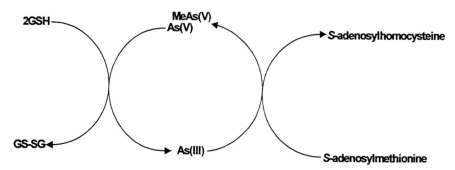

FIGURE 3-3 Biomethylation of arsenic: SAM as methyldonor, GSH as reducing agent. GSH, glutathione.

SAM is probably the source of the adenosyl group that is found in the arsenosugars (Francesconi and Edmonds 1997). The As(III) derivatives seem to have the unique ability to accept all three groups that are attached to sulfur in SAM, as illustrated in Figure 3-4.

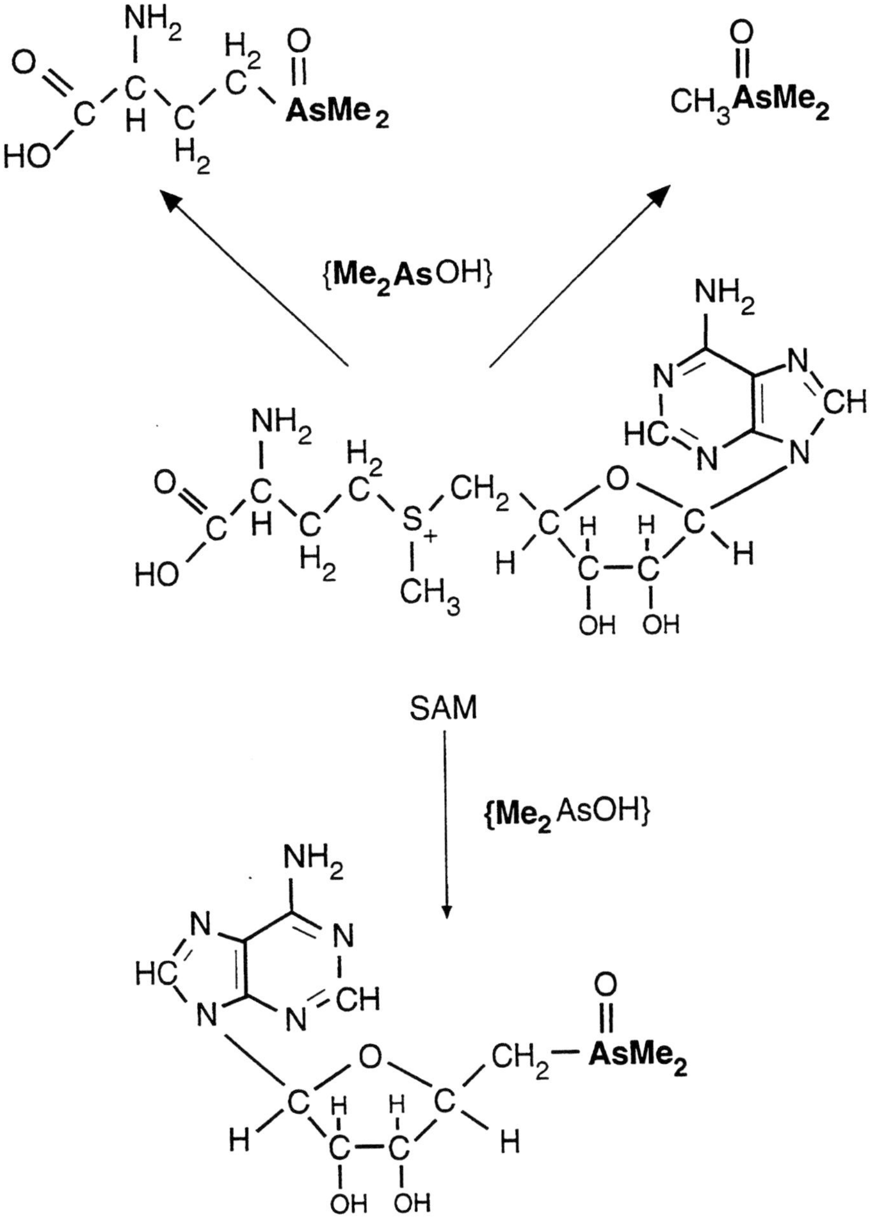

FIGURE 3-4 Reaction of As(III) derivatives with SAM. SAM, S-adenosylemthionine.

The As(III) species that are intermediates in the biotransformation of arsenic might well be toxic (Hocking and Jaffer 1969; Sheridan et al. 1973; Cullen et al. 1989b) (see Chapter 7). For example, glutathione reductase (GR) is a key enzyme in the metabolism of GSH and is inhibited by the methylarsenic(III) and As(III) species (Delnomdedieu et al. 1994). The action of GR is critical in maintaining the redox status of cells.

Some Geochemical Considerations: Absorption and Redox

As(III) exists in most natural water as As(OH)$_3$ (pKa = 9.2) and is more mobile than As(V) because it is less strongly absorbed on most mineral surfaces than the negatively charged As(V) oxyanions (H$_3$AsO$_4$; pKa = 2.22, 6.98, 11.53). Iron(III) oxy species are well known to have a high affinity for As(V) (Waychunas et al. 1993; Lumsdon et al. 1984), and As(III) also seems to be adsorbed on some iron(III) surfaces (Sun and Doner 1996).

Little is known about the adsorption of As(III) on the terrestrially abundant aluminum oxides and aluminosilicate minerals. Activated alumina has a twofold higher affinity for As(V) than for As(III) at pH 7 (Ghosh and Yuan 1987); negligible removal of As(III) from drinking water is achieved by coagulation with alum (Hering et al. 1997). Kaolinite and montmorillonite also have higher affinities for As(V) than for As(III) (Frost and Griffin 1977). Abiotic oxidation of As(III) is enhanced in the presence of the clay minerals kaolinite and illite, a process that results in strongly bound As(V) species (Manning and Goldberg 1997; Scott and Morgan 1995). Thus, long-term modeling of arsenic mobility in soils and aquifers must consider the effects of pH and mineral conditions, which will influence both adsorption and abiotic oxidation of As(III).

Little is known about the adsorption behavior of the organic arsenic species listed in Table 3-1 in spite of the use of the methylarsenicals MMA and DMA and their salts as pesticides, herbicides, and defoliants (Vallee 1973; Nriagu and Azcue 1990).

Microbial Activity and Arsenic Mobilization

Direct microbial reduction of arsenate to the more mobile arsenite is known for bacterial, algal, and fungal species (Cullen and Reimer 1989; Silver et al. 1993; Diorio et al. 1995). Microbial activity has been implicated in arsenic mobilization from sediments. Iron-reducing bacteria might cause arsenate dissociation from sediment that is solid as a consequence of iron oxide dissolution (Lovley et al. 1991). Sulfate-reducing bacteria produce hydrogen sulfide, which might promote arsenate reduction. In recent years, some arsenate-respiring bacteria have been isolated; those include the dissimilatory arsenate-reducer strain MIT-13 (Ahmann et al. 1994) and *Chrysiogenes arsenatis* native to gold-mine waters (Macy et al. 1996).

Ahmann et al. (1997) showed that arsenic-rich anoxic sediments from the Halls Brook storage area are mobilized by native microbial activity. In particular, strain MIT-13 is likely to catalyze that activity. In related experiments, Ahmann et al. (1997) found that microbial activity catalyzed rapid dissolution of arsenic, as As(III), from Fe(II) and Fe(III) arsenates.

Free Radical and Peroxy Species

It has been suggested that the observed tumor promotional activity of DMA might be due to the action of active oxygen-containing species, such as the dimethylarsenic peroxyl radical $(CH_3)_2As$-O-O (Rin et al. 1995; Yamanaka et al. 1996) (see Chapter 7). In fact, not much is known about peroxy species of arsenic, but the proposed As(III) species does not seem to be a plausible entity. Phenylarsonic acid, $C_6H_5AsO(OH)_2$, can act as an oxygen-transfer agent by reacting with peroxide to form the intermediate peroxy acid $C_6H_5AsO(OH)(OOH)$ (Jacobson et al. 1979a,b). One compound that was formulated as $(CH_3)_2As$-S-S-As$(CH_3)_2$, close in structure to the proposed peroxyl radical, turned out to have the structure $(CH_3)_2As(S)$-S-As$(CH_3)_2$, which has arsenic in two oxidation states (Camerman and Trotter 1964). On that basis and because of the ease of oxidation of DMA(III), $(CH_3)_2As(O)$-O or even $(CH_3)_2As(O)$-O-O might be more likely candidates for active oxygen-containing species. Related antimony peroxy species have been isolated and characterized (Dodd et al. 1992).

ANALYSIS OF ARSENIC COMPOUNDS

The discovery by Scheele in 1775 that arsenic compounds could react under reducing conditions to produce a volatile gas, arsine (AsH_3) (Partington 1962), provided a tool to counteract the use of arsenic, usually as the oxide As_2O_3, for homicide; that use had reached epidemic proportions during the Middle Ages. The discovery led to the development of the Marsh test for arsenic, in which arsine is volatalized out of the reaction mixture and is detected, for example, by decomposition to an arsenic mirror. Alternatively, in the Gutzeit modification, the arsine is brought into contact with a filter paper soaked with either silver nitrate or mercuric halide to produce a colored deposit. Both procedures can be made semiquantitative. They are the first applications of an analytical method now referred to as "hydride generation" that is widely applicable to the analysis of elements that form volatile hydrides when treated with an appropriate reducing agent, usually sodium borohydride (Vallee 1973).

In older studies, zinc and hydrochloric acid were used as reducing agents. The Gutzeit method was used in a recently published Japanese study (Tsuda et al. 1995) in which well water was found to contain arsenic in the parts-per-million range—the measurements were made in 1959. A variation of this method, Natelson's method (Natelson 1961), was used in the early study of arsenic in the well water of Taiwan (Tseng et al. 1968). That method uses colorimetric detection and is said to detect arsenic at $40\,\mu g/L$. Arsine produced from arsenate and arsenite is sometimes reacted with silver diethyldithiocarbamate solution to produce a red solution of undetermined chemical nature that can be measured colorimetrically (Vallee 1973; Irgolic 1994; see also Table 3-3). The colorimetric method is easy to use, is inexpensive in terms of equipment and operator costs, and is commonly used by the water-supply industry. For example, Saha (1995) used the colorimetric method for his work on the wells of Bengal, and the method was used in the Lane County, Oregon, study (Morton et al. 1976); however, it has limitations with regard to sensitivity and arsenic speciation.

Total-arsenic determination commonly involves oxidation of the sample, by using digestion or ashing, with a mixture of chemicals, including HNO_3-H_2SO_4-H_2O_2 or HNO_3-H_2SO_4-$HClO_4$ for wet digestion and MgO-$MgNO_3$ for dry ashing (Irgolic et al. 1995). The arsenic is then determined by using one of a number of methods ranging from hydride generation (colorimetric or spectroscopic detection or neutron activation) to spectrophotometry (e.g., graphite-furnace atomic absorption (GFAA) or inductively coupled plasma-atomic emission spectrometry (ICP-AES)).

Hydride Generation with Speciation

The commonly used hydride-generation method that is currently applied to the determination of arsenic species is outlined in Figure 3-5. Volatile arsines are produced from a range of inorganic and methylarsenicals in both oxidation states. The four arsines, AsH_3 and Me_xAsH_{3-x} ($x = 1$-3) are produced from their appropriate precursors and are then quantified following separation if necessary. Bramen and Foreback (1973) and Andreae (1977) were among the first to use this method for arsenic speciation in natural systems.

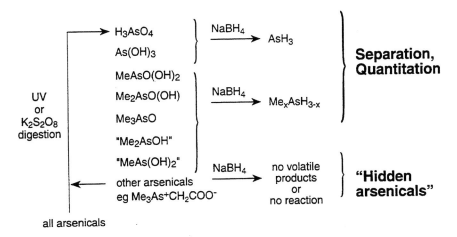

FIGURE 3-5 Hydride generation. Arsenic speciation by using hydride generation. UV, ultraviolet.

The method involves a derivatization technique, and the number of methyl groups in the evolved arsine, Me_xAsH_{3-x}, is generally the same as that in the arsenic species before reduction (Andreae 1977). The precursors to the arsines are also generally assumed to be the oxyspecies shown in Table 3-1. That is not necessarily correct. For example, in some sulfur-rich environments, the precursors to the arsines might be such compounds as $MeAs(SR)_2$ (Bright et al. 1994, 1996).

An important feature of the hydride-generation reaction is its pH dependence. All the As(III) compounds produce arsines at about pH 6 (Andreae 1977; Bright et al. 1994; Hasegawa 1997). At about pH 1, all the arsenicals are reduced to arsines. By using that difference in reactivity, As(III) and As(V) can be determined in a sample. In the absence of other confounding factors, at intermediate pHs (e.g., in acetic acid) further differentiation between species and oxidation state can be obtained (Cullen et al. 1994).

When a mixture of arsines is obtained following hydride generation, the arsines must be separated before quantification can be achieved. Often, in the usual batch-type operation mode, the arsines are trapped at liquid nitrogen temperature (cryofocused) and then separated by using gas chromatography. Alternatively, the cold trapped arsines are allowed to warm up slowly, and the differences in boiling points result in sequential presentation of the four compounds to the detector. In another variation, the hydrides are trapped in cold solvent, and aliquots of the resulting solution are injected into a gas chromatograph.

Many detectors have been used for the analysis of the separated arsines.

Element-specific detection is preferred, although flame ionization and electron capture have been used. The arsines are passed into a flame, a quartz-tube atomizer, or a graphite furnace for atomic absorption detection. A mass spectrometer or ICP-MS (inductively coupled plasma-mass spectroscopy) can be used as can ICP-AES. The detectors and their detection limits for AsH_3 are listed in Table 3-2. The detectors respond differently to different arsines, so separate calibration curves are usually needed. However, by adjusting such factors as pH and flow rate in a flow system, compromise conditions for hydride generation–atomic absorption (HG-AA) can be found so that the different arsines produce the same response (Le et al. 1994a) and separate calibration curves are not needed.

Hidden Arsenic Species

Figure 3-5 indicates that apart from the methylarsenicals and inorganic arsenic species listed in Table 3-1, all other arsenic species likely to be found in the environment do not form hydrides that can be quantified by using the usual technique. AsB is in that category. Compounds that are not detected by hydride generation are sometimes referred to as "hidden arsenic" species. That term originated in the era when hydride generation was the only method readily available for arsenic speciation. As indicated in Figure 3-3, all arsenicals can be decomposed to arsenate for analysis. Decomposition via ultraviolet (UV) irradiation (Cullen and Dodd 1988), microwave-assisted persulfate oxidation (Le et al. 1992), or UV irradiation combined with persulfate oxidation (Zhang et al. 1996a) are singled out because of their application to speciation methodology.

Arsenic(III) Species

Occasionally, specific As(III) species are extracted from aqueous solution by use of sodium diethyldithiocarbamate before determination by HG-AA, for example. (Chatterjee et al. 1995; Hasegawa 1996). This procedure involves a preconcentration step using chloroform.

Chromatographic Separation of Involatile Arsenic Species

As mentioned previously, hydride generation is a method that involves derivatization; hence, assumptions must be made about the nature of the

TABLE 3-2 Methods for the Determination of Total Arsenic in Drinking Water

| Method | Detection Limit | | Instrument cost, $ \times 10^{-3}$ | Operator Skill Level | Applicable Arsenic Limit | | | |
	Absolute	Concentration			50 μg/L	20 μg/L	2 μg/L	2 ng/L
Hydride Generation								
Colorimetric[a]	1 μg	10 μg/L (100 mL)	5	Low	Yes	No	No	No
Thermal conductivity		10 μg/L	40	High	Yes	Yes	Yes	No
Atomic fluorescence		20 ng/L	20	High	Yes	Yes	Yes	No
Graphite furnace AAS	0.2 ng	2 ng (100 mL)	60	High	Yes	Yes	Yes	No
Quartz-tube AAS	0.5 ng	32 ng/L (15 mL)	60	High	Yes	Yes	Yes	No
Helium discharge	0.1 ng	1 ng/L (100 mL)	20	High	Yes	Yes	Yes	No
Microwave plasma	20 pg	1.4 ng/L (15 mL)	20	High	Yes	Yes	Yes	No
DC-plasma	0.4 μg	4 μg/L (100 mL)	60	Very high	Yes	Yes	No	No
ICP emission	2 ng	20 ng/L (100 mL)	80	Very high	Yes	Yes	Yes	No
ICP-MS	10 pg	0.1 ng/L (100 mL)	200	Very high	Yes	Yes	Yes	No
Electrochemical								
Differential pulse polarography	20 ng	1 μg/L (20 mL)	20	High	Yes	Yes	No	No
Anodic stripping voltammetry	6 pg	0.3 ng/L (20 mL)	30	High	Yes	Yes	Yes	Yes
Spectroscopic								
Flame atomic absorption		1 mg/L	20	Low	No	No	No	No
Graphite furnace AAS		1 μg/L	80	High	Yes	Yes	No	No
DCP or ICP-AES		10 μg/L	80	Very high	Yes	Yes	No	No
ICP-MS		0.05 μg/L	200	Very high	Yes	Yes	Yes	No

[a]Silver diethyldithiocarbamate.

Abbreviations: AAS, atomic absorption spectroscopy; DC, direct current; ICP-MS, inductively coupled plasma–mass spectrometry; DCP, direct current plasma; AES, atomic emission spectroscopy.

Source: Adapted from Irgolic 1994.

analyte species. To minimize problems and examine all soluble arsenic species, some form of chromatography has been used for the initial separation of the arsenicals, and high-performance (pressure) liquid chromatography (HPLC) is rapidly becoming the method of choice. Ion exchange (cation and anion), size exclusion, and reversed-phase (with ion pairing) columns are used (Morita and Shibata 1990; Sheppard et al. 1992; Vela and Caruso 1993; Inoue et al. 1994; Kawabata et al. 1994; Kumar et al. 1995; Pergantis et al. 1995). Hydride-generation methods can be used to quantify the fractions separated from conventional chromatography columns, a procedure that has been used in many urine studies, as described below; however, investigators are now using HPLC for the separation coupled with an arsenic-specific detector, such as an ICP-MS or ICP-AES, for quantification. Hyphenated techniques, such as HPLC-ICP-MS or HPLC-ICP-AES, have the advantage in that, in principle, all species in the sample can be separated and detected with selectivity and sensitivity in the subnanogram-to-subpicogram range. Of the two detectors, the ICP-MS is more sensitive than the ICP-AES. The ICP-MS also has a wide linear range and high precision, but it is expensive. One inexpensive HPLC detector for arsenic species consists of a chamber in which the eluate is combusted in a hydrogen-oxygen flame, and then the products are entrained into a silica T tube situated in the light path of an AA spectrometer. Detection limits are in the subnanogram region (Monplaisir et al. 1994).

One promising development, in which hydride generation is still used, was published by Le et al. (1996). HPLC is used to separate the arsenicals, which are then decomposed on line to arsenate by using microwave-assisted persulfate oxidation. Arsenate is then converted to arsine, which is detected by using atomic fluorescence. This detector is much less expensive than the ICP-MS alternative, and the method has a detection limit for arsenic species in urine of 10 parts per billion (ppb).

Mass Spectrometry for Arsenic Speciation

The most recent development in speciation methodology has been to combine the separation capability of HPLC with the molecular-recognition capability of mass spectrometry. Electrospray mass spectrometry appears to offer important advantages (Siu et al. 1988; Siu et al. 1991; Florêncio et al. 1997; Pergantis et al. 1997a,b). In the most complete study to date, 10 arsenicals were separated and detected by using a microbore reversed-phase column coupled to an electrospray triple-quadrupole mass spectrometer (μ-HPLC-ESMS-MS). The electrospray mass spectrum of the compounds listed in Table 3-3 essentially consists of only protonated species (if not cationic to start with) or the cation (if cationic). The collision-induced dissociation (CID) fragment ions listed in Table 3-3 were obtained by using argon as the collision gas in the second quadrupole. The monitored CID reaction allows the analysis of the species even if the species is not separated completely by the chromatography. Thus, discrimination is achieved within the mass spectrometer. The detection limits are also listed in Table 3-3; these limits are becoming comparable to those obtainable with ICP-MS (Table 3-2); the instrument cost, however, is higher than the ICP-MS cost. AsB has been measured in a standard reference material, although matrix problems have been encountered (Pergantis et al. 1997b). A closely related ionization mode, ionspray (IS), has been incorporated into the hyphenated method HPLC-IS-MS-MS (Corr and Larsen 1996) with equally impressive results: arsenicals, including AsB and arsenosugars, were verified in flatfish and oyster tissues.

ARSENIC IN WATER

In 1994, Irgolic published a review of the methods for determining arsenic and arsenic species in drinking water (see also Irgolic et al. 1995). Irgolic concluded that drinking water normally contains arsenic as arsenate and, if the water is anaerobic, some arsenite. Methylated species (MMA and DMA) would rarely be present in water supplies. Unless special circumstances, such as pollution by arsenical herbicides or high biological activity, exist, Irgolic argued that determination of arsenic species in water supplies is unnecessary; knowledge of the inorganic arsenic content is sufficient for regulatory purposes. The subcommittee evaluated that conclusion, as described below.

Arsenic in Groundwater

Although it is widely believed that arsenate is the major water-soluble species in groundwater, there is increasing evidence (Korte and Fernando 1991) that arsenite might be more prevalent than anticipated. Improved methods of sampling, sample preservation, and analysis have contributed to that conclusion. For example, Anderson and Bruland (1991) found it necessary to trap AsH_3 generated from As(III) in the field and to store the sample in liquid nitrogen for later laboratory analysis. Significant differences were found between those samples and water samples collected, immediately frozen (-196°C), and later analyzed in the laboratory. Andreae (1977) claimed that speciation is unchanged in samples stored at -15°C or under dry ice, although an initial loss of arsenite (approximately 0.02 ppb) is experienced. Korte and Fernando (1991) listed other procedures that have been used for sample preservation.

TABLE 3-3 CID Fragment Ions and Selected Reactions Monitored for 10 Organic Arsenic Compounds

Compound	M_n[a]	Precursor Ion	CID Fragment Ions[b]	CID Reaction Monitored	Detection Limit (ppm)[c]
Methylarsonic acid	140	141	141(100); 123(15); 109(7); 91(5)	141→123	0.3
p-Arsanilic acid	217	218	218(100); 109(37); 108(13); 92(13)	218→109	0.1
4-Hydroxyphenylarsonic acid	218	219	219(100); 201(16); 110(31); 93(10)	219→110	0.3
Dimethylarsinic acid	138	139	139(100); 121(27); 108(8); 91(8)	139→121	0.07
3-Nitro-4-hydroxy-phenylarsonic acid	263	264	264(100); 246(12)	264→246	0.2
4-Nitrophenylarsonic acid	247	248	248(100); 230(12); 202(16); 122(5)	248→202	0.1
Arsenobetaine	178	179	179(100); 120(18)	179→120	0.002
Trimethylarsine oxide	136	137	137(100); 122(17); 107(23)	137→107	0.04
Arsenocholine	165	165	165(100); 121(5); 45(9)	165→45	0.02
Tetramethylarsonium ion	135	135	135(100); 120(44); 105(15)	135→120	0.02

[a]Nominal relative molecular mass; the monoisotopic molecular mass rounded to the nearest whole number.
[b]Numbers in parentheses correspond to percent relative intensity.
[c]Selected reaction monitoring, 1 μL injections.
Abbreviation: CID, collision-induced dissociation.
Source: Adapted from Pergantis et al. 1997b.

The use of excess Fe(II) and acidic pH at less than 2 has been suggested to suppress the oxidation of As(III) (Borho and Wilderer 1997). However, samples from different bodies of water usually have different redox potential and therefore require different amounts of Fe(II). Thus, this approach might be difficult to apply to all water samples without prior knowledge of the sample.

Yalcin and Le (1998) recently developed an interesting method in which As(III) and As(V) were separated on-site by using disposable cartridges. Immediately after collection, a measured volume of a water sample was pumped through a resin-based strong cation-exchange cartridge followed by a silica-based strong anion-exchange cartridge. The cation-exchange cartridge retained DMA and allowed other arsenic species to pass through. The anion-exchange cartridge retained MMA and As(V), and As(III) remained in the solution. The cartridges and the solution containing separate arsenic species were brought to a laboratory for analysis. The unretained arsenic in the solution was a measure of As(III) in the original water sample. Arsenic eluted from the cation-exchange cartridge with 1 M HCl was quantified for DMA. The anion-exchange cartridge was first eluted with 0.06 M acetic acid for the determination of MMA and then with 1 M HCl to elute As(V). If only inorganic As(III) and As(V) were present as the major arsenic species, the procedure could be simplified by using only the anion-exchange cartridge.

Chatterjee et al. (1995) also found that As(III) is about 50% of the total arsenic in the groundwater of many wells in six districts of West Bengal, India. (As(III) was separated from As(V) by extraction with sodium diethyldithiocarbamate.) No MMA or DMA was found. Total-arsenic concentrations ranged from 10 to 1,095 μg/L.

Hydride generation was used to speciate arsenic in groundwaters from Taiwan (Chen et al. 1994). In the blackfoot-disease (BFD) area, the average arsenic, predominantly As(III), concentration in three wells was 671 $\pm$ 149 μg/L. The ratio of As(III) to As(V) was 2.6:1. Outside the BFD area, the arsenic concentration dropped to 0.7 μg/L. No methylarsenic species were present (at less than 1 μg/L), and hidden arsenic species were not significant. Insoluble suspended arsenic accounted for about 3% of the total arsenic in the water from the three wells, and ultrafiltration revealed that about 11% of the soluble arsenic, mainly As(III), was associated with molecules of molecular mass greater than 300,000 daltons. Possibly, the material was humic. Much has been written on the possible connection between BFD, humic material, and arsenic (e.g., Lu 1990; Lu and Lee 1992; Lu et al. 1991, 1994; Yang et al. 1994).

The arsenic species detected in ground water by hydride generation generally are believed to be the oxy species $Me_xAsO(OH)_{3-x}$ or $As(OH)_3$.

However, that might not always be the case, especially in a reducing environment where arsenic and sulfur compounds would be expected to dominate (Cullen and Reimer 1989). The presence of the oxythioarsenate H_3AsO_3S in arsenic-rich terrain has been established, and one base extract contained arsenate at 2,616 $\mu g/kg$ of soil and the thio analogue at 115 $\mu g/kg$, as determined by capillary electrophoresis (Schwedt and Reickhoff 1996a,b).

Arsenic in Fresh Surface Water

An important study of the arsenic species in the Ottawa River, Canada (Sturgeon et al. 1989), opens with the statement, "Few data exist on the species distribution of arsenic in natural waters." At the time of publication, no reports had hinted at the possible presence of nonhydride-active organic arsenic species (hidden arsenic) in water. The Ottawa River samples were used in the preparation of the river-water reference material for trace metals, the Standard Laboratory Reference Sample (SLRS-1), for the National Research Council of Canada (NRCC 1986). Careful analysis of the standard gave the following results (species and concentration in micrograms per liter): As(III), 0.16; As(V), 0.18; MMA, less than 0.02; DMA, 0.05; AsC and TMAs, less than 0.01; nonhydride and inactive (hidden) species, 0.12; organically bound, less than 0.01; total arsenic, 0.52 ± 0.03. The certified value for that reference water was 0.55 ± 0.08 $\mu g/L$. The nonhydride and active species constituted 22% of the total arsenic, and the authors suggested that the compound or compounds are similar to AsB. However, the workup of the sample, which involved the use of a strong cation-exchange column, could have changed the species originally present. Arsenic speciation in the sterile water sample (pH 1.6) was stable for at least 13 months.

In a study of a number of U.S. lakes and estuaries (mostly Californian), Anderson and Bruland (1991) used the HG-AA method (Andreae 1977). Measurable amounts of methylarsenicals were detected, amounting to 1-59% of the total arsenic. With the exception of two highly alkaline lakes, Mono and Pyramid Lakes, the methylated forms constituted on average 24% of the total dissolved arsenic in lake surface water. In the Davis Creek Reservoir, a seasonally anoxic lake, DMA became the dominant surface arsenic species during the late er and fall. The study indicated that the DMA can be demethylated later in the yearly cycle. The total-arsenic concentration varied with the season, and arsenate was generally the predominant inorganic species, although appreciable amounts of arsenite were detected. For example, in October 1988, the ratio of total arsenic to As(V) to As(III) to DMA was 128:45:12:58. No attempt was made to look for hidden arsenic species in those waters.

Studies conducted on Lake Biwa, Japan (Hasegawa 1997; Sohrin et al. 1997), in which a more sophisticated form of hydride generation was used, revealed the presence of methylarsenic(III) species, possibly $MeAs(OH)_2$ and Me_2AsOH, in low concentrations. The authors also found that arsenic speciation and concentration varied with the season, particularly in the euphotic southern basin of the lake where DMA can become the dominant species. Seasonal variation in methylarsenic(III) and (V) species was also found in coastal waters (Hasegawa 1996). Similar compounds were seen in sediment pore water from Yellowknife, Canada (Bright et al. 1994, 1996), but hidden arsenic species were also present and were the major species in some samples.

Arsenic in Estuarine Water

Hydride generation was used for arsenic speciation in coastal waters of southern England (Howard and Comber 1989). The overall concentration of arsenic increased by approximately 25% when samples were irradiated with UV light, indicating that arsenicals undetectable by hydride generation become detectable following irradiation. In the opinion of the authors, those hidden arsenic species might be arsenosugars but are probably not AsB. Their maximum concentration occurred when biological activity was high. Targus Estuary, Portugal, also was found to contain hidden arsenic amounting to 19-25% of the total (de Bettencourt et al. 1994).

For most of the year, Howard and Apte (1989) found As(V) to be the only detectable arsenic species in the Itchen Estuary in southern England. In saline areas, the total-arsenic concentration was 0.7-1.0 μg/L and was 0.2 μg/L at a freshwater site. DMA was found in the river only in May and June. In the estuary, 30% of the total arsenic was in the form of methylated species when productivity was at a maximum (temperatures more than 12°C). At lower temperatures, the absence of methyl species might have been due to (1) lower general turnover of arsenic; (2) lower ability, or need, of organisms to excrete methylarsenicals; or (3) excretion of arsenicals not detected by hydride generation.

Practical Quantification Level for Arsenic in Drinking Water

A recent study (Eaton 1994) attempted to determine the practical quantification level (PQL) for total arsenic in drinking water. Twenty-five laboratories, commercial and utility, were involved. The laboratories used approved analytical methods: HG-AA and GFAA. The data indicated that a reasonable value for a minimum interlaboratory PQL for arsenic is 4 μg/L. At that concentration, a laboratory technician should be able to measure arsenic to an accuracy of better than $\pm 25\%$ for 95% confidence limits; individual laboratories might be capable of achieving much greater accuracy. The PQL of 4 μg/L is about the same as that expected from the data given in Table 3-2 (Irgolic 1994) for hydride generation but is lower than that estimated for the less-sensitive direct spectroscopic GFAA method. The detection limits suggested by Irgolic are conservative but realistic, and if the arsenic maximum contamination level (MCL) is set at 2 μg/L, GFAA will not be capable of reaching that target. HG-AA will still be of use, and the method has the advantage of being able to supply some speciation information if required. Hydride generation can achieve low-picogram arsenic detection limits with improved detection by ICP-MS. GFAA is limited in both sensitivity and speciation capabilities. Eaton (1994) found that below 4 μg/L, precision and bias degrade substantially, indicating that reliable interlaboratory measurements are not routinely possible below that concentration.

ARSENIC IN FOOD

Total-Arsenic Concentrations

One of the most comprehensive studies of arsenic in food was published in 1993 (Dabeka et al. 1993). Food collected in Canadian cities in the years 1985-1988 was analyzed for total arsenic, and the food groups containing the highest mean arsenic concentrations were fish (1,662 ng/g), meat and poultry (24.3 ng/g), bakery goods and cereals (24.5 ng/g), and fats and oils (19.0 ng/g). The average daily dietary ingestion of total arsenic by Canadians was estimated to be 38.1 μg (48.5 μg for adults) and varied from 14.9 μg for children 1-4 years old to 59.2 μg for males 20-39 years old. Previous estimates for Canadians were 16.7 μg per day and 30 μg per day (Dabeka et al. 1987).

Those figures are comparable with data from other countries: United States, 62 μg per day (Gartrell et al. 1985); United Kingdom, 89 μg per day (Food Additives and Contaminants Committee 1984); Austria, 27 μg per day (Pfannhauser and Pechanek 1977); and New Zealand, 55 μg per day (Dick et al. 1978). Assuming that those figures have general application, it is apparent that individuals receive a considerable daily dose of arsenic from food.

On the basis of the U.S. Food and Drug Administration (FDA) Total Diet Study, Adams et al. (1994) provided the most thorough analysis of arsenic in the U.S. diet to date. Out of about 5,000 foods regularly consumed in the United States, 234 were selected as being representative, and excess caloric diets were constructed from those foods for total diet studies. (The diet consisted of 82 foods from 11 food groups in quantities for a 14-day intake with excessive energy intake of 4,200 kcal per day.) The results indicate that food contributes 93% of the total intake of arsenic, and seafood contributes 90% of that 93% (see Table 3-4). Mean arsenic intakes by groups of individuals were estimated in 1982-1991, and those results are given in Table 3-5. The results from the latter years are generally lower than those from the peak period 1984-1986. Nriagu and Azcue (1990) arized the data from a number of studies on total dietary arsenic, and Jelinek and Corneliussen (1977) reported similar EPA data for the years 1967-1974.

Results of the most recent FDA Total Diet Study are shown in Table 3-6 (Tao and Bolger 1998). The total arsenic intake is divided into contributions from seafood and others. The estimates given in the final column are based on the assumption that 10% of the arsenic in seafood is inorganic and that 100% of the arsenic in the rest of the food is inorganic. The estimates of 10% and 100% are high but nevertheless set an upper bound. For example, a 25-30 year old 79-kg male will ingest 9.89 g of inorganic arsenic per day from food. The significance of the intake of inorganic arsenic from food increases as the concentration of arsenic in water decreases. If water contains 50 μg/L of inorganic arsenic, arsenic in food might not be significant. However, if water contains 5 μg/L of arsenic and 2 L per day is consumed, the contribution of inorganic arsenic from diet and water are comparable.

The average arsenic intakes reported in Table 3-6 are generally higher than those reported for earlier years (Table 3-5). The new numbers probably reflect an increase in the consumption of seafood (Table 3-4).

Studies of Arsenic Speciation in Food

In view of the arsenic concentrations in some foods, the nature of the arsenic species present is an important consideration. The simplest method that has been used for distinguishing between so-called "organic" arsenic in food and "inorganic" arsenic is to use hydrochloric acid as an extractant and reagent for isolating an arsenic-containing fraction. The HCl fraction is distillable from the remainder of the extract and is regarded as containing the inorganic arsenic originally present in the food. The question has been raised whether organic arsenic can be broken down to inorganic arsenic species during the HCl distillation (Mushak and Crocetti 1995), thus increasing the proportion of inorganic species in the sample. That seems unlikely: the arsenic-carbon bond in methylarsenicals is robust, and DMA, for example, is stable in hot nitric acid.

HCl distillation has been widely used for marine-animal arsenic speciation. Edmonds and Francesconi (1993) collected much of the available

TABLE 3-4 Foods Containing Arsenic at Concentrations above 50 ppb as Determined by the FDA Total Diet Study for Market Baskets Collected from 1990 through 1991

Fish	Meat	Vegetable
Tuna in oil	Turkey breast	Rice, cooked
Fish sticks		Rice cereal
Haddock, fried		Mushrooms, raw
Shrimp, boiled		Olive/safflower oil
Tuna noodle casserole		
Fish sandwich		
Clam chowder		

Source: Adams et al. 1994.

TABLE 3-5 Mean Total Daily Arsenic Intakes (μg/d) as Determined by the FDA Total Diet Study for Market Baskets Collected from April 1982 through April 1991

Population-Group Age (Sex)[a]	Arsenic Intake (μg/d) and Years of Collection (Number of Collections)				
	1982-84 (8)[b]	1984-86 (8)[c]	1986-88 (8)[c]	1988-90 (8)[c]	1990-91 (5)[c]
6-11 mo	4.9	7.4	6.2	3.6	3.2
2 yr	12.2	15.8	12.8	9.3	9.0
14-16 yr (F)	23.0	29.3	23.5	17.5	16.9
14-16 yr (M)	27.7	35.7	28.7	20.6	20.3
25-30 yr (F)	31.0	39.5	31.3	23.7	23.3
25-30 yr (M)	45.3	58.1	45.6	34.0	34.6
60-65 yr (F)	35.2	45.3	34.8	26.7	26.6
60-65 yr (M)	43.8	56.6	43.1	32.7	33.4

[a]F, female; M, male.
[b]In calculating intakes, "trace" concentrations were assigned a value of one-half the limit of quantitation; the "trace" concentration assigned to arsenic during those years was 0.01 mg/kg of diet.
[c]In calculating intakes for this time period, "trace" concentrations were estimated by the analyst.
Source: Adams et al. 1994.

information, and regression analysis of the data indicates that the proportion of inorganic arsenic falls from about 1% at very low total-arsenic concentrations to about 0.5% at total-arsenic concentrations of 20 mg/kg. These proportions contrast with the 2-10% proposed by WHO (1989) and GESAMP (1986) for the inorganic arsenic content of marine animals. The distillation method seems to provide minimum but useful and reliable information on speciation of arsenic in marine-animal food for routine work, but Edmonds and Francesconi (1993) suggested that more sophisticated methods should be used to establish the arsenic status of particular marine foods, such as algae, before approval for consumption.

TABLE 3-6 Estimated Average Inorganic Arsenic Intakes for Various Age and Sex Groups as Determined by the FDA Total Diet Study for Market Baskets Collected in 1991-1997

Population Group			Inorganic Arsenic Intake[a] (g/d)		Total Inorganic Arsenic Average Intake (μg/d)
Age (Sex)[b]	Weight (kg)[c]	Total Arsenic Intake (μg/d)	Seafood	Others	
6-11 mo	7	2.15	0.09	1.25	1.34
2 yr	13	23.4	2.11	2.30	4.41
6 yr	22	20.3	1.74	2.90	4.64
10 yr	64	13.3	1.01	3.20	4.21
14-16 yr (F)	53	21.8	1.85	3.30	5.15
14-16 yr (M)	64	15.4	1.21	3.30	4.51
25-30 yr (F)	62	27.5	2.46	2.90	5.36
25-30 yr (M)	79	56.6	5.19	4.70	9.89
40-45 yr (F)	67	36.8	3.38	3.00	6.38
40-45 yr (M)	81	46.8	4.28	4.00	8.28
60-65 yr (F)	67	72.1	6.93	2.80	9.73
60-65 yr (M)	81	92.1	8.84	3.70	12.54
70+ (F)	62	45.4	4.25	2.90	7.15
70+ (M)	74	69.4	6.63	3.10	9.70

[a]Based on the assumption that 10 % and 100% of the total arsenic is inorganic arsenic in seafood and all other foods, respectively. Seafood inclues seven TDS food items (tuna, fish sticks, haddock, shrimp, tuna noodle casserole, clam chowder, and fish sandwich).

[b]F, female; M, male.

[c]Self-reported weights from the data tapes of the U.S. Department of Agriculture.
Source: Tao and Bolger 1998.

The HCl extraction-distillation method was applied in two recent studies that included a range of food classes. In the first (Yost et al. 1998), 15 food samples from Canada were examined for inorganic and organic arsenic (arsenic in the residue after the distillation step) and total arsenic (arsenic in a wet digest, H_2SO_4-HNO_3-$HClO_4$, of the sample). The data used by Yost et al. (1998) was previously available as a report from the Ontario Ministry of the Environment (OME 1987). Yost and co-workers (1998) claimed that the data were misinterpreted when estimates of dietary arsenic were made for EPA's 1988 risk assessment. For example, although no potatoes or vegetables were analyzed, the data have been cited as indicating that arsenic in yams (EPA 1988) and vegetables (Mushak and Crocetti 1995) occurs primarily in organic form. Fifteen food groups were examined (OME 1987), but the study can only be regarded as preliminary (quality-assurance and quality-control (QA-QC) procedures were not described); only one sample per food group was analyzed, and some mass balances were poor. For example, 50% of the arsenic in bread, with arsenic at 0.024 mg/kg, is inorganic, yet the organic arsenic was undetectable. In the study, the HCl distillate was further treated with HNO_3 and H_2SO_4 before HG-AA analysis. No reason is given for following that procedure; perhaps the investigators believed it might be necessary to convert any methylarsenicals in the distillate to arsenate (a possibility that should be investigated) (see Table 3-7). As mentioned above, the organic arsenic was determined as the total arsenic in the residue left after the HCl distillation step. Some of the data are shown in Table 3-7. As expected, canned shrimp had a high total-arsenic content, but the inorganic content seems very high in view of the report of Edmonds and Francesconi (1993) described above. The concentrations of arsenic in rice seem low in view of the study described below. The results given in Table 3-7 together with those of Dabeka et al. (1993), Gunderson (1995), and Borum (1992) were used by Yost et al. (1998) to estimate daily dietary intakes of inorganic arsenic ranging from 8.3 to 14 μg per day in the United States and from 4.8 to 12.7 μg per day in Canada, on the basis that inorganic arsenic constitutes 20-40% of the total dietary intake. A previous estimate (EPA 1988) of 17 or 18 μg per day for inorganic arsenic includes arsenic from food, drinking water, and beverages.

TABLE 3-7 Arsenic Concentration in Food and Cigarettes (Values in ppm, Wet Weight)

Food (Sample No.)	Total	Inorganic	Organic	% Inorganic
Vanilla ice cream (1)	0.016	0.0042	<0.002	26
Cured pork (1)	0.013	0.018	<0.007	144
Pastrami (1)	0.024	0.024	<0.009	99
Chicken (1)	0.022	0.0090	0.012	41
Sole (1)	4	0.022	4.4	1
Tuna (1)	1.1	0.025	1.2	2
Pickerel (1)	0.14	0.022	0.086	15
Shrimp (1)	0.65	0.10	0.52	16
Rice (1)	0.24	0.1	0.16	43
Special K cereal (1)	0.27	0.070	0.15	26
Bread (1)	0.024	0.012	<0.006	50
Flour (1)	0.011	0.0076	<0.005	69
Apple juice (1)	0.012	0.0088	<0.002	73
Tea (1)	0.035	0.0091	0.025	26
Cigarettes (1)	0.18	0.11	0.03	61

Source: Adapted from Yost et al. 1998.

Schoof et al. (1998) concentrated on the arsenic species in Taiwanese rice and yams and used two methods of extraction claimed to yield similar results. In the first, 2 molar (M) HCl was used (12 hr, 80°C), and the extract was analyzed without further distillation for arsenic speciation by using HG-AA. In the second method, the sample was simply extracted with water (12 hr, 25°C) followed by HPLC-ICP-MS for speciation (an example of a higher-level speciation study; see following section). Table 3-8 presents some of the data from that study.

TABLE 3-8 Arsenic Species in Rice and Yams from Taiwan (Average Values in ppm, Dry Weight, 1995 Samples)

Extract (Sample No.)	As(T)[a]	MMA	DMA	As(V) and As(III) (% of total)	Recovery (%)
Rice					
HCl (>5)	0.13	0.021	0.021	0.083 (72%)	105
Water (5)	0.15	0.013	0.013	0.11 (69%)	86
Yam					
HCl (>15)	0.081	0.020	ND	0.058 (76%)	86
Water (1)	0.40	0.21	ND	0.13 (33%)	87

[a]Sum of species, not determined.
Abbreviations: As(T), arsenic total; ND, no data; MMA, monomethylarsonic acid; DMA, dimethylarsinic acid.
Source: Adapted from Schoof et al. 1998.

The average arsenic concentrations in rice and yams were 0.15 mg/kg and 0.11 mg/kg, respectively, for samples collected in 1995 and 1993. In contrast to Yost et al. (1998), who defined organic arsenic as the arsenic content of the residues after extraction on the basis of the OME (1987) data, Schoof et al. (1998) defined the organic arsenic fraction as the sum of MMA and DMA, species that are extracted and ignored the residues. Although the data vary from sample to sample (not an unusual finding; see Dabeka et al. 1993), they were used to estimate mean values of 31 μg per day and 19 μg per day for total inorganic intake from yams and rice, respectively, for a total of 50 μg per day within a range of estimates of 15-211 μg per day. That is considerably higher than previous estimates of 2 μg per day (EPA 1988; Abernathy et al. 1989).

In an earlier study from Taiwan (Li et al. 1979), most of the crop (95%) in 1975 was found to contain detectable amounts of arsenic mainly in the 0.1-0.7 mg/kg (total arsenic) range. The concentrations in some samples were said to exceed the "tolerance level" of 0.76 mg/kg and ranged up to 1.43 mg/kg. The rice was grown in arsenic-rich soil that had probably been treated with arsenical pesticides of unstated composition.

Higher-Level Speciation Studies of Food

Most dietary arsenic originates from fish, shellfish, and algal products. The arsenic speciation in those products from the marine environment has been comprehensively arized (Francesconi and Edmonds 1997). In general, the major arsenical found in the parts of fish that are usually eaten is AsB (see Table 3-9), which is believed to have low-to-negligible toxicity on the basis of studies with mice (the lethal dose for 50% of the test animals (LD_{50}) was more than 10 g/kg) (Kaise and Fukui 1992), and with humans (Vahter 1994). The arsenic in marine algae and algal products is mainly determined to be one or more of the four arsenosugars X, XI, XII and XIII (see Table 3-1). Little work has been done on the toxicity of those compounds, although the consensus seems to be that they are similar to AsB in that regard. However, arsenosugars are metabolized by humans, largely to DMA (Le et al. 1994b, 1996); therefore, the question of the toxicity of DMA should be addressed (e.g., Yamanaka et al. 1996).

In the case of marine shellfish, early studies of arsenic speciation indicated that AsB and the tetramethylarsonium ion were the main arsenicals present (Cullen and Reimer 1989). That understanding changed with the development of improved analytical methods and sampling procedures. Now, arsenosugars are found in molluscs, which are commonly eaten in North America, (Shibata et al. 1992; Reimer et al. 1994) at concentrations that are comparable to those of AsB.

Although total-arsenic concentrations are known to be lower in freshwater fish than in marine animals, little is known about arsenic speciation in freshwater fish (Cullen and Reimer 1989). Freshwater fish, including pike (arsenic at 0.05 μg/g), bass (at 0.12 μg/g), carp (at 0.18 μg/g), pickerel (at 0.04 μg/g), and white fish (at 0.02 μg/g), do not contain AsB or AsC but do contain soluble unidentified arsenic species amounting to approximately 70% of the total arsenic (Lawrence et al. 1986); however, in a recent abstract, Koch et al. (1998) report that AsB is found in all the freshwater fish studied and that arsenosugars are the major species in freshwater mussels, AsB being absent. Inorganic arsenic species were either not found or were present at trace concentrations. In salmon (with arsenic at 0.31 μg/g), approximately 50% of the soluble arsenic (90% of the total) is AsB and the rest is unknown (Lawrence et al. 1986). The concentrations are given on a fresh weight basis.

The major arsenic species in cultured rainbow trout (*Salmo gairdneri*) and wild Japanese smelt (*Hypomesus nipponensis*) is AsB. The AsB in the trout might originate from the commercial feed; that in the smelt is naturally derived. Of the total arsenic in the trout (1.46 μg/g) and smelt (1.08 μg/g), more than 95% was water soluble and was mainly AsB (Shiomi et al. 1995).

TABLE 3-9 Arsenobetaine in Marine Animals

Animal (No. of Species)	Arsenic Concentration (mg/kg, Wet Wt.)	Arsenobetaine Content (% of Total Arsenic)
Fish		
Elasmobranchs (7)	3.1-44.3	≥94
Teleosts (17)	0.1-166	48 to >95
Crustaceans		
Lobsters (4)	4.7-26	77 to >95
Prawns (5)	5.5-20.8	55 to >95
Crabs (6)	3.5-8.6	79 to >95
Molluscs		
Bivalves (4)	0.7-2.8	44-88
Gastropods (6)	3.1-116.5	58 to >95
Cephalopods (3)	49	72 to >95

Source: Francesconi and Edmonds 1997. Reprinted with permission from *Advances in Inorganic Chemistry*; copyright 1997, Academic Press.

Much is known about the ability of freshwater microalgae to grow in water containing high arsenic concentrations and to accumulate arsenic mainly as inorganic species with minor amounts of DMA and MMA (Maeda 1994). In contrast, the freshwater edible *Nostoc* species contain arsenic at a concentration of 3 ppm (dry-weight basis), but only 34% of that is extractable into water-methanol. For most marine algae, extraction efficiency is approximately 90% or better (Morita and Shibata 1990). Seasonal variations have been observed, however (Lai et al. 1998). The extracted arsenic in the *Nostoc* species consisted mainly of arsenosugar X (93%), the rest being DMA as determined by HPLC-ICP-MS.

That same method has been applied to determine arsenic species in mushrooms, the only other type of food for which significant speciation information is available. Most mushroom species contain arsenic at less than 0.1 ppm on a dry weight basis (Vetter 1994). Arsenic-accumulating mushrooms contain a range of arsenicals, depending on the fungus (Byrne et al. 1995). For example, *Sarcosphaera coronaria* (accumulating arsenic at up to 2,000 μg/g of dry weight) contained only MMA, and *Entoloma lividum* (with arsenic at 40 μg/g) contained only As(III) (8%) and As(V) (92%). Two *Agaricus* species (arsenic at 8 ppm) contained AsB as the major arsenic species. In the edible mushroom *Laccaria amethystina*, the arsenic (40 μg/g) was mainly in the form of DMA. Samples for the Byrne et al. (1995) study came from Switzerland and Slovenia. Kuehnelt et al. (1997a,b) showed that the arsenic species in *Collybia maculata* (30 ppm) is mainly AsB, as it is in *Collybia butracea* (11 ppm). AsB and AsC were found in the toxic mushroom *Amanita muscaria* (15-22 ppm and approximately 730 ppm in samples found growing on a contaminated site); AsB and

AsC were found at equal concentrations (15% each of the total arsenic). In addition, several unidentified arsenicals were present, amounting to 60% of the total arsenic. Those findings are the first reports of AsC and AsB in the terrestrial environment. In contrast to mushrooms, the concentration of AsC in marine animals is much less than that of AsB (Francesconi and Edmonds 1997). The mushroom results and others (Lai et al. 1997) suggest that AsB in the terrestrial environment might not originate from an arsenosugar precursor. That suggestion is contrary to the widely held view that the arsenosugars are precursors to AsB in the marine environment.

In meat and poultry, some of the high total-arsenic concentrations might result from the use of arylarsonic acids as growth promoters (Ledet and Buck 1978; Adams et al. 1994). It is also possible that the arsenic originates from fish meal present in the feed. Animal feeds often contain substantial amounts of arsenic (more than 0.1 ppm) even without supplements (Nriagu and Azcue 1990). When the arsenicals used as food supplements are administered orally, a considerable percentage is eliminated in the feces. Limited biotransformation can occur; for example, the nitro group of 3-NHPAA (Figure 3-1) can be reduced to an amino group (Dean et al. 1994). Retention of those arsenicals might be partly responsible for increased total-arsenic concentrations found in some poultry, but Dean et al. (1994) found that if the supplement is stopped for 7 days before slaughter (the time required by regulations), no arsenical can be detected in the muscle of chicken. That study used enzymatic digestion with trypsin at pH 8 to release the arsenical, 4-NHPAA, Roxarsone, from the flesh and used HPLC-ICP-MS for the analysis. Sensitive HPLC-MS and μ-HPLC-ESMS-MS methods are now available for that and other analyses (Pergantis et al. 1997a,b,c).

One study of arsenic speciation in rice was described above (Schoof et al. 1998). Odanaka et al. (1985) grew rice hydroponically in the presence of DMA (arsenic at 500 μg as the sodium salt in 500 mL of nutrient solution). A monomethylated species accumulated in the plants, mainly in the roots, at a concentration of up to 777 ppm. Translocation to the shoots seemed to be restricted—arsenic at 18 ppm accumulated as the monomethyl species, but little DMA was found. The loss of a methyl group is uncommon. Part of the monomethylated product seems to be complexed in the plant, as reported for other plants (e.g., Sckerl and Frans 1969; Pyles and Woolson 1982). In addition, part of the product might be a reduced form of MMA, as described by Nissen and Benson (1982). The arsenicals were extracted with methanol and water and identified with HG-AA.

Pyles and Woolson (1982) used methanol and water to extract arsenic from garden vegetables grown in arsenate-amended soil (arsenic at 100 ppm). The average arsenic recovery was only 28%. The most recalcitrant plants were beets, tomato, swiss chard, and potato flesh. Total arsenic in the edible plants ranged from trace amounts in cabbage and corn to 3.0 ppm in potato peel. MMA and As(V) were found in the extracts of broccoli, lettuce, potato flesh, potato peel, and swiss chard. Some extracts contained hidden arsenic that required digestion with hot 2 M NaOH before detection with HG-AA was possible. Most of the arsenic in the methanol-water phase appeared to be a complex organic arsenical. Nissen and Benson (1982) found that terrestrial plants, such as *Lycopersicon esculentum*, metabolize arsenic differently from freshwater plants, such as *Lemna minima*. The higher terrestrial plants take up and reduce arsenate, producing methylated arsenicals only when grown in nutrient-deficient conditions. Freshwater plants produce not only methylarsenic species but also more elaborate compounds that might be arsenosugars.

The fourth major food group with high arsenic content comprises fats and oils (see Total-Arsenic Concentrations above). Margarine and peanut butter have high concentrations of arsenic, but unfortunately, nothing is known about speciation in those types of foods.

The Nature of Arsenic in Plants

In many instances, recovering arsenic species from plants of terrestrial origin has proved to be difficult, explaining why most studies have been concerned with measuring total arsenic. That difficulty has given rise to speculation that arsenic in terrestrial plants is bound up in an organic form that is not bioavailable to humans as is the AsB found in seafood. However, it is worth considering some relevant chemistry. First, if the arsenic is truly an organometallic compound and contains As-C bonds, the organic moieties are most likely to be the same as or similar to those already known and listed in Table 3-1. Apart from arsenolipids, all those compounds are water soluble and should be easily extracted if they are not bound in some way to bigger organic moieties. Such bonding would likely be via oxygen or sulfur. As discussed previously, the As-OR links are not hydrolytically stable. Although the As-S bond is more stable than the As-OR bond, it is not particularly robust, especially in the As(V) state (Zingaro and Thomson 1973; Sagan et al. 1972). As-Se bonds are more robust. The arsenic-containing moieties in such compounds should be available to mild extractants unless there is some physical barrier, such as a cell wall, to the extractant. On the same basis, inorganic arsenic species should be extractable unless there is a barrier. Alternatively, the difficulty in the extraction could arise because the arsenic is bound up in a lipid-soluble species, possibly membrane located. The species could be related to the well-characterized arsenolipid shown in Table 3-1 where the tail of the arsenolipid is made up of palmitolate groups. Choline-based lipids are well known, so it is certainly possible that lipids could be based on AsC as the head group. Some investigators have postulated that lipid-like arsenic species are present in plants (e.g., Nissen and Benson 1982). Studies involving arsenical uptake by plant cell cultures of the Madagascan periwinkle found that after uptake methylarsenicals became invisible to NMR spectroscopy; that finding suggests that they become bound to large molecules or cell walls (Cullen and Hettipathirana 1993; Cullen et al. 1989a). The same studies found that arsenate is methylated by the cells but that repeated extraction was necessary to recover the species. The suggestion was made that the plant stores the unwanted arsenicals in the vacuole.

The use of enzymes for digestion of difficult samples should be explored (e.g., Dean et al. 1994). Microwave irradiation in the presence of tetramethyl-ammonium hydroxide has proved effective for the extraction of related organo-tin compounds (Schmitt et al. 1997).

ARSENIC IN URINE, BLOOD, HAIR, AND NAILS

Arsenic in Urine

As described in Chapters 5 and 6, some arsenic species are more toxic than others, so it is important to obtain information about the speciation of the arsenic absorbed (e.g., from food, water, and particulates), eliminated (e.g., by urine, feces, nails, and hair), and stored (e.g., in liver and kidney). Some information is available on the speciation of arsenic that is ingested (as described in the section Arsenic in Food) and eliminated (as described below), but little is known about what forms of arsenic might be stored in the body (e.g., Vahter et al. 1984; see Chapter 5).

Total Arsenic in Urine

Some foods, especially those of marine origin, have high concentrations of arsenic, and consumption results in a surge in the concentration of arsenic in the urine. That might not be of toxicological significance if the arsenic species (e.g., AsB) is nontoxic and is excreted rapidly unchanged in the urine (Vahter 1994; Le et al. 1994b). However, arsenosugars, which are present in algal products and many shellfish, are metabolized by humans to DMA and other arsenicals, presumably sugars (Le et al. 1994b). Thus, high urinary arsenic concentrations in an individual can indicate exposure to high concentrations of toxic inorganic arsenic species or recent consumption of certain foods. Depending on the nature and amount of arsenic species found in the food, recent consumption of certain foods might not represent a toxicological concern.

The concentration of total arsenic in urine is generally accepted as a good indicator of the absorbed amount of arsenicals, because excretion via urine is the primary route for elimination of most arsenic species from most animals (Buchet and Lauwerys 1983; Vahter 1994). However, ingestion of arsenic compounds might not be detected (see Chapter 5). Arsenic was not detected in the urine of a number of individuals following ingestion of As(III) sulfide in a herbal preparation for asthma (Tay and Seah 1975), possibly because of the low rate of absorption. Arsenic concentrations in urine samples from a group of volunteers usually increased following the ingestion of Nori, an algal food product containing arsenosugars (Le et al. 1994b). However, the amount of the increase and the rate of the elimination varied greatly for each subject. In the most extreme case, a 20-year-old female showed no increase in urine arsenic content (Le et al. 1994b). In other studies, mice fed partially purified arsenosugars eliminated most of the arsenic via the feces (86% of the dose eliminated in 48 hr) (Shiomi et al. 1990).

Repeated exposure of human volunteers to As(V) for 10 days (66 μg per day) established a constant speciation pattern, but only 48% of the dose was recovered over 18 days (Johnson and Farmer 1991). Generally, 40-60% of the daily intake of inorganic arsenic is excreted each day in urine (Buchet et al. 1981; Farmer and Johnson 1990).

Arsenic Species in Urine

In a recent study by Buchet et al. (1996), two methods were used to determine arsenic speciation. The first method was the same as that used by Foà et al. (1984) in a study in which 148 Italian male subjects who were not occupationally exposed to arsenic and reportedly did not eat seafood during the study period (Foà et al. 1984). Total arsenic was determined by HG-AA following dry ashing ($MgNO_3$ and MgO at 600°C). Arsenic species in the urine were isolated on a strong anion-exchange column. Elution with 0.5 M HCl, H_2O, NH_4OH (5%), and NH_4OH (20%) yielded in each fraction, respectively, As(V) and As(III), MMA, other forms (OF) of arsenic, and DMA. The OF fraction is said to represent dietary arsenic, such as AsB, that is not metabolized. That fraction can be analyzed following dry ashing but is usually ignored or determined by difference. The known species in the isolated fractions were determined by HG-AA. The QA-QC procedures were described and seem adequate. The results for this reference population are shown in Table 3-10. More than 60% of the urinary arsenic is present in the OF fraction. Only the concentration of DMA in urine correlated with blood arsenic concentrations (Foà et al. 1984). The second method (Buchet et al. 1996) used hydride generation to liberate the arsenic species, which were then separated on the basis of volatility. Total arsenic was determined following dry ashing, and OF arsenic was determined by difference. There was good agreement between the two methods, which were used in different laboratories, although detection limits were not reported. The results for subjects who refrained from eating seafood are given in Table 3-11. The results for smokers and nonsmokers do not differ. The OF fraction is again significant and is reflected in the data from 15 subjects who reportedly had not eaten seafood for 5 days before the 24-hr sampling: As(V) and As(III), mean value 0.6 μg per 24 hr (standard deviation (SD) 0.3); MMA, 0.5 μg (SD 0.2); DMA, 3.8 μg (SD 1.8); and total arsenic, 20 μg (SD 16). Here, OF arsenic represents 76% of the total arsenic excreted. Buchet et al. (1996) found increases in DMA concentrations following ingestion of mussels. That is not surprising in view of the high arsenosugar content in mussels (Le et al. 1994a,b).

TABLE 3-10 Total Arsenic in Blood and Arsenic Species in Urine in the Foà et al. (1984) Study[a]

Measure	Total Arsenic in Blood (µg/L)	Arsenic Species in Urine (µg/L)				
		As(V) and As(III)	MMA	DMA	OF	As(T)[b]
Mean	5.1	1.9	1.9	2.1	11.3	17.2
SD	6.9	1.2	1.4	1.5	10.1	11.1
Range	0.5-32	0.5-10	0.5-9	0.5-10	0-43	0.5-48

[a]Seafood was not consumed during the study.
[b]Sum of species, not determined.
Abbreviations: DMA, dimethylarsinic acid; MMA, monomethylarsonic acid; OF, other forms of arsenic determined by difference in this case; As(T), arsenic total; SD, standard deviation.

The first major U.S. study of arsenic species in urine was reported by Kalman et al. (1990), and some results are given in Table 3-12. In all, about 3,000 samples were collected from residents of a community surrounding an arsenic-emitting copper smelter. The work was carefully done, and HG-AA was used for speciation with a quantitation limit of 0.7 ppb. Unfortunately, total arsenic was not determined. The authors estimated that with no seafood consumption, the sum of the species should equal the total-arsenic output and be about 10 μg/L. The results are in agreement with that value.

Cation-exchange chromatography followed by HG-AA was used in a urinary study of patients with blackfoot disease (Lin and Huang 1995). A standard urine sample was used for QA-QC (total arsenic only; no certified

TABLE 3-11 Arsenic Species in Urine in the Buchet et al. (1996) Study[a]

Measure	Arsenic Species in Urine (μg/g of Creatinine)				
	As(V) and As(III)	MMA	DMA	OF	As(T)[b]
Mean	1.8	0.6	2.8	6.14	10.8
	(2.1)	(0.5)	(5.1)		(27.7)
SD	0.7	0.4	1.5		6.2
	(1.4)	(0.2)	(3.1)		(56.2)
Range	0.7-3.0	0.2-1.3	1.0-5.3		2.4-21.9
	(0.6-5.8)	(0.2-0.9)	(1.6-12.4)		(4.5-196.5)

[a]Seafood was not consumed during the study; 10 did not smoke and 11 smoked tobacco products. Values in parentheses are from smokers.
[b]Sum of species, not determined.
Abbreviations: DMA, dimethylarsinic acid; MMA, monomethylarsonic acid; OF, other forms of arsenic determined by difference in this case; As(T), arsenic total; SD, standard deviation.

TABLE 3-12 Control-Group Data on Arsenic Species in Urine in the Kalman et al. (1990) Study

Measure (Sample No.)	Arsenic Species in Urine (μg/L)			
	As(V) and As(III)	MMA	DMA	As(T)
Mean (696)[b]	1.3	1.6	6.4	9.2
SD	1.1	1.3	5.8	7.5
Mean (140)[c]	1.5	1.7	11.3	14.5
SD	1.2	1.4	9.4	11.2

[a]Sum of species, not determined.
[b]Samples with reported seafood consumption excluded.
[c]Samples with reported seafood consumption only.
Abbreviations: DMA, dimethylarsinic acid; MMA, monomethylarsonic acid; OF, other forms of arsenic determined by difference in this case; As(T), arsenic total (sum of species and is not determined); SD, standard deviation.

standards are available for speciation). The results for 30 patients and 30 controls are listed in Table 3-13. The authors stated that the OF data indicated that the high total-arsenic values were probably the result of diet.

Table 3-14 presents a comparison of those data (Lin and Huang 1995) with the data from studies in Japan (Yamauchi et al. 1989) and Italy (Foà et al. 1984); also included are data from studies in Argentina (Vahter et al. 1995). The similarity between the results of the Taiwanese and European studies is strong. The high values in the Japanese study are almost certainly associated with seafood consumption, and arsenosugars are a likely source of the DMA; however, the inorganic concentrations are noteworthy, and demethylation during storage or analyses could be a cause.

TABLE 3-13 Arsenic Species in Urine in the Lin and Huang (1995) Study

Measure (Subject No.)	Arsenic Species in Urine (μg/g of Creatinine)				
	As(V) and As(III)	MMA	DMA	OF	AsT
Patients with BFD (30)					
Mean	6.1	6.2	7.2	36.1	55.6
SD	2.8	2.3	4.5	10.5	13.1
Controls (30)					
Mean	3.4	3.9	6.4	26.3	40.1
SD	2.3	1.9	4.1	6.7	8.2

Abbreviations: DMA, dimethylarsinic acid; MMA, monomethylarsonic acid; OF, other forms of arsenic determined by difference in this case; AsT, arsenic total; BFD, blackfoot disease; SD, standard deviation.

TABLE 3-14 Comparison of Arsenic Species in Urine in Four Studies

Study (Subject No.)	Location	Arsenic Species in Urine (Mean µg/L ± SD)				
		As(V) and As(III)	MMA	DMA	OF	AsT
Lin and Huang 1995 (30)	Taiwan	1.7 ± 1.1	2.0 ± 1.0	3.3 ± 2.5	13.7	20.7 ± 7.0
Foà et al. 1984 (148)	Europe	1.9 ± 1.2	1.9 ± 1.4	2.1 ± 1.5	11.3	17.2 ± 11.2
Yamauchi et al. 1989 (102)	Japan	11.4 ± 5.9	3.6 ± 2.8	35.0 ± 20.8	71.0	121 ± 101
Vahter et al. 1995 (11)	Argentina	66 ± 41	7.1 ± 12	185 ± 110	13	274 ± 98

Abbreviations: DMA, dimethylarsinic acid; MMA, monomethylarsonic acid; OF, other forms of arsenic determined by difference in this case; AsT, arsenic total; SD, standard deviation.

The urinary arsenic concentrations are much higher in native Andean women exposed to high concentrations of arsenic in drinking water (Vahter et al. 1995, Table 3-14). Ion exchange chromatography in combination with HG-AA was used for speciation and for determination of total-arsenic concentration following dry ashing. A standard reference water (National Institute of Standards and Technology, USA, No. 1643a) was used for QA-QC, and the speciation method was validated in an interlaboratory comparison exercise (Crecelius and Yager 1997). A similar method was used in a study that involved Mexican individuals exposed to high arsenic concentrations in drinking water (408 μg/L) and controls (31 μg/L) (Del Razo et al. 1997) (Table 3-15). In both studies, the sum of the As(III) and As(V), MMA, and DMA concentrations is close to the total-arsenic concentrations, presumably because of diets without seafood.

Chatterjee et al. (1995) also used ion exchange, both cation and anion, and flow injection–HG-AA in a study of the urine of individuals living in the arsenic-rich region of West Bengal (up to 3,700 μg/L in well water and about 50% As(III)). In addition to MMA and DMA, inorganic As(V) and As(III) were found in the urine samples. The sum of those species is close to the measured total-arsenic values.

TABLE 3-15 Arsenic in Urine of Subjects in the Del Razo et al. (1997) Study

| Exposure Group (Subject No.) | Measure | Arsenic Species in Urine (μg/g of Creatinine) | | | |
		As(V) and As(III)	MMA	DMA	AsT
High (35)	Mean	171.8	63.5	303.6	561.3
	Confidence intervals	135.8-217.3	46.8-86.2	239.4-385.0	449.8-700.5
Low (35)	Mean	1.8	1.4	16.1	20.6
	Confidence intervals	1.3-2.5	1.1-1.7	11.5-22.6	15.1-28.0

Abbreviations: AsT, arsenic total; MMA, monomethylarsonic acid; DMA, dimethylarsinic acid.

The maximal total-arsenic concentration of 956 μg/g of creatinine was measured (hydride generation) in a group of occupationally exposed British workers (Farmer and Johnson 1990). For the most-exposed group, the average speciation pattern was 1-6% As(V), 11-14% As(III), 14-18% MMA, and 63-70% DMA. Significant concentrations of hidden arsenic were noted in some urine samples and were attributed to seafood consumption.

The development of modern techniques based on HPLC separation has enabled the identification of more arsenic species in urine, although no extensive studies are available to date. Some results for the urine standard-reference-material (SRM 2670, high concentration) species are as follows: AsB, 15 $\pm$ 3 μg/L; DMA, 49 $\pm$ 3 μg/L; MMA, 7 $\pm$ 2 μg/L; As(V), 443 $\pm$ 20 μg/L; total, 514 $\pm$ 23 μg/L. The certified value for total arsenic is 480 $\pm$ 100 μg/L (Le and Ma 1998).

An analytical method based on microwave decomposition and flow-injection analysis coupled to HG-AA has been used to differentiate between total arsenic in urine and hydride-producing and nonhydride-producing species (Le et al. 1993).

The nonhydride-producing species (OF in Tables 3-10, 3-11, 3-13 and 3-14) are generally assumed to be organic arsenicals of dietary origin (e.g., AsB from fish or mushrooms) rather than metabolites of inorganic arsenic.

A recent intercomparison of analytical methods for arsenic speciation in urine (Crecelius and Yager 1997) found that both accuracy and precision are relatively poor for arsenic concentrations of less than 5 μg/L. Hydride generation was used by five of the seven participating laboratories. It should be noted that this limit is just above the practical quantification level of 4 μg/L for inorganic arsenic in drinking water, reflecting the increased difficulty of the analyses (see previous section Practical Quantification Level for Arsenic in Drinking Water).

Collection and Storage of Urine Samples
for Arsenic Speciation Analysis

Important considerations for collection and storage of urine samples are the prevention of contamination and the minimization of loss of trace amounts of analytes. An additional prerequisite for obtaining reliable speciation information is to maintain the stability of chemical species in the sample.

Polyethylene containers are normally preferred to glass containers because the former is less adsorptive to arsenic (Schaller et al. 1991). To maintain the stability of arsenic species in the sample, refrigeration and frozen conditions have been repeatedly shown to be most effective for urine-sample storage (Schaller et al. 1991; Palacios et al. 1997; Le et al. 1998). Among the most common urinary arsenic species, DMA, MMA, and AsB are generally more stable than As(III) and As(V), which can interconvert (Larsen et al. 1993b; Palacios et al. 1997; Le et al. 1998).

Palacios et al. (1997) found that As(V), MMA, DMA, and AsB (each at 200 μg/L) in urine were stable for the entire test period of 67 days at 4°C without using any additives. AsC was oxidized to AsB. In dried urine residue, all of the five arsenic species tested were stable during the same testing period at 4 °C and at ambient temperature. This study did not test the stability of As(III) because other work (Larsen et al. 1993b) had shown a rapid oxidation of As(III) to As(V).

Le et al. (1998) compared the effects of the following storage conditions on the stability of As(III), As(V), MMA, DMA, and AsB (each at 50 μg/L): temperature (25°C, 4°C, and -20°C), storage time (1, 2, 4, and 8 months), and the use of additives (hydrochloric acid, sodium azide, benzoic acid, benzyltrimethylammonium chloride, and cetylpyridinium chloride). In replicate studies that used urine samples from male and female volunteers and from commercial sources, the authors found that all five arsenic species were stable for up to 2 months when urine samples were stored at 4°C and -20°C without additives. For 4 and 8 months of storage, the stability of arsenic species was dependent on urine matrices. Although the five arsenic species in some urine samples were stable for the entire 8 months at 4°C and -20°C, in other samples stored under identical conditions, there were significant changes in speciation. The use of additives did not improve the stability of arsenic species in urine. The addition of 0.1 M HCl to urine samples resulted in alterations of inorganic arsenite and arsenate concentrations and in some demethylation. Thus, an acidification procedure is not appropriate for speciation analysis, even though dilute acetic, hydrochloric, and nitric acids have traditionally been added to samples to minimize possible adsorption of trace elements onto sample containers.

Arsenic Species in Blood

Blood is a more difficult matrix than urine for chemical analysis, so until very recently, only total-arsenic concentrations in whole blood were reported. The sample was first decomposed by using wet or dry ashing, prior to analysis by conventional methods. However, a neutron-activation method, which involved a radiochemical separation and re-irradiation, was used in a study of the blood, plasma, cells, and whole blood of blackfoot-disease patients and others (Heydorn 1970) (see Table 3-16).

Dry ashing followed by HG-AA was used in a study by Vahter et al. (1995). They reported a mean arsenic concentration of 8.0 μg/L (a range of 2.7 to 18.3) in the blood of exposed Andean women and 1.5 μg/L (a range of 1.1 to 2.4) in controls. The mean value for blood arsenic in a reference population of 148 subjects was 5.1 μg/L (a range of 0.5 to 32) (Foà et al. 1984). Blood arsenic in 85 patients undergoing hemodialysis treatment had a mean value of 8.5 $\pm$ 1.8 μg/L versus that in 25 controls who had a mean value of 10.6 $\pm$ 1.3 μg/L (Mayer et al. 1993).

TABLE 3-16 Arsenic in Blood of Families with Blackfoot-Disease Patients and Control Subjects in the Heydorn (1970) Study

| Tissue | Measure | Arsenic in Blood (μg/L) | | |
		BFD Families (Subject No.)	Danish Controls (Subject No.)	Taiwanese Controls (Subject No.)
Plasma	Mean	38.1 (47)	2.4 (16)	15.4 (17)
	SD	1.90	1.9	1.39
Red blood cells	Mean	93 (11)	2.7 (7)	32.7 (5)
	SD	1.84	1.3	1.84
Whole blood	Mean	60 (11)	2.5	21.6 (5)
	SD	1.70	—	1.67

Abbreviations: BFD, blackfoot disease; SD, standard deviation.

Shibata et al. (1994) used HPLC-ICP-MS to detect, for the first time, AsB in human blood. The limit of detection was 0.3 $\mu g/L$, and the results for a 29-year-old male were as follows: plasma, 3.3 $\mu g/L$; serum, 4.6 $\mu g/L$; red blood cells, 10.1 $\mu g/L$. Only one additional high-molecular-weight compound was detected, but not identified, by gel-permeation chromatography. The HPLC method was developed in Japan and is described by Shibata et al. (1992). A less expensive but still sensitive method has been used to confirm the presence of AsB in human serum (Zhang et al. 1996a,b). Trace amounts of DMA are also found. The method uses ion-exchange HPLC to separate arsenicals. The next step is photo-oxidation (ultraviolet with persulfate) to arsenate, followed by HG-AA. (The method is similar to that described above for urine speciation (Le et al. 1996).) The detection limits in blood were 1.0, 1.3, 1.5, and 1.4 $\mu g/L$ for MMA, DMA, AsB, and AsC, respectively.

The rat accumulates arsenic in red blood cells as DMA (Lerman and Clarkson 1983). The speciation analysis involved the use of electrophoresis following dosing with radiolabeled arsenate and thin-layer chromatography (Odanaka et al. 1980).

Arsenic in Hair and Fingernails

Arsenic is believed to accumulate in hair and fingernails more than other tissues because of the high content of keratin (and the corresponding high content of cysteine) in those tissues. Consequently, arsenic is assumed to be bound as As(III). There are reports (Yamauchi and Yamamura 1984; Yamato 1988) that DMA(V) is present in both hair and nails, but the oxidation state is assumed; the species could well be DMA(III) (see Affinity of Arsenic for Sulfur, above).

Arsenic in hair and nails might be increased as a result of surface contamination. Harrison and Clemena (1972) and Agahian et al. (1990) developed elaborate schemes for the removal of arsenic on hair surfaces. The procedure was found to remove 98% of exogenous arsenic. However, it is not clear whether such procedures can remove arsenic that is bound to the surface of hair and nails as a result of contact with arsenic in the water. A method of determining externally bound arsenic on hair and nails on the basis of the generation of arsine (Gutzeit method) from undigested samples was proposed by Pirl et al. (1983). The authors showed that soaking hair in arsenate or arsenite (0.2% solution) results in the surface uptake of arsenic that cannot be removed by washing with water or 4 M HCl.

Hindmarsh (1998) claims that the source of arsenic on the outer surface of hair is both ingestion and external contamination, and that the two sources cannot be differentiated. External contamination can produce hair arsenic concentrations of several thousand parts per million. This work was done by using a nondestructive method, the proton-induced X-ray emission. According to this abstract, hair arsenic concentrations of up to 100 ppm are found in live patients with clinical arsenic poisoning even though concentrations of about 45 ppm can be associated with death. Hindmarsh (1998) recommends that hair samples should consist of at least 1 g of hair cut close to the scalp and derived from several sites on the head, and the whole sample should be analyzed.

Smith (1964) determined that the arsenic concentration in human hair was 0.62 ppm in a group of males and 0.37 ppm in a group of females. Direct neutron-activation analysis (Pan et al. 1993) of carefully washed samples of hair from 28 healthy subjects from Taiwan revealed an arsenic content of 0.27 $\pm$ 0.33 ppm. It is interesting that the antimony content of the hair of healthy Taiwanese and of patients with BFD was the same, about 0.08 ppm, and that for some individuals, the concentration of antimony was greater than that of arsenic. The crustal abundance of antimony is appreciably less than that of arsenic (Latimer and Hildebrand 1951).

In Hungary, 2,095 hair samples were washed and analyzed by wet digestion and flame atomic absorption (FAA) (Bozsai et al. 1989). The FAA method is not sensitive for arsenic, although the authors claimed a detection limit of 0.10 ppm for a 1-g sample of arsenic. Hair concentrations of 3 ppm were found in some individuals. In the United States, Kalman et al. (1990) found a mean hair arsenic concentration of 6.8 μg/g, median 0.5 μg/g (SD 27.7), in 32 individuals in the study's Tacoma control subgroup. Higher values (mean 15.2 μg/g, median 3.7 μg/g, SD 35.0) were found in 40 individuals living in Ruston, close to an arsenic-emitting copper smelter.

In a study in Japan, Yamato (1988) digested unwashed hair with 2 M NaOH at 95°C for 3 hr. That procedure was designed to extract the arsenicals with minimal change in speciation. HG-AA revealed the presence of inorganic arsenic and DMA. (That is likely to be DMA(III) as pointed out above.) The mean arsenic concentration was 0.08 ppm, ranging from 0.04 to 0.33 ppm in 100 samples. Inorganic arsenic accounted for 73% of the total, and DMA accounted for 27%. DMA was also found in the hair of hamsters (Yamauchi and Yamamura 1984).

Liebscher and Smith (1968) used neutron-activation analysis on the fingernails from a normal population of 124 subjects and established that total-arsenic concentrations are in the range of 0.02 to 2.90 ppm. In a more recent study (Agahian et al. 1990) in which acid digestion and HG-AA were used, the limit of detection was 1.5 μg/g. The results were as follows: no exposure, more than 1.5 ppm; low exposure, 2.0-3.0 ppm; medium exposure, 2.5-8.6 ppm; high exposure, 10.6-16.0 ppm.

SUMMARY AND CONCLUSIONS

A large number of arsenic-containing chemical compounds are known to be present in the terrestrial environment: they include the inorganic species arsenate, or As(V), and arsenite, or As(III), in addition to organic derivatives that usually contain As-methyl units. The brief account of the chemistry and biochemistry of the species emphasizes that their chemical and physical properties are greatly species dependent. Analytical methods used to identify arsenic species are described. Early investigations used a derivatization technique, hydride generation, that could be used to quantitate a limited number of water-soluble species. Recent developments permit the analysis of a much wider range of species, and examples of the use of HPLC-ICP-MS (separation with element-specific detection) and HPLC-ESMS-MS (separation with molecule-specific detection) are given.

The arsenic species present in groundwater and surface water are largely arsenate and arsenite, and the latter can amount to around 50% of the total arsenic present, as found in West Bengal and to a greater extent in Taiwan. In some surface water methylated arsenic species can achieve high concentrations presumably as a result of the biological conversion of the inorganic species. The practical quantitation limit (PQL) of the water industry for arsenic in drinking water apparently is 4 ppb. The reliable analysis of arsenic at lower concentrations will probably require skilled operators and more expensive instruments.

The highest concentrations of arsenic compounds in food (at more than 1 ppm) are found in products that originate from the marine environment. In such food as fish and shrimp, the major arsenical is arsenobetaine (AsB), an apparently nontoxic species that is not metabolized by humans and is rapidly excreted in the urine. A range of arsenic species that exist in shellfish include AsB, arsenosugar derivatives, and the tetramethylarsonium ion in varying proportions. Arsenosugars are the principal arsenic species present in most marine algal products, although up to 50% of the arsenic in certain algae is the more toxic arsenate. Arsenosugars are metabolized by humans mainly to DMA.

Fish and algal products from terrestrial sources contain low arsenic concentrations (less than 1 ppm), but little is known about the species content. AsB is present but is by no means ubiquitous. The available data indicate that, as in marine organisms, concentrations of inorganic arsenic in freshwater fish are probably low.

Mushrooms (total arsenic at more than 1 ppm) contain a wide range of arsenic species. Most of the arsenic in an edible mushroom species is found as DMA; AsB and AsC are present in a poisonous mushroom. The arsenic content of other foods is less than 1 ppm, but little is known about speciation. The arsenic species are usually difficult to extract intact, possibly because they are difficult to access or are bound to cellular components. This "food arsenic" is likely to be based largely on inorganic species. Crude separations into so-called "organic" and "inorganic" fractions have been based on methods that have been shown to be applicable to some food, such as fish, but the value of those separations when applied to other foods, such as meat and grain, is moot.

Many studies have been conducted on the arsenic species present in urine, because humans eliminate most ingested arsenic (e.g., 40-80% of ingested arsenite or arsenate) by this route. Speciation studies have mainly concentrated on the determination of inorganic species, MMA, DMA, and total arsenic, largely because of available hydride-generation methods. There are problems with both accuracy and precision of these measurements at low concentrations of arsenic species (less than 5 μg/L). In some populations (e.g., those in Mexico and Argentina), MMA, DMA, and inorganic arsenic are essentially the only species present, and the mean total-arsenic concentrations can be as much 561.3 μg/g of creatinine in an exposed population and 20.6 μg/g in controls. In other populations, high concentrations of additional species are found, for example, in Taiwan, where the mean total-arsenic concentration in the urine of one exposed group, 55.6 μg/g includes unidentified arsenic species at 36.1 μg/g. The additional species are believed to be largely AsB, which is not metabolized and which reflects consumption of seafood; however, unidentified species can be found even in the urine of individuals who claim not to have eaten seafood before the study. Individuals who eat algal products and shellfish seem to have increased concentrations of DMA, probably because the arsenosugars present in the food are metabolized to DMA. In general, total urinary arsenic concentrations and the concentrations of the arsenic species increase with exposure; however, in a given population, a wide range is seen in the concentration of each species and in the total-arsenic concentrations. More modern methods are now being applied to determine all arsenic species in urine, but at present, application is only at the research level.

The range of total-arsenic concentrations in human blood is smaller (up to 100 ppm) than that found in urine. Blood is a more-difficult matrix for speciation studies; however, DMA, AsB, and inorganic arsenic species have been identified in serum.

Arsenic concentrations in hair and nails also reflect exposure, but there are difficulties in ensuring that the arsenic is not adsorbed on the surface as a result of external exposure. According to a recent abstract (Hindmarsh 1998), the upper range of arsenic concentrations in hair and nails after excessive arsenic ingestion may be higher than previously reported (e.g., 100 versus 10 ppm).

RECOMMENDATIONS

Analytical techniques are needed to determine the arsenic species in various media (e.g. urine), including biological tissues. Quality-control data and certified standards for arsenic speciation are also needed to help legitimize interlaboratory and intralaboratory studies.

More comprehensive studies should be undertaken to determine the arsenic content in food, especially after food processing. These studies should focus on growth conditions, speciation, availability to humans, residence time in humans, and mass balances.

Other studies of less critical importance for assessing the risk of arsenic from drinking-water exposures but nonetheless important to fill critical data gaps include the following:

— Fundamental studies on the transport of arsenic species through membranes and cell walls.

— Studies investigating low-cost and easy-to-use methods for routine measurement of all arsenic species at concentrations below the current PLQ of 4 ppb in water.

REFERENCES

Abernathy, C.O., W. Marcus, H. Chen, and P. White. 1989. Report on Arsenic Work Group Meetings. U.S. Environmental Protection Agency, Office of Drinking Water, Washington, D.C.

Adams, M.A., P.M. Bolger, and E.L. Gunderson. 1994. Dietary intake and hazards of arsenic. Pp. 41-49 in Arsenic: Exposure and Health, W.R. Chappell, C.O. Abernathy, and C.R. Cothern, eds. Northwood, U.K.: Science and Technology Letters.

Agahian, B., J.S. Lee, J.H. Nelson, and R.E. Johns. 1990. Arsenic levels in fingernails as a biological indication of exposure to arsenic. Am. Ind. Hyg. Assoc. J. 51:646-651.

Ahmann, D., A.L. Roberts, L.R. Krumholz, and F.M. Morel. 1994. Microbe grows by reducing arsenic [letter]. Nature 371:750.

Ahmann, D., L.R. Krumholz, H.F. Hemond, D.R. Lovley, and F.M.M. Morel. 1997. Microbial mobilization of arsenic from sediments in the Aberjona watershed. Environ. Sci. Technol. 31:2923-2930.

Anderson, L., and K.W. Bruland. 1991. Biogeochemistry of arsenic in natural waters: The importance of methylated species. Environ. Sci. Technol. 25:420-427.

Andreae, M.O. 1977. Determination of arsenic species in natural waters. Anal. Chem. 49:820-823.

Berger, B.J., and A.H. Fairlamb. 1994. High-performance liquid chromatographic method for the separation and quantitative estimation of antiparasitic melaminophenyl arsenical compounds. Trans. R. Soc. Trop. Med. Hyg. 88:357-359.

Borho, M., and P. Wilderer. 1997. A reliable method for preservation and determination of arsenite(III) concentrations in groundwater and water works samples. Aqua 46(3):138-143.

Borum, D. 1992. Arsenic Exposure. Draft Report Background Paper. U.S. Environmental Protection Agency, Washington, D.C.

Bozsai, G., Z. Deak, M. Csanadi, J. Ring, A. Horvath, and Z. Karpati. 1989. Determination of arsenic content of hair samples to assess the role of drinking water in the arsenic load of population. Egészségtudomány 33:115-124.

Bramen, R.S., and C.D. Foreback. 1973. Methylated forms of arsenic in the environment. Science 182:1247-1249.

Bright, D.A., S. Brock, W.R. Cullen, G.M. Hewitt, J. Jafaar, and K.J. Reimer. 1994. Methylation of arsenic by anaerobic microbial consortia isolated from lake sediment. Appl. Organomet. Chem. 8:415-422.

Bright, D.A., M. Dodd, and K.J. Reimer. 1996. Arsenic in subarctic lakes influenced by gold mine effluent: The occurrence of organoarsenicals and "hidden" arsenic. Sci. Total Environ. 180:165-182.

Buchet, J.P., and R. Lauwerys. 1983. Evaluation of exposure to inorganic arsenic in man. Pp. 75-90 in Analytical Techniques for Heavy Metals in Biological Fluids, S. Facchetti, ed. Amsterdam: Elsevier.

Buchet, J.P., R. Lauwerys, and H. Roels. 1981. Urinary excretion of inorganic arsenic and its metabolites after repeated ingestion of sodium metaarsenite by volunteers. Int. Arch. Occup. Environ. Health 48:111-118.

Buchet, J.P., D. Lison, M. Ruggeri, V. Foa, and G. Elia. 1996. Assessment of exposure to inorganic arsenic, a human carcinogen, due to the consumption of seafood. Arch. Toxicol. 70:773-778.

Byrne, A.R., Z. Šlejkovec, T. Stijve, L. Fay, W. Gössler, J. Gailer, and K.J. Irgolic. 1995. Arsenobetaine and other arsenic species in mushrooms. Appl. Organomet. Chem. 9:305-313

Camerman, N. and J. Trotter. 1964. Stereochemistry of arsenic Part XI: "Cacodyl disulphide" dimethylarsino dimethyldithioarsinate. J. Chem

Soc. (London) 1964:219-227

Challenger, F. 1951. Biological methylation. Adv. Enzymol. 12:429-491.

Chatterjee, A., D. Das, B.K. Mandal, T.R. Chowdhury, G. Samanta, and D. Chakraborti. 1995. Arsenic in ground water in six districts of West Bengal, India: The biggest arsenic calamity in the world. Part 1. Arsenic species in drinking water and urine of the affected people. Analyst 120:643-650.

Chen, S.L., S.R. Dzeng, M.H. Yang, K.H. Chiu, G.M. Shieh, and C.M. Wai. 1994. Arsenic species in ground water of the blackfoot disease area, Taiwan. Environ. Sci. Technol. 28:877-881.

Corr, J.J., and E.H. Larsen. 1996. Arsenic speciation by liquid chromatography coupled with ionspray tandem mass spectrometry. J. Anal. Atom. Spectrom. 11:1215-1224.

Crecelius, E., and J. Yager. 1997. Intercomparison of analytical methods for arsenic speciation in human urine. Environ. Health Perspect. 105:650-653.

Cullen, W.R., and M. Dodd. 1988. The photooxidation of solutions of arsenicals to arsenate: a convenient analytical procedure. Appl. Organomet. Chem. 2:1-7.

Cullen, W.R., and K.J. Reimer. 1989. Arsenic speciation in the environment. Chem. Rev. 89:713-764.

Cullen, W.R., and D.I. Hettipathirana. 1993. The effect of arsenicals on alkaloid production by cell suspension cultures of Catharanthus roseus. Appl. Organomet. Chem. 7:477-486.

Cullen, W.R., B.C. McBride, and J. Reglinski. 1984. The reaction of methylarsenicals with thiols: Some biological implications. J. Inorg. Biochem. 21:179-194.

Cullen, W.R., D. Hettipathirana, and J. Reglinski. 1989a. The effect of arsenicals on cell suspension cultures of the Madagascar periwinkle (Catharanthus roseus). Appl. Organomet. Chem. 3:515-521.

Cullen, W.R., B.C. McBride, H. Manji, A.W. Pickett, and J. Reglinski. 1989b. The metabolism of methylarsine oxide and sulfide. Appl. Organomet. Chem. 3:71-78.

Cullen, W.R., H. Li, G. Hewitt, K.J. Reimer, and N. Zalunardo. 1994. Identification of extracellular arsenical metabolites in the growth medium of the microorganisms Apiotrichum humicola and Scopulariopsis brevicaulis. Appl. Organomet. Chem. 8:303-311.

Dabeka, R.W., A.D. McKenzie, and G.M.A. Lacroix. 1987. Dietary intakes of lead, cadmium, arsenic, and fluoride by Canadian adults: a 24-hour duplicate diet study. Food Addit. Contam. 4:89-101.

Dabeka, R.W., A.D. McKenzie, G.M. Lacroix, C. Cleroux, S. Bowe, R.A.

Graham, H.B. Conacher, and P. Verdier. 1993. Survey of arsenic in total diet food composites and estimation of the dietary intake of arsenic by Canadian adults and children. J. AOAC Int. 76:14-25.

Dean, J.R., L. Ebdon, M.E. Foulkes, H.M. Crews, and R.D. Massey. 1994. Determination of the growth promoter, 4-hydroxy-3-nitrophenylarsonic acid in chicken tissue by coupled high-performance liquid chromatography-inductively coupled plasma mass spectrometry. J. Anal. Atom. Spectrom. 9:615-618.

de Bettencourt, A.M., M.H. Florêncio, M.F.N. Duarte, M.L.R. Gomes, and L.F.C. Vilas Boas. 1994. Refractory methylated arsenic compounds in esturine waters: tracing back elusive species. Appl. Organomet. Chem. 8:43-56.

Delnomdedieu, M., M.M. Basti, M. Styblo, J.D. Otvos, and D.J. Thomas. 1994. Complexation of arsenic species in rabbit erythrocytes. Chem. Res. Toxicol. 7:621-627.

Del Razo, L.M., G.G. Garcia-Vargas, H. Vargas, A. Albores, M.E. Gonsebatt, R. Montero, P. Ostrosky-Wegman, M. Kelsh, and M.E. Cebrián. 1997. Altered profile of urinary arsenic metabolites in adults with chronic arsenicism: A pilot study. Arch. Toxicol. 71:211-217.

Dick, G.L., J.T. Hughes, J.W. Mitchell, and F. Davidson. 1978. Survey of trace elements and pesticide residues in the New Zealand diet. 1. Trace element content. NZ J. Sci. 21:57-69.

Diorio, C., J. Cai, J. Marmor, R. Shinder, and M.S. DuBow. 1995. An *Escherichia coli* chromosomal *ars* operon homolog is functional in arsenic detoxification and is conserved in gram-negative bacteria. J. Bacteriol. 177:2050-2056.

Dixon, H.B.F. 1997. The biochemical action of arsonic acids especially as phosphate analogs. Adv. Inorg. Chem. 44:191-227.

Dodd, M., S.L. Grundy, K.J. Reimer, and W.R. Cullen. 1992. Methylated antimony(V) compounds: Synthesis, hydride-generation properties, and implications for aquatic speciation. Appl. Organometal. Chem. 6:207-211.

Eaton, A.D. 1994. Determining the practical quantitation level for arsenic. J. Am. Water Works Assoc. 86(2):100-114.

Edmonds, J.S. and K.A. Francesconi. 1993. Arsenic in seafoods: Human health aspects and regulations. Marine Pollut. Bull. 26:665-674.

Edmonds, J.S., Y. Shibata, K.A. Francesconi, R.J. Rippingale, and M. Morita. 1997. Arsenic transformations in short marine food chains studied by HPLC-ICP MS. Appl. Organomet. Chem. 11:281-287.

EPA (U.S. Environmental Protection Agency). 1988. Special Report on Ingested Inorganic Arsenic: Skin Cancer; Nutritional Essentiality. EPA

625/3-87/013. U.S. Environmental Protection Agency, Risk Assessment Forum, Washington, D.C.

Farmer, J.G., and L.R. Johnson. 1990. Assessment of occupational exposure to inorganic arsenic based on urinary concentrations and speciation of arsenic. Br. J. Ind. Med. 47:342-348.

Fish, R.H., F.E. Brinckman, and K.L. Jewett. 1982. Fingerprinting inorganic arsenic and organoarsenic compounds in in situ oil shale retort and process waters using a liquid chromatograph coupled with an atomic absorption spectrometer as a detector. Environ. Sci. Technol. 16:174-179.

Florêncio, M.H., M.F. Duarte, A.M. Bettencourt, M.L. Gomes, and L.F. Vilas Boas. 1997. Electrospray mass spectra of arsenic compounds. Rapid Commun. Mass Spectrom. 11:469-473.

Foà, V., A. Colombi, M. Maroni, M. Buratti, and G. Calzaferri. 1984. The speciation of the chemical forms of arsenic in the biological monitoring of exposure to inorganic arsenic. Sci. Total Environ. 34:241-259.

Food Additives and Contaminants Committee. 1984. Report on the Review of the Arsenic in Food Regulations. Ministry of Agriculture, Fisheries and Foods, FAC/REP/39. London: Her Majesty's Stationary Office.

Francesconi, K.A. and J.S. Edmonds. 1997. Arsenic and marine organisms. Adv. Inorg. Chem. 44:147-189.

Frost, R.R. and R.A. Griffin. 1977. Effect of pH on adsorption of arsenic and selenium from landfill leachate by clay minerals. Soil Sci. Soc. Am. J. 41:53-57.

Gartrell, M.J., J.C. Craun, D.S. Podrebarac, and E.L. Gunderson. 1985. Pesticides, selected elements, and other chemicals in adult total diet samples, October 1979–September 1980. J. Assoc. Off. Anal. Chem. 68:862-875.

GESAMP (IMO/FAO/UNESCO/WMO/WHO/IAEA/UN/UNEP). 1986. Joint Group of Experts on the Scientific Aspects of Marine Pollution. Review of Potentially Harmful Substances; Arsenic, Mercury, and Selenium. Report and Studies. GESAMP Vol. 28.

Ghosh, M.M., and J.R. Yuan. 1987. Adsorption of inorganic arsenic and organoarsenicals on hydrous oxides. Environ. Progress 6:150-157.

Gunderson, E.L. 1995. FDA total diet study, July 1986–April 1991, dietary intakes of pesticides, selected elements, and other chemicals. J. AOAC Int. 78:1353-1363.

Harrison, W. W. and G.G. Clemena. 1972. Survey analysis of trace elements in human fingernails by spark source mass spectrometry. Clin. Chim. Acta 36:485-492.

Hasegawa, H. 1996. Seasonal changes in methylarsenic distribution in Tosa

Bay and Uranouchi Inlet. Appl. Organomet. Chem. 10:733-740.

Hasegawa, H. 1997. The behavior of trivalent and pentavalent methyl arsenicals in Lake Biwa. Appl. Organomet. Chem. 11:305-311.

Hering, J.G., P.Y. Chen, J.A. Wilkie, and M.L. Elimelech. 1997. Arsenic removal from drinking water during coagulation. J. Environ. Eng. 123:800-808.

Heydorn, K. 1970. Environmental variation of arsenic levels in human blood determined by neutron activation analysis. Clin. Chim. Acta 28:349-357.

Hindmarsh, J.T. 1998. Hair arsenic as an index of toxicity [abstract]. P. 7 in Book of Abstracts of the Third International Conference on Arsenic Exposure and Health Effects, July 12–15, San Diego, Calif.

Hocking, D., and A.A. Jaffer. 1969. Damping-off in pine nurseries: Fungicidal control by seed pelleting. Commonwealth Forest Rev. 48:355-363.

Howard, A.G., and S.C. Apte. 1989. Seasonal control of arsenic speciation in an estuarine ecosystem. Appl. Organomet. Chem. 3:499-507.

Howard, A.G., and S.D.W. Comber. 1989. The discovery of hidden arsenic species in coastal waters. Appl. Organomet. Chem. 3:509-514.

Inoue Y., K. Kawabata, H. Takahashi, and G. Endo. 1994. Determination of arsenic compounds using inductively coupled plasma mass spectrometry with ion chromatography. J. Chromatogr. A 675(1-2):149-154.

Irgolic, K.J. 1994. Determination of total arsenic and arsenic compounds in drinking water. Pp. 51-60 in Arsenic: Exposure and Health, W.R. Chappell, C.O. Abernathy, and C.R. Cothern, eds. Northwood, U.K.: Science and Technology Letters.

Irgolic, K.J., D. Spall, B.K. Puri, D. Ilger, and R.A. Zingaro. 1991. Determination of arsenic and arsenic compounds in natural gas samples. Appl. Organomet. Chem. 5:117-124.

Irgolic, K.J., H. Greschonig, and A.G. Howard. 1995. Arsenic. Pp 168-184 in Encyclopedia of Analytical Science, A. Townshend, ed. London: Academic.

Jacobson, S.E., F. Mares, and P.M. Zambri. 1979a. Biphase and triphase catalysis. Arsenated polystyrene as catalysts for Bayer-Villiger oxidation of ketones by aqueous hydrogen peroxide. J. Am. Chem. Soc. 101:6938-6946.

Jacobson, S.E., F. Mares, and P.M. Zambri. 1979b. Biphase and triphase catalysis. Arsenated polystyrene catalysts for the epoxidation of olefins by aqueous hydrogen peroxide. J. Am. Chem. Soc. 101:6946-6950.

Jauhiainen, M., K.J. Stevenson, and P.J. Dolphin. 1988. Human plasma lecithin-cholesterol acetyltransferase. The vicinal nature of cysteine 31 and cysteine 184 in the catalytic site. J. Biol. Chem. 263:6525-6533.

Jelinek, C.F., and P.E. Corneliussen. 1977. Levels of arsenic in the United

States food supply. Environ. Health Perspect. 19:83-87.

Johnson, L.R., and J.G. Farmer. 1991. Use of human metabolic studies and urinary arsenic speciation in assessing arsenic exposure. Bull. Environ. Contam. Toxicol. 46:53-61.

Kaise, T., and S. Fukui. 1992. The chemical form and acute toxicity of arsenic compounds in marine organisms. Appl. Organomet. Chem. 6:155-160.

Kalman, D.A., J. Hughes, G. van Belle, T. Burbacher, D. Bolgiano, K. Coble, N.K. Mottet, and L. Polissar. 1990. The effect of variable environmental arsenic contamination on urinary concentrations of arsenic species. Environ. Health Perspect. 89:145-151.

Kawabata, K., Y. Inoue, H. Takahashi, and G. Endo. 1994. Determination of arsenic species by inductively coupled plasma mass spectrometry with ion chromatography. Appl. Organomet. Chem. 8:245-248.

Knowles, F.C. and A.A. Benson. 1983a. Mode of action of a herbicide. Johnsongrass and methanearsonic acid Sorghum halepense, reduction of methanearsonate to arsenosomethane, inhibition of malic enzymes. Plant Physiol. 71:235-240.

Knowles, F.C. and A.A. Benson. 1983b. The biochemistry of arsenic. Trends Biochem. Sci. 8(5):178-180.

Koch, I., L. Wang, W.R. Cullen, C.A. Ollson, and K.J. Reimer. 1998. Arsenic Speciation in Yellowknife Biota: Impact on the Terrestrial Environment. Paper presented at the Third International Conference on Arsenic Exposure and Health Effects, July 12-15, San Diego, Calif.

Korte, N.E. and Q. Fernando. 1991. A review of arsenic(III) in groundwater. Crit. Rev. Environ. Control 21:1-40.

Kuehnelt, D., W. Goessler, and K.J. Irgolic. 1997a. Arsenic compounds in terrestrial organisms I. Collybia maculata, Collybia butyracea, and Amanita muscaria from arsenic smelter sites in Austria. Appl. Organomet. Chem. 11:289-296.

Kuehnelt, D., W. Goessler, and K.J. Irgolic. 1997b. Arsenic compounds in terrestrial organisms II: Arsenocholine in the mushroom Amanita muscaria. Appl. Organomet. Chem. 11:459-470.

Kumar, U.T., N.P. Vela, and J.A. Caruso. 1995. Multi-element detection of organometals by supercritical fluid chromatography with inductively coupled plasma mass spectrometric detection. J. Chromatogr. Sci. 33:606-610.

Lai, V.W.M., W.R. Cullen, C.F. Harrington, and K.J. Reimer. 1997. The characterization of arsenosugars in commercially available algal products including a Nostoc species of terrestrial origin. Appl. Organomet. Chem. 11:797-803.

Lai, V.W.M., W.R. Cullen, C.F. Harrington, and K.J. Reimer. 1998. Seasonal changes in the arsenic speciation in Fucus species. Appl. Organomet. Chem. 12:243-251.

Larsen, E.H., G. Pritzl, and S.H. Hansen. 1993a. Arsenic speciation in seafood samples with emphasis on minor constituents: An investigation using high-performance liquid chromatography with detection by inductively coupled plasma mass spectrometry. J. Anal. Atomic Spectrom. 8:1075-1084.

Larsen, E.H., G. Pritzl, and S.H. Hansen. 1993b. Speciation of eight arsenic compounds in human urine by high-performance liquid chromatography with inductively coupled plasma mass spectrometric detection using antimonate for internal chromatographic standardization. J. Anal. Atom. Spectrom. 8:557-563.

Latimer, W.M., and J.H. Hildebrand. 1951. Reference Book of Inorganic Chemistry, 3rd Ed. New York: Macmillan.

Lawrence, J.F., P. Michalik, G. Tam, H.B.S. Conacher. 1986. Identification of arsenobetaine and arsenocholine in Canadian fish and shellfish by high-performance liquid chromatography with atomic absorption detection and confirmation by fast atom bombardment mass spectrometry. J. Agric. Food Chem. 34:315-319.

Le, X.C., and M. Ma. 1998. Short-column liquid chromatography with hydride generation atomic fluorescence detection for the speciation of arsenic. Anal. Chem. 70:1926-1933.

Le, X.C., W.R. Cullen, and K.J. Reimer. 1992. Decomposition of organoarsenic compounds by using a microwave oven and subsequent determination by flow injection-hydride generation-atomic absorption spectrometry. Appl. Organomet. Chem. 6:161-171.

Le, X.C., W.R. Cullen, and K.J. Reimer. 1993. Determination of urinary arsenic and impact of dietary arsenic intake. Talanta 40:185-193.

Le, X.C., W.R. Cullen, and K.J. Reimer. 1994a. Effect of cysteine on the speciation of arsenic by using hydride generation atomic absorption spectrometry. Anal. Chim. Acta 285:277-285.

Le, X.C., W.R. Cullen, and K.J. Reimer, K. J. 1994b. Human urinary arsenic excretion after one time ingestion of seaweed, crab and shrimp. Clin. Chem. 40:617-625.

Le, X.C., M. Ma, and N.A. Wong. 1996. Speciation of arsenic compounds using high-performance liquid chromatography at elevated temperature and selective hydride generation atomic fluorescence detection. Anal. Chem. 68:4501-4506.

Le, X.C., M. Ma, S. Yalcin, N.A. Wong, J. Feldmann, V.W. Lai, and W.R. Cullen. 1998. Stability of Arsenic Species in Urine and Water. Paper presented at the Third International Conference on Arsenic Exposure and Health Effects, July 12–15, San Diego, Calif.

Ledet, A.E. and W.B. Buck. 1978. Toxicity of organic arsenicals in feed-stuffs. Pp. 375-391 in Toxicity of Heavy Metals in the Environment, Part 1. F. W. Oehme, ed. New York: Marcel Dekker.

Lerman, S., and T.W. Clarkson. 1983. The metabolism of arsenite and arsenate by the rat. Fundam. Appl. Toxicol. 3:309-314.

Li, G.C., W.C. Fei, and Y.P. Yen. 1979. Survey of arsenical residual levels in the rice grain from various locations in Taiwan. Natl. Sci. Council Monthly 7:700-706.

Li, J., and C.M. Pickart. 1995. Binding of phenylarsenoxide to Arg-tRNA protein transferase is independent of vicinal thiols. Biochemistry 34:15829-15837.

Liebscher, K., and H. Smith. 1968. Essential and nonessential trace elements. A method of determining whether an element is essential or nonessential in human tissue. Arch. Environ. Health 17:881-890.

Lin, T.H., and Y.L. Huang. 1995. Chemical speciation of arsenic in urine of patients with blackfoot disease. Biol. Trace Elem. Res. 48:251-261.

Lovley, D.R., E.J.P. Phillips, and D.J. Lonergan. 1991. Enzymatic versus nonenzymatic mechanisms for Fe(III) reduction in aquatic sediments. J. Environ. Sci. Technol. 25:1062-1067.

Lu, F.J. 1990. Fluorescent humic substances and blackfoot disease in Taiwan. Appl. Organomet. Chem. 4:191-195.

Lu, F.J., and Y.S. Lee. 1992. Humic acid: Inhibitor of plasmin. Sci. Total Environ. 114:135-139.

Lu, F.J., H.P. Hsieh, H. Yamauchi, and Y. Yamamura. 1991. Fluorescent humic substances-arsenic complex in well water in areas where blackfoot disease is endemic in Taiwan. Appl. Organomet. Chem. 5:507-512.

Lu, F.J., T.S. Huang, Y.S. Lin, V.F. Pang, and S.Y. Lin. 1994. Peripheral vasculopathy in rats induced by humic acids. Appl. Organomet. Chem. 8:223-228.

Lumsdon, D.G., R.A. Fraser, J.D. Russel, and N.T. Livesey. 1984. New infrared band assignments for the arsenate ion adsorbed on synthetic goethite (a-FeOOH) J. Soil Sci. 35:381-386.

Macy, J.M., K. Nunan, K.D. Hagen, D.R. Dixon, P.J. Harbour, M. Cahill, and L.I. Sly. 1996. *Chrysiogenes arsenatis* gen. nov., sp. nov., a new arsenate-respiring bacterium isolated from gold mine wastewater. Int. J. Syst. Bacteriol. 46:1153-1157.

Maeda, S. 1994. Biotransformation of arsenic in the freshwater environment. Pp. 155-187 in Arsenic in the Environment. Part 1: Cycling and Characterization, J.O. Nriagu, ed. New York: Wiley Interscience.

Manning, B.A. and S. Goldberg. 1997. Adsorption and stability of arsenic(III) at the clay mineral-water interface. Environ. Sci. Technol. 31:2005-2011.

Mayer, D.R., W. Kosmus, H. Pogglitsch, D. Mayer, and W. Beyer. 1993. Essential trace elements in humans: Serum arsenic concentrations in hemodialysis patients in comparison to healthy controls. Biol. Trace Elem. Res. 37:27-38.

Monplaisir, G.M., T. Lei, and W.D. Marshall. 1994. Performance of a novel silica T-tube interface. Anal. Chem. 66:3533-3539.

Morita, M., and Y. Shibata. 1990. Chemical form of arsenic in marine macroalgae. Appl. Organomet. Chem. 4:181-190.

Morton, W., G. Starr, D. Pohl, J. Stoner, S. Wagner, and P. Weswig. 1976. Skin cancer and water arsenic in Lane County, Oregon. Cancer 37:2523-2532.

Mushak, P., and A.F. Crocetti. 1995. Risk and revisionism in arsenic cancer risk assessment. Environ. Health Perspect. 103:684-689.

Natelson, S. 1961. Part II. Methodology. Pp. 113-116 in Microtechniques of Clinical Chemistry, 2nd Ed. Springfield, Ill.: Charles C Thomas.

Nissen, P., and A.A. Benson. 1982. Arsenic metabolism in freshwater and terrestrial plants. Physiol. Plant. 54:446-450.

NRCC (National Research Council of Canada). 1986. Certified Reference Materials. National Research Council of Canada, Institute for National Measurement Standards, Ottawa, Ont.

Nriagu, J.O., and J.M. Azcue. 1990. Food contamination with arsenic in the environment. Pp. 121-143 in Food Contamination from Environmental Sources. J.O. Nriagu and M.S. Simmons, eds. New York: John Wiley & Sons.

Odanaka, Y., O. Matano, and S. Goto. 1980. Biomethylation of inorganic arsenic by the rat and some laboratory animals. Bull. Environ. Contam. Toxicol. 24:452-459.

Odanaka, Y., N. Tsuchiya, O. Matano, and S. Goto. 1985. Characterization of arsenic metabolites in rice plant treated with DSMA (disodium methanearsonate). J. Agric. Food Chem. 33:757-763.

OME (Ontario Ministry of the Environment) 1987. Organic vs Inorganic Arsenic in Selected Food Samples. Rep. 87-48-450000-057. Ontario Ministry of the Environment, Hazardous Contaminants Coordination Branch, Toronto, Ont.

Palacios, M.A., M. Gomez, C. Camara, and M.A. Lopez. 1997. Stability studies of arsenate, monomethylarsonate, dimethylarsinate, arsenobetaine and arsenocholine in deionized water, urine and clean-up dry residue from urine samples and determination by liquid chromatography. Anal. Chim.

Acta 340:209-220.

Pan, T.C., T.H. Lin, C.L. Tseng, M.H. Yang, and C.W. Huang. 1993. Trace elements in hair of blackfoot disease. Biol. Trace Elem. Res. 39: 117-128.

Partington, J.R. 1962. VI. Chemistry in Scandinavia. II. Scheele. Pp. 205-234 in A History of Chemistry, Vol. 3. London: Macmillan.

Pergantis, S.A., E.M. Heithmar, and T.A. Hinners. 1995. Microscale flow injection and microbore high-performance liquid chromatography coupled with inductively coupled plasma mass spectrometry via a high-efficiency nebulizer. Anal. Chem. 67:4530-4535.

Pergantis, S.A.. W.R. Cullen, D.T. Chow, and G.K. Eigendor. 1997a. Liquid chromatography and mass spectrometry for the speciation of arsenic animal feed additives. J. Chromatogr. A 764:211-222.

Pergantis, S.A., W. Winnik, and D. Betowski. 1997b. Determination of ten organoarsenic compounds using microbore high-performance liquid chromatography coupled with electrospray mass spectrometry-mass spectrometry. J. Anal. Atom. Spectrom. 12:531-536.

Pergantis, S.A., E.M. Heithmar, and T.A. Hinners. 1997c. Speciation of arsenic animal-feed additives by microbore high-performance liquid chromatography with inductively coupled plasma mass spectrometry. Analyst 122:1063-1068.

Pfannhauser, W., and U. Pechanek. 1977. The contamination of food in Austria by toxic heavy metals [in German]. Lebensm. Ernähr. 30:88-92.

Pirl, J.N., G.F. Townsend, A.K. Valaitis, D. Grohlich, and J.J. Spikes. 1983. Death by arsenic: A comparative evaluation of exhumed body tissues in the presence of external contamination. J. Anal. Toxicol. 7:216-219.

Pyles, R.A. and E.A. Woolson. 1982. Quantitation and characterization of arsenic compounds in vegetables grown in arsenic acid treated soil. J. Agric. Food Chem. 30:866-870.

Reimer, K.J., X.C., Le, and W.R. Cullen. 1994. Speciation of arsenic compounds in some marine organisms. Environ. Sci. Technol. 28:1598-1604.

Rin, K., K. Kawaguchi, K. Yamanaka, M. Tezuka, N. Oku, and S. Okada. 1995. DNA-strand breaks induced by dimethylarsinic acid, a metabolite of inorganic arsenics, are strongly enhanced by superoxide anion radicals. Biol. Pharmacol. Bull. 18:45-48.

Sagan, L.S., R.A. Zingaro, and K.J. Irgolic. 1972. Alkoxy-, alkylthio-, and (organyseleno)dialkylarsines. J. Organomet. Chem. 39:301-311.

Saha, K.C. 1995. Chronic arsenical dermatoses from tube-well water in West Bengal during 1983-87. Ind. J. Dermatol. 40:1-12.

Schaller, K.H., M. Fleischer, J. Angerer, and J. Lewalter. 1991. Arsenic determination in urine. Pp. 69-80 in Analyses of Hazardous Substances in Biological Materials, J. Angerer and K.H. Schaller, eds. Weinheim, Germany: VCH.

Schmitt, V.O., J. Szpunar, O.F. Donard, and R. Lobinski. 1997. Microwave accelerated sample preparation for speciation analysis of organotin compounds in biomaterials. Can. J. Anal. Sci. Spectrosc. 42:33-68.

Schoof, R.A., L.J. Yost, E. Crecelius, K. Irgolic, W. Goessler, H.R. Guo, and H. Greene. 1998. Dietary arsenic intake in Taiwanese districts with elevated arsenic in drinking water. Hum. Ecol. Risk Assess. 4:117-135.

Schwedt, G., and M. Reickhoff. 1996a. Analysis of oxothio arsenic species in soil and water. J. Prakt. Chem. 338:55-59.

Schwedt, G., and M. Reickhoff. 1996b. Separation of thio- and oxothio-arsenates by capillary zone electrophoresis and ion chromatography. J. Chromatogr. A 736:341-350.

Sckerl, M.M., and R.E. Frans 1969. Translocation and metabolism of MMA-^{14}C in johnsongrass and cotton-D. Weed Sci. 17:421-427.

Scott, M.J., and J.J. Morgan. 1995. Reactions of oxide surface. Oxidation of As(III) by synthetic birnessite. Environ. Sci. Technol. 29:1898-1905.

Sheppard, B.S., J.A. Caruso, D.T. Heitkemper, and K.A. Wolnik. 1992. Arsenic speciation by ion chromatography with inductively coupled plasma mass spectrometric detection. Analyst 117:971-975.

Sheridan, J.E., J.D. Whitehead, and A.G. Spiers. 1973. Control of mercury-resistant Pyrenophora avenae on seed oats with methyl arsenic sulphide. N.Z. J. Exp. Agric. 1:127-130.

Shibata, Y., M. Morita, and K. Fuwa. 1992. Selenium and arsenic in biology: Their chemical forms and biological functions. Adv. Biophys. 28:31-80.

Shibata, Y., J. Yoshinaga, and M. Morita. 1994. Detection of arsenobetaine in human blood. Appl. Organomet. Chem. 8:249-251.

Shiomi, K., M. Chino, and T. Kikuchi. 1990. Metabolism in mice of arsenic compounds contained in the red alga Porphyra yezoensis. Appl. Organomet. Chem. 4:281-286.

Shiomi, K., Y. Sugiyama, K. Shimakura, and Y. Nagashima. 1995. Arsenobetaine as the major arsenic compound in the muscle of two species of freshwater fish. Appl. Organomet. Chem. 9:105-109.

Silver, S., G. Ji, S. Broer, S. Dey, D. Dou, and B. R. Rosen. 1993. Orphan enzyme or patriarch of a new tribe: The arsenic resistance ATPase of bacterial plasmids. Mol. Microbiol. 8:637-642.

Siu, K.W.M., G.J. Gardner, and S.S. Berman. 1988. Atmospheric pressure chemical ionization and electrospray mass spectrometry of some organoarsenic species. Rapid Commun. Mass Spec. 2:69-71.

Siu, K.W.M., R. Guevremont, J.C.Y. le Blanc, G.J. Garnder, and S.S. Berman. 1991. Electrospray interfacing for the coupling of ion exchange and ion-pairing chromatography to mass spectrometry. J. Chromatogr. 554(1/2):27.

Smith, H. 1964. The interpretation of the arsenic content of human hair. Forsensic Sci. Soc. J. 4:192-199.

Sohrin, Y., M. Matsui, M. Kawashima, M. Hojo, and H. Hasegawa. 1997. Arsenic biogeochemistry affected by eutrophication in Lake Biwa, Japan. Environ. Sci. Technol. 31:2712-2720.

Sturgeon, R.E., M.K.W. Siu, S.N. Willie, and S.S. Berman. 1989. Quantification of arsenic species in a river water reference material for trace metals by graphite furnace atomic absorption spectrometric techniques. Analyst 114:1393-1396.

Sun, X., and H.E. Doner. 1996. An investigation of arsenate and arsenate bonding structures on goethite by FTIR. Soil Sci. 161:865-872.

Tao, S.H., and P.M. Bolger. 1998. Dietary Intakes of Arsenic in the United States. Paper presented at the Third International Conference on Arsenic Exposure and Health Effects, July 12–15, San Diego, Calif.

Tay, C.H., and C.S. Seah. 1975. Arsenic poisoning from anti-asthmatic herbal preparations. Med. J. Aust. 2:424-428.

Tseng, W.P., H.M. Chu, S.W. How, J.M. Fong, C.S. Lin, and S. Yeh. 1968. Prevalence of skin cancer in an endemic area of chronic arsenicism in Taiwan. J. Natl. Cancer Inst. 40:453-463.

Tsuda, T., A. Babazono, E. Yamamoto, N. Kurumatani, Y. Mino, T. Ogawa, Y. Kishi, and H. Aoyama. 1995. Ingested arsenic and internal cancer: A historical cohort study followed for 33 years. Am. J. Epidemiol. 141:198-209.

Vahter, M. 1994. Species differences in the metabolism of arsenic compounds. Appl. Organomet. Chem. 8:175-182.

Vahter, M., E. Marafante, and L. Dencker. 1984. Tissue distribution and retention of ^{74}As-dimethylarsinic acid in mice and rats. Arch. Environ. Contam. Toxicol. 13:259-264.

Vahter, M., G. Concha, B. Nermell, R. Nilsson, F. Dulout, and A.T. Natarajan. 1995. A unique metabolism of inorganic arsenic in native Andean women. Eur. J. Pharmacol. Environ. Toxicol. Pharmacol. 293:455-462.

Vallee, B.L. 1973. Arsenic. Air Quality Monographs, No. 73-18. Washington, D.C.: American Petroleum Institute.

Vela, N.P. and J.A. Caruso. 1993. Potential of liquid chromatography-inductively coupled plasma mass spectrometry for trace metal speciation.

J. Anal. Atom. Spect. 8:787-794.

Vetter, J. 1994. Data on arsenic and cadmium contents of some common mushrooms. Toxicon 32:11-15.

Waychunas G.A., B.A. Rea, C.C. Fuller, and J.A. Davis. 1993. Surface chemistry of ferrihydrite: Part 1. EXAFS studies of the geometry of co-precipitated and adsorbed arsenate. Geochim. Cosmochim. Acta 57:2251-2269.

WHO (World Health Organization). 1989. Arsenic. Pp 155-162. In: Toxicological Evaluation of Certain Food Additives and Contaminants. WHO Food Additive Ser. 24. Cambridge, U.K.: Cambridge University Press.

Yalcin, S., and X.C. Le. 1998. Preconcentration and speciation of arsenic species via solid phase extraction cartridges. Paper 384 presented at the 81st Canadian Society for Chemistry Conference and Exhibition, Whistler, B.C., May 31–June 4, 1998.

Yamanaka, K., K. Ohtsubo, A. Hasegawa, lH. Hayashi, H. Ohji, M. Kanisawa, and S. Okada. 1996. Exposure to dimethylarsinic acid, a main metabolite of inorganic arsenics, strongly promotes tumorigenesis initiated by 4-nitroquinoline 1-oxide in the lungs of mice. Carcinogenesis 17:767-770.

Yamato, N. 1988. Concentration and chemical species of arsenic in human urine and hair. Bull. Environ. Contam. Toxicol. 40:633-640.

Yamauchi, H., and Y. Yamamura. 1984. Metabolism and excretion of orally administered dimethylarsinic acid in the hamster. Toxicol. Appl. Pharmacol. 74:134-140.

Yamauchi, H., K. Takahashi, M. Mashiko, and Y. Yamamura. 1989. Biological monitoring of arsenic exposure of gallium arsenide- and inorganic arsenic-exposed workers by determination of inorganic arsenide and its metabolites in urine and hair. Am. Ind. Hyg. Assoc. J. 50:606-612.

Yang, H.L., S.C. Tu, F.J. Lu, and H.C. Chiu. 1994. Plasma protein C activity is enhanced by arsenic but inhibited by fluorescent humic acid associated with blackfoot disease. Am. J. Hematol. 46:264-269.

Yost, L.J., R.A. Schoof, and R. Aucoin. 1998. Intake of inorganic arsenic in the North American diet. Hum. Ecol. Risk Assess. 4:137-152.

Zhang, X., R. Cornelis, J. De Kimpe, and L. Mees. 1996a. Arsenic speciation in serum of uraemic patients based on liquid chromatography with hydride generation atomic absorption spectrometry and on-line UV photo-oxidation digestion. Anal. Chim. Acta 319:177-185.

Zhang, X., R. Cornelis, J. De Kimpe, L. Mees, V. Vanderbiesen, A. De Cubber, and R. Vanholder. 1996b. Accumulation of arsenic species in serum of patients with chronic renal disease. Clin. Chem. 42(8 Pt 1):1231-1237.

Zingaro, R.A., and J.K. Thomson. 1973. Thio and seleno sugar esters of
    dialkylarsinous acids. Carbohydr. Res. 29:147-152.

4

Health Effects of Arsenic

THIS chapter presents the subcommittee's review of the evidence of health effects in humans resulting from ingestion of inorganic arsenic. The source of exposure in the large majority of studies reviewed is drinking water contaminated with inorganic arsenic from natural sources. A few studies involve other sources of exposure, however, such as industrially contaminated drinking water, medicinal use of arsenic, and arsenical pesticides. The focus of the chapter is on causal inference, which in risk-assessment terminology is often referred to as hazard identification. The chapter first provides the evidence for cancer and then other effects.

Although evidence for dose-response relationships is presented as it relates to causal inference, the actual quantification of dose-response relationships has not been undertaken in this chapter. Statistical issues in dose-response quantification for risk-assessment purposes are presented in Chapter 10.

CANCER EFFECTS

The carcinogenic role of arsenic compounds was first noted over 100 years ago in the Hutchinson (1887) observation that an unusual number of skin tumors develop in patients treated with arsenicals. In a 1980 review of arsenic, the International Agency for Research on Cancer (IARC 1980) determined that inorganic arsenic compounds are skin and lung (via inhalation) carcinogens in humans. Data suggesting an increased risk for cancer at other sites were noted to be inadequate for evaluation. Since 1980, several additional studies of cancer and exposure to arsenic in drinking water have been completed.

The epidemiological studies outlined in this chapter clearly show associations of arsenic with several internal cancers at exposure concentrations of several hundred micrograms per liter of drinking water. However, they provide few data about the degree of association at exposure concentrations below a few hundred micrograms per liter.

An extensive literature describes cases of skin and internal cancers following medicinal treatment with potassium arsenite (Fowler's solution) for a variety of conditions (Sommers and McManus 1953; Rosset 1958; Robson and Jelliffe 1963; Jackson and Grainge 1975; Popper et al. 1978; Prystowsky et al. 1978; Reymann et al. 1978; Nagy et al. 1980; Falk et al. 1981; Roat et al. 1982; Robertson and Low-Beer 1983), exposure to arsenical pesticides (Sommers and McManus 1953; Kjeldsberg and Ward 1972; Popper et al. 1978), or consumption of industrially contaminated drinking water or pesticide-contaminated wine (Roth 1957). The case reports and case series do not provide the needed data for quantitative risk assessment. However, the occurrence of these tumors in high numbers after long-term ingestion of arsenic in relatively young patients, or at anatomic sites where cancer is an extremely rare occurrence (e.g., liver angiosarcoma), increases the likelihood that many of the documented cancers were induced by arsenic. The observations also assist in identifying major cancer end points. The most common types of malignancy described in the reports are skin cancer, lung cancer, angiosarcoma of the liver (probably noted because of its rarity), prostate cancer, and bladder cancer. Reports of other cancers also appear: leukemia; other hematopoietic cancers; and cancers of the breast, colon, stomach, parotid gland, nasopharynx, larynx, buccal cavity, kidney, and others. Additional case reports describe internal cancers after the appearance of Bowen's disease, a type of superficial intraepidermal carcinoma that has been linked with arsenic exposure (Graham and Helwig 1959; Epstein 1960; Peterka et al. 1961; Hugo and Conway 1967).

The second group of studies comprises epidemiological investigations. Most of them did not provide the informational quality necessary for interpretation of dose-response relationships. However, many of the studies included data that are valuable in establishing the level of risk of particular internal cancers associated with a range of likely arsenic exposures (see Table 4-1). The form of arsenic was not specified in the epidemiological studies cited except for Cuzick et al. (1992), who observed mortality in a cohort of patients medicinally treated with potassium arsenite. Ecological studies are considered first, followed by cohort studies. Studies are summarized in Tables 4-1 through 4-6. When evaluating the epidemiological evidence to help judge whether arsenic in drinking water is a likely cause of internal cancers or other diseases, the subcommittee used the evaluation criteria that have been discussed by Hill (1965) and others (Cox 1972; Susser 1973; Rothman 1986).

The primary criteria that were used in attempting to distinguish causal from noncausal associations included (1) strength of the association (the magnitude of the risk ratio between exposed and nonexposed populations); (2) temporality (the disease must follow the exposure); (3) biological gradient (exposure to higher concentrations of arsenic or exposure for longer periods should result in a greater effect than low-concentration exposures or exposures of short duration); and (4) epidemiological coherence (are similar observations made in diverse populations?).

TABLE 4-1 Summary of Cancer End Points Available for Quantitative Risk Assessment of Cancer and Ingested Arsenic Exposures

Study	Cancer Site							
	Skin	Bladder	Lung	Kidney	Nasal	Liver	Prostate	Other
Ecological studies								
Tseng et al. 1968	✓							
Wu et al. 1989	✓	✓	✓	✓	✓	✓	✓	
Chen and Wang 1990	✓	✓	✓	✓	✓	✓	✓	
Guo et al. 1997		✓		✓				
Hopenhayn-Rich et al. 1996, 1998	✓	✓	✓	✓				
Smith et al. 1998	✓	✓	✓	✓		✓		
Cohort studies								
Cuzick et al. 1992	✓	✓	✓			✓		
Tsuda et al. 1995		✓	✓			✓		✓
Chiou et al. 1995		✓	✓					
Case-control studies								
Bates et al. 1995		✓						

✓, cancer end points.

Ecological Studies

Summary results of the ecological studies are shown in Tables 4-2, 4-3, and 4-4.

TABLE 4-2 Bladder-Cancer Mortality, Urinary-Cancer Incidence, and Arsenic Exposure in Ecological Studies

Study	Location	Exposure	Cases, No.	Study Outcome	Comments
Mortality studies					
Chen and Wang 1990	Taiwan	Data from 83,656 wells, national survey	National data	β(SE) from regression: Male 3.9 (0.5) Female 4.2 (0.5)	Mortality, 1972-1983 in 314 precincts and townships; regression-coefficient (β) estimates increase in age-adjusted mortality per 100,000 per increase in arsenic at 100 µg/L of water
Wu et al. 1989	SW Taiwan	Average arsenic: <0.30 ppm 0.30-0.59 ppm ≥0.60 ppm	Male Female 23 30 36 36 26 30	Rate: Male Female 22.6 25.6 61.0 57.0 92.7 111.3	Mortality, 1973-1986 in 42 villages in Taiwan
Hopenhayn-Rich et al. 1996, 1998	Cordoba Province, Argentina	Few high concentration Scattered high concentration 178 µg/L average	Male Female 113 39 93 24 131 27	SMR: Male Female 0.80 (0.7-1.0) 1.21 (0.9-1.6) 1.42 (1.1-1.7) 1.58 (1.0-2.4) 2.14 (1.8-2.5) 1.82 (1.2-2.6)	Mortality, 1986-1991; national rates for 1989 used as the standard for the SMR; SMR for COPD below the expected level, indicating low smoking rates; also no trend with stomach cancer SMR
Smith et al. 1998	Region II, Northern Chile	420 µg/L average; 5-yr average ranged from below 100 µg/L after 1980 to 569 µg/L in 1955-1959; by city and 5-yr period, range was 40-870 µg/L	Male Female 93 64	SMR: Male Female 6.0 (4.8-7.4) 8.2 (6.3-10.5)	Mortality, 1989-1993; national rates for 1991 used as the standard for the SMR; arsenic concentration is population-weighted average for major cities or towns in Region II, 1950-1974; information in paper adequate to calculate increase in risk per unit exposure

Incidence studies

| Guo et al. 1997[a] | Taiwan | Data from 83,656 wells, national survey: <0.05 ppm 0.05-0.08 ppm 0.09-0.16 ppm 0.17-0.32 ppm 0.33-0.64 ppm >0.64 ppm | β(SE) from regression: Mixed results for exposure levels; at >0.64 ppm, the β(SE) was Male 0.57 (0.07) / Female 0.33 (0.04) National rates | Incidence, 1980-1987; results shown are for transitional-cell carcinoma, the most common form of bladder cancer |

[a] Transitional-cell carcinoma only.
Abbreviations: β(SE), regression coefficient (standard error); SMR, standardized mortality ratio; COPD, chronic obstructive pulmonary disease.

TABLE 4-3 Kidney-Cancer Mortality, Urinary-Cancer Incidence, and Arsenic Exposure in Ecological Studies

Study	Location	Exposure	Cases, No. Male	Female	Study Outcome		Comments
Mortality studies							
Chen et al. 1985	SW Taiwan	Blackfoot-disease endemic area	42	62	SMR: Male 772	Female 1,119	SMRs; age-specific Taiwan rates as standard
Chen and Wang 1990	Taiwan	Data from 83,656 wells; national survey	National data		β(SE) from regression: Male 1.1 (0.2)	Female 1.7 (0.2)	Mortality, 1972-1983 in 314 precincts and townships; regression-coefficient (β) estimates increase in age-adjusted mortality per 100,000 per increase in arsenic at 100 µg/L of water
Wu et al. 1989	SW Taiwan	Average arsenic: <0.30 ppm 0.30-0.59 ppm ≥0.60 ppm	9 11 6	4 13 16	Rate: Male 8.42 18.90 25.26	Female 3.42 19.42 57.98	Mortality, 1973-1986 in 42 villages in Taiwan
Hopenhayn-Rich et al. 1996, 1998	Cordoba Province, Argentina	County group: Low Medium High	66 66 53	38 34 27	SMR: Male 0.87 1.33 1.57	Female 1.00 1.36 1.81	SMRs using national age-specific rates as the standard

Incidence studies

Guo et al. 1997[a]	Taiwan	Data from 83,656 wells; national survey: <0.05 ppm 0.05-0.08 ppm 0.09-0.16 ppm 0.17-0.32 ppm 0.33-0.64 ppm >0.64 ppm	β(SE) from regression: Mixed results for exposure levels; at >0.64 ppm, the β(SE) was Male Female National rates 0.03 (0.02) 0.142 (0.013)	Incidence, 1980-1987; results shown are for renal-cell carcinoma only

[a]Transitional-cell carcinoma only.

Abbreviations: β(SE), regression coefficient (standard error); SMR, standardized mortality ratio.

TABLE 4-4 Lung-Cancer Mortality and Arsenic Exposure in Ecological Studies

Study	Location	Exposure	Cases, No.		Study Outcome		Comments
Chen and Wang 1990	Taiwan	1974-1976 data from 83,656 wells, national survey: average for each of 314 precincts or townships	National data		β(SE) from regression: Male 5.3(0.9)	Female 5.3(0.7)	Mortality, 1972-1983 in 314 precincts and townships; regression-coefficient (β) estimates increase in age-adjusted mortality per 100,000 per increase in arsenic at 100 µg/L of water
Wu et al. 1989	SW Taiwan	Average arsenic: <0.30 ppm 0.30-0.59 ppm ≥0.60 ppm	Male 53 62 32	Female 43 40 38	Rate: Male 49.16 100.67 104.08	Female 36.71 60.82 122.16	Mortality, 1973-1986 in 42 villages in Taiwan
Smith et al. 1998	Region II, Northern Chile	420 µg/L average; 5-yr average ranged from below 100 µg/L after 1980 to 569 µg/L in 1955-1959; by city and 5-yr period, range was 40-870 µg/L	Male 544	Female 154	SMR: Male 3.8(3.5-4.1)	Female 3.1(2.7-3.7)	Mortality, 1989-1993; national rates for 1991 used as the standard for the SMR; arsenic concentration is population-weighted average for major cities and towns in Region II, 1950-1974; information in paper adequate to calculate increase in risk per unit exposure

Hopenhayn-Rich et al. 1998	Cordoba Province, Argentina	County group:	Male	Female	SMR: Male	Female	Mortality, 1986-1991; national rates for 1989 used as the standard for the SMR; SMR for COPD below the expected level, indicating low smoking rates; also no trend with stomach cancer SMR
		Low	826	194	0.92(0.85-0.98)	1.24(1.06-1.42)	
		Medium	914	138	1.54(1.44-1.64)	1.34(1.12-1.58)	
		High	708	156	1.77(1.63-1.90)	2.16(1.83-2.52)	

Abbreviations: β(SE), regression coefficient (standard error); SMR, standardized mortality ratio.

Villages in southwestern coastal Taiwan switched from surface to ground-water (artesian wells) for drinking in the 1920s, motivated by the need to improve the microbiological quality of drinking water. Unexpectedly, aquifers were contaminated with naturally occurring arsenic, and the shift resulted in widespread exposure to relatively high concentrations. Tseng et al. (1968) and Tseng (1977) conducted individual medical examinations, with an emphasis on skin lesions, of 40,421 inhabitants of 37 villages in that area of Taiwan by the end of 1965. The arsenic content of well water ranged from 0.01 to 1.82 parts per million (ppm); most wells had arsenic concentrations of 0.4-0.6 ppm. Prevalence of skin cancer, keratoses, and hyperpigmentation were calculated for villages in three exposure groups: 0.0-0.29 ppm, 0.30-0.59 ppm, and 0.60 ppm and over. Hyperpigmentation was the most common condition (183.5/1,000), followed by keratosis (71.0/1,000) and skin cancer (10.6/1,000). In both sexes in three broad age groups, the prevalence of skin lesions increased with exposure to arsenic. For example, among males 60 and over, the prevalence of skin cancer per 1,000 persons was 46.1 in the 0.0-0.29-ppm group, 163.4 in the 0.30-0.59-ppm group, and 255.3 in the 0.60-ppm-and-over group. Among females 60 years of age and over, skin-cancer prevalence was 9.1, 62.0, and 110.1 per 1,000 persons in the three exposure groups. Study results were used by EPA for a risk assessment of ingested arsenic (EPA 1988). The primary limitation of this study, beyond the problems common to ecological studies, is related to the lack of detail and specificity provided for exposure estimates. Those issues are discussed in Chapter 2 of this report.

Arsenic-related risks of internal and skin cancers were studied by Chen et al. (1985). This study reported standardized mortality ratios (SMRs) in 84 villages in four townships in southwestern Taiwan where blackfoot disease was prevalent and where earlier studies had detected increased skin-cancer rates. Mortality over the period 1968-1986 was compared with expected mortality based on nationwide age- and sex-specific rates. Significantly increased mortality was observed among males and females for bladder, kidney, skin, lung, liver, and colon cancers as follows: bladder-cancer SMRs = 11.0 (95% confidence interval (CI) = 9.3-12.7) for males (M) and 20.1 (95% CI = 17.0-23.2) for females (F); kidney-cancer SMRs = 7.7 (95% CI = 5.4-10.1) (M) and 11.2 (95% CI = 8.4-14) (F); skin-cancer SMRs = 5.3 (95% CI = 3.8-6.9) (M) and 6.5 (95% CI = 4.7-8.4) (F); lung-cancer SMRs = 3.2 (95% CI = 2.9-3.5) (M) and 4.1 (95% CI = 3.6-4.7) (F); liver-cancer SMRs = 1.7 (95% CI = 1.5-1.9) (M) and 2.3 (95% CI = 1.9-2.7) (F); colon-cancer SMRs = 1.6 (95% CI = 1.2-2.0) (M) and 1.7 (95% CI = 1.3-2.1) (F). Other cancer sites (small intestine, esophagus, nasopharynx, rectum, stomach, and thyroid) did not show statistically meaningful associations. The

SMR for leukemia was 1.4 (95% CI = 1.0-1.8) for men and 0.9 (95% CI = 0.5-1.3) for women. Concentrations of arsenic in the drinking water were not presented in the Chen et al. (1985) report. However, an exposure-response gradient for risk of bladder, kidney, skin, lung, and liver cancers was noted in evaluating the risk in areas with shallow wells (presumably low arsenic exposure), both shallow and artesian wells (intermediate exposure), and artesian wells only (highest exposure). In villages with artesian wells, SMRs were approximately 30.0, 9.0, 10.0, 5.0, and 2.0 (CIs not reported) for bladder, kidney, skin, lung, and liver cancers, respectively.

Wu et al. (1989) provided quantitative information on arsenic concentrations in the drinking water of 42 villages in southwestern Taiwan and calculated age-adjusted cancer mortality during the period 1973-1986 within three groups of villages stratified by exposure concentration (less than 0.30 mg/L, 0.30-0.59 mg/L, and 0.60 mg/L or more). Among males, mortality increased with increasing arsenic concentrations in water for cancers of all sites combined, and cancers of the bladder, kidney, skin, lung, liver, prostate, and leukemia when considered separately. Among females, increases in mortality were observed for all sites combined and cancers of the bladder, kidney, skin, lung, and liver. Nationwide mortality rates for those cancers were not provided by Wu et al. (1989). However, age-adjusted mortality for Taiwan was noted by Chen et al. (1985) for the years 1968-1982. Among males, the ratio of mortality in high-arsenic-exposure villages compared with national mortality, varied with increases of about 3-fold for liver cancer and 30-fold and over for bladder cancer. Among females, analogous mortality ratios increased more than 80-fold for bladder cancer.

Chen and Wang (1990) analyzed nationwide mortality data from Taiwan using water arsenic concentrations from 83,656 wells located in 314 precincts and townships from 1974 to 1976. Using a multiple regression approach, the authors compared age-adjusted mortality for 1972-1983 with the arsenic concentrations in those locations. A significant association with arsenic concentration was found for cancers of the liver, nasal cavity, lung, skin, bladder, and kidney in both sexes and for prostate cancer in males. Using multiple linear regression models, Chen and Wang calculated a regression coefficient indicating the change in age-adjusted mortality per 100,000 person-years for every 0.1-ppm increase in arsenic in well water, after adjusting for indices of industrialization and urbanization. The regression coefficients were 6.8, 0.7, 5.3, 0.9, 3.9, and 1.1 for men and 2.0, 0.4, 5.3, 1.0, 4.2, and 1.7 for women for cancers of the liver, nasal cavity, lung, skin, bladder, and kidney, respectively. The regression coefficient for prostate cancer was 0.5. Regression models included indices of urbanization and industrialization and were weighted by the square root of person-years at risk in each place. The number of wells per precinct or township ranged from 12 to 3,160. In more than 90% of precincts and towns, more than 50 wells were examined. The method for calculating average exposure for each geographic area was not presented. Chen and Wang (1990) stated that "there was a significant intra-area homogeneity and interarea heterogeneity in arsenic concentration." Supporting data were not presented. High concentrations of arsenic were found in water in the northeast of Taiwan and in the coastal area in the south-west of Taiwan, where other studies have been conducted.

Guo et al. (1997) used tumor registry data along with the same exposure data from the 1974-1976 nationwide water-quality survey used previously by Chen and Wang (1990). The authors used arsenic concentrations in drinking water from 243 townships with about 11.4 million residents. The annual incidence of bladder and kidney cancers for townships in 1980-1987 and subcategories of those cancer diagnoses were regressed against a model that included six variables for the proportions of wells in each of six categories of arsenic concentration in each township. Sex-specific models were adjusted for age and included an urbanization index and the annual number of cigarettes sold per capita. Regression models were weighted by the total population of each township. A total of 1,962 bladder, 726 kidney, 170 ureter, and 57 urethral cancers were included. Guo et al. (1997) found associations of high arsenic concentrations (more than 0.64 ppm) in both sexes with transitional-cell carcinomas of the bladder, kidney, and ureter and all urethral cancers combined, but they did not present relative risk estimates, so the results cannot be compared directly with other studies. Associations of the township propor-tion of wells with arsenic at concentrations lower than 0.64 ppm were not significant, and some regression coefficients were negative. No association was found with cigarette sales, but a positive link was observed with urbaniza-tion. The overall crude annual bladder-cancer incidence rate (2.15 per 100,000 population) reported by Guo et al. (1997) is far below that of compa-rable Asian populations, suggesting under-ascertainment of newly diagnosed bladder cancer in the voluntary national cancer registry. Cancer reporting is likely to be better in urbanized areas than in rural areas, such as the high-arsenic regions of southwest and northeast Taiwan. Uncertainties in exposure estimates previously cited apply also to this study.

In two reports, Hopenhayn-Rich et al. (1996, 1998) examined SMRs for bladder, kidney, lung, liver, skin, and stomach cancers for 1986-1991 in the 26 counties of Cordoba Province, Argentina. The authors grouped counties into three strata according to the arsenic concentration in their drinking water. The low and intermediate exposure groups were defined qualitatively by the authors. In the highest exposure group, comprising two counties, arsenic exposure data were presented in tabular form by town. Arsenic concentrations ranged from 40 to 433 μg/L of drinking water in the towns of one county and 50 to 353 μg/L in those of the other. Separate average concentrations in each county were 181 and 174 μg/L. SMRs were calculated using sex- and age-specific rates for Argentina as the referent. Significant increases with exposure concentration were found for the following cancers: bladder-cancer SMRs = 0.80 (95% CI = 0.66-0.96), 1.42 (95% CI = 1.14-1.74), and 2.14 (95% CI = 1.78-2.53) (M) and 1.21 (95% CI = 0.85-1.64), 1.58 (95% CI = 1.01-2.35), and 1.82 (95% CI = 1.19-2.64) (F); lung-cancer SMRs = 0.92 (95% CI = 0.85-0.98), 1.54 (95% CI = 1.44-1.64), and 1.77 (95% CI = 1.63-1.90) (M) and 1.24 (95% CI = 1.06-1.42), 1.34 (95% CI = 1.12-1.58), and 2.16 (95% CI = 1.83-2.52) (F); and kidney-cancer SMRs = 0.87 (95% CI = 0.66-1.10), 1.33 (95% CI = 1.02-1.68), and 1.57 (95% CI = 1.17-2.05) (M) and 1.00 (95% CI = 0.71-1.37), 1.36 (95% CI = 0.94-1.89), and 1.81 (95% CI = 1.19-2.64) (F). Skin-cancer (risk did not increase monotonically with exposure) SMRs = 2.04 (95% CI = 1.38-2.89), 1.49 (95% CI = 0.83-2.45), and 1.49 (95% CI = 0.71-2.73) (M) and 0.85 (95% CI = 0.42-1.51), 0.82 (95% CI = 0.32-1.68), and 2.78 (95% CI = 1.61-4.44) (F). Skin cancers due to arsenic are generally not fatal, and with the small numbers of deaths, the confidence intervals were broad. The information presented above is in terms of relative risk. When considered in absolute risk terms, the major component of risk was lung cancer. For example, for men in the high exposure counties, there were 708 lung cancer deaths observed, with 400.73 expected, from which the excess number of deaths can be calculated to be 307. The corresponding excess number of deaths for bladder cancer was 70, indicating that the number of excess lung cancer deaths was over 4 times that for bladder cancer. Among women, the number of excess lung cancer deaths was 84 in the high exposure counties, which is 7 times more than the corresponding number of 12 for bladder cancer. Deaths from chronic obstructive pulmonary disease (COPD) were not related to arsenic concentrations in drinking water, indicating that smoking is an unlikely confounder of the lung, bladder, and kidney cancer results. This study has limitations shared by most ecological investigations.

Smith et al. (1998) examined bladder and lung-cancer mortality (1989-1993) among persons 30 years of age and over in a region of northern Chile (Region II) with a population of about 400,000. Concentrations of arsenic in drinking water were well-documented and had been high in all major population centers of Region II, especially before 1975. The population-weighted average in the years 1950-1974 was 420 μg/L, the maximum being 870 μg/L in Antofagasta, the largest city, between 1955 and 1969. SMRs for Region II were increased for every 10-year age group for each sex, using national rates as the standard. For bladder cancer, the overall SMRs were 6.0 (95%

CI = 4.8-7.4) for men and 8.2 (95% CI = 6.3-10.5) for women. Lung-cancer SMRs were 3.8 (95% CI = 3.5-4.1) for men and 3.1 (95% CI = 2.7-3.7) for women. As in Argentina, the main contribution to cancer risks involved lung cancer. The reported number for excess lung cancer deaths among men (400.8) was about 5 times that for bladder cancer (77.5). Among women, the number of excess lung cancer deaths (105) was about twice that for bladder cancer (56.2). Although having the limitations of an ecological design, this study has several strengths. Population exposures to arsenic were well defined compared with several other exposed populations, and mortality due to COPD was low, indicating low smoking rates in the population. The importance of the Hopenhayn-Rich studies in Argentina (1996, 1998) and the Smith study in Chile (1998) is that they confirmed earlier observations from Taiwan of increased risk for bladder and lung cancers after exposure to inorganic arsenic in drinking water.

Cohort Studies

The results of the cohort studies are shown in Tables 4-5 and 4-6.

Cuzick et al. (1992) observed excess bladder-cancer mortality among 478 patients medicinally treated with potassium arsenite in 1945-1969; 5 deaths occurred. Based on age-, sex-, and calendar-year-adjusted rates for England and Wales, 1.6 bladder-cancer deaths were expected ($p < 0.05$). Among the five cases, total arsenic doses were 224, 504, 963, 1,901, and 3,324 mg. The SMR was 5.00 (95% CI = 2.0-15) for the four patients treated with more than 500 mg of arsenic. No excess of lung-cancer deaths was observed (14 observed, 14.0 expected). Relatively little opportunity existed for bias in this follow-up study. Cigarette-smoking habits among patients were not described, but it is unlikely that smoking could have accounted for the excess, even if all bladder-cancer patients had smoked. With circulatory diseases as indicators (SMR = 0.91; 95% CI = 0.74-1.1), smoking rates in the overall cohort do not appear to be unusual.

Tsuda et al. (1995) found excess mortality due to the following cancers among a cohort of 113 persons exposed to arsenic above 1.0 mg/L of industrially contaminated drinking water in villages of Niigata Prefecture, Japan: urinary-tract cancer (3 observed, 0.10 expected) SMR = 31.18 (95% CI = 8.62-91.75), lung cancer (8 observed, 0.51 expected) SMR = 15.69 (95% CI = 7.38-31.02), liver cancer (2 observed, 0.28 expected) SMR = 7.17 (95% CI = 1.28-26.05), and uterine cancer (2 observed, 0.15 expected) SMR = 13.47 (95% CI = 2.37-48.63). The observed-to-expected ratios were near or below expectation among persons exposed to arsenic at less than 0.05 mg/L.

TABLE 4-5 Lung-Cancer Mortality or Incidence and Arsenic Ingestion in Cohort Studies

Study	Location	Exposure	Cases, No.	Study Outcome	Comments
Cuzick et al. 1992	United Kingdom		14	SMR: 1.00 (0.5-1.7)	478 patients treated with Fowler's solution (potassium arsenite)
Chiou et al. 1995	SW Taiwan	Cumulative arsenic:		Relative risk:	Incidence among a cohort of 2,556 subjects (263 blackfoot-disease patients and 2,293 healthy individuals) followed for 7 yr
		<0.1 mg/L/yr	3	1.0	
		0.1-19.9 mg/L/yr	7	3.1 (0.8-12.2)	
		≥20 mg/L/yr	7	4.7 (1.2-18.9)	
		Average arsenic:			
		<0.05 mg/L	5	1.0	
		0.05-0.70 mg/L	7	2.1 (0.7-6.8)	
		≥0.71 mg/L	7	2.7 (0.7-10.2)	
Tsuda et al. 1995	Niigata Prefecture, Japan			SMR:	Exposure among 113 persons who drank from contaminated wells for approximately 5 yr (1955-1959), then followed for 33 yr
		<0.05 µg/L	0	0.0 (0-2.4)	
		0.05-0.99 µg/L	1	2.3 (0.1-13.4)	
		≥1.0 µg/L	8	15.7 (7.4-31.0)	

Abbreviation: SMR, standardized mortality ratio.

TABLE 4-6 Bladder-Cancer Mortality or Incidence and Arsenic Ingestion in Cohort Studies

Study	Location	Exposure	Cases, No.	Study Outcome	Comments
Cuzick et al. 1992	United Kingdom	224 mg 504 mg 963 mg 1,901 mg 3,324 mg	1 1 1 1 1	SMR: 1.20 (0.04-7.0) 5.00 (2.0-15) (exposure ≥500 mg)	478 patients treated with Fowler's solution (potassium arsenite); also, one death at age 85 and mention of bladder cancer as contributing cause to another death
Chiou et al. 1995	SW Taiwan	Cumulative arsenic: <0.1 mg/L/yr 0.1-19.9 mg/L/yr 20+ mg/L/yr Average arsenic: <0.05 mg/L 0.05-0.70 mg/L 0.71+ mg/L	4 7 9 6 7 7	Relative risk: 1.0 2.1 (0.6-7.2) 5.1 (1.5-17.3) 1.0 1.8 (0.6-5.3) 3.3 (1.0-11.1)	Incidence among a cohort of 2,556 subjects (263 blackfoot-disease patients and 2,293 healthy individuals) followed for 7 yr
Tsuda et al. 1995	Niigata Prefecture, Japan	<0.05 μg/L 0.05-0.99 μg/L ≥1.0 μg/L	0 0 3	SMR: 0.0 (0-12.5) 0.0 (0-47.1) 31,2 (8.6-91.8)	Exposure among 113 persons who drank from contaminated wells for approximately 5 yr (1955-1959), then followed for 33 yr

Abbreviation: SMR, standardized mortality ratio.

Results in this low-exposure group were statistically unstable. Expected deaths numbered less than two for each cancer cause of death. Expected numbers of deaths were based on sex-, age-, and cause-specific mortality in Niigata Prefecture from 1960 to 1989.

Chiou et al. (1995) followed 2,556 subjects in the blackfoot-disease area of southwestern Taiwan for periods ranging up to 7.7 years (an average of 4.97 years) from 1986 to 1993. In contrast to many other studies that evaluate mortality, incident cancer was the outcome of interest. Followup occurred many years after exposure to elevated arsenic concentrations in drinking water ended. Blackfoot-disease patients numbered 263, and healthy individuals numbered 2,293. Information was gathered in individual interviews. Several measures of exposure were evaluated, including average concentration of arsenic in artesian wells and cumulative arsenic exposure from drinking artesian well water. Relative risks were calculated using Cox's proportional hazards regression analysis (Cox 1972). For average arsenic concentrations of less than 0.05 mg/L, 0.05-0.70 mg/L, and 0.71 mg/L or more, relative risks were as follows: bladder cancer, 1.0 (referent), 1.8 (95% CI = 0.6-5.3), and 3.3 (95% CI = 1.0-11.1); lung cancer, 1.0 (referent), 2.1 (95% CI = 0.7-6.8), and 2.7 (95% CI = 0.7-10.2). For cumulative arsenic exposures of 0, 0.1-19.9, and 20 mg/L or more times the number of years, relative risks were as follows: bladder cancer, 1.0 (referent), 2.1 (95% CI = 0.6-7.2), and 5.1 (95% CI = 1.5-17.3); lung cancer, 1.0 (referent), 3.1 (95% CI = 0.8-12.2); and 4.7 (95% CI = 1.2-18.9). Results were adjusted for cigarette-smoking habit and thus are likely to be more precise than those of other studies. A weakness of this study, shared with others from the same geographic area, is the small number of precise estimates of arsenic in drinking water.

Case-Control Studies

Bates et al. (1995) used information from 117 bladder-cancer cases and 266 population-based controls in the State of Utah to evaluate bladder-cancer risk after relatively low-level exposure to arsenic in drinking water. Subjects were interviewed in 1978 as part of the National Bladder Cancer Study sponsored by the National Cancer Institute. Individual exposures to arsenic in drinking water were estimated by linking residential-history information with water-sampling information from public-water supplies. Eighty-one of the 88 Utah study towns (92%) had arsenic at concentrations of less than 10 μg/L, and only one town had water with arsenic at more than 50 μg/L. Overall, no association was found between bladder-cancer risk and arsenic exposure. Using cumulative dose as the exposure metric, relative to a lifetime exposure of less than 19 mg, odds ratios were 1.56 (95% CI = 0.8-3.2), 0.95 (95% CI = 0.4-2.0), and 1.41 (95% CI = 0.7-2.9) for exposures of 19 to less than 33 mg, 33 to less than 53 mg, and 53 mg or more, respectively. However, among smokers, increased risk was suggested in time-window analyses of exposures occurring for years 20-29 (16 cases in the highest-exposure group) and 30-39 years (9 high-exposure cases) before the interview. The exposure index in this instance was expressed as the product of micrograms per liter and years of exposure.

Occupational Studies

Inhaled inorganic arsenic is a recognized cause of lung cancer. That effect is pertinent to arsenic ingestion and lung cancer because it supports the biological plausibility of a causal relationship between ingested inorganic arsenic and lung cancer. In addition, dose-response patterns observed between inhalation of inorganic arsenic and lung-cancer risk might be applicable to ingested arsenic and cancer risk and thus useful in assessing risk of ingested inorganic arsenic. At least five major studies of occupationally exposed individuals have reported excess risk of lung cancer from inhalation of arsenic (Ott et al. 1974; Lee-Feldstein 1986; Enterline et al. 1987; Jarup et al. 1989; Taylor et al. 1989). The question of the dose-response relationships found in those study populations was examined by most investigators. In one case, urinary arsenic levels were available to estimate exposures (Enterline et al. 1987). Enterline's first analysis of mortality data from a cohort of smelter workers (Enterline and Marsh 1982) indicated a supralinear dose-response relationship, based on estimates of airborne exposure. However, a reanalysis of the data using urinary arsenic levels was consistent with a linear dose-response association (Enterline et al. 1987). Data from the five studies were investigated by Hertz-Picciotto and Smith (1993). The data from each study were consistent with a supralinear dose-response relationship when exposures were estimated from air concentrations of inorganic arsenic in each workplace. The finding of linearity by Enterline et al. (1987) raises the possibility that the supralinear shape of the dose-response curve was due to misclassification of exposure based on air concentrations; such misclassification might have been due to workers avoiding exposure as much as possible (e.g., with the use of respirators) when air concentrations were high. In summary, the data from occupational studies suggest that the risk of lung cancer after inhalation of inorganic arsenic compounds is at least linear with exposure.

This observation might have implications for dose-response relationships with ingested arsenic.

NONCANCER EFFECTS

Arsenic exposure interferes with the action of enzymes, essential cations, and transcriptional events in cells throughout the body, and a multitude of multisystemic noncancer effects might ensue. This discussion focuses on selected noncancer effects from chronic ingestion of arsenic in drinking water that are most relevant to the effect on health. Because experimental animals appear to be less sensitive than humans to the chronic effects of arsenic (Byron et al. 1967; Heywood and Sortwell 1979), data from human studies are emphasized. Potential reproductive and developmental effects associated with chronic ingestion of arsenic are discussed in a later section.

Cutaneous Effects

In contrast to many of the early nonspecific multisystemic signs and symptoms of chronic arsenic poisoning that are challenging to diagnose, the classic cutaneous manifestations are distinctive and characteristic. Their appearance usually follows a temporal progression, beginning with hyperpigmentation, then progressing to palmar-plantar hyperkeratoses. As discussed further below, patients might subsequently develop a variety of nonmelanoma skin cancers, occasionally, but not always, at pre-existing areas of hyperkeratosis. Although cutaneous manifestations have been most commonly reported following ingestion of arsenic containing groundwater (Yeh 1973; Zaldivar 1974; Cebrian et al. 1983; Chakraborty and Saha 1987) medicinals (Black 1967; Tay 1974), or contaminated grape beverages (Luchtrath 1983), cohorts primarily exposed via inhalation have also been affected (Perry et al. 1948; Hamada and Horiguchi 1976).

The hyperpigmentation of chronic arsenic poisoning commonly appears in a finely freckled, "raindrop" pattern that is particularly pronounced on the trunk and extremities but that might also involve mucous membranes such as the tongue or buccal mucosa (Black 1967; Yeh 1973; Tay 1974; Saha 1995). The raindrop appearance results from the presence of numerous rounded hypopigmented maculas (typically 2-4 mm in diameter) widely dispersed against a tan-to-brown hyperpigmented background (Tay 1974). Although less common, other patterns include diffuse hyperpigmentation (Tay 1974; Saha 1995); localized or patchy pigmentation, particularly affecting skinfolds (Tay 1974; Szuler et al. 1979; Luchtrath 1983); and so-called leukoderma or

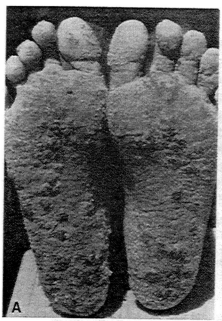

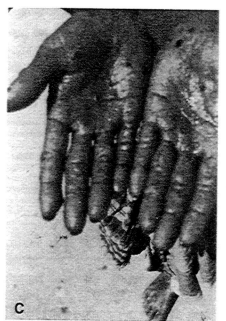

FIGURE 4-1 Photographs of West Bengal patients with arsenic-induced skin lesions. (A) Arsenic keratosis on plantar aspect of the feet. (B) Arsenic keratosis on the dorsum of feet and hands. (C) Arsenic keratosis on palm. Source: Subramanian and Kosnett (1998). Photos courtesy of Dr. D. Chakraborti, School of Environmental Studies, Jadavpur University, Calcutta. Reprinted with permission from the *International Journal of Occupational and Environmental Health*; copyright 1998, Hanley & Belfus, Philadelphia.

leukomelanosis, in which the hypopigmented maculas take on a spotty, white appearance. Mandal et al. (1996) reported that raindrop pigmentation might evolve to leukomelanosis several years after the subject is no longer exposed. Pigmentation is not histopathologically related to arsenical hyperkeratoses, nor is it a direct precursor to cancer.

Arsenical hyperkeratoses appear predominantly on the palms and the plantar aspects of the feet, although involvement of the dorsum of the extremities and the trunk has also been described. In early stages, the involved skin might have an indurated, gritlike character that can be best appreciated by palpation; however, the lesions usually advance to form raised, punctate, 2-4 mm wartlike keratoses that are readily visible (Tay 1974). Occasional lesions might be larger (approximately 1 cm) and have a nodular or horny appearance. Histological examination of the lesions typically reveals hyperkeratosis with or without parakeratosis, acanthosis, and enlargement of the rete ridges. In some cases, there might be evidence of cellular atypia, mitotic figures, or large vacuolated epidermal cells (Black 1967; Tay 1974; Ratnam et al. 1992; Alain et al. 1993). Yeh (1973) classified arsenical keratoses into two types: a benign type A, further subgrouped into those with no cell atypia and those with mild cellular atypia; and a malignant type B. Lesions of Bowen's disease (intraepithelial carcinoma, or carcinoma in situ), basal-cell carcinoma, or squamous-cell carcinoma might arise in the hyperkeratotic areas or might appear on nonkeratotic areas of the trunk, extremities, or head (Sommers and McManus 1953; Yeh 1973). The concurrent appearance of multiple skin cancers, particularly in non-sun-exposed areas, is particularly characteristic of arsenic causation (Tseng 1977; Zaldivar et al. 1981).

The magnitude of arsenic dose and the time frame of exposure necessary to induce the hyperpigmentation and hyperkeratoses characteristic of chronic arsenic intoxication have undergone limited investigation. Among the population exposed to arsenic in drinking water in the Antofagasta region of Chile, cases of cutaneous arsenicism, apparently including both hyperpigmentation and hyperkeratoses, have been described in children as young as 2 years of age (Rosenberg 1974; Zaldivar and Guillier 1977). The estimated mean arsenic dose in Antofagasta was estimated to be approximately 0.06 mg/kg per day for subgroups of children aged 3.13 ± 3.33 years but was approximately 0.02 mg/kg per day for subgroups in their teens and twenties and 0.006 mg/kg per day for a subgroup in their sixties, indicating an inverse relationship between daily arsenic dose rate per kilogram of body weight and age (Zaldivar and Ghai 1980). In the cohort of 40,421 inhabitants of southeastern Taiwan investigated by Tseng and colleagues, the youngest subjects found to have hyperpigmentation and hyperkeratosis were reported to be ages 3 and 4, respectively, in an early report (Tseng et al. 1968) and 5 and 15′ in a later account (Tseng 1977). The concentration of arsenic consumed by those children was not specified. Foy et al. (1992) reported palmar-plantar hyperkeratosis in a 4-year-old child residing in a region of southern Thailand with a mean well-water arsenic content of 0.82 mg/L. In a clinical evaluation conducted among 296 residents of Region Lagunera in northern Mexico where ingested groundwater contained a mean arsenic concentration of approximately 0.4 mg/L, the shortest time of exposure associated with "hypopigmentation" was 8 years, increasing to 12 years for hyperpigmentation and palmar-plantar hyperkeratosis (Cebrian et al. 1983). Wagner et al. (1979) reported a patient who presented with anemia, peripheral neuropathy, and palmar-plantar hyperkeratoses 4 months after ingesting arsenic from well water at a dose estimated to be between 3.4 and 3.9 mg per day.

In a long-term follow-up of patients who had consumed medicinal arsenic in the form of Fowler's solution (potassium arsenite), the median total arsenic dose among 69 subjects with cutaneous signs of arsenicism (keratoses, hyperpigmentation, or skin cancer) was 672 mg, compared with a median arsenic dose of 448 mg in 73 subjects without skin signs (Cuzick et al. 1982). Those patients were drawn from a larger cohort that ingested arsenic for a mean duration of 8.92 months at a dose rate of approximately 8.3 mg per day. Subjects were evaluated at a mean follow-up time of 20.3 years, and the latency period for onset of cutaneous signs was not evaluated. In a retrospective study of 262 adults treated with Fowler's solution, Fierz (1965) reported the minimal latency period for hyperkeratoses to be 2.5 years, following ingestion of approximately 2.2 g of arsenite. Other case reports of adults ingesting medicinal arsenic have described doses and latencies associated with the onset of cutaneous manifestations. Rattner and Dorne (1943) reported the development of hyperpigmentation within 6-12 months of the start of treatment with arsenite at a dose of 4.75 mg day. Hyperkeratoses appeared at approximately 3 years. Pascher and Wolf (1952) described a 24-year-old asthmatic individual who was found to have hyperpigmentation and hyperkeratoses when examined 3 months after termination of a 15-month course of arsenite taken at a dose of 10 mg per day. Silver and Wainman (1952) reported a patient with the onset of "freckling of the skin and darkening of the nipples" 13 months after taking an asthma mixture delivering arsenic at a dose of 9 mg per day for 9 months, followed by 4.5 mg per day for 4 months. Ribard et al. (1986) reported a subject who presented with chronic arsenic intoxication, including hyperpigmentation, after 18 months of ingestion of an anti-asthma remedy at a dose of 2.8 mg of arsenic per day.

Limited evidence indicates that hyperpigmentation and keratoses due to arsenic exposure might serve as markers of susceptibility for other outcomes, including skin cancers and internal cancers. A small study in England of cancer among patients treated with medicinal arsenic noted that cancer deaths occurred only among those with prior skin manifestations due to arsenic (Cuzick et al. 1982, 1984). In a further follow-up of that cohort, a threefold increased risk of bladder-cancer mortality was found, and all five deaths occurred in patients with previous signs of arsenic poisoning (Cuzick et al. 1992). However, Tsuda et al. (1995) found an SMR for bladder cancer of 10.34 (95% CI = 2.82-30.37) among the subcohort of arsenic-exposed subjects without skin findings (see Tsuda et al. 1995, Table 5). In studies that have observed a positive relationship between arsenic ingestion and cancer, the doses of ingested arsenic were of a sufficient magnitude to cause cutaneous signs of arsenicism (hyperpigmentation or hyperkeratoses) in at least some members of the study population. At the present time, epidemiological data are insufficient to demonstrate an observed risk of cancer in populations exposed to ingested arsenic at doses too low to result in overt nonmalignant cutaneous effects.

Gastrointestinal Effects

With acute or subacute exposure (greater than several milligrams of inorganic arsenic per day), arsenic might induce overt gastrointestinal disturbances, ranging from mild abdominal cramping and diarrhea to severe life-threatening hemorrhagic gastroenteritis associated with shock. Mild-to-moderate hepatocellular necrosis, evidenced by increases in serum transaminase, might occur.

With chronic exposure to arsenic, overt gastrointestinal symptoms are often absent; however, chronic concentrations might nonetheless be associated with important organ-system pathology. Noncirrhotic portal hypertension is an uncommon but relatively specific gastrointestinal manifestation associated with chronic inorganic arsenic ingestion via medications or groundwater. Because hepatic function remains intact, the condition might not come to clinical attention until advanced stages when the patient might present with gastrointestinal hemorrhage secondary to esophageal varices (Morris et al. 1974; Szuler et al. 1979; Upshaw et al. 1979; Robertson and Low-Beer 1983; Nevens et al. 1990). Physical examination of affected patients might reveal hepatic or splenic enlargement (Guha Mazumder et al. 1997), but that finding is not invariable. Cutaneous signs of chronic arsenic poisoning are usually apparent. Liver-function tests are generally normal. Histopathological examination of the liver might find periportal fibrosis associated with slight-to-moderate enlargement of the portal tracts and mild or no inflammatory-cell infiltration. Obliterative intimal hypertrophy of intrahepatic venules have been reported which results in obstruction of portal venous flow, increased splenic pressures, and hypersplenism (Morris et al. 1974; Nevens et al. 1990). Hepatic arsenic content may also be markedly increased (Morris et al. 1974; Datta 1976; Guha Mazumder et al. 1997).

A few case reports noted the evolution of noncirrhotic portal hypertension to cirrhosis in patients exposed to arsenite-containing medicines (Franklin et al. 1950; Cowlishaw et al. 1979; Upshaw and Claiborne 1995). A high prevalence of cirrhosis has been reported in an autopsy series of former vineyard workers who ingested Haustrunk, a wine substitute made from an aqueous infusion of pressed grapes contaminated with arsenic insecticide residues (Luchtrath 1972, 1983). It is also noteworthy that two cohorts of arsenic-exposed copper-smelter workers have experienced increased mortality from cirrhosis of the liver (Axelson et al. 1978; Welch et al. 1982), albeit the number of cases was small and other smelter cohorts have not been similarly affected. Unfortunately, in most reports of arsenic-associated cirrhosis the authors have not been able to determine subjects' ethanol consumption, the most common cause of cirrhosis. Therefore, the etiological link with arsenic remains uncertain.

Cardiovascular Effects

Acute or subacute exposure to inorganic arsenic in the range of milligrams to grams per day have induced the rapid appearance of serious overt cardiovascular manifestations, including hypotension, congestive heart failure, and cardiac arrhythmias. The latter are often preceded by electrocardiographic prolongation of the Q-T interval, occasionally leading to polymorphic ventricular tachycardia (torsades de pointe) (Zettel 1943; Glazener et al. 1968). These acute or subacute effects are reversible.

Chronic ingestion of inorganic arsenic, most notably from drinking-water sources and arsenic-contaminated wine or wine substitutes, has been associated with the insidious development of peripheral vascular disease. The most prominent reports of arsenic-related peripheral vascular disease have originated from southwestern Taiwan, where the ingestion of arsenic-containing artesian well water from the early 1900s through the late 1950s to early 1960s was associated with the development of more than 1,000 cases of blackfoot disease. A severe manifestation of peripheral vascular insufficiency resulted in gangrene of the extremities, particularly the feet (Tseng et al. 1961; Tseng 1977). In the villages with the highest number of cases, the reported arsenic concentration of the well water ranged from 0.35 to 1.14 ppm, with a median value of 0.78 ppm (Chen et al. 1962). Clinically, the disease begins with patients' subjective complaints of coldness or numbness in the extremities (usually the feet) and intermittent claudication, progressing over the course of several years to ulceration, gangrene, and spontaneous amputation (Tseng et al. 1961). Histological examination of tissue from affected limbs revealed evidence of thromboangiitis obliterans and arteriosclerosis obliterans, particularly affecting small vessels (Yeh and How 1963; Yu et al. 1984). Blackfoot disease usually occurs in combination with the classic cutaneous manifestations of chronic arsenic poisoning: among 360 cases reported by Tseng et al. (1968), 280 (78%) had hyperpigmentation and 135 (38%) had hyperkeratoses. Although humic substances isolated from artesian well water in the blackfoot-disease endemic areas of Taiwan have been associated with thrombogenic actions in experimental models (Lu 1990; Yang et al. 1996), there is no epidemiological or human histopathological data linking humic substances to blackfoot disease (Chen 1990; Engel et al. 1994).

An increased prevalence of signs and symptoms of peripheral vascular disease has also been reported among the residents of Antofagasta, Chile, where the public drinking-water supply from the mid-to-late 1950s through 1970 contained inorganic arsenic at a mean concentration of approximately 0.6 ppm (Zaldivar 1974). Borgono et al. (1977) compared the prevalence of several manifestations of cardiovascular disease in 146 Antofagasta residents with abnormal skin pigmentation, and 36 with normally pigmented skin. Among those with abnormal pigmentation, there was an increased prevalence of Raynaud's syndrome (38.8% versus 9.3%), acrocyanosis (24.3% versus 12.5%), and hyperkeratosis (43.7% versus 3.1%). In a clinical evaluation of 100 children with cutaneous manifestations of chronic arsenic poisoning, 19 had arterial spasms in the fingers and toes, one had gangrene of a finger, and four had ischemia of the tongue (Zaldivar and Guillier 1977). Autopsies performed on five children, aged 1 to 7 years, with cutaneous manifestations of chronic arsenic poisoning yielded findings that included mesenteric artery thrombosis, cerebrovascular disease, and coronary artery occlusions (Zaldivar 1974). An autopsy series on five Antofagasta children reported by Rosenberg (1974) described arterial intimal thickening comparable to that seen in the blackfoot-disease patients of Taiwan. Similarly, the postmortem findings on five children reported by Borgono and Greiber (1971) were noteworthy for extensive coronary or cerebrovascular occlusions, as well as ischemia of the tongue in a 2-year-old child, and Raynaud's syndrome and gangrene of the toe in a 4-year-old child.

In a recent extensive review of the vascular effects of arsenic, Engel et al. (1994) cited several German reports of overt peripheral vascular disease, including thromboangiitis obliterans and overt gangrene of the extremities, in German vintners with chronic arsenic poisoning from consumption of arsenic-contaminated wine substitutes (Butzengeiger 1940, as cited in Engel et al.

1994; Roth 1957; Grobe 1976, as cited in Engel et al. 1994). Hotta (1989) described a case study of 125 patients diagnosed with chronic arsenic poisoning as a result of occupational or environmental exposure to arsenic from smelter emissions contaminating the air, surface drinking water, and the residential environment of an arsenic mining and refining area in Toruku, Japan. The magnitude of exposure to arsenic and to other suspected pollutants, such as sulfur dioxide and other metals and particulates, was not quantified, but 93% of the subjects had melanosis, 92% had hyperkeratosis, and approximately 45% had Bowen's disease. Hypertension was reported in 68% of the subjects, Raynaud's syndrome in 26%, and gangrene of the extremities in two male subjects, neither of whom had a history of diabetes. Tsuda et al. (1990) investigated the mortality experience of 141 certified arsenic-poisoning patients, with a mean age of 60.8 ± 10.4 years and followed for an average of 9.3 ± 4.0 years in Toruku from 1972 to 1990. The SMR for ischemic heart disease was 214 (95% CI = 100-437), and the SMR for cerebrovascular disease was 77 (95% CI = 36-153).

Although extensive environmental exposure to arsenic in drinking water, accompanied by cutaneous manifestations, has also been reported in Region Lugunera in northern Mexico, the Cordova and Salta provinces of Argentina, and recently in West Bengal, India, investigators in those regions have reported little, if any, evidence of an excess prevalence of overt peripheral vascular disorders. A brief report by Cebrian (1987) refers to a 4% prevalence of "peripheral vascular alterations" and a 0.7% prevalence of blackfoot disease, apparently in reference to a study population of 296 residents of Region Lugunera exposed to a mean arsenic concentration in drinking water of 0.41 ppm (Cebrian et al. 1983; Engel et al. 1994). A recent angiographic study of 12 patients with cutaneous arsenic poisoning from the Argentina Salta Province (Torres Soruco et al. 1991, as cited in Engel et al. 1994) found evidence of microangiopathies in all patients, half of whom were under age 25, but overt peripheral vascular disease in that region has not been apparent.

Three other studies examined subclinical vascular effects of arsenic. Lagerkvist et al. (1986) detected a heightened vasospastic response to an experimental cooling of the fingers in 47 arsenic-exposed smelter workers compared with controls. Arsenic exposure of the subjects at the time of the study was estimated to be 300 μg or less per day, with a mean cumulative average uptake of 4 g. In a follow-up study of 21 of the affected workers, the vasospastic tendency displayed no change before and after 4-8 weeks of summer vacation, suggesting that cumulative rather than recent arsenic exposure was a determining factor (Lagerkvist et al. 1988). Tseng et al. (1995) used laser Doppler flowmetry to assess baseline and heat-induced cutaneous perfusion of the big toe in 45 long-term residents of the blackfoot-disease endemic area of Taiwan and 51 age-matched controls. All subjects were nonsmokers and were selected on the basis of the absence of any overt signs or symptoms or history of cardiac or peripheral vascular disease. The exposed subjects, with a mean age of 60 years, consumed artesian well water with high arsenic content for at least 30 years ending 20-30 years ago. The presence of cutaneous signs of chronic arsenic poisoning and the magnitude of past or current arsenic exposure were not reported. Both basal and heat-induced cutaneous perfusion was substantially lower in the formerly exposed subjects, suggesting that subclinical microcirculatory changes associated with chronic arsenic ingestion can persist long after exposure has ended.

Chen et al. (1995) recently examined the relationship between cumulative ingestion of arsenic in drinking water and the prevalence of hypertension among residents of the endemic area of blackfoot disease in Taiwan. Hypertension was defined as a systolic blood pressure equal to 160 mm Hg, a diastolic blood pressure equal to 95 mm Hg, or a history of treatment with antihypertensive drugs. Compared with several other reports of morbidity associated with chronic ingestion of arsenic in drinking water, this study was distinguished by an attempt to characterize each individual's cumulative arsenic exposure by use of detailed interviews and a geographical database of the arsenic content of the region's artesian wells. Data on 898 subjects over 30 years of age were analyzed, including 119 subjects who had never ingested artesian well water. Two analytical approaches found ingestion of arsenic to be associated with an increased risk of hypertension. In a multiple logistic regression model controlling for age, sex, diabetes, proteinuria, body-mass index, and fasting serum concentrations of triglycerides, cumulative arsenic exposure was associated with a significantly increased odds ratio for hypertension, peaking at 3.8 (95% CI = 1.4-10.3) for subjects with arsenic exposure at 14.8-18.5 mg/L-yr compared with subjects with no exposure. Alcohol consumption, cigarette smoking, physical activity at work, and duration of dried-sweet-potato consumption as a staple food were not found to be significant risk factors. In a second analytical approach, subjects from the endemic blackfoot-disease area were found to have a 1.5-fold increase in age- and sex-adjusted prevalence of hypertension compared with residents from a non-endemic area that were studied in separate but comparable investigations. Chen et al. (1995) did not present data on the relationship between cutaneous manifestations of chronic arsenic poisoning and hypertension prevalence in their study subjects.

In 1982, the Michigan Department of Public Health conducted a pilot health study of individuals who consumed water from private wells within an area of Huron County found on a prior environmental survey to contain arsenic at a concentration of greater than 50 μg/L. Of 221 eligible residents,

163 participated in the health study. Medical histories, limited physical examinations, and 24-hr urine collections were conducted on 53 males (mean age of 49.3 years) and 61 females (mean age of 46 years). Well-water arsenic concentrations ranged from 31 to 335 μg/L, with a median of 75 μg/L, for the 51 wells in the 60 households included in the study. The magnitude of typical daily arsenic consumption was calculated from questionnaire responses and well-water arsenic analysis, but duration of well-water use was not determined. Arsenic consumption amounts were found to be substantially higher for subjects (25 of the 114) who indicated having had "high blood pressure," but comparative exposure data, urine values, medication usage, and blood-pressure measurements were not reported. No relationship was reported between electrocardiogram findings and indices of arsenic exposure (Michigan Department of Public Health 1982).

Because hypertension and vascular occlusion are risk factors for death from ischemic heart disease or other cardiovascular illnesses, several investigators have examined the association between arsenic exposure and cardiovascular mortality. The experience in cohorts occupationally exposed to arsenic by inhalation has been inconsistent. Welch et al. (1982) found a risk ratio of 1.77 (95% CI = 1.32-2.31) for mortality from ischemic heart disease in a heavily exposed subgroup of smelter workers in Anaconda, Montana, and Wall (1980) reported a risk ratio of 1.32 (95% CI = 1.20-1.44) for mortality from circulatory disease among smelter workers in Ronnskar, Sweden. However, no such increase has been observed in other cohort studies of arsenic-exposed smelter workers (Rencher et al. 1977; Enterline and Marsh 1982) or insecticide manufacturers (Mabuchi et al. 1980; Sobel et al. 1988). Assessing those studies and others on cardiovascular mortality in occupational cohorts exposed to arsenic by inhalation, Engel et al. (1994) noted that the risk ratio for mortality from circulatory diseases in most cases exceeds unity, a relationship that might in fact be underestimated because of the healthy-worker effect.

Cuzick et al. (1992) reported cause-specific mortality through 1990 in a cohort of 478 dermatological clinic patients who were treated with Fowler's solution, an oral medication containing 1% potassium arsenite, between 1945 and 1969. Duration of treatment ranged from 2 weeks to 12 years. The magnitude of each subject's daily exposure was not stated but, on the basis of therapeutic practices in dermatology, can be estimated to have ranged from 5 to 10 mg of arsenite daily. The SMRs were less than 1.0 for all circulatory diseases (SMR = 0.91, 95% CI = 0.74-1.1), ischemic heart disease (SMR = 0.85, 95% CI = 0.6-1.1), and cerebrovascular diseases (SMR = 0.72, 95% CI = 0.4-1.1).

The relationship between arsenic ingestion in drinking water and cardiovascular-disease mortality has been examined in populations in Taiwan and the United States. Chen et al. (1988) examined the mortality experience of a cohort of 789 blackfoot-disease patients residing in four townships in southwestern Taiwan with high arsenic content in artesian wells. The diagnosis of blackfoot disease was based on a physician-confirmed finding of objective and subjective evidence of peripheral vascular insufficiency. The nonconcurrent cohort consisted of prevalent cases of blackfoot-disease patients alive on January 1, 1968, and all new cases registered after that date, followed through December 31, 1983. A total of 7,578 person-years was investigated. Death certificates and family interviews were used to determine cause of death, and SMRs for different end points were determined using age- and sex-specific mortality for all of Taiwan and, in a separate analysis, for the blackfoot-disease endemic area. In addition to finding increased SMRs for several malignancies, statistically significant SMRs of 1,243 (CIs not specified) for peripheral vascular disease and 209 (CIs not specified) for cardiovascular diseases were noted. Using the mortality of the blackfoot-disease endemic area as standard rates, the SMRs decreased to 351 for peripheral vascular disease and 160 for cardiovascular diseases. Causes of death from cardiovascular diseases in this study included endocarditis and pulmonary embolism, as well as end points more closely related to coronary atherosclerosis. SMRs for cerebrovascular disease were 118 (compared with all of Taiwan) and 107 (compared with the blackfoot-disease endemic area) and were statistically nonsignificant.

A large ecological study in the blackfoot endemic area of southwestern Taiwan (Wu et al. 1989) examined the relationship between arsenic well-water concentration and age-adjusted cause-specific mortality (as assessed from death certificates) from 1973 to 1986. A statistically increased trend was observed for increased mortality from peripheral vascular disease and cardiovascular disease with increasing median arsenic concentrations in well water in the decedent's community. The rates in the highest-arsenic-exposure areas (0.60 ppm) were approximately double those in the lowest-arsenic-exposure areas (less than 0.30 ppm). A smaller trend was observed in increased cerebrovascular accident mortality, a trend that was statistically nonsignificant.

Chen et al. (1996) reported the results of ischemic-heart-disease mortality in a prospective cohort study of 263 blackfoot-disease patients and 2,293 other residents of the blackfoot-disease endemic area. For each subject, lifetime residence histories, measurement data on arsenic in well water throughout Taiwan, and age-specific estimates of well-water consumption were used to generate exposure variables of average concentration of arsenic in drinking water and cumulative arsenic exposure from drinking water. In Cox's proportional-hazards regression analyses, the impact of arsenic exposure on ischemic-heart-disease mortality during an average follow-up period of 5 years (beginning in the late 1980s) was determined after adjusting for the covariates of age, sex, cigarette smoking, body-mass index, serum concentrations of cholesterol and triglycerides, hypertension, and diabetes. Relative risks were 2.46 (95% CI = 0.53-11.37), 3.97 (CI = 1.01-15.59), and 6.47 (CI = 1.88-22.24) for subjects with a cumulative arsenic exposure of 0.1-9.9 mg/L-yr, 10.0-19.9 mg/L-yr, and 20.0 mg/L-yr or more, respectively, compared with those without arsenic exposure. Adjusting for cumulative arsenic consumption and other listed covariates, the relative risk associated with blackfoot disease was 2.48 (CI = 1.14-5.40).

The relationship between the prevalence of cerebrovascular disease and ingestion of inorganic arsenic in drinking water was investigated by Chiou et al. (1997) in a cross-sectional study of 8,102 men and women 40 years of age and over residing in the Layang Basin at the northeastern coast of Taiwan. Residents of this study area were reported to have commonly used shallow wells (less than 40 m deep) as a source of drinking water from the 1940s through the 1990s, when a tapwater system began to be used by some area residents. The well-water arsenic concentration in the region's villages ranged from "undetectable" to 3.59 mg/L (median values in these villages ranged from undetectable to 0.14 mg/L). Subjects were recruited from a registry of all adult residents within 18 villages, but the criteria for village selection, methods of recruitment, and percentage participation were not stated. Medical history, cerebrovascular risk factors, and detailed lifetime history of residential village-water consumption according to water source and duration were obtained by individual subject interviews. A well-water sample obtained from each household (3,901 in number) was analyzed for arsenic by hydride-generation flameless-atomic-absorption spectrophotometry. The sensitivity and precision of the laboratory analyses were not stated, a major concern given that the data analyses categorized some samples as containing more than, or less than 0.1 μg/L, a value that is usually below the limit of detection of this method (see further comments on analytical precision on page 8-5). The water analyses and lifetime water-consumption histories were used to calculate cumulative lifetime arsenic consumption from drinking water and average arsenic consumption from water for each subject. The investigators stated that cases of cerebrovascular disease identified by personal interview were verified by review of hospital medical records, according to World Health Organization (WHO) criteria. However, quantitative data were not reported on the subdivision of suspected cases into "definite stroke," "no stroke," or "insufficient data" according to the WHO MONICA study criteria (Asplund et al. 1988), a key consideration in prevalence studies given that a recent investigation of hospital discharge summaries found a false-positive rate for stroke of 31.5% (Stegmayr and Asplund 1992). The basis for identifying a reported diagnostic subcategory of "cerebral infarction" in the Layang Basin cohort was not specified; that designation requires confirmation by computerized-tomography scan under the WHO MONICA criteria.

In a multivariate logistic regression model of cerebrovascular-disease prevalence, the adjusted odds ratio were 2.26 (95% CI = 1.23-4.15) and 2.69 (95% CI = 1.35-5.38) for cumulative arsenic exposures of 0.1-4.9 mg/L-yr and 5.0 mg/L-yr or more, respectively, compared with less than 0.1 mg/L-yr. Odds ratios were adjusted for age, sex, cigarette smoking, alcohol consumption, hypertension, and diabetes mellitus. The adjusted odds ratios were 2.53 (95% CI = 1.47-4.35), 2.78 (95% CI = 1.55-4.97), and 3.60 (95% CI = 1.83-7.11) for lifetime average drinking-water arsenic concentrations of 0.1-50 μg/L, 50.1-299.9 μg/L, and 300 μg/L or more, respectively, compared with less than 0.1 μg/L. Interestingly, the authors reported that although one-third of their study subjects were exposed to arsenic at an average concentration of 50 μg/L or more in well water, the age-adjusted prevalence rates of cerebrovascular disease in the entire study cohort (15.8/1,000 for males, 13.2/1,000 for females) were still similar to those of the general population in Taiwan.

Engel and Smith (1994) investigated the ecological relationship between cardiovascular mortality and arsenic in drinking water in 30 counties in the United States where the average arsenic concentration was greater than 5 μg/L. The mean arsenic concentration in the public-drinking-water-supply systems in those counties ranged from 5.4 to 91.5 μg/L. County-specific and national mortality figures from 1968 to 1984 were derived from data from the National Center for Health Statistics, and population demographics were obtained from records from the U.S. Census Bureau. In the five counties where the mean arsenic value exceeded 20 μg/L, SMRs for diseases of arteries, arterioles, and capillaries (DAAC) were 1.9 (90% CI = 1.7-2.1) for females and 1.6 (90% CI = 1.5-1.8) for males. However, mortality from ischemic heart disease for both sexes was decreased in those 5 counties and in 10 counties with mean arsenic values of 10-20 μg/L. SMRs were 0.8 (90% CI = 0.8-0.9) for females and 0.7 (90% CI = 0.7-0.7) for males. SMRs for cerebrovascular disease, all malignant neoplasms, and lung cancer were close to unity.

Hematological Effects

Acute and chronic arsenic poisoning might result in anemia, leukopenia, and thrombocytopenia. Effects on those cell lineages can be simultaneous and can appear within a week of high-dose acute arsenic poisoning. The anemia, a consequence of hemolysis or marrow suppression, might be normocytic or megaloblastic.   Basophilic stippling of erythrocytes and erythrocyte karyorrhexis can be present on bone-marrow examination or peripheral blood smear (Kyle and Pease 1965; Lerman et al. 1980; Eichner 1984).   Reticulo-cytosis is a common but not invariable finding.   The marrow can also reveal erythroid hyperplasia, with megaloblastic features in both erythroid and myeloid maturation.   Leukopenia can be characterized by neutropenia or lymphopenia, and relative eosinophilia is common (Kyle and Pease 1965; Westhoff et al. 1975; Feussner et al. 1979).   In practically all cases, the hematological abnormalities are reversible; normalization of most cell lineages occurs within weeks of termination of exposure (Rezuke et al. 1991).

The hematological consequences of subacute and chronic arsenic poison-ing can appear similar to that resulting from acute arsenic poisoning.   Thus, Mizuta et al. (1956) detected frequent anemia and leukopenia in the peripheral blood of 32 subjects after 2-3 weeks of ingesting approximately 3 mg of arsenic per day in contaminated soy sauce.   The hematological effects were characterized as "slight," with red-blood-cell (RBC) counts of 3-4.5 $\times$ 10^6 and white-blood-cell (WBC) counts of 3-6 $\times$ 10^3.   Accounts of anemia or leuko-penia in patients treated with 1-10 mg of inorganic arsenic per day in the form of potassium arsenite (Fowler's solution) or arsenic sulfide have been reported (Tay and Seah 1975; Swanson and Cook 1977).   Terada et al. (1962) de-scribed a characteristic pattern of anemia, leukopenia, and thrombocytopenia among 55 individuals exposed to arsenic in drinking water in the Niigata Perfecture of Japan.   Underground disposal of arsenic trioxide and arsenic trisulfide from a nearby factory was the source of the exposure, which oc-curred for approximately 5 years (Tsuda et al. 1995).   The magnitude of exposure to patients examined by Terada et al. (1962) was not specified, but the arsenic concentration of some wells in the area exceeded 1,000 μg/L, and approximately half the subjects had characteristic arsenic-related skin lesions.

Winski and Carter (1998) recently examined the effect of inorganic arsenate and arsenite on human erythrocyte morphology in an in vitro model. Slight hemolysis (approximately 1.2%) occurred after 5 hr of incubation with 10 mM of sodium arsenate but was not detected after incubation with the same amount of sodium arsenite.   Sodium arsenate induced dose-dependent echino-cytic transformation beginning at a concentration of 0.1 mM, and irreversibly transformed sphero-echinocytes appeared at concentrations of 5 mM and 10 mM of arsenate.   The morphological effects induced by sodium arsenite were less severe and were reported only after incubation at a concentration of 10 mM.   The observed morphological changes were noted to be consistent with the effects of adenosine triphosphate (ATP) depletion, and spectrophotometric measurements confirmed that arsenate incubation induced a dose-dependent depletion in erythrocyte ATP at concentrations of 0.01 mM and higher. By comparison, arsenite incubation had little effect on erythrocyte ATP. Based on those measurements, the authors estimated that human erythrocytes are at least 1,000 times more sensitive to arsenate, or As(V), than to arsenite, or As(III). The results suggest that arsenic-induced changes in erythrocyte membrane integrity and deformability could contribute to microvascular occlusion and related peripheral vascular effects of chronic arsenic exposure (see Cardiovascular Effects above). However, as noted in Chapter 6, the blood arsenic concentration reported in human populations with chronic exposure to arsenic in drinking water has been on the order of 0.0001 to 0.001 mM, and therefore, the direct clinical relevance of the study is uncertain.

Rodent models of arsenic exposure have demonstrated disturbances in heme biosynthesis, characterized particularly by an increase in urinary uroporphyrin excretion (Woods and Fowler 1978; Martinez et al. 1983; Conner et al. 1995). In a study of the effect of arsenic on human urinary porphyrin excretion, Garcia-Vargas et al. (1994) compared urinary porphyrin profiles in 36 subjects consuming water with an arsenic concentration of 400 μg/L to profiles in 31 control subjects consuming water with an arsenic concentration of 20 μg/L. A linear relationship between total urinary porphyrin concentration and urinary arsenic was limited to subjects whose spot-urine arsenic concentration exceeded 1,000 μg/g of creatinine. Compared with controls, more subjects in the high-arsenic-exposure group had a coproporphyrin-to-uroporphyrin ratio of less than 1.0, as well as a decreased ratio of coproporphyrin III to coproporphyrin I. Cutaneous signs of arsenic poisoning were present in 15 of the 36 subjects from the town with high arsenic concentrations in water, but porphyrin profiles and clinical findings were not associated in the report.

Harrington et al. (1978) examined complete blood counts from 183 subjects drawn from 59 households in the Ester Dome area of Alaska where well water contained a mean arsenic concentration of 0.22 mg/L (range of 0.001 to 2.45). No associations were found between estimated daily arsenic ingestion and any hematological abnormality. Morse et al. (1979) found no hematological abnormalities, nor correlation of blood counts or white-cell differential with urinary arsenic concentrations (mean 47.5 μg/L) in 132 children (mean age 10.9 years) in the copper smelter town of Ajo, Arizona. The children were exposed to varying amounts of arsenic in drinking water and dust. Among 73 of the children consuming groundwater with a mean arsenic concentration of 0.09 mg/L, urinary arsenic concentrations measured 59.0 $\pm$ 41.9 μg/L. Dermatological and neurological examinations were negative. Southwick et al. (1983) (see Neurological Effects below) found no increased prevalence of anemia or significant difference in hematocrit in 137 subjects from two arsenic-exposed towns in Utah (mean arsenic drinking-water concentrations of 0.180 mg/L and 0.270 mg/L) and in 100 subjects from a control town (mean arsenic drinking-water concentration of 0.019 mg/L). In the 1982 health survey of residents of Huron County, Michigan, where well-water arsenic concentrations ranged from 0.031 to 0.335 mg/L (median 0.075 mg/L) (Michigan Department of Health 1982), hemoglobin concentrations were significantly correlated with log urinary arsenic concentration ($r = -0.22$, $p = 0.03$, 103 samples), but not daily arsenic consumption ($r = -0.05$, p not specified, 86 samples). Other measurements within the complete blood count (WBC, RBC, hematocrit, mean cell volume, mean cell hemoglobin, and mean cell hemoglobin concentration) were not significantly correlated with either mean well-water arsenic concentration, daily arsenic consumption, or log urinary arsenic excretion.

Pulmonary Effects

The possible role of chronic arsenic ingestion in the genesis of nonmalignant pulmonary disease has been suggested in a few case series describing medical problems among individuals chronically exposed to increased concentrations of arsenic in drinking water. Among a total study cohort of 180 residents of Antofagasta, Chile, exposed to drinking water containing arsenic at 0.8 mg/L, 38.8% of 144 subjects with "abnormal skin pigmentation" complained of chronic cough, compared with 3.1% of 36 subjects with normal skin (Borgono et al. 1977). In autopsies of five children from the Antofagasta region with an antecedent history of cutaneous arsenicism and postmortem findings of extensive (nonpulmonary) vascular disease, two of the subjects were noted to have slight pulmonary fibrosis (Rosenberg 1974). In a study of arsenic in drinking water in West Bengal, India, Guha Mazumder et al. (1997) noted a complaint of cough in 89 (57%) of 156 patients with arsenical hyperpigmentation. Lung-function tests performed on 17 of those patients showed features of restrictive lung disease in 9 (53%) and combined obstructive and restrictive disease in 7 (41%) (Guha Mazumder et al. 1997). The results of more-extensive investigation to characterize the nature of the pulmonary disease among patients with chronic arsenic poisoning in West Bengal have not been reported.

In an ecological investigation of the relationship of arsenic in drinking water to vascular-disease mortality in 30 U.S. counties (see above), standardized mortality ratios for both chronic airway obstruction and emphysema were significantly increased (in the range of 1.2 to 1.7) (Engel and Smith 1994). However, as noted by the authors, the lack of any significant increase in lung cancer or ischemic heart disease in the same counties suggests the possibility that the increased pulmonary disease mortality might not be attributable to smoking, the most common underlying cause of death from chronic obstructive pulmonary disease. In like manner, in a recent ecological investigation of mortality in a region in northern Chile, which formerly had increased concentrations of arsenic in drinking water, a striking increase was observed in chronic obstructive disease mortality that was limited to the age category of 30-39 years (Smith et al. 1998). From 1989 to 1993, four deaths occurred in men, compared with 0.8 expected deaths, and six deaths occurred in women, compared with 0.1 expected deaths. The authors noted that the decedents would have been young children during the period 1955-1970, when arsenic concentrations in the region's drinking water were at their peak (approximately 0.57 mg/L).

Immunological Effects

Immunomodulating and immunotoxic effects of arsenic have been demonstrated in several experimental models in vitro and in vivo. McCabe et al. (1983) measured the response of in vitro cultures of human and bovine peripheral lymphocytes to phytohemagglutinin (PHA) stimulation in the presence of several concentrations of sodium arsenite and sodium arsenate. At low doses of arsenite (2×10^{-6} M) and arsenate (5×10^{-6} M), PHA-induced stimulation of cultured human lymphocytes was increased 49% with arsenite and 19% with arsenate. Conversely, at high doses of arsenite (1.9×10^{-5} M) and arsenate (6×10^{-4} M), PHA-induced stimulation was completely inhibited.

Gonsebatt et al. (1992) studied the response to PHA stimulation of peripheral blood lymphocytes from healthy human volunteers incubated with arsenite and arsenate at concentrations of 10^{-9} M, 10^{-8} M, or 10^{-7} M, concentrations equivalent to those observed in the blood of arsenic-exposed human populations. Delays in cell-cycle kinetics, assessed by the proportion of PHA-treated cells in M1, M2, and M3 phases, were observed at all concentrations of arsenite and arsenate in a dose-dependent pattern. Arsenite and arsenate did not differ in their capacity to effect cell proliferation.

In a follow-up study, Gonsebatt et al. (1994) compared lymphocyte-replicating ability in 33 individuals consuming drinking water with a mean arsenic concentration of 412 μg/L and in 30 control subjects consuming water with a mean arsenic concentration of 37 μg/L. Arsenic concentrations from first-morning-void urine from the exposed and control groups yielded means of 758 μg/L and 37 μg/L, respectively. The peripheral blood lymphocyte count of the arsenic-exposed subjects was slightly increased relative to the controls ($3.1 \pm 1.0 \times 10^6$ versus $2.6 \pm 1.1 \times 10^6$). The progression of lymphocytes from the S phase of the cell cycle to the M phase following PHA incubation was decreased in the exposed subjects, suggesting an impairment of immune response.

Sikorski et al. (1989) examined the effect of a single intratracheal dose of sodium arsenite at 10 mg/kg (the maximally tolerated dose with respect to mortality) on several immune responses in female mice. The immunoglobulin M (IgM) antibody response of splenocytes to T-dependent antigen sheep red blood cells was decreased 24% but without a change in splenic weight or cell number. The proliferate response of splenocytes to mitogens and the mixed lymphocyte response to DBA/2 spleen cells were not affected. Arsenite diminished by 47% the delayed hypersensitivity response to an intradermally injected antigen. The functional ability of peritoneal exudate cells to phagocytize chicken red blood cells was substantially increased. Host resistance to intraperitoneal injections of bacteria and tumor cells (B16F10 melanoma) was not decreased.

Gainer and Pry (1972) examined the effect of inorganic arsenic on host resistance to viral challenge in mice. Mice given drinking water containing 0.002 M arsenate for 2 weeks experienced a greater than 3-fold increase in mortality from a subsequent intraperitoneal challenge of pseudorabies virus. Impaired host resistance was also demonstrated in additional experiments using subcutaneous arsenic injections and intraperitoneal exposure to encephalomyocarditis virus and St. Louis encephalitis virus. Resistance to Western encephalitis virus increased when arsenic was administered at the time of viral inoculation (a possible direct antiviral effect of the arsenic) but decreased if arsenic exposure followed the inoculation by 1 day.

From the late eighteenth through the mid-twentieth century, oral preparations of inorganic arsenic were used therapeutically for a variety of health problems, particularly for such illnesses as asthma, rheumatic fever, and skin conditions (eczema and psoriasis) (Stockman 1902; Pope 1902) in which an immunosuppressant effect might have contributed to an improvement in symptoms. An immunosuppressant action might also have been responsible for a common side effect of medicinal arsenic, the development of herpes zoster (Farquharson 1880; Reynolds 1901; Costello 1942). Long-term daily ingestion of medicinal arsenite in those cases probably ranged from 5 to 10 mg (Stockman 1902; Pope 1902). An epidemic increase in the number of cases of herpes zoster led to the initial suspicion of arsenic as a cause of poisoning among several thousand beer drinkers in the Manchester beer incident of 1900 (Reynolds 1901), when arsenic ingestion might have been 1-5 mg per day for weeks or months. An increased incidence of herpes labialis has been reported in acute poisoning incidents from other arsenic contaminated foodstuffs, including a single acute exposure to 1-3 g of arsenic in cider (Lawson et al. 1925) or 2-3 weeks of exposure to 3 mg of arsenic per day in soy sauce (Mizuta et al. 1956).

In the 1982 Huron County, Michigan, health survey of residents exposed to arsenic in drinking water (see description in Cardiovascular Effects above), 37 of 114 adult participants (32.5%) related a history of "cold sores" (herpes labialis), making it the most common health problem reported in the study. The daily consumption of arsenic in drinking water and the log-transformed concentration of arsenic in urine were higher for the eight subjects who reported a history of shingles (herpes zoster) than for the other subjects (Michigan Department of Health 1982).

Neurological Effects

Acute inorganic arsenic intoxication that produces initial gastrointestinal or cardiovascular symptoms can be followed by the delayed onset of central or peripheral nervous-system involvement. The central-nervous-system effects, which generally occur within 1-5 days of acute poisoning, can range from headache and mild confusion to florid encephalopathy, seizures, and coma (O'Shaughnessy and Kraft 1976; Freeman and Couch 1978; Greenberg et al. 1979; Fincher and Koerker 1987; Levin-Scherz et al. 1987). Evidence of peripheral neuropathy, a more common but not invariable finding, emerges within 1-4 weeks (Heyman et al. 1956; Le Quesne and McLeod 1977; Donofrio et al. 1987). Initial neuropathic symptoms typically consist of sensory dysesthesias in a symmetric stocking-glove distribution, but can be accompanied by ascending weakness and flaccid paralysis in severe cases. Histopathological examination of the peripheral nerves is consistent with a sensorimotor axonopathy (Ota 1970; Le Quesne and McLeod 1977), although electrophysiological testing can sometimes suggest segmental demyelination (Murphy et al. 1981; Donofrio et al. 1987).

In subacute or chronic exposure, arsenic can occasionally result in sub-clinical or overt peripheral neuropathy in the absence of antecedent gastrointestinal or cardiovascular signs or symptoms (Buchanan 1901; Heyman et al. 1956; Feldman et al. 1979; Lagerkvist and Zetterlund 1994).

Prominent arsenical peripheral neuropathy has been reported following subacute ingestion of drinking water containing arsenic at a concentration of 10 mg/L or more. Ingestion of well water containing arsenic at concentrations of 11.8-21.0 mg/L, apparently from pesticide contamination, resulted in multisystemic illness, including neuropathy, in several subjects exposed over a 10-week period (Feinglass 1973). A 36-year-old male developed a slowly progressive sensorimotor peripheral axonopathy 4 months after daily consumption of well water containing arsenic of geological origin at a concentration of 25 mg/L (Kosnett and Becker 1988). Multisystemic illness, including neuropathy, occurred in a husband and wife consuming well water containing arsenic at 9.0-10.9 mg/L (Franzblau and Lilis 1989). Wagner et al. (1979) described a 41-year-old female who developed subacute multisystemic arsenical intoxication, including lower-extremity paresthesias, following 4 months of consumption of well water found to contain arsenic at a concentration of only 1.2 mg/L. However, a conservative estimate of her intake of coffee prepared from the well water was 12-14 cups per day.

The occurrence of peripheral neuropathy is inconsistent in individuals chronically exposed to arsenic in drinking water at concentrations of 0.1-1.0 mg/L. As noted and reviewed by Hotta (1989), peripheral neuropathy has not been identified as a common or significant finding in the cohorts affected by chronic arsenical dermatitis from well water in southeastern Taiwan; Cordoba, Argentina; or Antofagasta, Chile. Basu et al. (1996) recently described a sensory predominant distal polyneuropathy in eight patients with arsenical dermatoses in West Bengal, India, where there is chronic consumption of well water containing arsenic at concentrations of 0.2-2.0 mg/L. Hindmarsh et al. (1977) reported electromyographic findings in 32 of 110 members of a Canadian community consuming well water containing arsenic at a concentration of more than 0.05 mg/L (range of 0.06 to 1.40 mg/L) and in 12 control subjects who used wells with arsenic at less than 0.05 mg/L. Seven of 14 subjects exposed to well-water arsenic exceeding 0.10 mg/L had abnormal electromyograms, compared with 3 of 18 subjects exposed to well-water arsenic at 0.05-0.10 mg/L and none of the 12 control subjects.

Kreiss et al. (1983) conducted blinded clinical neurological examinations and nerve-conduction-velocity (NCV) measurements on 147 subjects from Ester Dome, Alaska, a community in which many residences use wells containing increased concentrations of arsenic (mean 0.347 mg/L; range of 0.001 to 4.78). Subjects had a mean age of 36.3 years (range of 17 to 57 years) and had lived an average of 74 months in their residence. An index of usual daily arsenic consumption in water for each subject ranged from 0.0 to 4,521 μg per day (one outlying value was 14,479 μg per day) and correlated closely with first-morning-void and spot-urine arsenic concentrations (Pearson correlation coefficient for log values = 0.730, $p < 10^{-5}$). When daily water arsenic consumption was divided into three categories (0-100 μg, 101-1,000 μg, and 1,001-15,000 μg), no significant differences were found in the prevalence of subjects with an abnormal neurological examination or abnormal NCV. Neurological findings on physical examination and NCV results were poorly correlated. Kreiss et al. (1983) concluded that there was no evidence of arsenic-induced clinical or subclinical neuropathy in the study cohort.

Southwick et al. (1983) conducted a controlled cross-sectional study of the effects of chronic arsenic ingestion in drinking water among residents of Millard County, Utah. Participants included 145 residents of two exposed communities whose well-water arsenic concentration averaged 0.180 mg/L and 0.270 mg/L and 105 control subjects whose well water averaged 0.019 mg/L. On the basis of individual interviews, the annual arsenic ingestion in the exposed subjects was found to average 152.4 mg per year (0.42 mg per day), compared with 24.2 mg per year (0.07 mg per day) in the controls. Blinded dermatological examinations did not reveal any apparent evidence of arsenic-related skin manifestations. Among a subset of participants undergoing NCV measurements, 13 of 83 exposed subjects (15.7%) and 8 of 67 controls (11.9%) were found to have at least one nerve with abnormal conduction. Blinded neurological examinations showed that the mean NCV for each particular nerve was not significantly different in the exposed subjects and the control subjects. In a regression analysis, the annual arsenic dose was not significantly associated with NCV.

Endocrinological Effects

Inhibition of the pyruvate dehydrogenase enzyme complex and the consequent effects on carbohydrate metabolism and cellular respiration have long been recognized as major effect of acute arsenic intoxication (Stocken and Thompson 1949). Experimental studies of the effect of arsenicals on glucose metabolism have yielded considerable interspecies differences. For example, acute and subacute exposure of rats to relatively high doses of sodium arsenite (i.e., 10 mg/kg intraperitoneally for 1-7 days) has been associated with hyperglycemia and impaired glucose tolerance (Ghafghazi et al. 1980), whereas exposure of mice to a single dose of sodium arsenite (10 mg/kg intraperitoneally) induces hypoglycemia (Boquist et al. 1988). Similarly, the organic arsenical phenylarsine oxide inhibits insulin-stimulated glucose transport in the rat skeletal muscle, but increases the same process in human skeletal muscle in vitro (Carey et al. 1995). Neither hyperglycemia nor hypoglycemia has been described in human accounts of overt subacute arsenic intoxication in humans (Mizuta et al. 1956; Terada et al. 1960; Armstrong et al. 1984; Franzblau and Lilis 1989).

Lai et al. (1994) investigated the relationship between cumulative arsenic exposure from artesian well water and the prevalence of diabetes mellitus in 891 adults who were over 30 years of age and residing in the blackfoot-disease hyperendemic area of southeastern Taiwan in 1989. Most (78.3 %) of the subjects had begun residing in the area before 1960, when median well-water arsenic concentrations ranged from 0.70 to 0.93 mg/L. Cumulative lifetime ingestion of arsenic in drinking water (parts per million-years) could be estimated for 718 (80.6%) of the subjects. The presence of diabetes mellitus in all subjects was assessed by a fasting blood glucose test, an oral glucose tolerance test, or a history of insulin or sulfonylurea medication. In a multiple logistic regression analysis controlling for age, sex, body-mass index, and physical activity at work, the odds ratio (95% CI) for diabetes mellitus was 6.61 (0.86-51.0) and 10.05 (1.30-77.9) for cumulative arsenic exposures of 0.1-15.0 ppm-yr and more than 15.0 ppm-yr, respectively. The prevalence of diabetes mellitus in 108 unexposed subjects was only 0.9 %, considerably lower than the 5.1% background prevalence cited by the authors as characteristic of the rural population of Taiwan at ages of 40 years or older. The study did not report a logistic model that included an apparent age-sex interaction or a continuous (rather than categorical) arsenic-exposure variable, and detailed recruitment information describing the relationship of the study subjects to the total population at risk was not supplied.

Prompted by the Taiwanese report, Swedish investigators (Rahman and Axelson 1995) examined the relationship between diabetes mellitus and arsenic exposure in two occupational cohorts. In a nested case-control study of a history of diabetes mellitus among 116 deceased male residents of a northern Swedish parish who had been employed at a copper smelter, the Mantel-Haenszel age-adjusted odds ratio associated with job-related arsenic exposure was 3.3 (95% CI = 0.5-30). Cases consisted of 12 decedents with diabetes mellitus noted in the death certificates or the employment medical records; the selected controls were 31 decedents who the authors considered to be free from diagnoses potentially related to arsenic ingestion (i.e., any cancer, cardiovascular, or cerebrovascular disease). The odds ratios associated with increasing arsenic exposure categories were (reference level, 1) 2.0, 4.2, and 7.0. The 95% CIs for each strata of exposure included unity; however, the test for trend was statistically significant ($X^2(1) = 4.68$, $p = 0.03$). Rahman et al. (1996) conducted a case-control study of diabetes mellitus as an underlying or contributing cause of death between 1950 and 1982 of 5,498 decedents who resided in the glass-producing area of southeastern Sweden. Controls were decedents without any indication on their death certificates of cancer, cardiovascular disease, or diabetes. A history of employment as a glassblower, (glass) foundry worker, or unspecified glass worker (job categories with probable arsenic exposure) was associated with a Mantel-Haenszel odds ratio for diabetes mellitus of 1.4 (95% CI = 0.92-2.2; 209 subjects). The unspecified glass workers, thought to include persons with high arsenic exposure, carried the highest risk (Mantel-Haenszl odds ratio 1.8, 95% CI = 1.1-2.8).

Rahman et al. (1998) conducted a cross-sectional study in western Bangladesh of the prevalence of diabetes mellitus among residents who had hyperkeratosis attributed to consumption of tube well water containing increased concentrations of arsenic. Arsenic-exposed subjects 30 years of age or older with keratoses (163 subjects) were recruited by a door-to-door survey in seven villages known to have arsenic contaminated drinking water, and unexposed subjects (854 subjects) were recruited by a similar door-to-door method in four suburbs of Dhaka, which has no arsenic contamination (i.e., arsenic in drinking water was less than 0.01 mg/L). The presence of diabetes mellitus was determined by a history of symptoms, previously diagnosed diabetes, glucosuria, and blood glucose after oral glucose challenge. There were 21 confirmed cases of diabetes mellitus in the 163 arsenic-exposed subjects with keratosis. The crude prevalence ratio for diabetes mellitus among the arsenic exposed subjects with keratosis was 4.4 (95% CI = 2.5-7.7), which increased to 5.2 (95% CI = 2.5-10.5) after adjustment for age, sex, and body-mass index. When current well-water arsenic content and historical well-usage data were used to estimate the time-weighted-average drinking-water arsenic concentration, a dose-response pattern emerged. Using the control population's age- and sex-adjusted prevalence as a reference (1.0), the prevalence ratios for diabetes mellitus were calculated to be 2.6, 3.9, and 8.8 for time-weighted-average arsenic-exposure categories of less than 0.5 mg/L, 0.5-1.0 mg/L, and greater than 1.0 mg/L.

Reproductive and Developmental Effects

Epidemiological Associations

Very few studies have been conducted on arsenic and reproductive success in humans, and nothing conclusive can be stated from those studies. Nordstrom et al. (1978a,b) reported an increase in spontaneous abortions and low birth weight in populations living near a copper smelter, which emitted considerable arsenic. Tabacova et al. (1994) reported similar findings in Bulgaria, where pregnancy complications and perinatal deaths attributable to congenital malformations were higher in women living near a copper smelter than in those living in a less-exposed region (as cited in Zelikoff et al. 1995). However, copper smelters are also a source of other metals, including mercury, lead, zinc, and copper. Some reports have made associations between arsenic concentration in drinking water and adverse pregnancy outcomes and birth defects. Reported effects include coarctation of the aorta, but not other heart abnormalities (Zierler et al. 1988), and spontaneous abortion (Aschengrau et al. 1989). On the other hand, Swan et al. (1995) reported no association between occupational exposure to arsenic in the semiconductor industry and miscarriage.

Investigators in Hungary reported a correlation between increased concentrations of arsenic in well water (60-270 μg/mL) and increased incidence of spontaneous abortion and perinatal death without an increase in premature births from 1980 to 1987 (Dési 1992). The arsenic content of the drinking water in the affected region has subsequently been lowered. Another series of evaluations of demographic data from 1970 to 1987 indicated that frequency of stillbirths and spontaneous abortions was increased in a population drinking from wells with arsenic concentrations exceeding 100 μg/L (Börzsönyi et al. 1992; Rudnai et al. 1996).

Animal Data

Arsenic has been shown to be teratogenic and embryotoxic in several commonly used animal models, including rats, mice, hamsters, rabbits, and chicks. The syndrome of malformations includes neural tube, eye, skeletal, and urogenital abnormalities. This syndrome is reasonably consistent across species, although the incidence varies. The potency of the different forms of arsenic also varies across species. The inorganic forms, arsenite and arsenate, are more toxic than the methylated forms.

Arsenic teratogenicity was first reported in studies on chick embryos in which tail-bud abnormalities were observed after arsenic administration (Ancel and Lallemand 1941). The teratogenic potential of arsenic in mammals was investigated almost three decades later. Ferm and Carpenter (1968) demonstrated that intravenous administration of sodium arsenate to pregnant golden hamsters on gestation day 8 produced exencephaly (a neural-tube defect comparable to anencephaly in humans) in embryos. Exposure at 20 mg/kg produced exencephaly in 66% of the embryos. That concentration also produced a 35% incidence of embryo lethality; 40 mg/kg was lethal to 100% of the embryos. Sodium arsenate administered at 5 mg/kg did not produce malformations, although the resorption (embryonic death) incidence of 16% was somewhat higher than that in the control group. Definitive conclusions cannot be drawn from that experiment because only three litters were evaluated. A repetition of the experiment using 20 mg/kg intravenously on gestation day 8 confirmed the previous results; 49% of the embryos in the later experiment were malformed (Holmberg and Ferm 1969).

Ferm et al. (1971) extended those observations in hamsters by intravenous administration of sodium arsenate at 15-25 mg/kg in the morning, afternoon, or evening of gestation day 8. In addition to exencephaly and encephalocele (another defect of the developing central nervous system), renal agenesis and other urogenital abnormalities, rib malformations, cleft lip and palate, and anophthalmia were observed. Neural-tube defects and rib abnormalities decreased with administration later on day 8, and urogenital anomalies occurred at roughly the same rate irrespective of administration time. Constant infusion of arsenate beginning on one of gestation days 4-7 and continuing until at least day 9 produced comparable malformations (Ferm and Hanlon 1985). The malformations were correlated with dose but not with duration of exposure.

The developmental toxicity of arsenite has also been evaluated in hamsters. Arsenite was more embryotoxic than arsenate: an intravenous injection of sodium arsenite at 10 mg/kg on gestation day 8 killed 90% of the embryos; at 20 mg/kg, sodium arsenate killed 44% (Willhite 1981). Sodium arsenite exposure at 2 mg/kg resulted in only a 4% incidence of resorptions (not different from background) but still produced malformations. The syndrome of malformations was comparable to that produced by arsenate. Oral gavage of sodium arsenite at 25 mg/kg on gestation day 8, 11, or 12 increased the death rate in fetuses exposed on gestation day 8 or 12 and decreased the weights of the surviving fetuses exposed on day 12 (Hood and Harrison 1982).

Mice are also sensitive to the developmental effects of arsenic. Intraperitoneal injection of sodium arsenate at 45 mg/kg on one of gestation days 6-12 in Swiss-Webster mice caused terata, resorptions, and decreased fetal weight. Resorption incidence was highest with later exposure and was as high as 78% on gestation day 12. Malformation incidence was highest in the litters of animals exposed on day 9—63% of the live fetuses had malformations. The spectrum of malformations was dependent on gestational stage at exposure and included exencephaly, hydrocephalus, anophthalmia, micrognathia, cleft lip, micromelia, ectrodactyly, and various skeletal abnormalities (Hood and Bishop 1972). The authors reported that exposure at 25 mg/kg had no effect. The same laboratory compared the effects of oral gavage and intraperitoneal administration of sodium arsenate in mice. Arsenate was given intraperitoneally at a dose of 40 mg/kg or by mouth at a dose of 120 mg/kg to CD-1 mice on one of gestation days 7-15. Those doses produced comparable maternal toxicity, and preliminary results with lower oral doses indicated that up to 100 mg/kg was without developmental effect. The intraperitoneal administration produced results that were comparable to the earlier study. Oral exposure to arsenate significantly decreased fetal weight when administered on gestation days 10, 11, or 15 but not on other days. The only statistically significant increase in resorption incidence was in the group exposed on day 11. No significant increases in malformation rates occurred after oral exposure (Hood et al. 1978).

The developmental toxicity of arsenic acid (the acid form of arsenate) was evaluated in mice using the regulatory standard Segment II testing protocol, which involves dosing pregnant animals daily through the period of major organogenesis, occurring on days 6-15 in this species (Nemec et al. 1998). The compound was administered by gavage at doses of 7.5, 24, and 48 mg/kg per day. The highest concentration was maternally toxic and increased the rate of resorptions and decreased fetal weight. There was a 2.03% malformation incidence in that group compared with a 0.98% incidence in controls. The malformations were exencephaly and thoracogastroschisis. No significant effects were observed at the two lowest concentrations, although one case of exencephaly and two of thoracogastroschisis occurred in those groups. Neither malformation was observed in the controls. The authors concluded that these malformations were not treatment-related and that the no-observed-adverse-effect level (NOAEL) for developmental effects for arsenic acid is 7.5 mg/kg per day (equivalent to arsenic at 3 mg/kg per day). In a separate review, Golub (1994) concluded that the malformations were attributable to arsenic and that the NOAEL was less than that value. Although these conflicting opinions cannot be resolved in this report, it is clear that the NOAEL for arsenic must be close to 3 mg/kg. The effects of arsenic acid were also evaluated in a two-generation study in mice in which it was added to the diet at concentrations of 20, 100, and 500 ppm (approximate daily doses of 0.5, 2.7, and 13.3 mg/kg) (Hazelton Laboratories 1990, as cited in Golub et al. 1998). The highest concentration was severely maternally toxic and had profound effects on litter size, offspring growth, and viability. The intermediate dose resulted in a mild (approximately 10%) growth retardation in offspring during the suckling period, and the lowest concentration was without effect. The fertility of adults appeared to be unaffected.

Recently completed studies reported in abstract form describe the results of oral and inhalation developmental toxicity tests using arsenic trioxide in rats. In the inhalation test, arsenic trioxide was administered at concentrations up to 10 mg/m^3 for 6 hr per day, 7 days per week, beginning 14 days before mating and continuing throughout gestation. No effect on any developmental measurement was observed (Stump et al. 1998a). In the oral test, arsenic trioxide was again administered 14 days before mating and daily throughout gestation. A concentration of 10 mg/kg per day caused a decrease in fetal weight and an increase in two skeletal variants; that dose also produced some maternal toxicity. A concentration of 5 mg/kg per day was without observable developmental or maternal effect (Stump et al. 1998b). In a recent review Golub et al. (1998) confirmed that the primary effect of arsenic was increased prenatal mortality and decreased fetal weight.

Arsenite was more potent than arsenate in the mouse. Intraperitoneal injection of sodium arsenite at 10-12 mg/kg to Swiss-Webster mice on one of gestation days 7-12 increased the resorption rate at all injection times, decreased fetal weight after injection on gestation days 7-11, and increased malformation incidence especially after injection on days 9 and 10. Malformations were similar to those seen after arsenate exposure: exencephaly, open eyes, and micrognathia; and rib, vertebral, and tail defects (Hood 1972). Sodium arsenite was given by gavage to CD-1 mice on one of days 8-15 of gestation at doses of 20, 40, or 45 mg/kg. The lowest dose was reported to be without effect. The two highest doses produced a 19% and 36% incidence of maternal deaths, respectively, and also decreased fetal weights and increased resorption incidence. There was also a small increase above the control rate in malformations (exencephaly and open eyes) after dosing on gestation days 8-10 (Baxley et al. 1981). In a multigeneration study in which arsenite at a concentration of 5 ppm was added to the diets of CD mice for three generations, fertility or generation time were not affected, the number of offspring per litter decreased slightly, abnormalities were not observed, and the sex ratio was skewed in favor of males in one of the three generations (Schroeder and Mitchener 1971). Because numerous other studies examining the developmental effects of arsenic have not noted anything similar to the last observation, it should be viewed as uncorroborated and unlikely.

Beaudoin (1974) confirmed the teratogenicity of intraperitoneal sodium arsenate in the rat. Doses of 20-50 mg/kg given to Wistar rats on one of gestation days 7-12 were evaluated. Embryo lethality was complete at 50 mg/kg. The lowest doses also increased the resorption rate and the malformation rate in surviving fetuses. The highest rate of malformation was after dosing on gestation day 9. Eye defects, exencephaly, renal agenesis, gonadal agenesis, and rib and vertebral abnormalities were the most commonly observed malformations.

A Segment II study was conducted in rabbits using gavaged arsenic acid at doses of 0.19, 0.75, and 3.0 mg/kg per day on gestation days 6-18 (Nemec et al. 1998). Seven of 18 animals in the highest-dose group died as a result of exposure. No effects on fetal weight were observed, and malformation rates were low in all groups. One case of renal agenesis was observed at the highest concentration, and three cases (all from the same litter) of fused ribs were observed at the intermediate concentration. Those effects are consistent with the effects of arsenic in other species but are also observed spontaneously in rabbits, particularly fused ribs, which occur at a mean rate of 0.3% of fetuses in 225 studies compiled from industry and contract laboratory records from 1989 to 1992 (MARTA 1996). Therefore, 1 mg/kg per day is a NOAEL for developmental toxicity in the rabbit study.

The developmental effects of other forms of arsenic have been studied. Arsine gas had no developmental effects in rats or mice exposed at up to 2.5 ppm by inhalation for 6 hr per day on gestation days 6-15, even though evidence of hemolysis was observed in the dams exposed at the highest concentration (Morrissey et al. 1990). Dimethylarsinic acid (cacodylic acid) administered by gavage to rats and mice on gestation days 6-15 was developmentally toxic. All the doses administered to mice (200-600 mg/kg per day) decreased maternal weight gain, and the highest dose produced over 50% maternal mortality. Developmental effects including decreased fetal weight and increased incidence of cleft palate at 400 and 600 mg/kg per day. Maternal weight gain in rats decreased at 40 mg/kg per day and above, and lethality began at 50 mg/kg per day. Fetal weight decreased at 40 mg/kg per day, and variations in palate structure were noted at 15 mg/kg per day and above but not at 7.5 mg/kg per day (Rogers et al. 1981). Variations of palate structure are considered within the range of normal variability in response to a stressor and are typically classified as nonadverse effects. Neither monomethylarsonic acid (MMA) nor dimethylarsinic acid (DMA) produced developmental toxicity in hamsters (Willhite 1981).

In summary, the animal data indicate that arsenic in a variety of forms has the potential to cause developmental toxicity, including malformations, in a variety of species. The spectrum of malformations that has been produced is remarkably consistent across species. Arsenite has been repeatedly shown to be more potent than arsenate, and organic forms appear to be considerably less potent than the inorganic forms. Along with other manifestations of developmental toxicity, malformation rates are highest after parenteral administration but have been observed after oral administration. The test regimen in a two-generation study in mice in which arsenic was administered in the diet as arsenic acid probably represents the closest of any of the test regimens to expected chronic human exposure to arsenic in drinking water, although it should be noted that mice convert organic arsenic to DMA much more efficiently than do humans (see Chapter 5). In that study, arsenic at a concentration of 20 ppm (approximately 0.5 mg/kg per day) was clearly without effect, and 100 ppm (approximately 2.65 mg/kg per day) had a reversible effect on growth during early life. Fertility of adult animals appears to be unaffected, although assessment of adult reproductive health has not been comprehensive. In marmoset monkeys, which do not methylate inorganic arsenic (Vahter et al. 1982), and in mice and hamsters, which are efficient in arsenic methylation (Lindgren et al. 1982), arsenic accumulates in the epididymis. In contrast to the rodents, the marmoset accumulated arsenic in the testis as well. Thus, there is reason to investigate the effects of arsenic exposure on male reproductive health.

Placental Transfer

Arsenic appears to move freely across the placenta, and substantial concentrations of arsenic have been measured in the embryo after oral or intraperitoneal administration of arsenate or arsenite in mice (Hood et al. 1987, 1988). This transfer occurs during all stages of gestation. During the embryonic period in the mouse and marmoset, accumulation of arsenic is especially great in the neuroepithelium, as assessed by autoradiography. During the fetal period, arsenate, but not arsenite, is distributed to developing bone, and both forms are distributed to the skin, liver, and gastrointestinal tract (Lindgren et al. 1984). The distribution of arsenic to those organs might be attributable to the in vivo reduction of arsenate to arsenite (see Chapter 5).

Recent studies found that arsenic readily crosses the human placenta, giving rise to arsenic concentrations that are about as high in cord blood as in maternal blood (Concha et al. 1998). However, more than 90% of the arsenic in plasma and urine was in the form of DMA, a percentage that was significantly higher in pregnant women than in nonpregnant women. That finding indicated an increased methylation of arsenic during pregnancy. Thus, the fetus seems to be exposed mainly to DMA, at least at term. As mentioned above, animal data indicate that less developmental toxicity is caused by the methylated metabolites of arsenic than by arsenite.

Pathogenesis and Possible Mechanisms of Teratogenesis

A few studies have evaluated the pathogenesis and potential mechanisms of action of arsenic-induced teratogenesis. Observations in hamster embryos several hours after parenteral administration of arsenate showed a delay in the elevation of the neural folds (Willhite 1981; Carpenter 1987), an event that precedes neural-tube closure. A paucity of cephalic mesoderm was also reported (Willhite 1981), along with a shortening and abnormal folding of the notochord (Marin-Padilla 1979), which is the structure that organizes and induces the neural plate, the precursor of the central nervous system. In addition to those effects on the mesoderm, the neuroepithelium was reported to thin in response to arsenate exposure (Marin-Padilla 1980). That effect was also observed in rat embryos, in which an increase in apoptosis of the neuro-ectoderm was observed several hours after maternal arsenate exposure (Takeuchi 1979).

Histological studies of the developing urogenital system in rat embryos after maternal arsenate exposure revealed that the first observable change is a retardation in the growth of the mesonephric duct. The retardation led to absence of the ureteric bud (which arises from the mesonephric duct) and resulted in the absence of the vas deferens, seminal vesicle, and part of the epididymis (Burk and Beaudoin 1977).

Neural-tube closure and mesonephric-duct elongation involve morphogenetic movements affected by cytoskeletal elements and cell-adhesion molecules. The function of these proteins is dependent in part on ionic and sulfhydryl interactions, both of which are known to be affected by arsenic. Therefore, it would be an interesting hypothesis to test for altered function of these molecules in arsenic-exposed embryos.

The adverse developmental effects of arsenic were frequently observed in conjunction with maternal toxicity. There are instances in which the maternal toxicity, and not the exogenous insult per se, is the causative factor in abnormal development (Daston 1994). One common mechanism by which that occurs is through the induction of metallothionein in the maternal liver, leading to a systemic redistribution of zinc and a transitory, but developmentally adverse, embryonic zinc deficiency. Arsenate has produced those effects in the pregnant rat (Taubeneck et al. 1994). However, explanted rodent embryos exposed to arsenic in the absence of the maternal system developed abnormally (Chaineau et al. 1990; Mirkes and Cornel 1992; Zelikoff et al. 1995), indicating that arsenic exposure has direct effects. In addition, Golub (1994) thoroughly analyzed the literature for maternal- and developmental-toxicity relationships and found the correlation to be less than perfect. Therefore, arsenic is likely to have direct embryotoxicity in vivo, but its effects might be exacerbated by maternal toxicity.

SUMMARY AND CONCLUSIONS

Ingestion of inorganic arsenic is an established cause of skin cancer. Recent studies strengthen the evidence that ingestion of arsenic can also cause cancers of the lung and the urinary bladder. Based on findings of increased risks of bladder- and lung-cancer mortality in three countries (Taiwan, Argentina, and Chile), the subcommittee believes that the evidence is now sufficient to include bladder and lung cancer among the cancers that can be caused by ingestion of inorganic arsenic. With minor exception, the epidemiological evidence for cancer comes from places where exposed populations were exposed to arsenic concentrations in drinking water of at least several hundred micrograms per liter. Few data address the degree of cancer risk at lower concentrations of ingested arsenic. Studies of lung cancer among workers exposed to airborne arsenicals indicate a linear dose-response relationship over a broad range of exposure.

Increased risks of other cancers, such as kidney and liver cancer, have

Increased risks of other cancers, such as kidney and liver cancer, have also been reported. However, the strength of the association for these sites is not as strong as for lung and bladder cancers, and increased risk for some have not been noted in all studies. Thus, further confirmatory studies are needed to establish arsenic as a cause of the other cancers.

Data derived from population-based studies, clinical-case series, and case reports relating to the ingestion of inorganic arsenic in drinking water, medications, or contaminated food or beverages show the capacity of arsenate and arsenite to adversely affect multiple-organ systems. The clinical appearance of the noncancer manifestations of arsenic intoxication in humans is dependent on the magnitude of the dose and the time course of exposure. Although the toxicokinetic and toxicodynamic interaction between those two measures has not been well characterized, several general findings emerge from the available data. Diffuse or spotted hyperpigmentation, the initial nonmalignant cutaneous effect of chronic arsenic ingestion, can first appear within 6 months to 3 years of chronic ingestion at concentrations in excess of approximately 0.04 mg/kg per day. Lower exposure rates, on the order of 0.01 mg/kg per day or higher, can also result in hyperpigmentation after intervals as long as 5 to 15 years. Palmar-plantar hyperkeratoses, the other principal nonmalignant cutaneous manifestation of chronic arsenic exposure, usually follows the initial appearance of arsenical hyperpigmentation within a period of years.

Weeks to months of ongoing ingestion of inorganic arsenic at doses of approximately 0.04 mg/kg per day or higher can result in overt nonspecific gastrointestinal complaints, such as diarrhea and cramping, and hematological effects, including anemia and leukopenia. A sensory predominant axonal peripheral neuropathy can also occur after months to years of this level of exposure. Such gastrointestinal, hematological, and neurological effects generally improve or resolve following cessation of exposure. Irreversible noncirrhotic portal hypertension appears to have occurred after years of arsenic ingestion at concentrations of 0.01 to 0.02 mg/kg per day or higher. Recent studies from Mexico suggest that those low concentration rates can also perturb porphyrin metabolism; however, the impact of this disturbance on clinical function is not fully determined.

Peripheral vascular disease has been associated with chronic arsenic ingestion in epidemiological studies conducted in populations exposed via drinking water in Taiwan. Clinical-case series and case reports also linked arsenic ingestion to peripheral vascular disease in subjects exposed to arsenic in drinking water in Latin America and northern Mexico and to arsenic from multiple sources in Japan and Germany (Moselle vintners). The patients with peripheral vascular disease were drawn from populations in areas where arsenic exposure occurred over a period of years at concentrations sufficient to result in cutaneous manifestations. However, data on the latency and progression of arsenic-induced peripheral vascular disease remain sparse.

Recent epidemiological investigations in the arsenic-affected areas of southwestern Taiwan associated cumulative arsenic ingestion with a risk of hypertension and cardiovascular disease mortality. Although investigators estimated individual arsenic doses in several studies, the reports do not reveal the extent of the cardiovascular risk, in the absence of cutaneous effects, from exposure to low concentrations of arsenic. A small cross-sectional study conducted in Michigan suggested a possible link between chronic exposure to low concentrations of arsenic and hypertension. However, a cohort study of individuals exposed to higher concentrations of arsenic in medication revealed no evidence of increased cardiovascular mortality. Cohort studies of occupational arsenic exposure have suggested a small increase in cardiovascular-related mortality, but the relationship has not been found consistently. Recently, a study conducted in the Layang Basin of northeastern Taiwan reported that chronic ingestion of groundwater containing arsenic at a concentration as low as 0.1 to 50 $\mu g/L$ was associated with an increased prevalence of cerebrovascular disease. However, uncertainties relating to that study's design and negative findings in other cohorts require that the relationship between arsenic exposure and cerebrovascular disease undergo further evaluation.

Recent studies in southwestern Taiwan and Bangladesh associated chronic arsenic ingestion in drinking water with an increased risk of diabetes mellitus. The study subjects were drawn from populations with overt cutaneous signs of arsenic intoxication; information is lacking on the magnitude of the potential risk associated with exposure to low concentrations of arsenic. Two small Swedish case-control studies suggested that arsenic exposure of smelter workers and art glass workers might also be associated with an increased risk of diabetes mortality.

Inorganic arsenic has been shown to have immunomodulating and immunotoxic effects in experimental models. Subacute or chronic arsenic exposure at high doses (more than 0.05 mg/kg per day) has been associated with a decline in peripheral leukocytes, and as discussed in Chapter 8, the capacity of arsenic to suppress aspects of the immune response might have formed the basis for its former use as a therapeutic agent. The potential effect of exposure to low concentrations of arsenic on immune function has not been adequately investigated in field research; however a small cross-sectional study from Michigan is consistent with an immunomodulating effect. The potential effect of ingested arsenic on respiratory function has been suggested by studies from Chile, West Bengal, and the United States, but the specific pathology of the effect has not been investigated.

Arsenic administered parenterally has been shown to be teratogenic in a number of mammalian species, but there is little evidence to suggest teratogenicity by oral or inhalation routes. Although some studies show an association between arsenic exposure and adverse pregnancy outcomes, they are inadequate to draw firm conclusions. No effects on fertility were observed in a multigeneration study in mice; however, arsenic does accumulate in the epididymides of hamsters, mice, and marmosets and in the testes of marmosets, suggesting that potential reproductive effects of arsenic should be investigated further.

RECOMMENDATIONS

Epidemiological studies are needed to characterize the dose-response relationship for arsenic-associated cancer and noncancer end points, especially at low doses. Such studies are of critical importance for improving the scientific validity of risk assessment. With respect to cancer, studies are recommended to define the dose-response relationship between arsenic ingestion and cancer of the skin, bladder, and lung, and to investigate the effect of arsenic on cancer at other sites. With respect to noncancer effects, particular emphasis should be placed on epidemiological study of arsenic-associated cutaneous effects, cardiovascular and cerebrovascular disease, diabetes mellitus, and adverse reproductive outcomes. Data related to latency and the relationship between magnitude of dose and time course of exposure should be obtained. Other studies of less critical importance but nonetheless needed to fill important data gaps include the following:

— Detailed clinical studies and preliminary epidemiological studies to better characterize the effect of low-to-moderate chronic arsenic exposure (0.01 to 0.03 mg/kg per day) on immune function, porphyrin metabolism, and respiratory function.

— Studies investigating the possible role of certain nonmalignant arsenic-associated effects as biomarkers of susceptibility to arsenic-induced malignancies. Such effects could include specific cutaneous manifestations or elaboration of specific gene products.

REFERENCES

Alain, G., J. Tousignant, and E. Rozenfarb. 1993. Chronic arsenic toxicity. Int. J. Dermatol. 32:899-901.

Ancel, P., and S. Lallemand. 1941. Sur l'arret de developpement du borgeon caudal obtenu experimentalement chez l'embryon de poulet. Arch. Phys. Biol. 15:27-29.

Armstrong, C.W., R.B. Stroube, T. Rubio, E.A. Siudyla, and G.B. Miller, Jr. 1984. Outbreak of fatal arsenic poisoning caused by contaminated drinking water. Arch. Environ. Health 39:276-279.

Aschengrau, A., S. Zierler, A. and Cohen. 1989. Quality of community drinking water and the occurrence of spontaneous abortion. Arch. Environ. Health 44:283-290.

Asplund, K., J. Tuomilehto, B. Stegmayr, P.O. Wester, and H. Tunstall-Pedoe. 1988. Diagnostic criteria and quality control of the registration of stroke events in the MONICA project. Acta. Med. Scand. 728(Suppl.):26-39.

Axelson, O., E. Dahlgren, C.D. Jansson, and S.O. Rehnlund. 1978. Arsenic exposure and mortality: A case-referent study from a Swedish copper smelter. Br. J. Ind. Med. 35:8-15.

Basu, D., J. Dasgupta, A. Mukherjee and D.N. Guha Mazumder. 1996. Chronic neuropathy due to arsenic intoxication from geo-chemical source—A five-year follow-up. JANEI. 1:45-47.

Bates, M.N., A.H. Smith, and K.P. Cantor. 1995. Case-control study of bladder cancer and arsenic in drinking water. Am. J. Epidemiol. 141:523-530.

Baxley, M.N., R.D. Hood, G.C. Vedel, W.P. Harrison, and G.M. Szczech. 1981. Prenatal toxicity of orally administered sodium arsenite in mice. Bull. Eviron. Contam. Toxicol. 26:749-756.

Beaudoin, A.R. 1974. Teratogenicity of sodium arsenate in rats. Teratology 10:153-157.

Black, M.M. 1967. Prolonged ingestion of arsenic. Pharm. J. (Dec. 9):593-597.

Boquist, L., S. Boquist, and I. Ericsson. 1988. Structural B-cell changes and transient hyperglycemia in mice treated with compounds inducing inhibited citric acid cycle enzyme activity. Diabetes 37:89-98.

Borgono, J.M., and R. Greiber. 1971. Epidemiological study of arsenicism in the city of Antofagasta [in Spanish]. Rev. Med. Chil. 99:702-707.

Borgono, J.M., P. Vicent, H. Venturino, and A. Infante. 1977. Arsenic in the drinking water of the city of Antofagasta: Epidemiological and clinical study before and after the installation of the treatment plant. Environ. Health Perspect. 19:103-105.

Börzsönyi, M., A. Berecsky, P. Rudnai, M. Csanady, and A. Horvath. 1992. Epidemiological studies on human subjects exposed to arsenic in drinking water in southeast Hungary. Arch. Toxicol. 66:77-78.

Buchanan, R.J.M. 1901. Cases of arsenical peripheral neuritis. Lancet (Jan. 19):170-172.

Burk, D., and A.R. Beaudoin. 1977. Arsenate-induced renal agenesis in rats. Teratology 16:247-259.

Butzengeiger, K.H.   1940.   Uber periphere Zirkulationsstorungen bei chronischer Arsenvergiftung. Klin Wochenschr. 22:523-527.

Byron, W.R., G.W. Bierbower, J.B. Brouwer, and W.H. Hansen. 1967. Pathologic changes in rats and dogs from two-year feeding of sodium arsenite or sodium arsenate. Toxicol. Appl. Pharmacol. 10:132-147.

Carey, J.O., J.L. Azevedo, P.G. Morris, W.J. Pories, and G.L. Dohm. 1995. Okadaic acid, vanadate, and phenylarsine oxide stimulate 2-deoxyglucose transport in insulin-resistant human skeletal muscle. Diabetes 44:682-688.

Carpenter, S.J. 1987. Developmental analysis of cephalic axial dysraphic disorders in arsenic-treated hamster embryos. Anat. Embryol. 176:345-365

Cebrian, M. 1987.   Some Potential Problems in Assessing the Effects of Chronic Arsenic Exposure in North Mexico [preprint extended abstract]. Preprint of paper presented at the 194th National Meeting of the American Chemical Society, Aug. 30–Sept. 4, 1987, New Orleans, La.

Cebrian, M.E., A. Albores, M. Aguilar, and E. Blakely. 1983.   Chronic arsenic poisoning in the north of Mexico. Hum. Toxicol. 2:121-133.

Chaineau, E., S. Binet, D. Pol, B. Chatellier, and V. Meininger.   1990. Embryotoxic effects of sodium arsenite and sodium arsenate on mouse embryos in culture. Teratology 41:105-112.

Chakraborty, A.K., and K.C. Saha.   1987.   Arsenical dermatosis from tubewell water in West Bengal. Indian J. Med. Res. 85:326-334.

Chen, C.J. 1990. Blackfoot disease [letter]. Lancet 336(8712):442.

Chen, C.J., and C.J. Wang. 1990. Ecological correlation between arsenic level in well water and age-adjusted mortality from malignant neoplasms. Cancer Res. 50:5470-5474.

Chen, C.J., Y.C. Chuang, T.M. Lin, and H.Y. Wu. 1985. Malignant neoplasms among residents of a blackfoot disease-endemic area in Taiwan: High-arsenic artesian well water and cancers. Cancer Res. 45:5895-5899.

Chen, C.J., M.M. Wu, S.S. Lee, J.D. Wang, S.H. Cheng, and H.Y. Wu. 1988. Atherogenicity and carcinogenicity of high-arsenic artesian well water. Multiple risk factors and related malignant neoplasms of blackfoot disease. Arteriosclerosis 8:452-460.

Chen, C.J., Y.M. Hsueh, M.S. Lai, M.P. Shyu, S.Y. Chen, M.M. Wu, T.L. Kuo, and T.Y. Tai. 1995. Increased prevalence of hypertension and long-term arsenic exposure. Hypertension 25:53-60.

Chen, G.Q., J. Zhu, X.G. Shi J.H. Ni, H.J. Zhong, G.Y. Si, X.L. Jin, W. Tang, X.S. Li, S.M. Xong, Z.X. Shen, G.L. Sun, J. Ma, P. Zhang, T.D. Zhang, C. Gazin, T. Naoe, S.J. Chen, Z.Y. Wang, and Z. Chen. 1996.

In vitro studies on cellular and molecular mechanisms of arsenic trioxide (As_2O_3) in the treatment of acute promyelocytic leukemia: As_2O_3 induces NB_4 cell apoptosis with downregulation of *Bcl-2* expression and modulation of PML-RARα/PML proteins. Blood 88:1052-1061.

Chen, K.P., H.Y. Wu, and T.C. Wu. 1962. Epidemiologic studies on blackfoot disease in Taiwan. 3. Physicochemical characteristics of drinking water in endemic blackfoot disease areas. Mem. Coll. Med. Natl. Taiwan Univ. 8:115-129.

Chiou, H.Y., Y.M. Hsueh, K.F. Liaw, S.F. Horng, M.H. Chiang, Y.S. Pu, J.S. Lin, C.H. Huang, and C.J. Chen. 1995. Incidence of internal cancers and ingested inorganic arsenic: A seven-year follow-up study in Taiwan. Cancer Res. 55:1296-1300.

Chiou, H.Y., Y.M. Hsueh, L.L. Hsieh, L.I. Hsu, Y.H. Hsu, F.I. Hsieh, M.L. Wei, H.C. Chen, H.T. Yang, L.C. Leu, T.H. Chu, C. Chen-Wu, M.H. Yang, and C.J. Chen. 1997. Arsenic methylation capacity, body retention, and null genotypes of glutathione *S*-transferase M1 and T1 among current arsenic-exposed residents in Taiwan. Mutat. Res. 386:197-207.

Concha, G., G. Vogler, D. Lezcano, B. Nermell, and M. Vahter. 1998. Exposure to inorganic arsenic metabolites during early human development. Toxicol. Sci. 44:185-190.

Conner, E.A., H. Yamauchi, and B.A. Fowler. 1995. Alterations in the heme biosynthetic pathway from the III-V semiconductor metal, indium arsenide (InAs). Chem.-Biol. Interact. 93:273-285.

Costello, M.J. 1942. Herpes zoster following administration of mapharsen. Arch. Dermatol. Syphilol. 45:1188-89.

Cowlishaw, J.L., E.J. Pollard, A.E. Cowen, and L.W. Powell. 1979. Liver disease associated with chronic arsenic ingestion. Aust. NZ J. Med. 9:310-313.

Cox, D.R. 1972. Regression models and life-tables. J. R. Stat. Soc. Ser. B 34:187-220.

Cuzick, J., S. Evans, M. Gillman, and D.A. Price Evans. 1982. Medicinal arsenic and internal malignancies. Br. J. Cancer 45:904-911.

Cuzick, J., R. Harris, and P.S. Mortimer. 1984. Palmar keratoses and cancers of the bladder and lung. Lancet i(8376):1530-1533.

Cuzick, J., P. Sasieni, and S. Evans. 1992. Ingested arsenic, keratoses, and bladder cancer. Am. J. Epidemiol. 136:417-421.

Daston, G.P. 1994. Relationships between maternal and developmental toxicity. Pp.189-212 in Developmental Toxicology, 2nd Ed., C.A. Kimmel, and J. Buelke-Sam, eds. New York: Raven.

Datta, D.V. 1976. Arsenic and non-cirrhotic portal hypertension [letter].

Lancet i(7956):433.

Dési, I. 1992. Arsenic contamination of drinking water in south-east Hungary. Geogr. Med. 22:45-53.

Donofrio, P.D., A.J. Wilbourn, J.W. Albers, L. Rogers, V. Salanga and H.S. Greenberg. 1987. Acute arsenic intoxication presenting as Guillain-Barre-like syndrome. Muscle Nerve 10:114-120.

Eichner, E.R. 1984. Erythroid karyorrhexis in the peripheral blood smear in severe arsenic poisoning: A comparison with lead poisoning. Am. J. Clin. Pathol. 81:533-537.

Engel, R.R., and A.H. Smith. 1994. Arsenic in drinking water and mortality from vascular disease: An ecological analysis in 30 counties in the United States. Arch. Environ. Health 49:418-427.

Engel, R.R., C. Hopenhayn-Rich, O. Receveur, and A.H. Smith. 1994. Vascular effects of chronic arsenic exposure: A review. Epidemiol. Rev. 16:184-209.

Enterline, P.E. and G.M. Marsh. 1982. Cancer among workers exposed to arsenic and other substances in a copper smelter. Am. J. Epidemiol. 116:895-911.

Enterline, P.E., V.L. Henderson, and G.M. Marsh. 1987. Exposure to arsenic and respiratory cancer: A reanalysis. Am. J. Epidemiol. 125:929-38.

EPA (U.S. Environmental Protection Agency). 1988. Special Report on Inorganic Arsenic: Skin Cancer; Nutritional Essentiality. EPA 625/3-87/013. U.S. Environmental Protection Agency, Risk Assessment Forum, Washington, D.C.

Epstein, E. 1960. Association of Bowen's disease with visceral cancer. Arch. Dermatol. 82:349-351.

Falk, H., J. Herbert, S. Crowley, K.G. Ishak, L.B. Thomas, H. Popper, and G.G. Caldwell. 1981. Epidemiology of hepatic angiosarcoma in the United States: 1964-1974. Environ. Health Perspect. 41:107-113.

Farquharson, R. 1880. On the use of arsenic in skin-diseases. Br. Med. J. (May 29) 802-804.

Feinglass, E.J. 1973. Arsenic intoxication from well water in the United States. N. Engl. J. Med. 268:828-830.

Feldman, R.G., C.A. Niles, M. Kelly-Hayes, D.S. Sax, W.J. Dixon, D.J. Thompson, and E. Landau. 1979. Peripheral neuropathy in arsenic smelter workers. Neurology 29:939-944.

Ferm, V.H., and S.J. Carpenter. 1968. Malformations induced by sodium arsenate. J. Reprod. Fertil. 17:199-201.

Ferm, V.H., and D.P. Hanlon. 1985. Constant rate exposure of pregnant hamsters to arsenate during early gestation. Environ. Res. 37:425-432.

Ferm, V.H., A. Saxon, and B.M. Smith. 1971. The teratogenic profile of sodium arsenate in the golden hamster. Arch. Environ. Health 22:557-560.

Feussner, J.R., J.D. Shelburne, S. Bredehoeft and H.J. Cohen. 1979. Arsenic-induced bone marrow toxicity: Ultrastructural and electron-probe analysis. Blood. 53:820-827.

Fierz, U. 1965. Catamnestic investigations of the side effects of therapy of skin diseases with inorganic arsenic [in German]. Dermatologica 131:41-58.

Fincher, R.E., and R.M. Koerker. 1987. Long-term survival in acute arsenic encephalopathy: Follow-up using newer measures of electrophysiologic parameters. Am. J. Med. 82:549-552.

Foy, H.M., S. Tarmapai, P. Eamchan, and O. Metdilogkul. 1992. Chronic arsenic poisoning from well water in a mining area in Thailand. Asia Pacific. J. Public Health 6(3):150-152.

Franklin, M., W. Bean and R.C. Harden. 1950. Fowler's solution as an etiologic agent in cirrhosis. Am. J. Med. Sci. 219:589-596.

Franzblau, A., and R. Lilis. 1989. Acute arsenic intoxication from environmental arsenic exposure. Arch. Environ. Health. 44:385-390.

Freeman, J.W. and J.R. Couch. 1978. Prolonged encephalopathy with arsenic poisoning. Neurology 28:853-855.

Gainer, J.H., and T. W. Pry. 1972. Effects of arsenicals on viral infections in mice. Am. J. Vet. Res. 33:2299-2307.

Garcia-Vargas, G.G., L.M. Del Razo, M.E. Cebrian, A. Albores, P. Ostrosky-Wegman, R. Montero, M.E. Gonsbatt, C.K. Lim, and F. De Matteis. 1994. Altered urinary porphyrin excretion in a human population chronically exposed to arsenic in Mexico. Hum. Exp. Toxicol. 13:839-847.

Ghafghazi, T., J.W. Ridlington, and B.A. Fowler. 1980. The effects of acute and subacute sodium arsenite administration on carbohydrate metabolism. Toxicol. Appl. Pharmacol. 55:126-130.

Glazener, F.S., J.G. Ellis, and P.K. Johnson. 1968. Electrocardiographic findings with arsenic poisoning. Calif. Med. 109:158-162.

Golub, M.S. 1994. Maternal toxicity and the identification of inorganic arsenic as a developmental toxicant. Reprod. Toxicol. 8:283-295.

Golub, M.S., M.S. Macintosh, and N. Baumrind. 1998. Developmental and reproductive toxicity of inorganic arsenic: Animal studies and human concerns. J. Toxicol. Environ. Health B Crit Rev. 1:199-241.

Gonsebatt, M.E., L. Vega, L.A. Herrera, R. Montero, E. Rojas, M.E. Cebrian, and P. Ostrosky-Wegman. 1992. Inorganic arsenic effects on human lymphocyte stimulation and proliferation. Mutat. Res. 283:91-95.

Gonsebatt, M.E., L. Vega, R. Montero, G. Garcia-Vargas, L.M. Del Razo,

A. Albores, and M.E. Cebrian. 1994. Lymphocyte replicating ability in individuals exposed to arsenic via drinking water. Mutat. Res. 313:293-299.

Graham, J.H., and E.B. Helwig. 1959. Bowen's disease and its relationship to systemic cancer. Arch. Dermatol. 80:133-159.

Greenberg, C., S. Davies, T. McGowan, A. Schorer, and C. Drage. 1979. Acute respiratory failure following severe arsenic poisoning. Chest 76:596-598.

Grobe, J.V. 1976. Peripheral circulatory disorders and acrocyanosis in arsenic exposed Moselle wine-growers.[in German]. Berufsdermatosen 24(3):78-84.

Guha Mazumder, D.N., J. Das Gupta, A. Santra, A. Pal, A. Ghose, S. Sarkar, N. Chattopadhaya, and D. Chakraborti. 1997. Non-cancer effects of chronic arsenicosis with special reference to liver damage. Pp.112-123 in Arsenic: Exposure and Health Effects, C.O. Abernathy, R.L. Calderon, and W.R. Chappell, eds. London: Chapman & Hall.

Guha Mazumder, D.N., R. Haque, N. Ghosh, B.K. De, A. Santra, D. Chakraborty, and A.H. Smith. 1998. Arsenic levels in drinking water and the prevalence of skin lesions in West Bengal, India. Int. J. Epidemiol. 27:871-877.

Guo, H.R., H.S. Chiang, H. Hu, S.R. Lipsitz, and R.R. Monson. 1997. Arsenic in drinking water and incidence of urinary cancers. Epidemiology 8:545-550.

Hamada T., and S. Horiguchi. 1976. Occupational chronic arsenical poisoning: On the cutaneous manifestations. Jpn. J. Ind. Health 18(2):103-115.

Harrington, J.M., J.P. Middaugh, D.L. Morse, and J. Housworth. 1978. A survey of a population exposed to high concentrations of arsenic in well water in Fairbanks, Alaska. Am. J. Epidemiol. 108:377-385.

Hazelton Laboratories. 1990. Two-generation dietary reproductive study with arsenic acid in mice. Study No. HLA 6120-138. Hazleton Laboratories America, Vienna, Va.

Hertz-Picciotto, I., and A.H. Smith. 1993. Observations on the dose-response curve for arsenic exposure and lung cancer. Scan. J. Work Environ. Health 19:217-226.

Heyman, A. J.B. Pfeiffer, R.W. Willett, and H.M. Taylor. 1956. Peripheral neuropathy caused by arsenical intoxication: A study of 41 cases with observations on the effects of BAL (2,3 dimercapto-propanol). N. Engl. J. Med. 254:401-409.

Heywood, R., and R.J.Sortwell. 1979. Arsenic intoxication in the rhesus monkey. Toxicol. Lett. 3:137-144.

Hill, A.B. 1965. The environment and disease: Association or causation? Proc. R. Soc. Med. 58:295-300.

Hindmarsh, J.T., O.R. McLetchie, L.P. Heffernan, O.A. Hayne, H.A. Ellenberger, R.F. McCurdy, and H.J. Thiebaux. 1977. Electromyographic abnormalities in chronic environmental arsenicalism. J. Anal. Toxicol. 1:270-276.

Holmberg, R.E., and V.H. Ferm. 1969. Interrelationships of selenium, cadmium, and arsenic in mammalian teratogenesis. Arch. Environ. Health 18:873-877.

Hood, R.D. 1972. Effects of sodium arsenite on fetal development. Bull. Environ. Contam. Toxicol. 7:216-222.

Hood, R.D., and S.L. Bishop. 1972. Teratogenic effects of sodium arsenate in mice. Arch. Environ. Health 24:62-65.

Hood, R.D., and W.P. Harrison. 1982. Effects of prenatal arsenite exposure in the hamster. Bull. Environ. Contam. Toxicol. 29:679-687.

Hood, R.D., G.T. Thacker, B.L. Patterson, and G.M. Szczech. 1978. Prenatal effects of oral versus intraperitoneal sodium arsenate in mice. J. Environ. Pathol. Toxicol. 1:671-678.

Hood, R.D., G.C. Vedel-Macrander, M.J. Zaworotko, F.M. Tatum, and R.G. Meeks. 1987. Distribution, metabolism and fetal uptake of pentavalent arsenic in pregnant mice following oral or intraperitoneal administration. Teratology 35:19-25.

Hood, R.D., G.C. Vedel, M.J. Zaworotko, and R.G. Meeks, 1988. Uptake, distribution, and metabolism of trivalent arsenic in the pregnant mouse. J. Toxicol. Environ. Health 25:423-434.

Hopenhayn-Rich, C., M.L. Biggs, A. Fuchs, R. Bergoglio, E.E. Tello, H. Nicolli, and A.H. Smith. 1996. Bladder cancer mortality associated with arsenic in drinking water in Argentina. Epidemiology 7:117-124.

Hopenhayn-Rich C., M.L. Biggs, and A.H. Smith. 1998. Lung and kidney cancer mortality associated with arsenic in drinking water in Córdoba, Argentina. Int. J. Epidemiol. 27:561-569.

Hotta, N. 1989. Clinical aspects of chronic arsenic poisoning due to environmental and occupational pollution in and around a small refining spot [in Japanese]. Nippon Taishitsugaku Zasshi [Jpn. J. Const. Med.] 53(1/2):49-70.

Hugo, N.E., and H. Conway. 1967. Bowen's disease: Its malignant potential and relationship to systemic cancer. Plast. Reconstr. Surg. 39:190-194.

Hutchinson, J. 1887. Arsenic cancer. Br. Med. J. 2:1280-1281.

IARC (International Agency for Research on Cancer). 1980. Some Metals and Metallic Compounds. IARC Monographs on the Evaluation of

Carcinogenic Risks to Humans, Vol. 23. Lyon, France: International Agency for Research on Cancer.

Jackson, R. and J.S. Grainge. 1975. Arsenic and cancer. Can. Med. Assoc. J. 113:396-401.

Jarup, L., G. Pershagen, and S. Wall. 1989. Cumulative arsenic exposure and lung cancer in smelter workers: A dose-response study. Am. J. Ind. Med. 15:31-41.

Kjeldsberg, C.R. and H.P. Ward. 1972. Leukemia in arsenic poisoning. Ann. Intern. Med. 77:935-937.

Kosnett, M.J., and C.E. Becker. 1988. Dimercaptosuccinic acid: Utility in acute and chronic arsenic poisoning [abstract]. Vet. Hum. Toxicol. 30:369.

Kreiss, K., M.M. Zack, P.J. Landrigan, R.G. Feldman, C.A. Niles, J. Chirico-Post, D.S. Sax, M.H. Boyd, and D.H. Cox. 1983. Neurologic evaluation of a population exposed to arsenic in Alaskan well water. Arch. Environ. Health. 38:116-121.

Kyle, R.A., and G.L. Pease. 1965. Hematologic aspects of arsenic intoxication. N. Engl. J. Med. 273:18-23.

Lagerkvist, B.J., and B. Zetterlund. 1994. Assessment of exposure to arsenic among smelter workers: A five year follow-up. Am. J. Ind. Med. 25:477-488.

Lagerkvist, B., H. Linderholm, and G.F. Nordberg. 1986. Vasospastic tendency and Raynaud's phenomenon in smelter workers exposed to arsenic. Environ. Res. 39:465-474.

Lagerkvist, B.E., H. Linderholm, and G.F. Nordberg. 1988. Arsenic and Raynaud's phenomenon: Vasospastic tendency and excretion of arsenic in smelter workers before and after the summer vacation. Int. Arch. Occup. Environ. Health. 60:361-364.

Lai, M.S., Y.M. Hsueh, C.J. Chen, M.P. Shyu, S.Y. Chen, T.L. Kuo, M.M. Wu, and T.Y. Tai. 1994. Ingested inorganic arsenic and prevalence of diabetes mellitus. Am. J. Epidemiol. 139:484-492.

Lawson, G.B., W.P. Jackson, and G.S. Cattanach. 1925. Arsenic poisoning: Report of twenty-eight cases. JAMA 35:24-26.

Lee-Feldstein, A. 1986. Cumulative exposure to arsenic and its relationship to respiratory cancer among copper smelter employees. J. Occup. Med. 28:296-302.

Le Quesne, P.M., and J.G. McLeod. 1977. Peripheral neuropathy following a single exposure to arsenic. Clinical course in four patients with electrophysiological and histological studies. J. Neurol. Sci. 32:437-451.

Lerman, B.B., N. Ali, and D. Green. 1980. Megaloblastic, dyserythropoietic anemia following arsenic ingestion. Ann. Clin. Lab. Sci. 10:515-517.

Levin-Scherz, J.K., J.D. Patrick, F.H. Weber, and C. Garabedian, Jr. 1987. Acute arsenic ingestion. Ann. Emerg. Med. 16:702-704.

Lindgren, A., M. Vahter, and L. Dencker. 1982. Autoradiographic studies on the distribution of arsenic in mice and hamster administered [74]As-arsenite or -arsenate. Acta Pharmacol. Toxicol. 51:253-365.

Lindgren, A., B.R. Danielsson, L. Dencker, and M. Vahter. 1984. Embryotoxicity of arsenite and arsenate: Distribution in pregnant mice and monkeys and effects on embryonic cells in vitro. Acta Pharmacol. Toxicol. 54:311-320.

Lu F.J. 1990. Blackfoot disease: arsenic or humic acid? Lancet 336(8707): 115-116.

Luchtrath, H. 1972. Cirrosis of the liver in chronic arsenical poisoning of vintners. Ger. Med. 2:127-128.

Luchtrath, H. 1983. The consequences of chronic arsenic poisoning among Moselle wine groweres. Pathoanatomical investigations of post-mortem examinations performed between 1960 and 1977. J. Cancer Res. Clin. Oncol. 105:173-182.

Mabuchi, K., A.M. Lilienfeld and L.M. Snell. 1980. Cancer and occupational exposure to arsenic: A study of pesticide worker. Prev. Med. 9:51-77.

Mandal, B.K., T.R. Chowdhury, G. Samanta, G.K. Basu, P.P. Chowdhury, C.R. Chanda, D. Lodh, N.K. Karan, R.K. Dhar, D.K. Tamili, D. Das, K.C. Saha, and D. Chakraborti. 1996. Arsenic in groundwater in seven districts of West Bengal, India—The biggest arsenic calamity in the world. Curr. Sci. (Bangalore) 70:976-986.

Marin-Padilla, M. 1979. Notochordal-basichondrocranium relationships: abnormalities in experimental axial skeletal (dysraphic) disorders. J. Embryol. Exp. Morphol. 53:15-38.

Marin-Padilla, M. 1980. Morphogenesis of experimental encephalocele (cranioschisis occulta). J. Neurol. Sci. 46:83-99.

MARTA (Middle Atlantic Reproduction and Teratology Society). 1996. Historical control data. Pp. 713-733 in Handbook of Developmental Toxicology, R.D. Hood, ed. Boca Raton, Fla.: CRC Press.

Martinez, G., M. Cebrian, G. Chamorro, and P. Jauge. 1983. Urinary uroporphyrin as an indicator of arsenic exposure in rats. Proc. West. Pharmacol. Soc. 26:171-174.

McCabe, M., D. Maguire, and M. Nowak. 1983. The effects of arsenic compounds on human and bovine lymphocyte mitogenesis in vitro. Environ. Res. 31:323-331.

Michigan Department of Public Health. 1982. Arsenic in Drinking Water—A Study of Exposure and a Clinical Survey. Division of Environmental Epidemiology, Bureau of Disease Control and Laboratory Services.

Environmental Health Statistics Unit, Technical Services Section, Office of Vital and Health Statistics, Department of Public Health, Lansing, Mich.

Mirkes, P.E., and L. Cornel. 1992. A comparison of sodium arsenite- and hyperthermia-induced stress responses and abnormal development in cultured postimplantation rat embryos. Teratology 46:251-259

Mizuta, N., M. Mizuta, F. Ito, T. Ito, H. Uchida, Y. Watanabe, H. Akama, T. Murakami, F. Hayashi, K. Nakamura, T. Yamaguchi, W. Mizuia, S. Oishi and H. Matsumura. 1956. An outbleak of acute arsenic poisoning caused by arsenic-contaminated soy-sauce (shoyu): A clinical report of 220 cases. Bull. Yamaguchi Med. Sch. 4(2):131-149.

Morris, J.S., M. Schmid, S. Newman, P.J. Scheuer, M.R.C. Path and S. Sherlock. 1974. Arsenic and noncirrhotic portal hypertension. Gastroenterology 66:86-94.

Morrissey, R.E., B.A. Fowler, M.W. Harris, M.P. Moorman, C.W. Jameson, and B.A. Schwetz. 1990. Arsine: Absence of developmental toxicity in rats and mice. Fundam. Appl. Toxicol. 15:350-356.

Morse D.L., J.M.. Harrington, J. Housworth, P.J. Landrigan, A. Kelter. 1979. Arsenic exposure in multiple environmental media in children near a smelter. Clin Toxicol 14(4):389-399.

Murphy, M.J., L.W. Lyon, and J.W. Taylor. 1981. Subacute arsenic neuropathy: Clinical and electrophysiological observations. J. Neurol. Neurosurg. Psychiatry 44:896-900.

Nagy, G., A. Nemeth, F. Bodor, and E. Fiscor. 1980. Cases of bladder cancer caused by chronic arsenic poisoning [in Hungarian]. Orv. Hetil. 121:1009-1011.

Nemec, M.D., J.F. Holson, C.H. Farr, and R.D. Hood. 1998. Developmental toxicity assessment of arsenic acid in mice and rabbits. Reprod. Toxicol. 12:647-658.

Nevens, F., J. Fevery, W. Van Steenbergen, R. Sciot, V. Desmet, and J. De Groote. 1990. Arsenic and non-cirrhotic portal hypertension: A report of eight cases. J. Hepatol. 11:80-85.

Nordstrom, S., L. Beckman, and I. Nordenson. 1978a. Occupation and environmental risks in and around a smelter in northern Sweden. I. Variations in birth weight. Hereditas 88:43-46.

Nordstrom, S., L. Beckman, and I. Nordenson. 1978b. Occupation and environmental risks in and around a smelter in northern Sweden. III. Frequencies of spontaneous abortion. Hereditas 88:51-54

O'Shaughnessy, E., and G.H. Kraft. 1976. Arsenic poisoning: Long-term follow-up of a nonfatal case. Arch. Phys. Med. Rehabil. 57:403-406.

Ota, M. 1970. Ultrastructure of sural nerve in a case of arsenical neuropathy. Acta Neuropathol. 16:233-242.

Ott, M.G., B.B. Holder, and H.L. Gordon. 1974. Respiratory cancer and occupational exposure to arsenicals. Arch. Environ. Health 29:250-255.

Pascher, F., and J. Wolf. 1952. Cutaneous sequelae following treatment of bronchial asthma with inorganic arsenic: Report of two cases. JAMA 148:734-736.

Perry, K., R.G. Bowler, H.M. Buckell, H.A. Druett, and R.S.F. Schilling. 1948. Studies in the incidence of cancer in a factory handling inorganic compounds of arsenic: II. Clinical and environmental investigations. Br. J. Ind. Med. 5:6-15.

Peterka, E.S., F.W. Lynch, and R.W. Goltz. 1961. An association between Bowen's disease and internal cancer. Arch. Dermatol. 84:623-629.

Pope, F.M. 1902. Arsenic in the treatment of chorea. Br. Med. J. 2:1229-1230.

Popper, H., L.B. Thomas, N.C. Telles, H. Falk, and I.J. Selikoff. 1978. Development of hepatic angiosarcoma in man induced by vinyl chloride, thorotrast, and arsenic. Am. J. Pathol. 92:349-369.

Prystowsky, S.D., G.J. Elfenbein and S.I. Lamberg. 1978. Nasopharyngeal carcinoma associated with long-term arsenic ingestion. Arch. Dermatol. 114:602-603.

Rahman, M., and O. Axelson. 1995. Diabetes mellitus and arsenic exposure: a second look at case-control data from a Swedish copper smelter. Occup. Environ. Med. 52:773-774.

Rahman, M., G. Wingren, and O. Axelson. 1996. Diabetes mellitus among Swedish art glass workers—An effect of arsenic exposure? Scand. J. Work Environ. Health 22:146-149.

Rahman, M., M. Tondel, S.A. Ahmad, and O. Axelson. 1998. Diabetes mellitus associated with arsenic exposure in Bangladesh. Am. J. Epidemiol. 148:198-203.

Ratnam, K.V., M.J. Espy, S.A. Muller, T.F. Smith, and W.P. Su. 1992. Clinicopathologic study of arsenic-induced skin lesions: No definite association with human papillomavirus. J. Am. Acad. Dermatol. 27:120-122.

Rattner, H., and M. Dorne. 1943. Arsenical pigmentation and keratoses. Arch Dermatol. Syphilol. 48:458-460.

Rencher, A.C., M.W. Carter, and D.W. McKee. 1977. A retrospective epidemiological study of mortality at a large western copper smelter. J. Occup. Med. 19:754-758.

Reymann, F., R. Moller, and A. Nielsen. 1978. Relationship between arsenic intake and internal malignant neoplasms. Arch. Dermatol. 114:378-381.

Reynolds, E.S. 1901. An account of the epidemic outbreak of arsenical poisoning occurring in beer-drinkers in the north of England and the midland counties in 1900. Lancet (Jan. 19):166-170.

Rezuke, W.N., C. Anderson, W.T. Pastuszak, S.R. Conway and S.I. Firshein. 1991. Arsenic intoxication presenting as a myelodysplastic syndrome: A case report. Am. J. Hematol. 36:291-293.

Ribard, P., J.F. Bergman, V.G. Levy, and M. Thomas. 1986. Chronic self-poisoning by arsenic [in French] [letter]. Presse Med. 15(36):1833.

Roat, J.W., A. Wald, H. Mendelow, and K.I. Pataki. 1982. Hepatic angiosarcoma associated with short-term arsenic ingestion. Am. J. Med. 73:933-936.

Robertson, D.A.F., and T.S. Low-Beer. 1983. Long term consequences of arsenical treatment for multiple sclerosis. Br. Med. J. 286:605-606.

Robson, A.O., and A.M. Jelliffe. 1963. Medicinal arsenic poisoning and lung cancer. Br. Med. J. 5351:207-209.

Rogers, E.H., N. Chernoff, and B.J. Kavlock. 1981. The teratogenic potential of cacodylic acid in the rat and mouse. Drug Chem. Toxicol. 4:49-61.

Rosenberg, H.G. 1974. Systemic arterial disease and chronic arsenicism in infants. Arch. Pathol. 97(6):360-365.

Rosset, M. 1958. Arsenical keratoses associated with carcinomas of the internal organs. Can. Med. Assoc. J. 78:416-419.

Roth, F. 1957. The sequelae of chronic arsenic poisoning in Moselle vintners. Germ. Med. Monthly. 2:172-175.

Rothman, K.J. 1986. Modern Epidemiology. Boston: Little, Brown. 358 pp.

Rudnai, P., M. Csanády, E. Sárkány, V. Kiss, and G. Mucsi. 1996. Association between arsenic levels of drinking water in reproductive outcomes in Hungary [abstract]. International Seminar on Arsenic Exposure: Health Effects, Remediation Methods in Treatment Costs. Universidad de Chile, Oct. 8-10.

Saha, K.C. 1995. Chronic arsenical dermatoses from tube-well water in West Bengal during 1983-87. Ind. J. Dermatol. 40:1-12.

Schroeder H.A., and M. Mitchener. 1971. Toxic effects of trace elements on the reproduction of mice and rats. Arch. Environ. Health 23:102-106.

Sikorski, E.E., J.A. McCay, K.L. White, Jr., S.G. Bradley, and A.E. Munson. 1989. Immunotoxicity of the semiconductor gallium arsenide in female B6C3F$_1$ mice. Fundam. Appl. Toxicol. 13:843-858.

Silver, A.S., and P.L. Wainman. 1952. Chronic arsenic poisoning following use of an asthma remedy. JAMA 150:584-585.

Smith, A.H., M. Goycolea, R. Haque, and M.L. Biggs. 1998. Marked increase in bladder and lung cancer mortality in a region of northern Chile due to arsenic in drinking water. Am. J. Epidemiol. 147:660-669.

Sobel, W., G.G. Bond, C.L. Baldwin, and D.J. Ducommun. 1988. An update of respiratory cancer and occupational exposure to arsenicals. Am. J. Ind. Med. 13:263-270.

Sommers, S.C., and R.G. McManus. 1953. Multiple arsenical cancers of skin and internal organs. Cancer 6:347-359.

Southwick, J.W., A.E. Western, M.M. Beck, T. Whitley, R. Isaacs, J. Petajan and C.D. Hansen 1983. An epidemiological study of arsenic in drinking water in Millard County, Utah. Pp. 210-225 in Arsenic: Industrial, Biomedical, Environmental Perspectives, W.H. Lederer and R.J. Fensterheim, eds. New York: Van Nostrand Reinhold.

Stegmayr, B., and K. Asplund. 1992. Measuring stroke in the population: Quality of routine statistics in comparison with a population-based stroke registry. Neuroepidemiology. 11(4-6):204-213.

Stocken, L.A., and R.H.S. Thompson. 1949. Reactions of British anti-lewisite with arsenic and other metals in living systems. Physiol. Rev. 29:168-194.

Stockman, R. 1902. The therapeutic value of arsenic and the justification of its continued use in the light of recent observations concerning its toxic action. Br. Med. J. (Oct. 18):1227-1229.

Subramanian, K.S., and M.J. Kosnett. 1998. Human exposures to arsenic from consumption of well water in West Bengal, India. Int. J. Occup. Environ. Health 4:217-230.

Stump, D.G., C.E. Ulrich, J.F. Holson, and C.H. Farr. 1998a. An inhalation developmental toxicity study of arsenic trioxide in rats. Teratology 57(4-5):216.

Stump, D.G., K.J. Clevidence, J.F. Knapp, J.F. Holson, and C.H. Farr. 1998b. An oral developmental toxicity study of arsenic trioxide in rats. Teratology 57(4-5):216-217.

Susser, M. 1973. Causal Thinking in the Health Sciences: Concepts and Strategies of Epidemiology. New York: Oxford University Press. 181 pp.

Swan, S.H., J.J. Beaumont, S.K. Hammond, J. Von Behren, R.S. Green, M.F. Hallock, S.R. Woskie, C.J. Hines, and M.B. Schenker. 1995. Historical cohort study of spontaneous abortion among fabrication workers in the Semiconductor Health Study: Agent-level analysis. Am. J. Ind. Med. 28:751-769.

Swanson, M., and R. Cook. 1977. Drugs, Chemicals and Blood Dyscrasias: A summary of blood abnormalities associated with exposure to specific drugs and chemicals. Hamilton, Ill.: Drug Intelligence Publications.

Szuler, I.M., C.N. Williams, J.T. Hindmarsh, and H. Park-Dinesoy. 1979. Massive variceal hemorrhage secondary to presinusoidal portal hypertension due to arsenic poisoning. Can. Med. Assoc. J. 120:168-171.

Tabacova, S., D.D. Baird, L. Balabaeva, D. Lolova, and I. Petrov. 1994. Placental arsenic and cadmium in relation to lipid peroxides and glutathione levels in maternal-infant pairs from a copper smelter area. Placenta 15:873-881.

Takeuchi, I.K. 1979. Embryotoxicity of arsenic acid: Light microscopy and electron microscopy of its effect on neurulation-stage rat embryo. J. Toxicol. Sci. 4:405-416.

Taubeneck, M.W., G.P. Daston, J.M. Rogers, and C.L. Keen. 1994. Altered maternal zinc metabolism following exposure to diverse developmental toxicants. Reprod. Toxicol. 8:25-40.

Tay, C.H. 1974. Cutaneous manifestations of arsenic poisoning due to certain Chinese herbal medicine. Australas. J. Dermatol. 15(3):121-131.

Tay, C.H., and C.S. Seah. 1975. Arsenic poisoning from anti-asthmatic herbal preparations. Med. J. Aust. 2:424-428.

Taylor, P.R., Y.L. Qiao, A. Schatzkin, S.X. Yao, J. Lubin, B.L. Mao, J.Y. Rao, M. McAdams, X.Z. Xuan, and J.Y. Li. 1989. Relation of arsenic exposure to lung cancer among tin miners in Yunnan Province, China. Br. J. Ind. Med. 46:881-886.

Terada, H., K. Katsuta, T. Sasakawa, H. Saito, H. Shirota, K. Fukuchi, C. Skiya, Y. Yokoyama, S. Hirokawa, G. Watanabe, K. Hasegawa, T. Oshina, and C. Sekiguchi. 1960. Clinical observations of chronic toxicosis by arsenic [in Japanese]. Nihon Rinsho 118:2394-2403. Translation Doc. TR 74-106 by Leo Kanner Associates, Redwood City, Calif., for the U.S. Environmental Protection Agency.

Terada, H., T. Sasagawa, H. Saito, H. Shirata and T. Sekiya. 1962. Chronic arsenical poisoning and hematopoietic organs. Acta Med. Biol. 9(4):279-292.

Torres Soruco, C.A., R.E. Bagini, and M.A. Salvador. 1991. Arteriopatía en pacientes con hidroarsenicismo crónico. La Semana Med. 175:35-38.

Tseng, W.P. 1977. Effects and dose-response relationships of skin cancer and blackfoot disease with arsenic. Environ. Health Perspect. 19:109-119.

Tseng, W.P., W.Y. Chen, J.L. Sung, and J.S. Chen. 1961. A clinical study of blackfoot disease in Taiwan: An epidemic peripheral vascular disease. Mem. Coll. Med. Natl. Taiwan Univ. 7:1-18

Tseng, W.P., H.M. Chu, S.W. How, J.M. Fong, C.S. Lin, and S. Yeh. 1968. Prevalence of skin cancer in an endemic area of chronic arsenicism in Taiwan. J. Natl. Cancer Inst. 40:453-463.

Tseng, C.H., C.K. Chong, C.J. Chen, B.J. Lin, and T.Y. Tai. 1995. Abnormal peripheral microcirculation in seemingly normal subjects living in blackfoot-disease-hyperendemic villages in Taiwan. Int. J. Microcirc. Clin. Exp. 15:21-27.

Tsuda, T., T. Nagira, M. Yamamoto, and Y. Kume. 1990. An epidemiological study on cancer in certified arsenic poisoning patients in Toroku. Ind. Health 28(2):53-62.

Tsuda, T., A. Babazono, E. Yamamoto, N. Kurumatani, Y. Mino, T. Ogawa, Y. Kishi, H. Aoyama. 1995. Ingested arsenic and internal cancer: A historical cohort study followed for 33 years. Am. J. Epidemiol. 141:198-209.

Upshaw, C.B., and T.S. Claiborne. 1995. Medicinal arsenic poisoning: 27 year follow-up. South. Med. J. 88:892-893.

Upshaw, C.B., M.F. Bryant, and T.S. Claiborne. 1979. Noncirrhotic portal hypertension after arsenic ingestion. South. Med. J. 72:1332-1334.

Vahter, M., E. Marafante, A. Lindgren, and L. Dencker. 1982. Tissue distribution and subcellular binding of arsenic in marmoset monkeys after injection of ^{74}As-arsenite. Arch. Toxicol. 51:65-77.

Wagner, S.L, J.S. Maliner, W.E. Morton, and R.S. Braman. 1979. Skin cancer and arsenical intoxication from well water. Arch. Dermatol. 115:1205-1207.

Wall, S. 1980 Survival and mortality pattern among Swedish smelter workers. Int. J. Epidemiol. 9:73-87.

Welch, K., I. Higgins, M. Oh, C. Burchfiel. 1982. Arsenic exposure, smoking and respiratory cancer in copper smelter workers. Arch. Environ. Health 37:325-335.

Westhoff, D.D., R.J. Samaha, and A. Barnes. 1975. Arsenic intoxication as a cause of megaloblastic anemia. Blood 45:241-246.

Willhite, C.C. 1981. Arsenic-induced axial skeletal (dysraphic) disorders. Exp. Mol. Pathol. 34:145-158.

Winski, S.L., and D.E. Carter. 1998. Arsenate toxicity in human erythrocytes: characterization of morphologic changes and determination of the mechanism of damage. J. Toxicol. Environ. Health. 53:345-355.

Woods, J.S., and B.A. Fowler. 1978. Altered regulation of mammalian hepatic heme biosynthesis and urinary porphyrin excretion during prolonged exposure to sodiium arsenate. Toxicol. Appl. Pharmacol. 43:361-371.

Wu, M.M., T.L. Kuo, Y.H. Hwang, and C.J. Chen. 1989. Dose-response relation between arsenic concentration in well water and mortality from cancers and vascular diseases. Am. J. Epidemiol. 130:1123-1132.

Yang, H.L., H.C. Chiu, and F.J. Lu. 1996. Effects of humic acid on the viability and coagulant properties of human umbilical vein endothelial cells. Am. J. Hematol. j51:200-206.

Yeh, S. 1973. Skin cancer in chronic arsenicism. Hum. Pathol. 4:469-485.

Yeh, S., and S.W. How. 1963. Rep. Inst. Pathol. Natl. Taiwan Univ. 14:25-73.

Yu, H.S., H.M. Sheu, S.S. Ko, L.C.Chiang, C.H. Chien, S.M. Lin, B.R. Tserng, C.S. Chen. 1984. Studies on blackfoot disease and chronic arsenism in southern Taiwan: with special reference to skin lesions and fluorescent substances. J. Dermatol. 11:361-370.

Zaldivar, R. 1974. Arsenic contamination of drinking water and food-stuffs causing endemic chronic poisoning. Beitr. Pathol. 151:384-400.

Zaldivar, R., and G.L. Ghai. 1980. Mathematical model of mean age, mean arsenic dietary dose and age-specific prevalence rate from endemic chronic arsenic poisoning: A human toxicology study. Zentralbl. Bakteriol. Abt. 1 Orig. B 170(5-6):402-408.

Zaldivar, R., and A. Guillier. 1977. Environmental and clinical investigations on endemic chronic arsenic poisoning in infants and children. Zentralbl. Bakteriol. Parasitenkd. Infektionskr. Hyg. Abt. 1 Orig. Reihe B 165(2):226-234.

Zaldivar R, L. Prunes, and G. Ghai. 1981. Arsenic dose in patients with cutaneous carcinomata and hepatic hemangio-endothelioma after environmental and occupational exposure. Arch. Toxicol. 47:145-154.

Zelikoff, J.T., J.E. Bertin, T.M. Burbacher, E.S. Hunter, R.K. Miller, E.K. Silbergeld, S. Tabacova, and J.M. Rogers. 1995. Health risks associated with prenatal metal exposure. Fundam. Appl. Toxicol. 25:161-170.

Zettel, H. 1943. Der einfluss chronischer arsenschadigung auf herz und gefasse. Z. Klin. Med. 142:689-703.

Zierler S., M. Theodore, A. Cohen, and K.J. Rothman. 1988. Chemical quality of maternal drinking water and congenital heart disease. Int. J. Epidemiol. 17:589-594.

5

Disposition of Inorganic Arsenic

THIS chapter reviews the data regarding the absorption, biotransformation, distribution, and elimination of arsenic in animals and humans. Physiologically based pharmacokinetic (PB-PK) models that incorporate that information are described in the section Kinetic Model. The implications of the subcommittee's conclusions for a risk assessment for arsenic in drinking water are presented in the section Summary and Conclusions.

ABSORPTION

When ingested in dissolved form, inorganic arsenic is readily absorbed. About 80-90% of a single dose of arsenite As(III) or arsenate As(V) was absorbed from the gastrointestinal tract of humans and experimental animals (Pomroy et al. 1980; Vahter and Norin 1980; Freeman et al. 1995). A much lower degree of gastrointestinal absorption was reported for arsenic-contaminated soil (Freeman et al. 1995), although the form of arsenic in the soil, as well as the type of soil, can be assumed to influence the degree of arsenic absorption. Also, arsenic compounds of low solubility (e.g., arsenic selenide) (Mappes 1977), arsenic trisulfide and lead arsenate (Marafante et al. 1987), and gallium arsenide (Webb et al. 1984; Yamauchi et al. 1986) are absorbed much less efficiently than is dissolved arsenic. There is a lack of data on the bioavailability of inorganic arsenic in various types of foods.

No controlled studies have been conducted on the rate of absorption of inorganic arsenic through intact human skin. However, reported systemic toxicity in persons having extensive acute dermal contact with solutions of inorganic arsenic indicates that skin can be a route of exposure (Hostynek et al. 1993). In vitro studies in which water solutions of radiolabeled arsenate were topically applied to human skin or the skin of rhesus monkeys showed that about 2-6% of the applied arsenic was absorbed in 24 hr (Wester et al. 1993). Similar in vitro studies using dorsal skin of mice showed a much higher absorption; 30% of the applied dose of radiolabeled arsenate in aqueous solution (100-200 ng/L) was absorbed in 24 hr (Rahman et al. 1994). A large percentage, on average 60-90%, of the absorbed arsenic was retained in the skin. That result indicates that inorganic arsenic can bind externally to skin and hair. Rapid binding of ^{74}As to the skin and epithelium of the upper gastrointestinal tract in the marmoset fetus has also been observed 8 hr after maternal exposure to ^{74}As-arsenite (Lindgren et al. 1984). Taken together, those results indicate a low degree of systemic absorption of arsenic via the skin. Some further information on the skin absorption of arsenic in humans may be obtained from a study in Fairbanks, Alaska, where arsenic was found in home water at 345 μg/L (Harrington et al. 1978). One group of people who drank bottled water only but used the arsenic-rich water for other purposes had about the same low concentrations of the sum of arsenic metabolites in urine (average 43 μg/L) as people with less than 50 μg/L in their home water (average 38 μg/L in urine), indicating a low degree of skin absorption. However, the hair arsenic concentrations were clearly elevated in the group drinking bottled water (5.7 μg/g compared with 0.43 μg/g in the low-arsenic-water group), suggesting that arsenic is bound externally to hair and probably also to skin during washing with arsenic-rich water.

BIOTRANSFORMATION

In this section, arsenate reduction and arsenite methylation are described. Species differences are reviewed, as are other factors influencing the metabolism of arsenic. Variations in arsenic methylation in humans are reviewed in more detail in Chapter 7.

Arsenate Reduction and Arsenite Methylation

In humans and in most experimental animals, inorganic arsenic is methylated to monomethylarsonic acid (MMA) and dimethylarsinic acid (DMA). Compared with inorganic arsenic, the methylated metabolites are less reactive with tissue constituents, less acutely toxic, less cytotoxic, and more readily excreted in the urine (Buchet et al. 1981a; Vahter and Marafante 1983; Vahter et al. 1984; Yamauchi and Yamamura 1984; Marafante et al. 1987; Moore et al. 1997; Rasmussen and Menzel, 1997; Concha et al. 1998a; Hughes and

Kenyon 1998; Sakurai et al. 1998). In addition, experimental studies showed that inhibition of the methylation reactions results in increased tissue concentrations of arsenic (Marafante and Vahter 1984; Marafante et al. 1985).

In the 1930s, Challenger found that microorganisms grown in the presence of arsenite, MMA, or DMA released trimethylarsine (Challenger 1945). Essentially the same sequence of alternating reduction and methylation reactions was postulated for various mammals exposed to inorganic arsenic (Challenger 1945). However, considerable variation in methylation products is found among species. For example, DMA is the major end point of arsenic biomethylation in most mammals, while in many microorganisms, trimethylarsine is the end product. In mice, hamsters, and humans exposed to DMA, a small fraction was further methylated and excreted in the urine as trimethylarsine oxide (Marafante et al. 1987). However, the formation of trimethylarsine or its oxide has not been demonstrated following exposure to inorganic arsenic.

As noted in Chapter 3, methylation of inorganic arsenate to DMA involves alternating reduction of pentavalent arsenic to trivalent arsenic and addition of methyl groups (Vahter and Envall 1983; Cullen et al. 1984; Marafante et al. 1985; Vahter and Marafante 1988; Buchet and Lauwerys 1988; Hirata et al. 1990; Thompson 1993). Although all the steps and mechanisms in the arsenic biotransformation have not been elucidated, experimental animal studies performed in vivo or with animal tissue preparations in vitro indicate that the methylation takes place by transfer of methyl groups from S-adenosylmethionine (SAM) to arsenic in its trivalent oxidation state (Marafante and Vahter 1984; Buchet and Lauwerys 1985; Marafante et al. 1985; Styblo et al. 1995, 1996; Zakharyan et al. 1995). Probably, glutathione (GSH) plays an important role in the reduction of As(V) to As(III). The produced As(III) can form a complex with GSH (Delnomdedieu et al. 1994a,b). Also, cysteine or dithiothreitol (DTT) can reduce pentavalent arsenic, as shown in studies with purified rabbit-liver enzyme preparations (Zakharyan et al. 1995) or rat-liver cytosols (Buchet and Lauwerys 1985; Styblo et al. 1996).

Studies with mice, rabbits, and marmoset monkeys showed that a substantial fraction of absorbed As(V) is rapidly reduced, probably mainly in the blood, to As(III) (Vahter and Envall 1983; Vahter and Marafante 1985; Marafante et al. 1985), most of which is then methylated to MMA and DMA (Marafante et al. 1985). As(V) might also be reduced in the stomach or intestine, but quantitative experimental data are not available. Because of the rapid reduction, chronic exposure to arsenite and arsenate will result in fairly similar metabolite distribution in the body. However, the distribution pattern will differ for the two forms if the reducing capacity is exceeded by acute high-dose exposure (Vahter 1981; Lindgren et al. 1982). If the newly formed trivalent arsenic is not completely methylated, the reduction of As(V) to As(III) results in enhanced retention in most tissues, because trivalent arsenic is more reactive with tissue constituents than is pentavalent arsenic (Vahter and Marafante 1983; Bogdan et al. 1994; Styblo et al. 1995).

Following ingestion of MMA(V) by humans, only about 10% is further methylated and excreted as DMA in the urine (Buchet et al. 1981a). Similar results were obtained in vitro with rat-liver cytosols, while more than 90% of added MMA in reduced form, MMA(III), was further methylated to DMA (Styblo et al. 1995). That result indicates that MMA is not reduced as easily as arsenate or that there is a slow cellular uptake of MMA in vivo (Delnomdedieu et al. 1995; Mann et al. 1996a).

The kinetics of arsenic methylation in vivo has not been completely elucidated. In rabbits exposed to inorganic arsenic, DMA appeared in the liver before appearing in other tissues (Marafante et al. 1985). Further support for the finding that the liver is an important initial site of arsenic methylation is obtained in studies conducted in experimental animals and humans. Orally administered inorganic arsenic, most of which initially passes through the liver following absorption, was found to be methylated more efficiently than inorganic arsenic administered subcutaneously or intravenously (Charbonneau et al. 1979; Vahter 1981; Buchet et al. 1984). Also the fact that the methylation of arsenic injected in patients with end-stage liver disease improved markedly with liver transplantation suggests that the liver plays an important role in arsenic metabolism (Geubel et al. 1988). The site of methylation might also depend on the rate of reduction of As(V) to As(III). Studies on isolated rat hepatocytes showed that arsenite, but not arsenate, is readily taken up and methylated by the liver cells (Lerman et al. 1983). That might occur because the trivalent inorganic arsenic is in non-ionized form (arsenous acid) at physiological pH, and the pentavalent form is ionized (see Chapter 3). On the other hand, studies with kidney slices showed that about five times more DMA is produced from arsenate than from arsenite (Lerman and Clarkson 1983), indicating that the arsenate that is not initially reduced to arsenite can be taken up by the kidney cells, reduced and methylated to DMA intracellularly, and then excreted in the urine. Reabsorption and reduction of arsenate in the kidney tubule were demonstrated in dogs (Ginsburg 1965).

In vitro studies investigating the methylation capacity of different tissues had varying results. Buchet and Lauwerys (1985) reported that the methylating capacity of red blood cells, brain, lung, intestine, and kidneys of rats was insignificant compared with that of the liver. In vitro studies using arsenite methyltransferases from mouse tissues showed that the highest amount of methylating activity is in the testes, followed by kidney, liver, and lung (Healy et al. 1998). The amounts of methyltransferases vary in different tissues and animal species (Aposhian 1997). Although the methylating capacity of tissues in vitro does not reflect in vivo methylation, when the kinetics of the arsenic species plays an important role, the results indicate that arsenite initially bound to tissue constituents can be methylated and released. That could explain the observed slow elimination phase that follows the initial rapid phase; the slow elimination phase might involve the continuous release of arsenic from most binding sites (Marafante et al. 1981; Vahter and Marafante 1983).

In vitro studies using rat-liver preparations showed that the methylating activity is localized in the cytosol and that SAM is the main methyl donor (Buchet and Lauwerys, 1985; Zakharyan et al. 1995; Styblo and Thomas 1997). Added vitamin B12, coenzyme B12, and methylcobolamin could also act as methyl donors, and the latter could produce MMA even in the absence of enzymatic activity. Research on the purification and characterization of arsenic methyltransferases (Zakharyan et al. 1995, 1996) indicated that the rabbit arsenite and MMA methyltransferase activities are in the same protein. Using the 2,000-fold purified protein, the investigators found no evidence that the activities were on different proteins (Zakharyan et al. 1995). SAM was used as the methyl source, as previously shown by in vivo studies and in vitro studies using tissue cytosol. The arsenite and the MMA methyltransferase had a molecular mass of 60 kDa, as determined by gel-size-exclusion chromatography but had different pH optima and different saturation concentrations for their substrates. Neither arsenate nor selenate, selenite, or selenide was methylated by the purified enzyme preparations.

Species Differences

There are major species differences in the biotransformation of inorganic arsenic (Vahter 1994). A number of studies, in which the metabolites of inorganic arsenic in human urine have been speciated, consistently show average values of 10-30% inorganic arsenic, 10-20% MMA, and 55-75% DMA (for a review, see Hopenhayn-Rich et al. 1993). Those results were found in human subjects exposed to inorganic arsenic in the general environment and in those exposed at work. However, in recent studies of people exposed to arsenic via drinking water in northern Argentina, urinary arsenic consisted of only 2% MMA on average (Vahter et al. 1995a; Concha et al. 1998a). Variations in arsenic methylation in humans is reviewed in more detail in Chapter 7.

Many experimental animals excrete less MMA and more DMA in the urine than do humans. Mice and dogs methylate inorganic arsenic efficiently, and in general, more than 80% of the administered dose is excreted, mainly as DMA, in the urine within a few days (Charbonneau et al. 1979; Vahter 1981). The rat also methylates inorganic arsenic efficiently, but a major portion of the DMA produced is retained in the erythrocytes (Odanaka et al. 1980; Lerman et al. 1983), giving rise to a slow urinary excretion of DMA and a tissue-distribution pattern that is different from that in most other species (Vahter et al. 1984). In addition, the rat shows an extensive biliary excretion of arsenic, about 800 and 37 times more than the dog and rabbit, respectively (Klaassen 1974).

With respect to arsenic methylation, the rabbit (Marafante et al. 1981; Vahter and Marafante 1983; Maiorino and Aposhian 1985) and the hamster (Charbonneau et al. 1980; Yamauchi and Yamamura 1984, 1985; Marafante and Vahter 1987) are more similar than other investigated animal species to humans, although more DMA and less MMA is excreted by rabbits and hamsters than by humans. The Flemish giant rabbit (De Kimpe et al. 1996) and a New Zealand rabbit (Bogdan et al. 1994) were found to excrete MMA in amounts similar to those in humans.

The two animal species that were first shown not to methylate inorganic arsenic, the marmoset monkey (Vahter et al. 1982; Vahter and Marafante 1985) and the chimpanzee (Vahter et al. 1995b), in general have a metabolism most similar to that of humans. The cynomolgus monkey, on the other hand, seems to methylate inorganic arsenic well (S.M. Charbonneau, Health and Welfare Canada, Ottawa, Ont., personal commun., 1983; cf. Vahter 1983). Another unique feature of the marmoset monkey is that it accumulates arsenic in the liver, apparently firmly bound to the rough microsomal fraction (Vahter et al. 1982). The first phase of elimination has a fairly short half-time. In the second phase, as much as 70% of the administered dose is eliminated at a very slow rate.

In the chimpanzee, excretion also seems to be biphasic, and the half-time of the second phase is similar to that observed in the marmoset; however, much less of the total administered dose is eliminated. In spite of the lack of methylation of arsenic in the chimpanzee, about 50% of an intravenous dose was excreted within 2 to 4 days in the urine (Vahter et al. 1995b). That is similar to that in humans, who excrete about half of a low dose of arsenite or arsenate in the urine within about 4 days (Tam et al. 1979; Pomroy et al. 1980; Buchet et al. 1981b), indicating that other factors influence the tissue retention and excretion of arsenic.

Arsenite methyltransferase activity, tested by incubation of liver preparations with arsenite in vitro, has been detected in the liver of the rabbit, rat, mouse, hamster, pigeon, and rhesus monkey but not in the liver of the marmoset monkey, tamarin monkey, squirrel monkey, chimpanzee, and guinea pig

(Zakharyan et al. 1995, 1996; Healy et al. 1997). With human liver preparations, no methylated arsenic metabolites were detected. As humans do methylate inorganic arsenic in vivo, the reason for the negative in vitro test is not known. In the case with marmoset monkeys and chimpanzees the negative in vitro test is in concordance with in vivo studies showing no methylation of inorganic arsenic in those animals (Vahter et al. 1982; Vahter et al. 1995b).

The rhesus monkey, hamster, rat, mouse, and pigeon, have ample amounts of such methyltransferase activity. In decreasing order, the species with liver arsenite methyltransferase activity are the pigeon, rhesus monkey, mouse, hamster, rabbit, marmoset monkey, squirrel monkey, and tamarin monkey. In addition, when guinea pigs were injected intraperitoneally with radioactive arsenate, five of six guinea pigs did not have methylated arsenic species in their urine (Healy et al. 1997). The sixth animal had minimal but measurable amounts of DMA in its urine. Analysis of liver cytosol showed that the guinea pigs were deficient in liver arsenic methyltransferase activities (Healy et al. 1997). All the species had ample arsenate reductase activity, however.

Factors Influencing the Metabolism of Arsenic

It is likely that factors influencing the methylation of arsenic can modify the tissue retention and toxicity of arsenic, because the biomethylation of inorganic As(III) produces metabolites that have low reactivity toward most tissues and that are readily excreted in the urine. This section describes the experimental evidence for effects on the methylation of arsenic by such factors as the chemical form and dose of arsenic absorbed protein binding, nutrition, and genetic polymorphism. The observed variation in human methylation of arsenic in relationship to dose, sex, ethnicity, and recreational habits is discussed in Chapter 7.

In some experimental animal studies, exposure to arsenite resulted in a higher degree of methylation and more DMA in the urine than did exposure to arsenate (Vahter 1981; Vahter and Marafante 1983). However, in spite of the fact that the reduction of arsenate is not complete, the total amount of arsenic excreted in the urine is slightly higher following arsenate exposure than following arsenite exposure, as shown by experimental studies on human volunteers (Pomroy et al. 1980; Buchet et al. 1981a). Most likely, the reason for this is that As(V) is less reactive with tissue constituents and more readily excreted in the urine than is As(III) (Vahter and Marafante 1983). The differences in retention of arsenic following exposure to arsenate and arsenite decrease with decreasing dose (Vahter 1981), because a large part of the arsenate is reduced rapidly following absorption.

Studies on mice showed that as the dose of inorganic arsenic increases substantially, the methylation rate decreases and the tissue concentrations of arsenic increase (Vahter 1981; Hughes et al. 1994). Also, in humans acutely intoxicated by very high doses of inorganic arsenic, there is a marked delay in the urinary excretion of DMA (Mahieu et al. 1981; Foà et al. 1984). In one case of attempted suicide, a person ingested about 3 g of As_2O_3 in water and was admitted to the hospital 2 hr later (Foà et al. 1984). The relative percentage of urinary DMA increased from about 30% on the 8th day to 78% on the 13th day after ingestion. In three persons who ingested 100-500 mg of arsenic in the form of As_2O_3, which was mistakenly used instead of sugar, urinary DMA increased from about 10% the first days after ingestion (blood arsenic concentrations of 190-800 $\mu g/L$) to about 75% after a week (Mahieu et al. 1981). However, in the case of exposure to arsenic via drinking water, even at very high arsenic concentrations, the methylation of arsenic seems to be relatively unaffected by the concentration of the dose. According to an abstract of a study by Kosnett and Becker (1988), following subacute exposure to drinking water containing arsenic at a concentration of 25,000 $\mu g/L$, a 36-year-old man yielded a urinary arsenic collection containing 6,025 μg per 24 hr, 26% as inorganic arsenic and 74% as methylated metabolites. A further discussion of the dose-dependence of arsenic methylation in humans exposed via drinking water is presented in Chapter 8.

Results from in vitro studies suggested that the delay in urinary excretion of DMA might occur because of the high tissue concentrations of arsenite inhibit the methyltransferase catalyzing the second methylation step (Buchet and Lauwerys 1985). Methylation capacity might also have been overloaded by the high tissue concentrations of As(III). However, in both human studies, BAL was administered for several days, which might have influenced the methylation of arsenic (see below).

Protein binding is another factor in arsenic mechanism. Bogdan et al. (1994) found three arsenite-binding proteins in rabbit liver. They were 450 kilodaltons (kDa), 100 kDa, and less than 2,000 kDa in size. Inorganic arsenite was firmly bound to them. The affinity of arsenite for those proteins was 20 times greater than that for arsenate.

Experimental studies on mice and rabbits showed that inhibition of SAM-dependent methylation reactions by treatment with periodate-oxidized adenosine, which inhibits the metabolism of S-adenosylhomocysteine, results in decreased methylation and increased tissue concentrations of arsenic (Marafante and Vahter 1984; Marafante et al. 1985). That finding indicates that a low tissue concentration of SAM (e.g., as a result of low intake of precursors to SAM) might give rise to a low rate of methylation of arsenic. In fact, studies on rabbits fed diets with low amounts of methionine, choline, or proteins showed a marked decrease in urinary excretion of DMA, accompanied by a 2-3 times increase in tissue concentrations of arsenic, especially in the liver (Vahter and Marafante 1987). A decrease in urinary excretion of arsenic was also observed in mice fed a choline-deficient diet (Tice et al. 1997). In particular, arsenic concentrations were increased in liver microsomes of the rabbits on the methyl-deficient diet (Vahter and Marafante 1987), a result similar to that seen in the marmoset monkeys (Vahter et al. 1982). Thus, nutritional factors might influence the subcellular distribution of arsenic.

The methylation of arsenic appears to be affected by hepatic disease. Various liver diseases (i.e., alcoholic cirrhosis, chronic hepatitis, homochromatosis, postnecrotic cirrhosis, steatosis, and biliary cirrhosis) decreased the proportion of MMA (in relationship to the total urinary excretion of metabolites of inorganic arsenic) and increased the proportion of DMA in urine following injection of a single dose of sodium arsenite (Buchet et al. 1984; Geubel et al. 1988). The overall effect was a more efficient methylation of the injected arsenic in individuals with liver disease than in healthy controls or controls with other types of diseases.

The effect of the chelating agent 2,3-dimercapto-1-propanesulfonic acid (DMPS; 300 mg of Dimaval given by mouth after an overnight fast) on the urinary arsenic metabolite pattern was studied in people living in the Atacama desert in northeastern Chile, where the concentration of arsenic in drinking water is 600 μg/L (Aposhian et al. 1997). During the 2-hr period following administration, the content of metabolites of inorganic arsenic in urine consisted of 20-22% inorganic arsenic, 42% MMA, and 37-38% DMA. The usual range of MMA in human urine is 10-20% and that of DMA 60-80%. A similar increase in the percentage of MMA was found in the control subjects exposed to arsenic at 20 μg/L of drinking water. DMPS increased the total urinary arsenic excretion by about 5-6 times during the 6-hr period after administration. The mechanism for the increase in MMA excretion is not known.

In vitro studies on arsenic methylation in rat-liver cytosol showed that chelating agents, such as DMSA and DMPS (0.05-0.5 mM), almost completely inhibit the methylation of inorganic arsenic to DMA (Buchet and Lauwerys 1985, 1988). Addition of DTT (dithiothreitol) and 2-mercaptoethanol of up to 0.5 mM stimulated in vitro methylation, but resulted in inhibition at higher concentrations. Also, EDTA (1 mM) was shown to inhibit preferentially DMA formation from [74]As-As(III) (carrier-free) in vitro (Styblo and Thomas 1997). Possibly, the administration of chelating agents results in an inhibition of the second step of the methylation of the inorganic arsenic released from tissues, giving rise to more MMA being excreted in the urine.

TRANSPORTATION, DISTRIBUTION, AND ELIMINATION

In this section, the transportation of arsenic in blood, its distribution in tissues, and its elimination from the body are described.

Transportation in Blood

Absorbed arsenic is transported in the blood, mainly bound to sulfhydryl (SH) groups in proteins and low-molecular-weight compounds such as gluta-thione (GSH) and cysteine, to the organs in the body. Formation of complexes between trivalent arsenicals and GSH, probably mainly in the form of $As(GS)_3$, has been demonstrated in water solutions (Scott et al. 1993; Delnomdedieu et al. 1994a), rabbit erythrocytes (Delnomdedieu et al. 1994b), and rat bile (Anundi et al. 1982). However, As(III) can be transferred easily from the $As(GS)_3$ complex to binding sites of higher affinity. Recently, inorganic arsenic was reported to be the main form of arsenic bound to serum proteins in patients on continuous ambulatory peritoneal dialysis, and transferrin was the main carrier (Zhang et al. 1997, 1998a,b).

Most of the arsenic in blood is rapidly cleared, following a three-exponential clearance curve (Mealey et al. 1959; Pomroy et al. 1980). The majority of arsenic in blood is cleared with a half-time of about 1 hr. The half-times of the second and third phases are about 30 and 200 hr, respectively. Experimental data on animals and data on patients with uremia indicate that the concentration of arsenic in red blood cells is severalfold that in plasma at low or background exposure concentrations but is close to onefold at increased blood concentrations (Lindgren et al. 1982; Versieck 1985; De Kimpe et al. 1993). The ratio between plasma and the red blood cells might also depend on the exposure form of arsenic; studies on rabbits found that As(III) is more easily taken up by erythrocytes than is As(V), MMA, or DMA (Delnomdedieu et al. 1995). Early studies on healthy individuals with no known exposure to arsenic indicate similar concentrations (about 2.5 μg/L) in plasma and whole blood (Heydorn 1970). People from the area in Taiwan with arsenic-rich water had about 15 μg/L in plasma and 22 μg/L in whole blood. Patients with blackfoot disease and their families had about 30 μg/L in plasma and 60 μg/L in whole blood (Heydorn 1970).

Arsenic concentrations were found to be significantly higher in the serum and erythrocytes of chronic hemodialysis patients compared with controls (De Kimpe et al. 1993). Serum had a median arsenic concentration of 12 μg/L versus 0.38 μg/L in controls, and erythrocytes had a median of 9.5 μg/L versus 3.2 μg/L in controls. A single hemodialysis treatment did not change the arsenic concentrations. In a similar study, Zhang et al. (1996) reported a mean total arsenic concentration of 5.1 μg/L in nonhemodialysis patients and 6.5 μg/L in hemodialysis patients, compared with 0.96 μg/L in a control group of healthy subjects. DMA and arsenobetaine (AsB) were the major arsenic species in serum, the mean values being about 1 μg/L for DMA and 3.5 μg/L for AsB. Serum concentrations of inorganic arsenic and MMA were below the detection limits. In the control group, serum arsenic concentrations were too low for speciation. Hemodialysis treatment removed 68% of total arsenic in serum and 16% in erythrocytes. The efficiency was similar for DMA and AsB.

There are major species differences in the half-time of arsenic in blood. In the rat, arsenic is retained in the blood considerably longer than in other species because of the accumulation of DMA in the red blood cells, apparently bound to hemoglobin (Odanaka et al. 1980; Lerman and Clarkson 1983; Vahter 1983; Vahter et al. 1984). The accumulation of arsenic in the rat erythrocytes was first reported more than 50 years ago (Hunter et al. 1942), although at that time DMA was not known to be the main form of arsenic retained. Lanz and co-workers (1950) reported that the cat also had higher concentrations of arsenic in the blood than most other species, although not as high as the rat. Whether it is DMA that accumulates in the red blood cells of the cat is not known.

Even though inorganic arsenic is not methylated in the chimpanzee, the clearance of arsenic from the plasma, following a single intravenous dose of [73]As-arsenate, was shown to be fast, with a half-time of about 1 hr (Vahter et al. 1995b). The elimination from red blood cells was slower, with a half-time of about 5 hr. Essentially, all [73]As in the plasma was ultrafiltrable, indicating a low degree of binding to high-molecular-weight proteins (above 25,000 daltons). Those findings indicate that the rate of clearance of arsenic from blood might be affected by factors other than methylation.

Tissue Distribution

In the body, As(III) is mainly bound to SH groups. In particular, As(III) forms high-affinity bonds with vicinal thiols, as demonstrated with lipoic acid and DMSA (Cullen and Reimer 1989; Delnomdedieu et al. 1993). Experimental animal studies found that the binding of arsenic is mainly to high-molecular-weight proteins in various tissues; however, arsenic is continuously released from most intracellular binding sites over time following exposure (Marafante et al. 1981; Vahter et al. 1982). Probably, As(III) is bound to proteins before undergoing subsequent methylation-reduction reactions. Whether the protein is methyltransferase is not known. Compounds of the type Me_2AsSR, formed following addition of the second methyl group, are easily oxidized to DMA (Cullen and Reimer 1989), which is then excreted in the urine. However, the stability might vary, and DMA complexes have been detected in urine (Marafante et al. 1987). A very stable complex appears to be formed between DMA and hemoglobin in the rat (Lerman et al. 1983). In vitro studies indicate the formation of mixed protein hemoglobin–GSH complex with As(III) (Winski and Carter 1995).

In experimental studies on mammals exposed to inorganic arsenic, the tissues with the longest retention of arsenic were skin, hair, squamous epithelium of the upper gastrointestinal tract (oral cavity, tongue, esophagus, and stomach wall), epididymis, thyroid, skeleton, and the lens of the eye (Lindgren et al. 1982, 1984; Vahter et al. 1982). Except for the skeleton, all the tissues mentioned contained higher concentrations of arsenite than arsenate shortly after administration of either. Following administration of arsenate to mice, immediate accumulation and long-term retention of arsenic were observed in the calcified areas of the skeleton, probably reflecting the substitution of phosphate by arsenate in the apatite crystals in bone because of the chemical similarities between arsenate and phosphate (see Chapter 3). However, the differences in distribution in relationship to the exposure form of arsenic decreased over time following exposure. A few days after the administration of arsenic, the distribution pattern was essentially the same irrespective of the form of arsenic administered. The similar pattern of distribution following administration of fairly low doses of arsenate and arsenite might be explained by the rapid in vivo reduction of As(V) to As(III), as demonstrated in various mammalian species (Ginsburg 1965; Vahter and Envall 1983; Marafante et al. 1985).

Most likely, inorganic arsenic, mainly As(III), is the form bound to SH groups of keratin in the skin, hair, oral mucosa, and esophagus. That was evident from the distribution pattern of arsenite in the marmoset monkey, which does not methylate inorganic arsenic (Vahter et al. 1982). Furthermore, chemical inhibition of the transfer of methyl groups from S-adenosylmethionine in mice and rabbits resulted in increased arsenic concentrations in most tissues, especially the skin (Marafante and Vahter 1984). The half-time in skin seems to be more than 1 month (Du Pont et al. 1941). Scott (1958) used neutron-activation analysis to assess the arsenic content of benign and malignant skin lesions of 14 patients exposed at least 4 years earlier to several years of inorganic arsenical medication. Arsenic content of the biopsied skin ranged from 0.8 to 8.9 ppm, and on average exceeded the arsenic content of normal skin and malignant skin lesions from six subjects with no history of arsenic intake (range 0.4 to 1.0 ppm). In contrast to the rodents, the marmoset monkey showed an accumulation of arsenic in the testes, mainly localized to the spermatogenetic epithelium (Vahter et al. 1982). Accumulation of arsenic in the liver of marmosets was also pronounced.

The tissue retention of MMA and DMA is much lower than that of inorganic arsenic. Following administration of ^{74}As-DMA to mice, its concentrations decreased rapidly in most tissues (Vahter et al. 1984). The tissues with the longest retention of DMA were the lungs, thyroid, intestinal mucosa, and the lens of the eyes. Accordingly, there was no localization of arsenic in the thyroid and ocular lens of the marmoset monkey, which did not methylate the administered inorganic arsenic (Vahter et al. 1982).

In human subjects exposed to normal environmental concentrations of arsenic, the hair and nails had the highest concentrations of arsenic (0.02-1 mg/kg of dry weight), and fairly high concentrations were found in the skin and lungs (0.01-1 mg/kg of dry weight) (Liebscher and Smith 1968; Cross et al. 1979; Das et al. 1995). Thus, arsenic appears to concentrate in tissues with a high content of cysteine-containing proteins. The arsenic concentrations in skin and kidneys of adults in Japan were reported to be 2-3 times higher than those in 1-year-old children (Kadowaki 1960). In West Bengal, India, where people are exposed to arsenic in drinking water (district average arsenic values of 200-700 μg/L), arsenic concentrations in skin scale, hair, and nails were 1.9-5.5, 3.6-9.6, and 6.1-23 mg/kg of dry weight, respectively (Das et al. 1996). However, the concentration of arsenic in skin, hair, and nails that is due to external contact with arsenic in water is not known.

Experimental animal studies showed that inorganic arsenic, trivalent as well as pentavalent, and the methylated metabolites cross the placenta during the entire gestational period (Lindgren et al. 1984; Hood et al. 1982, 1987). Administration of arsenite showed somewhat less placental transfer of arsenic in a marmoset monkey (known not to methylate arsenic) than in mice (Lindgren et al. 1984). The tissue distribution of arsenic was similar in fetus and mother. In a study of pregnant women living in a village in northwestern Argentina where drinking water contains arsenic at about 200 μg/L, arsenic concentrations were about as high in cord blood (on average 9 μg/L) as in maternal blood, indicating that arsenic readily reaches the human fetus (Concha et al. 1998b). The placentas also had clearly increased arsenic concentrations. However, more than 90% of the arsenic in urine and plasma of the newborns and their mothers (at the time of delivery) was in the form of DMA, indicating that arsenic methylation is induced during pregnancy and that the fetus is exposed mainly to DMA, at least in late gestation. The fetal toxicity of arsenic, however, remains to be elucidated. In pregnant women with no known arsenic exposure, the concentration of arsenic in cord blood was found to be about the same (average 2-3 μg/L) as that in maternal blood (Kagey et al. 1977). Increased concentrations of arsenic have been detected in the placentas of women living near smelters (Tabacova et al. 1994).

The studies of women living in northwestern Argentina indicated a low degree of arsenic excretion in human breast milk (Concha et al. 1998c). The average concentration of arsenic in milk was 2 μg/kg, compared with 10 μg/L in maternal blood and 320 μg/L in maternal urine. Breast feeding was shown to decrease the concentrations of arsenic in the urine in the newborn child (Concha et al. 1998c). The arsenic concentrations found in human breast milk were slightly higher than the lowest concentrations reported in previous studies (Byrne et al. 1983; Dang et al. 1983; Parr et al. 1991). The arsenic exposure of the women in those studies was not reported, and the form of arsenic in breast milk is not known. An average breast-milk arsenic concentration of about 19 μg/kg was reported from the Philippines (Parr et al. 1991), indicating that organic arsenic compounds originating from seafood might be excreted in the milk.

Intracellular Distribution

In rabbits and mice exposed to radiolabeled arsenic, a major part of the arsenic in liver, kidneys, and lungs was present in the nuclear and soluble fractions (Marafante et al. 1981; Marafante and Vahter 1984). A different intracellular distribution was observed in the liver of the marmoset monkey, which is unable to methylate inorganic arsenic (Vahter et al. 1982; Vahter and Marafante 1985). Almost 50% of the arsenic was present in the microsomal fraction, apparently in a very strong association, leading to a long half-time of arsenic in the liver. Chemically induced inhibition of arsenic methylation did not change the intracellular binding of arsenic in rabbit tissues (Marafante and Vahter 1984; Marafante et al. 1985). However, in rabbits fed diets with low contents of methionine, choline, or proteins, leading to a decrease in arsenic methylation and an increase in tissue concentrations of arsenic, especially in the liver, there was an increase in arsenic in the microsomal fraction of the liver (Vahter and Marafante 1987) similar to that in the marmoset monkey. Mice fed a choline-deficient diet showed a similar decrease in the urinary excretion of DMA, but the arsenic-induced DNA damage shifted from the liver to the skin (Tice et al. 1997). These studies indicate that nutritional status might influence the intracellular distribution of arsenic and possibly its toxic effects.

Elimination

The major route of excretion of most arsenic compounds is via the urine. Following exposure to inorganic arsenic, the biological half-time is about 4 days. It is slightly shorter following exposure to As(V) than to As(III) (Yamauchi and Yamamura 1979; Tam et al. 1979; Pomroy et al. 1980; Buchet et al. 1981a). In six human subjects who ingested radiolabeled [74]As-arsenate, 38% of the dose was excreted in the urine within 48 hr and 58% within 5 days (Tam et al. 1979). The results indicate that the data were best fit to a three-compartment exponential function, with 66% excreted with a half-time of 2.1 days, 30% with a half-time of 9.5 days, and 3.7% with a half-time of 38 days (Pomroy et al. 1980). In three subjects, each of whom ingested 500 μg of arsenic in the form of arsenite in water, about 33% of the dose was excreted in the urine within 48 hr, and 45% within 4 days (Buchet et al. 1981a). The methylated metabolites MMA and DMA are excreted in the urine faster than the inorganic arsenic. In humans, about 78% of MMA and 75% of DMA were excreted in the urine within 4 days of ingestion of the dose (Buchet et al. 1981a). Similar results were reported for mice in which the half-time of MMA and DMA was about 1 hr (Hughes and Kenyon 1998). The 24-hr whole-body retention was about 2% of the dose.

Although absorbed arsenic is removed from the body mainly via the urine, small amounts of arsenic are removed via other routes (e.g., skin, sweat, hair, and breast milk). The average concentration of arsenic in sweat induced in a hot and humid environment was 1.5 μg/L, and the hourly loss was 2 μg (Vellar 1969). With an average arsenic concentration in the skin of 0.18 mg/kg, Molin and Wester (1976) estimated that the daily loss of arsenic through desquamation was 0.1-0.2 μg in males with no known exposure to arsenic. As mentioned above, the excretion of arsenic in breast milk is low.

KINETIC MODEL

A physiologically based pharmacokinetic (PB-PK) model for exposure to inorganic arsenic (orally, intravenously, and intratracheally) in hamsters and rabbits has been developed (Mann et al. 1996a). It consists of five tissue compartments (i.e., liver, kidney, lungs, skin, and other organs) and takes into consideration the absorption, distribution, metabolism, and excretion of arsenate, arsenite, MMA, and DMA; the four major metabolites of inorganic arsenic. The model was found to simulate accurately the excretion of arsenic metabolites in urine and feces.

The model has been extended to a PB-PK model for humans by taking into consideration species differences in absorption and metabolic rate constants (Mann et al. 1996b). It describes the absorption and distribution of arsenic following oral intake or inhalation of As(III), As(V), or both. The extended model was validated against empirical data on the urinary excretion of the different metabolites of inorganic arsenic following repeated oral intake of arsenite, intake of inorganic arsenic via drinking water, and occupational exposure to arsenic trioxide. Predicted variation in urinary excretion of arsenic metabolites in relationship to form of arsenic absorbed, route of absorption, and time of urine sampling needs to be validated further. The model predicted a slight decrease in the percentage of DMA in urine with increasing single-dose exposure (highest dose of arsenic at 15 μg/kg of body weight), especially following exposure to As(III), and an almost corresponding increase in the percentage of MMA. A decrease in the percentage of DMA of about 10% corresponded to an increase in the arsenic dose of about 1,000 μg.

One major objective of the model was to compare the urinary excretion of arsenic metabolites under different exposure conditions. Examples showed that consumption of drinking water containing arsenic at 50 μg/L by adults results in a higher urinary excretion of arsenic than that following occupational exposure at 10 μg/m^3 (Mann et al. 1996b).

A PB-PK model for ingested arsenate in mice (Menzel et al. 1994; Menzel 1997) assumed efficient absorption of arsenate in the gastrointestinal tract and metabolism of arsenic mainly in the liver. Because the tissue concentrations of As(III) could not be explained by absorption of As(III) from the blood (the concentration in blood was very low), all organs were assumed to have some capacity to metabolize As(V) to DMA. Tissue binding was mainly in the form of As(III), and the binding constant was calculated from experimental data. The model involved complex elimination from the kidneys.

SUMMARY AND CONCLUSIONS

When ingested in dissolved form, inorganic arsenic is readily absorbed in the gastrointestinal tract. Arsenic appears to be poorly absorbed through intact human skin but can bind externally to skin and hair. Absorbed arsenic is transported in the blood, bound to SH groups in proteins and low-molecular-weight compounds such as GSH or cysteine, to the organs in the body. Studies on blood arsenic concentrations in hemodialysis patients indicate that part of arsenic is bound to transferrin. The extent of the binding in healthy individuals is not known. Most of the arsenic in blood is cleared with a half-time of about 1 hr. The whole-body half-time of ingested arsenite is about 4 days, urine being the major excretory pathway.

In humans, inorganic arsenic is methylated to MMA(V) and DMA(V), which are less reactive with tissue constituents, less acutely toxic, and more readily excreted in the urine than inorganic arsenic. The methylation involves addition of methyl groups from S-adenosylmethionine to arsenic in its trivalent oxidation state. A major part of absorbed pentavalent arsenic is reduced probably by GSH or cysteine. Thus, the tissue distribution, retention and toxicity of arsenic following exposure to moderate doses of arsenite and arsenate are similar. At very high doses, more arsenic is retained following exposure to arsenite than to arsenate. The liver is an important initial site of arsenic methylation, but most tissues seem to have methylating capacity. There are major differences in the biotransformation of inorganic arsenic between animal species and population groups. Most experimental animals methylate arsenic more efficiently and excrete less MMA in the urine than do humans. Some mammals (e.g., chimpanzee, marmoset monkey, and guinea pig) have been identified that do not methylate inorganic arsenic at all. Although the rat efficiently methylates arsenic, a major part of the DMA produced is retained in the erythrocytes. That response and the unusual biliary excretion of arsenic in the rat make it a less-suitable animal model for studies of arsenic disposition in humans.

In people occupationally, experimentally, or environmentally exposed to inorganic arsenic, the urinary content of metabolites of inorganic arsenic generally consists of 10-30% inorganic arsenic, 10-20% MMA, and 55-75% DMA. Some groups of people who excrete only a few percent of MMA have been identified. That response, together with marked individual variations, can indicate a genetic polymorphism in the arsenic methyltransferases. Experimental studies indicate that the methylation of arsenic might also be influenced by the arsenic species absorbed, by acute high-level exposures, as well as by nutritional factors and diseases.

Animal studies have shown retention of arsenic in the skin, hair, squamous epithelium of the upper gastrointestinal tract, epididymis, thyroid, skeleton, and lens of the eye. Arsenite is the main form interacting with tissue constituents, except the skeleton. In human subjects, the hair and nails have the highest concentrations of arsenic (0.02-1 mg/kg of dry weight), and the skin and lungs have fairly high concentrations (0.01-1 mg/kg of dry weight). Data extrapolated from animal studies permit the development and validation of a suitable PB-PK model for inorganic arsenic for humans.

Experimental animal studies show that both inorganic arsenic and the methylated metabolites pass the placenta. In humans exposed to arsenic via drinking water, arsenic concentration in cord blood was similar to that in maternal blood. DMA was the main form of arsenic in plasma of mothers and newborns. The excretion of arsenic in human milk is low, and in areas with high arsenic concentrations in the water, an infant is less exposed to arsenic via breast feeding than via formula prepared from the water.

RECOMMENDATIONS

Because of interspecies differences in the amounts of various arsenic species excreted in the urine and the amounts of methyltransferases in tissues, extrapolation of animal data to humans is generally not possible. More human studies are needed, including research using human tissues, to answer some of the questions concerning the disposition and toxic effects of arsenic. Factors influencing methylation, tissue retention, and excretion of arsenic in humans (e.g., arsenic-binding proteins) also need to be investigated.

Other studies of less critical importance but nonetheless needed to fill important data gaps include the following:

— Studies to determine whether the methylation of arsenic in vivo results in the formation of reactive intermediates that are distributed to tissues.

— Studies to identify the gene or genes for arsenic methyltransferases so that nucleotide probes can be used to examine the relationships between the polymorphism of arsenic methyltransferases and the phenotype (excretion of arsenic metabolites in urine), as well as between the polymorphism of arsenic methyltransferases and the signs and symptoms of arsenic toxicity.

— Studies on the bioavailability of inorganic arsenic in various types of food.

— Studies to examine fetal exposure to various arsenic metabolites during different stages of development.

— Studies using arsenic methyltransferase knock-out mice to determine whether methylation alters inorganic arsenite toxicology.

REFERENCES

Anundi, I, J. Högberg, and M. Vahter. 1982. GSH release in bile as influenced by arsenite. FEBS Lett. 145:285-288.

Aposhian, H.V. 1997. Enzymatic methylation of arsenic species and other new approaches to arsenic toxicity. Annu. Rev. Pharmacol. Toxicol. 37:397-419.

Aposhian, H.V., R. Zakharyan, Y. Wu, S. Healy, and M.M. Aposhian. 1997.

Enzymatic methylation of arsenic compounds: II—An overview. Pp. 296-321 in Arsenic: Exposure and Health Effects, C.O. Abernathy, R.L. Calderon, and W.R. Chappell, eds. London: Chapman & Hall.

Bogdan, G.M., A. Sampayo-Reyes, and H.V. Aposhian. 1994. Arsenic binding proteins of mammalian systems: I. Isolation of three arsenite-binding proteins of rabbit liver. Toxicology 93:175-193.

Buchet, J.P., and R. Lauwerys. 1985. Study of inorganic arsenic methylation by rat liver in vitro: Relevance for the interpretation of observations in man. Arch. Toxicol. 57:125-129.

Buchet, J.P., and R. Lauwerys. 1988. Role of thiols in the in vitro methylation of inorganic arsenic by rat liver cytosol. Biochem. Pharmacol. 37:3149-3153.

Buchet, J.P., R. Lauwerys, and H. Roels. 1981a. Comparison of the urinary excretion of arsenic metabolites after a single dose of sodium arsenite, monomethylarsonate or dimethylarsinate in man. Int. Arch. Occup. Environ. Health 48:71-79.

Buchet, J.P., R. Lauwerys, and H. Roels. 1981b. Urinary excretion of inorganic arsenic and its metabolites after repeated ingestion of sodium metaarsenite by volunteers. Int. Arch. Occup. Environ. Health 48:111-118.

Buchet, J.P., A. Geubel, S. Pauwels, P. Mahieu, and R. Lauwerys. 1984. The influence of liver disease on the methylation of arsenite in humans. Arch. Toxicol. 55:151-154.

Byrne, A.R., L. Kosta, M. Dermelj, and M. Tusek-Znidaric. 1983. Aspects of some trace elements in human milk. Pp. 21-35 in Trace Element Analytical Chemistry In Medicine And Biology, Vol. 2, P. Brätter and P. Schramel. Berlin: Walter de Gruyter.

Challenger, F. 1945. Biological methylation. Chem. Rev. 36:315-361.

Charbonneau, S.M., G.K.H. Tam, F. Bryce, Z. Zawidzka, and E. Sandi. 1979. Metabolism of orally administered inorganic arsenic in the dog. Toxicol. Lett. 3:107-114.

Charbonneau, S.M., J.G. Hollins, G.K.H. Tam, F. Bryce, J.M. Ridgeway, and R.F. Willes. 1980. Whole-body retention, excretion and metabolism of [^{74}As]arsenic acid in the hamster. Toxicol. Lett. 5:175-182.

Concha, G., B. Nermell, and M. Vahter. 1998a. Metabolism of inorganic arsenic in children with chronic high arsenic exposure in northern Argentina. Environ. Health Perspect. 106:355-359.

Concha, G., G. Vogler, D. Lezeano, B. Nermell, and M. Vahter. 1998b. Exposure to inorganic arsenic metabolites during early human development. Toxicol. Sci. 44:185-190.

Concha, G., G. Vogler, B. Nermell, and M. Vahter. 1998c. Low arsenic excretion in breast milk of native Andean women exposed to high levels of arsenic in the drinking water. Int. Arch. Occup. Environ. Health 71:42-46.

Cross, J.D., I.M. Dale, A.C.D. Leslie, and H. Smith. 1979. Industrial exposure to arsenic. J. Radioanal. Chem. 48:197-208.

Cullen, W.R., and K.J. Reimer. 1989. Arsenic speciation in the environment. Chem. Rev. 89:713-764.

Cullen, W.R., B.C. McBride, and J. Reglinski. 1984. The reaction of methylarsenicals with thiols: Some biological implications. J. Inorg. Biochem. 21:171-194.

Dang, H.S., D.D. Jaiswal, and S. Somasundaram. 1983. Distribution of arsenic in human tissues and milk. Sci. Total Environ. 29:171-175.

Das, D., A. Chatterjee, B.K. Mandal, G. Samanta, D. Chakraborti, and B. Chanda. 1995. Arsenic in ground water in six districts of West Bengal, India: The biggest arsenic calamity in the world. Part 2. Arsenic concentration in drinking water, hair, nails, urine, skin-scale and liver tissue (biopsy) of the affected people. Analyst 120:917-924.

Das, D., G. Samanta, B.K. Mandal, T.R. Chowdhury, C.R. Chanda, P.P. Chowdhury, G.K. Basu, and D. Chakraborti. 1996. Arsenic in ground water in six districts of West Bengal, India. Environ. Geochem. Health 18:5-15.

De Kimpe, J., R. Cornelis, L. Mees, S. Van Lierde, and R. Vanholder. 1993. More than tenfold increase of arsenic in serum and packed cells of chronic hemodialysis patients. Am. J. Nephrol. 13:429-434.

De Kimpe, J, R. Cornelis, L. Mees, and R. Vanholder. 1996. Basal metabolism of intraperitoneally injected carrier-free [74]As-labeled arsenate in rabbits. Fundam. Appl. Toxicol. 34:240-248.

Delnomdedieu, M., M.M. Basti, J.D. Otvos, and D.J. Thomas. 1993. Transfer of arsenite from glutathione to dithiols: A model of interaction. Chem. Res. Toxicol. 6:598-602.

Delnomdedieu, M., M.M. Basti, J.D. Otvos, and D.J. Thomas. 1994a. Reduction and binding of arsenate and dimethylarsinate by glutathione: a magnetic resonance study. Chem.-Biol. Interact. 90:139-155.

Delnomdedieu, M., M.M. Basti, M. Styblo, J.D. Otvos, and D.J. Thomas. 1994b. Complexation of arsenic species in rabbit erythrocytes. Chem. Res. Toxicol. 7:621-627.

Delnomdedieu, M., M. Styblo, and D.J. Thomas. 1995. Time dependence of accumulation and binding of inorganic and organic arsenic species in rabbit erythrocytes. Chem.-Biol. Interact. 98:69-83.

Du Pont, O., I. Ariel, and S.L. Warren. 1941. The distribution of radioactive arsenic in the normal and tumor-bearing (Brown-Pearce) rabbit. Am. J. Syph. Gonorrhea Vener. Dis. 26:96-118.

Foà, V., A. Colombi, M. Maroni, M. Buratti, and G. Calzaferri. 1984. The speciation of the chemical forms of arsenic in the biological monitoring of exposure to inorganic arsenic. Sci. Total Environ. 34:241-259.

Freeman, G.B., R.A. Schoof, M.V. Ruby, A.O. Davis, J.A. Dill, S.C. Liao, C.A. Lapin, and P.D. Bergstrom. 1995. Bioavailability of arsenic in soil and house dust impacted by smelter activities following oral administration in *Cynomologus* monkeys. Fundam. Appl. Toxicol. 28:215-222.

Geubel, A.P., M.C. Mairlot, J.P. Buchet, and R. Lauwerys. 1988. Abnormal methylation capacity in human liver cirrhosis. Int. J. Clin. Pharmacol. Res. 8:117-122.

Ginsburg, J.M. 1965. Renal mechanism for excretion and transformation of arsenic in the dog. Am. J. Physiol. 208:832-840.

Harrington J.M., J.P. Middaugh, D.L. Morse, and J. Housworth. 1978. A survey of a population exposed to high concentrations of arsenic in well water in Fairbanks, Alaska. Am. J. Epidemiol. 108:377-385.

Healy, S.M., R.A. Zakharyan, and H.V. Aposhian. 1997. Enzymatic methylation of arsenic compounds: IV. In vitro and in vivo deficiency of the methylation of arsenite and monomethylarsonic acid in the guinea pig. Mutat. Res. 386:229-239.

Healy, S.M., E.A. Casarez, F. Ayala-Fierro, and H.V. Aposhian. 1998. Enzymatic methylation of arsenic compounds v. arsenite methyltransferase activity in tissues of mice. Toxicol. Appl. Pharmacol. 148:65-70.

Heydorn, K. 1970. Environmental variation of arsenic levels in human blood determined by neutron activation analysis. Clin. Chim. Acta 28:349-357.

Hirata, M., A. Tanaka, A. Hisanaga, and N. Ishinishi. 1990. Effects of glutathione depletion on the acute nephrotoxic potential of arsenite and on the arsenic metabolism in the hamster. Toxicol. Appl. Pharmacol. 106:469-481.

Hood, R.D., W.P. Harrison, and G.C. Vedel. 1982. Evaluation of arsenic metabolites for prenatal effects in the hamster. Bull. Environ. Contam. Toxicol. 29:679-687.

Hood R. D., G.C. Vedel-Macrander, M.J. Zaworotko, F.M. Tatum, and R.G. Meeks. 1987. Distribution, metabolism and fetal uptake of pentavalent arsenic in pregnant mice following oral or intraperitoneal administration. Teratology 35:19-25.

Hopenhayn-Rich, C., A.H. Smith, and H.M. Goeden. 1993. Human studies do not support the methylation threshold hypothesis for the toxicity of inorganic arsenic. Environ. Res. 60:161-177.

Hostynek, J.J., R.S. Hinz, C.R. Lorence, M. Price, and R.H. Guy. 1993. Metals and the skin. Crit. Rev. Toxicol. 23:171-235.

Hughes, M.F., and E.M. Kenyon. 1998. Dose-dependent effects on the disposition of monomethylarsonic acid and dimethylarsinic acid in the mouse after intravenous administration. J. Toxicol. Environ. Health 53:95-112.

Hughes, M.F., M. Menache, and D.J. Thompson. 1994. Dose-dependent disposition of sodium arsenite in mice following acute oral exposure. Fundam. Appl. Toxicol. 22:80-89.

Hunter F.T., A.F. Kip, and J.W. Irvine. 1942. Radioactive tracer studies on arsenic injected as potassium arsenite. J. Pharmacol. Exp. Ther. 76:207-220

Kadowaki, K. 1960. Studies on the arsenic contents in organ-tissues of the normal Japanese [in Japanese with English summary]. J. Osaka City Med. Cent. 9:2083-2099.

Kagey, B.T., J.E. Bumgarner, and J.P. Creason. 1977. Arsenic levels in maternal-fetal tissue sets. Pp. 252-256 in Trace Substances in Environmental Health—XI, Proceedings of the University of Missouri's 11th Annual Conference on Trace Substances in Environmental Health, D.D. Hemphill, ed. Columbia, Mo.: University of Missouri Press.

Klaassen, C.D. 1974. Biliary excretion of arsenic in rats, rabbits and dogs. Toxicol. Appl. Pharmacol. 29:447-457.

Kosnett, M., and C.E. Becker. 1988. Dimercaptosuccinic acid: Utility in acute and chronic arsenic poisoning [abstract]. Vet. Hum. Toxicol. 30:369.

Lanz, H. Jr., P.C. Wallace, and J.G. Hamilton. 1950. The metabolism of arsenic in laboratory animals using As^{74} as a tracer. Univ. Calif. Publ. Pharmacol. 2:263-282.

Lerman, S., and T.W. Clarkson. 1983. The metabolism of arsenite and arsenate by the rat. Fundam. Appl. Toxicol. 3:309-314.

Lerman, S.A., T.W. Clarkson, and R.J. Gerson. 1983. Arsenic uptake and metabolism by liver cells is dependent on arsenic oxidation state. Chem.-Biol. Interact. 45:401-406.

Liebscher, K., and H. Smith. 1968. Essential and nonessential trace elements. A method of determining whether an element is essential or nonessential in human tissue. Arch. Environ. Health 17:881-890.

Lindgren, A., M. Vahter, and L. Dencker. 1982. Autoradiographic studies on the distribution of arsenic in mice and hamster administered ^{74}As-arsenite or -arsenate. Acta Pharmacol. Toxicol. 51:253-365.

Lindgren, A., B. R. G. Danielsson, L. Dencker, and M. Vahter. 1984. Embryotoxicity of arsenite and arsenate: Distribution in pregnant mice and monkeys and effects on embryonic cells in vitro. Acta Pharmacol. Toxicol. 54:311-320.

Mahieu, P., J.P. Buchet, H.A. Roels, and R. Lauwerys. 1981. The metabolism of arsenic in humans acutely intoxicated by As_2O_3. Its significance for the duration of BAL therapy. Clin. Toxicol. 18:1067-1075.

Maiorino, R.M., and H.V. Aposhian. 1985. Dimercaptan metal-binding agents influence the biotransformation of arsenite in the rabbit. Toxicol. Appl. Pharmacol. 77:240-250.

Mann, S., P.O. Droz, and M. Vahter. 1996a. A physiologically based pharmacokinetic model for arsenic exposure: I. Development in hamster and rabbits. Toxicol. Appl. Pharmacol. 137:8-22.

Mann, S., P.O. Droz, and M. Vahter. 1996b. A physiologically based pharmacokinetic model for arsenic exposure: II. Validation and application in humans. Toxicol. Appl. Pharmacol. 140:471-486.

Mappes, R. 1977. Experiments on the excretion of arsenic in urine. Int. Arch. Occup. Environ. Health 40:267-272.

Marafante, E., and M. Vahter. 1984. The effect of methyltransferase inhibition on the metabolism of (^{74}As)arsenite in mice and rabbits. Chem.-Biol. Interact. 50:49-57.

Marafante, E., and M. Vahter. 1987. Solubility, retention and metabolism of intratracheally and orally administered inorganic arsenic compounds in the hamster. Environ. Res. 42:72-82.

Marafante, E., J. Rade, E. Sabbioni, F. Bertolero, and V. Foa. 1981. Intracellular interaction and metabolic fate of arsenite in the rabbit. Clin. Toxicol. 18:1335-1341.

Marafante, E., M. Vahter, and J. Envall. 1985. The role of the methylation in the detoxication of arsenate in the rabbit. Chem.-Biol. Interact. 56:225-238.

Marafante, E., M. Vahter, H. Norin, J. Envall, M. Sandström, A. Christakopoulos, and R. Ryhage. 1987. Biotransformation of dimethylarsinic acid in mouse, hamster and man. J. Appl. Toxicol. 7:111-117.

Mealey J., G.L.Brownell, and W.H. Sweet. 1959. Radioarsenic in plasma, urine, normal tissue, and intracranial neoplasms. Arch. Neurol. Psychiatr. 81:310-320.

Menzel, D.B., M. Ross, S.V. Oddo, P. Bergstrom, H. Greene, and R.N. Roth. 1994. A physiologically based pharmacokinetic model for ingested arsenic. Environ. Geochem. Health 16:209-218.

Menzel, D.B. 1997. Some results of a physiologically based pharmacokinetic modeling approach to estimating arsenic body burdens. Pp. 349-368 in Arsenic: Exposure and Health Effects, C.O. Abernathy, R.L. Calderon, and W.R. Chappell, eds. London: Chapman & Hall.

Molin, L., and P.O. Wester. 1976. The estimated daily loss of trace elements from normal skin by desquamation. Scand. J. Clin. Lab. Invest. 36:679-682.

Moore, M.M., K. Harrington-Brock, and C.L. Doerr. 1997. Relative genotoxic potency of arsenic and its methylated metabolites. Mutat. Res. 386:279-290.

Odanaka, Y., O. Matano, and S. Goto. 1980. Biomethylation of inorganic arsenic by the rat and some laboratory animals. Bull. Environ. Contam. Toxicol. 24:452-459.

Parr, R.M., E.M. De Maeyer, V.G. Iyengar, A.R. Byrne, G.F. Kirkbright, G. Schöch, L. Niinistö, O. Pineda, H.L. Vis, Y. Hofvander, and A. Omololu. 1991. Minor and trace elements in human milk from Guatemala, Hungary, Nigeria, Philippines, Sweden and Zaire. Results from a WHO/IAEA Joint Project. Biol. Trace Elem. Res. 29:51-75.

Pomroy, C., S. M. Charbonneau, R.S. McCullough, and G.K.H. Tam. 1980. Human retention studies with [74]As. Toxicol. Appl. Pharmacol. 53:550-556.

Rahman, M.S., L.L. Hall, and M.F. Hughes. 1994. In vitro percutaneous absorption of sodium arsenate in B6C3F$_1$ mice. Toxicol. In Vitro 8:441-448.

Rasmussen, R.E., and D.B. Menzel. 1997. Variation in arsenic-induced sister chromatid exchange in human lymphocytes and lymphoblastoid cell lines. Mutat. Res. 386:299-306.

Sakurai, T., T. Kaise, and C. Matsubara. 1998. Inorganic and methylated arsenic compounds induce cell death in murine macrophages via different mechanisms. Chem. Res. Toxicol. 11:273-283.

Scott, A. 1958. The retention of arsenic in the late cutaneous complications of its administration. Br. J. Dermatol. 70:195-200.

Scott, N., K.M. Hatlelid, N.E. MacKenzie, and D.E. Carter. 1993. Reactions of arsenic(III) and arsenic(V) species with glutathione. Chem. Res. Toxicol. 6:102-106.

Styblo, M., and D.J. Thomas. 1997. Factors influencing in vitro methylation of arsenicals in rat liver cytosol. Pp. 283-295 in Arsenic: Exposure and Health Effects, C.O. Abernathy, R.L. Calderon, and W.R. Chappell, eds. London: Chapman & Hall.

Styblo, M., H. Yamauchi, and D.J. Thomas. 1995. Comparative in vitro methylation of trivalent and pentavalent arsenicals. Toxicol. Appl. Pharmacol. 135:172-178.

Styblo, M., M. Delnomdedieu, and D.J. Thomas. 1996. Mono- and dimethylation of arsenic in rat liver cytosol in vitro. Chem.-Biol. Interact. 99:147-164.

Tabacova, S., D.D. Baird, L. Balabaeva, D. Lolova, and I. Petrov. 1994. Placental arsenic and cadmium in relation to lipid peroxides and glutathione levels in maternal-infant pairs from a copper smelter area. Placenta 15:873-881.

Tam, G.K.H., S.M. Charbonneau, F. Bryce, C. Pomroy, and E. Sandi. 1979.

Metabolism of inorganic arsenic ([74]As) in humans following oral ingestion. Toxicol. Appl. Pharmacol. 50:319-322.

Thompson, D.J. 1993. A chemical hypothesis for arsenic methylation in mammals. Chem.-Biol. Interact. 88:89-114.

Tice, R.R., J.W. Yager, P. Andrews, and E. Crecelius. 1997. Effect of hepatic methyl donor status on urinary excretion and DNA damage in B6C3F1 mice treated with sodium arsenite. Mutat. Res. 386:315-334.

Vahter, M. 1981. Biotransformation of trivalent and pentavalent inorganic arsenic in mice and rats. Environ. Res. 25:286-293.

Vahter, M. 1983. Metabolism of Inorganic Arsenic in Relation to Chemical Form and Animal Species. Doctoral Thesis. Karolinska Institutet, Stockholm.

Vahter, M. 1994. Species differences in the metabolism of arsenic compounds. Appl. Organomet. Chem. 8:175-182.

Vahter, M., and J. Envall. 1983. In vivo reduction of arsenate in mice and rabbits. Environ. Res. 32:14-24.

Vahter, M., and E. Marafante. 1983. Intracellular interaction and metabolic fate of arsenite and arsenate in mice and rabbits. Chem.-Biol. Interact. 47:29-44.

Vahter, M., and E. Marafante. 1985. Reduction and binding of arsenate in marmoset monkeys. Arch. Toxicol. 57:119-124.

Vahter, M., and E. Marafante. 1987. Effects of low dietary intake of methionine, choline or proteins on the biotransformation of arsenite in the rabbit. Toxicol. Lett. 37:41-46.

Vahter M., and E. Marafante. 1988. In vivo methylation and detoxication of arsenic. Pp. 105-119 in Biological Alkylation of Heavy Metals, P.J. Craig and F. Glockling, eds. London: Royal Society of Chemistry.

Vahter M., and H. Norin. 1980. Metabolism of [74]As-labeled trivalent and pentavalent inorganic arsenic in mice. Environ. Res. 21:446-457.

Vahter, M., E. Marafante, A. Lindgren, and L. Dencker. 1982. Tissue distribution and subcellular binding of arsenic in marmoset monkeys after injection of [74]As-arsenite. Arch. Toxicol. 51:65-77.

Vahter, M., E. Marafante, and L. Dencker. 1984. Tissue distribution and retention of [74]As-dimethylarsinic acid in mice and rats. Arch. Environ. Contam. Toxicol. 13:259-264.

Vahter, M., G. Concha, B. Nermell, R. Nilsson, F. Dulout, and A.T. Natarajan. 1995a. A unique metabolism of inorganic arsenic in native Andean women. Eur. J. Pharmacol. 293:455-462.

Vahter, M., R. Couch, B. Nermell, and R. Nilsson. 1995b. Lack of methylation of inorganic arsenic in the chimpanzee. Toxicol. Appl. Pharmacol. 133:262-268.

Vellar, O.D. 1969. Nutrient Losses Through Sweating. Thesis. Oslo University, Oslo, Norway.

Versieck, J. 1985. Trace elements in human body fluids and tissues. Crit. Rev. Clin. Lab. Sci. 22:97-184.

Webb, D.R., I.G. Sipes, and D.E. Carter. 1984. In vitro solubility and in vivo toxicity of gallium arsenide. Toxicol. Appl. Pharmacol. 76:96-104.

Wester, R.C., H.I. Maibach, L. Sedik, J. Melendres, and M. Wade. 1993. In vivo and in vitro percutaneous absorption and skin decontamination of arsenic from water and soil. Fundam. Appl. Toxicol. 20:336-340.

Winski, S.L., and D.E. Carter. 1995. Interactions of rat red blood cell sulfhydryls with arsenate and arsenite. J. Toxicol. Environ. Health 46:379-397.

Yamauchi, H., and Y. Yamamura. 1979. Dynamic change of inorganic arsenic and methylarsenic compounds in human urine after oral intake as arsenic trioxide. Ind. Health 17:79-84.

Yamauchi, H., and Y. Yamamura. 1984. Metabolism and excretion of orally administered dimethylarsinic acid in the hamster. Toxicol. Appl. Pharmacol. 74:134-140.

Yamauchi, H., and Y. Yamamura. 1985. Metabolism and excretion of orally administrated arsenic trioxide in the hamster. Toxicology 34:113-121.

Yamauchi, H., K. Takahashi, and Y. Yamamura. 1986. Metabolism and excretion of orally and intraperitoneally administered gallium arsenide in the hamster. Toxicology 40:237-246.

Zakharyan, R.A., Y. Wu, G.M. Bogdan, and H.V. Aposhian. 1995. Enzymatic methylation of arsenic compounds: Assay, partial purification, and properties of arsenite methyltransferase and monomethylarsonic acid methyltransferase of rabbit liver. Chem. Res. Toxicol. 8:1029-1038.

Zakharyan, R.A., E. Wildfang, and H.V. Aposhian. 1996. Enzymatic methylation of arsenic compounds: III. The marmoset and tamarin, but not the rhesus, monkeys are deficient in methyltransferases that methylate inorganic arsenic. Toxicol. Appl. Pharmacol. 140:77-84.

Zhang, X., R. Cornelis, J. De Kimpe, L. Mees, V. Vanderbiesen, A. De Cubber, and R. Vanholder. 1996. Accumulation of arsenic species in serum of patients with chronic renal disease. Clin. Chem. 42:1231-1237.

Zhang, X., R. Cornelis, J. De Kimpe, L. Mees, and N. Lameire. 1997. Speciation of arsenic in serum, urine, and dialysate of patients on continuous ambulatory peritoneal dialysis. Clin. Chem. 43:406-408.

Zhang, X., R. Cornelis, J. de Kimpe, L. Mees, and N. Lameire. 1998a. Study of arsenic-protein binding in serum of patients on continuous ambulatory peritoneal dialysis. Clin. Chem. 44:141-147.

Zhang, X., R. Cornelis, L. Mees, R. Vanholder, and N. Lameire. 1998b.

Chemical speciation of arsenic in serum of uraemic patients. Analyst 123:13-17.

6

Biomarkers of Arsenic Exposure

ASSESSMENT of arsenic exposure via drinking water is often based on the measured concentrations in the drinking water and estimations of the amount of water consumed. For estimation of population averages, default values are often used for water consumption (e.g., 2 liters of water per day for an adult person). Data on individual consumption require information on the actual amount of water each individual uses for drinking and preparation of foods and beverages, as well as information on the water sources used and the arsenic concentration in each source. Unless the consumption data are based on actual measurements over several days by the duplicate portion technique, such data are estimates, the uncertainty of which will depend on the method used.

Biological monitoring provides data on the absorbed dose for each individual studied. In this chapter, the subcommittee evaluates various biomarkers (e.g., arsenic in urine, blood, hair, and nails) as meaningful measures of the absorbed dose of inorganic arsenic. A discussion is provided on the suitability of the various biomarkers to serve as indicators of acute or chronic exposure to inorganic arsenic and the various factors (e.g., dietary intake of arsenic compounds) that can influence the indicators.

ARSENIC IN URINE

The concentration of total arsenic in urine has often been used as an indicator of recent exposure because urine is the main route of excretion of most arsenic species (see, e.g., Buchet et al. 1981; Vahter 1994). The half-time of inorganic arsenic in human subjects is about 4 days (see Chapter 5). However, the total urinary arsenic concentration does not provide information on the form of arsenic absorbed. As mentioned in Chapter 3, some foods, especially those of marine origin, often have high concentrations of arsenic mainly in the form arsenobetaine, which is not metabolized in the body but is rapidly excreted in the urine (Vahter et al. 1984; Vahter 1994). Thus, ingestion of such foods results in a rapid increase in the concentration of total arsenic in the urine; that increase would invalidate urinary arsenic as an indicator of exposure to inorganic arsenic. One serving of seafood might give rise to urinary arsenic concentrations of more than 1,000 μg/L (Norin and Vahter 1981). In comparison, concentrations of 5-50 μg/L are found in the urine of subjects with no intake of seafood arsenic or excessive exposure to inorganic arsenic in drinking water or in the working environment. Certain other foods (e.g., chicken) also might contain arsenobetaine if fish meal is used as a source of protein in the feed.

A better measurement of the intake of inorganic arsenic can be obtained from the concentration of inorganic arsenic and its metabolites mono-methylarsonic acid (MMA) and dimethylarsinic acid (DMA) in the urine (see Chapters 3 and 5). Exposure to MMA, DMA, or both will influence the estimate, but other than occupational exposure to pesticides containing DMA, such exposure seems to be very low in most countries. However, certain types of seafood, especially seaweed and some shellfish, might contain DMA (Mohri et al. 1990; Arbouine and Wilson 1992; Yamauchi et al. 1992) or arsenosugars, which are partly metabolized in the body to DMA (Le et al. 1994; Ma and Le 1998). Thus, consumption of such foods might result in increased urinary concentrations of DMA, and those increases might be interpreted as exposure to inorganic arsenic. In fact, consumption of seafood has been shown to cause a slight increase in the concentration of metabolites of inorganic arsenic in the urine (Norin and Vahter 1981; Vahter and Lind 1986; Arbouine and Wilson 1992; Mürer et al. 1992; Larsen et al. 1993; Buchet et al. 1994). Therefore, the intake of seafood, especially seaweed, should be investigated when urinary metabolites of arsenic are to be used for evaluation of exposure to inorganic arsenic. If such food is common, people should be asked to refrain from eating seafood a couple of days before urine sampling.

Reported data on average background concentrations of metabolites of inorganic arsenic (inorganic arsenic + MMA + DMA) in the urine are generally below 10 μg/L in European countries (Apel and Stoeppler 1983; Valkonen et al. 1983; Foà et al. 1984; Vahter and Lind 1986; Andrén et al. 1988; Jensen et al. 1991; Buchet et al. 1996; Trepka et al. 1996; Kristiansen et al. 1997; Kavanagh et al. 1998), somewhat higher in some parts of the United States (Smith et al. 1977; Morse et al. 1979; Binder et al. 1987), and around 50 μg/L in Japan (Yamauchi and Yamamura 1979; Yamauchi et al.

1992). In certain areas in the United States, an average concentration of metabolites of inorganic arsenic at 10 μg/L or less has been reported for children (Kalman et al. 1990; Pollisar et al. 1990; Gottlieb et al. 1993). Urinary arsenic concentrations among occupationally exposed subjects can reach hundreds of micrograms per liter (Cant and Legendre 1982; Vahter et al. 1986; Yamauchi et al. 1989; Hakala and Pyy 1992; Offergelt et al. 1992; Yager et al. 1997).

In a population, group-average concentrations of arsenic metabolites in the urine correlate with the average concentrations of arsenic in drinking water. However, the relationship can vary considerably depending on the amount of water consumed and the amount of water used for cooking. In studies carried out in California and Nevada, a water arsenic concentration of 400 μg/L corresponded to about 230 μg/L in the urine (as total urinary arsenic), and 100 μg/L in the water corresponded to about 75 μg/L in the urine (Valentine et al. 1979). Similarly, people in Alaska where the arsenic concentration was about 400 μg/L in drinking water had on average 180 μg/L in urine, and those exposed to 50-100 μg/L (average 75 μg/L) had on average 45 μg/L (Harrington et al. 1978). Among native Andean people in northwestern Argentina where the local water contains arsenic at about 200 μg/L, the average concentration of arsenic metabolites in urine was much higher, on the average of 250-450 μg/L, mainly because fluids other than the water are generally not consumed and most of the food is prepared with the water (Vahter et al. 1995; Concha et al. 1998a,b). In northeastern Taiwan, people living in villages with arsenic concentrations of 50-300 μg/L in drinking water had an average of 140 μg/L in urine (Chiou et al. 1997).

Studies have also reported a relationship between airborne concentrations of arsenic and urinary excretion of inorganic arsenic metabolites (inorganic arsenic + MMA + DMA) among workers occupationally exposed to arsenic (Smith et al. 1977; Vahter et al. 1986; Offergelt et al. 1992; Yager et al. 1997). The urinary concentrations of arsenic metabolites were found to increase steadily during the first day of the workweek (2-3 days after the end of the previous workweek), after which they reached a steady state (Vahter et al. 1986). The concentrations in the late evening were very similar to those of the following early morning, and both correlated well with the total daily excretion. Hakala and Pyy (1995) reported a significant correlation between airborne concentrations of arsenic in a copper smelter and an arsenic trioxide refinery plant and urinary concentrations of inorganic arsenic. The urinary DMA correlated poorly with airborne arsenic, apparently because of the influence of dietary arsenic compounds that resulted in increased urinary DMA.

As in other studies measuring concentrations of exposure markers in the urine, an important question is whether to collect 24-hr urine samples, spot urine samples, or first-morning urine samples. Ideally, the amount of arsenic excreted over a certain period of time should be assessed. Usually that is done by measuring the excretion of arsenic in all urine produced in 24 hr. However, obtaining complete 24-hr urine collections is difficult (Bingham and Cummings 1983; Johansson et al. 1998). It requires supervision and validation. Because of those difficulties and other problems (e.g., the risk of contamination of the urine during sampling), the first-morning urine or spot urine samples are generally collected for determination of the urinary concentration of arsenic or arsenic metabolites. To evaluate the concentration properly, especially in the case of spot urine samples, the dilution of the urine has to be considered. The urine flow is highly variable, being dependent on numerous factors, such as body size, body water content, solute intake, physical activity, and diurnal variations (Diamond 1988). A short time after the consumption of large amounts of fluid, the urine is very diluted and has a low solute content. To compensate for the dilution, the concentration of arsenic can be related to the concentration of creatinine or the specific gravity. A disadvantage of using the creatinine-adjusted urinary arsenic measurement is that it is dependent on the muscle mass and thus is often quite different for men and women. Protein intake might also influence urinary creatinine concentrations.

In a study of bladder-cell micronuclei in people exposed to arsenic via drinking water in northern Chile, creatinine-adjusted urinary arsenic measurements showed the strongest correlation with intake estimates (average daily intake over the previous 4 months), and unadjusted urinary arsenic (sum of inorganic arsenic metabolites) showed the strongest correlation with bladder-cell micronuclei (Biggs et al. 1997). At the most, 67% of the variation in urinary arsenic was explained by the intake estimate, probably because urinary arsenic reflected exposure over the previous 1-2 days and the intake estimate reflected the average for the previous 4 months, and the daily intake of water and water-derived food is likely to vary considerably. A comparison with 24-hr recall data was not reported. The results might also reflect the difficulties in correctly estimating the intake of water without direct measurements (i.e., by duplicate portion collections).

ARSENIC IN BLOOD

Most of the absorbed inorganic and organic arsenic has a short half-time in blood (see Chapter 5); arsenic concentrations in blood are increased only for a very short time following absorption. If exposure is continuous and steady, as is often the case with exposure through drinking water, the blood arsenic concentration might reach a steady-state and then reflect the degree of exposure.

Blood is a difficult matrix for chemical analysis (see Chapter 3), so in general, only total arsenic concentrations are reported. Partial speciation of arsenic in blood has been reported in a few cases (Zhang et al. 1996; Concha et al. 1998b). When using total arsenic in blood as an indicator of exposure to inorganic arsenic, the interference from organic arsenic compounds originating from seafood has to be considered. Furthermore, because of the low concentrations, the analytical error might be significant, unless the more-sensitive methods are used.

Data on concentrations of arsenic in blood in people with no known exposure to arsenic cover quite a wide range—0.3-2 μg/L (Bencko and Symon 1977; Heydorn 1970; Kagey et al. 1977; Olguín et al. 1983; Hamilton et al. 1994; Vahter et al. 1995; Concha et al. 1998a,b). In a population in northern Argentina with no known exposure to inorganic arsenic and very little fish intake, the average blood arsenic concentration was 0.9 μg/L in children and 1.5 μg/L in adults (Vahter et al. 1995; Concha et al. 1998a,b). The average blood arsenic concentration in people in Belgium was reported to be about 0.4 μg/L; that in red blood cells was 1.8 μg/L (Versieck 1985; Versieck and Vanballenberghe 1985). In areas where consumption of seafood is common, mean blood arsenic concentrations of 5-10 μg/L have been reported (Foà et al. 1984; Yamauchi et al. 1992). Similarly, the blood arsenic concentration was much higher in people living in coastal municipalities in Norway with high fish consumption than in people living in inland areas with low fish consumption (average values 7-18 μg/L versus 1 μg/L; Blekastad et al. 1984). Heydorn (1970) sampled blood from four individuals every 4 hr to determine the arsenic content in blood. No signs of circadian variation occurred, but following a supper of flatfish, blood arsenic concentrations rapidly increased in one subject by more than an order of magnitude (18 μg/L), followed by an approximately exponential decrease with a half-time of about 8 hr. The baseline blood arsenic concentrations in the four subjects were 0.3, 1.2, 1.6, and 4.5 μg/L, respectively.

In subjects exposed to arsenic via drinking water, blood arsenic concentrations are clearly increased and might reach several tens of micrograms per liter (Heydorn 1970; Valentine et al. 1979; Vahter et al. 1995). In people exposed to arsenic in drinking water (200 μg/L) in northern Argentina, arsenic concentration in blood was about 10 μg/L on average (Vahter et al. 1995; Concha et al. 1998a,b). In studies carried out in California and Nevada, an arsenic concentration of 400 μg/L in the water corresponded to about 13 μg/L in the blood, and 100 μg/L in the water corresponded to 3-4

μg/L in the blood (Valentine et al. 1979). Obviously, compared with urine, blood is a much less sensitive biomarker of exposure to arsenic via drinking water.

ARSENIC IN HAIR AND NAILS

Arsenic concentrations are normally higher in hair and nails than in other parts of the body because of the high content of keratin, the SH groups of which might bind trivalent inorganic arsenic (Curry and Pounds 1977; Hopps 1977; Hostýnek et al. 1993). The concentration of arsenic in the root of the hair is in equilibrium with the concentration in the blood. Hair might be considered an excretory pathway, and once incorporated in the hair, the arsenic is not biologically available. Arsenobetaine, the major organic arsenic compound in seafood, is not accumulated in hair (Vahter et al. 1983). That implies that arsenic in hair reflects exposure to inorganic arsenic only. Experimental studies in which radiolabeled DMA was administered to mice and rats showed very low incorporation of DMA in skin and hair compared with that of inorganic arsenic (Vahter et al. 1984). However, in one study, the presence of DMA in hair and nails has been reported (Yamauchi and Yamamura 1983; Yamato 1988).

Segmental hair analysis (i.e., determination of the concentration along the length of the hair) might provide valuable information on the time of acute arsenic exposure (Smith 1964; Toribara et al. 1982; Koons and Peters 1994). For example, Smith (1964) reported a case in which a single fatal ingestion of 0.8 g of arsenic trioxide gave rise to a concentration of only 0.86 mg/kg for the whole length of hair, 30 cm long. Further analysis showed that the concentration of arsenic in the first millimeter, including the root, was 90 mg/kg. In another fatal case of arsenic poisoning, centimeter segmental analysis revealed that the concentrations of arsenic varied between 28 and 226 mg/kg (Poklis and Saady 1990).

The main disadvantage of using hair and nails as indicators of exposure to arsenic is that the arsenic concentrations might be influenced by external contamination via air, water, soaps, and shampoos. That was clearly demonstrated in studies on people living in Fairbanks, Alaska, where the water contained arsenic at 345 μg/L (Harrington et al. 1978). One group of people drinking essentially only bottled water, resulting in low concentrations of arsenic in urine (average 43 μg/L), had high arsenic concentrations in hair (average 5.7 μg/g). In areas with low concentrations of arsenic in drinking water (less than 50 μg/L in water, 38 μg/L in urine), the concentration in hair was 0.4 μg/g, on average. Thus, the concentrations in hair varied by a factor of 14 at similar concentrations in urine. Apparently, arsenic was bound to the hair during washing with the arsenic-rich water. As discussed in Chapter 3, methods for cleaning hair and nails externally contaminated by arsenic have been proposed. It is not clear whether such procedures can remove the arsenic that is bound to the surface of hair and nails as a result of contact with arsenic in the water. Experimental absorption and desorption experiments have shown that the amount of externally deposited arsenic removed from hair by various washing protocols is variable and virtually always incomplete (Smith 1964; Atalla et al. 1965; Bate 1966; Maes and Pate 1977; Van den Berg et al. 1968). Moreover, attempts to remove externally deposited arsenic by washing may result in removal of arsenic contained in the hair as a result of in vivo incorporation (Atalla et al. 1965; Van den Berg et al. 1968). In addition, the influence on the accumulation and external binding of arsenic by hair treatment (e.g., permanent waving and dying) is not known. Therefore, although the determination of arsenic concentrations in the hair might be useful for the detection of arsenic exposure, its use as an indicator of the degree of exposure to arsenic on an individual basis is limited.

Another problem with using hair arsenic concentrations as an indicator of absorbed dose of arsenic is related to the fact that the concentration of arsenic in the hair over the head of the same person might vary considerably (Cornelis 1973).

In people with no known exposure to arsenic, the concentration of arsenic in hair is generally 0.02-0.2 mg/kg (Valentine et al. 1979; Olguín et al. 1983; Narang et al. 1987; Takagi et al. 1988; Koons and Peters 1994; Wang et al. 1994; Wolfsperger et al. 1994; Vienna et al. 1995; Raie 1996; Paulsen et al. 1996; Rogers et al. 1997; Kurttio et al. 1998). The concentrations of arsenic in hair are clearly increased in people drinking water with high arsenic concentrations. For example, concentrations ranging from 3 to 10 mg/kg are reportedly common in people in areas in West Bengal that have high arsenic concentrations in drinking water (Das et al. 1995).

On a group basis, a few reports indicate that the correlation between the concentration of arsenic in drinking water and the concentration in hair is fairly good, although it is not known how much of the arsenic in hair originates from arsenic in blood and how much is bound due to external contact with the water, as discussed above. The range of reported relationships is significant. In studies carried out in California and Nevada, a concentration of 400 μg/L in drinking water corresponded to about 1.2 μg/g in hair, and 100 μg/L in water corresponded to about 0.5 μg/g in hair (Valentine et al. 1979). In Alaska, an average of 400 μg/L in drinking water corresponded to 3.3 μg/g in hair (Harrington et al. 1978). In Hungary, people with drinking-water concentrations ranging from 50 to 100 μg/L had an average hair concentration of 3 μg/g (Börzsönyi et al. 1992). The highest hair arsenic concentrations were found in children. In Canada, 50% of 86 individuals using well water with arsenic concentrations above 50 μg/L had hair arsenic concentrations above 1 μg/g (Grantham and Jones 1977). Of the 33 people using wells with arsenic concentrations above 100 μg/L, 94% had hair concentrations above 1 μg/g.

Data on arsenic in nails are sparse, but normal values appear to range from 0.02 to 0.5 μg/g (Narang et al. 1987; Takagi et al. 1988). Several tens of micrograms per gram have been reported in cases of chronic poisoning (Pounds et al. 1979; Das et al. 1995). A single dose of arsenic can be detected at the distal tip of the nails about 100 days after exposure (Pounds et al. 1979; Pirl et al. 1983). Presumably, arsenic is deposited in the nail roots from the blood and then migrates distally as the nails grow (at about 0.12 mm a day). As with hair, external contamination can increase the arsenic concentrations in nails.

SUMMARY AND CONCLUSIONS

Arsenic exposure via drinking water is often estimated from the concentrations in the drinking water, sometimes in combination with information on the consumed amounts of water via drinking and food preparation. The latter measurement might include marked uncertainties, especially concerning individual data, depending on the method used. The concentration of arsenic metabolites (inorganic arsenic, MMA, and DMA) in urine reflects the absorbed amount of inorganic arsenic and serves as a useful measurement of an individual's recent (previous day) or ongoing exposure (e.g., via drinking water). Total urinary arsenic is a less useful biomarker of exposure to inorganic arsenic, unless ingestion of certain foods, especially those of marine origin, can be excluded. Ingestion of such foods can result in a rapid increase in the concentration of total arsenic in the urine, and even small amounts of seafood can invalidate total urinary arsenic as an indicator of exposure to inorganic arsenic. Certain seafood, especially seaweed and mussels, might increase in the concentration of DMA in urine. If such exposure is common, the people under study should be asked to refrain from eating such food at least 5 days before urine sampling. This is particularly important if the exposure to inorganic arsenic is low.

Because of the variations in the proportions of different arsenic metabolites in urine, the concentration of the sum of the metabolites is a better indicator of exposure than is the concentration of inorganic arsenic or DMA in urine. The exact reasons for the variations are largely unknown, but probably are influenced by age, sex, health status, genetic factors, and analytical variability.

Few reports have been published on urinary concentrations of arsenic metabolites in populations living in the Unites States.

In the case of continuous exposure to arsenic, there is an association between the absorbed dose and the concentration in blood. Because intake of food containing organic arsenic compounds of marine origin might cause a substantial increase in the concentration of arsenic in blood and because it is difficult to speciate arsenic in this matrix, blood is not a useful biomarker of exposure to inorganic arsenic. In addition, because of the lower concentrations in blood compared with urine, blood arsenic is less sensitive as a biomarker of exposure. Also, the half-time of arsenic in blood is in the order of a few hours compared with a few days in urine. Thus, the time between the last exposure and the sampling can affect the results.

Arsenic concentrations in hair and nails have often been used as indicators of exposure to inorganic arsenic. Arsenic externally deposited onto hair and nails cannot be consistently removed by washing methods nor distinguished from arsenic present as a result of internal incorporation. Therefore, measurement of arsenic in hair and nails will have very limited use as a quantitative biomarker of internal exposure unless the potential for external exposure can be definitively excluded. Speciation is of less importance because the major forms of organic arsenic compounds in food (i.e., arsenobetaine, arsenocholine, and arsenosugars) are not accumulated in hair or nails. In the case of acute exposure to arsenic, an advantage of the hair biomarker is that the time of exposure can be estimated by determining the arsenic concentrations along the length of a hair strand. The main disadvantage of using hair and nails as biomarkers of arsenic exposure is that it is difficult to distinguish between arsenic incorporated into the hair and nail from the systemic circulation and that bound externally (e.g., when washing with water containing arsenic). In addition to water, arsenic in dust can also contaminate hair externally. Thus, arsenic concentrations in hair and nails can be used as markers of exposure rather than markers of absorbed dose. The variation in accumulation in hair and nails between individuals is unknown.

RECOMMENDATIONS

More data are needed that tie biomarkers of absorbed dose (especially urinary concentrations of arsenic metabolites) to arsenic exposure concentrations, tissue concentrations, and the clinical evidence of arsenic toxicity. Data are particularly lacking for people living in different parts of the United States.

The relationship between arsenic in urine and arsenic in whole blood or serum needs to be clarified as well as between those biomarkers and arsenic in hair and nails, taking into consideration the possibility of external contamination.

REFERENCES

Andrén P., A. Schütz, M. Vahter, R. Attewell, L. Johansson, S. Willers, and S. Skerfving. 1988. Environmental exposure to lead and arsenic among children living near a glassworks. Sci. Total Environ. 77:25-34.

Apel, M., and M. Stoeppler. 1983. Speciation of arsenic in urine of occupationally non-exposed persons. Pp. 517-520 in International Conference Heavy Metals in the Environment, Heidelberg- September 1983. Vol. 1. Edingburgh: CEP Consultants

Arbouine, M.W., and H.K. Wilson. 1992. The effect of seafood consumption on the assessment of occupational exposure to arsenic by urinary arsenic speciation measurements. J. Trace Elem. Electrolytes Health Dis. 6:153-160.

Atalla, L.T., C.M. Silva, F.W. Lima. 1965. Activation analysis of arsenic in human hair—Some observations on the problems of external contamination. Ann. Acad. Brasil. Cien. 37:432-441.

Bate, L.C. 1966. Adsorption and elution of trace elements on human hair. Int. J. Appl. Radiat. Isot. 17:417-423.

Bencko, V., and K. Symon. 1977. Health aspects of burning coal with a high arsenic content: Arsenic in hair, urine, and blood in children residing in a polluted area. Environ. Res. 13:378-385.

Biggs, M.L., D.A. Kalman, L.E. Moore, C. Hopenhayn-Rich, M.T. Smith, and A.H. Smith. 1997. Relationship of urinary arsenic to intake estimates and a biomarker of effect, bladder cell micronuclei. Mutat. Res. 386:185-195.

Binder, S., D. Forney, W. Kaye, and D. Paschal. 1987. Arsenic exposure in children living near a former copper smelter. Bull. Environ. Contam. Toxicol. 39:114-121.

Bingham, S., and J.H. Cummings. 1983. The use of 4-aminobenzoic acid as a marker to validate the completeness of 24 h urine collection in man. Clin. Sci. 64:629-635.

Blekastad, V., J. Jonsen, E. Steinnes, and K. Helgeland. 1984. Concentrations of trace elements in human blood serum from different places in Norway determined by neutron activation analysis. Acta Med. Scand. 216:25-29.

Börzsönyi, M., A. Berecsky, P. Rudnai, M. Csanady, and A. Horvath. 1992. Epidemiological studies on human subjects exposed to arsenic in drinking water in southeast Hungary. Arch. Toxicol. 66:77-78.

Buchet, J.P., R. Lauwerys, and H. Roels. 1981. Comparison of the urinary excretion of arsenic metabolites after a single dose of sodium arsenite, monomethylarsonate or dimethylarsinate in man. Int. Arch. Occup. Environ. Health 48:71-79.

Buchet, J.P., J. Pauwels, and R. Lauwerys. 1994. Assessment of exposure to inorganic arsenic following ingestion of marine organisms by volunteers. Environ. Res. 66:44-51.

Buchet, J.P., J. Staessen, H. Roels, R. Lauwerys, and R. Fagard. 1996. Geographical and temporal differences in the urinary excretion of inorganic arsenic: A Belgian population study. Occup. Environ. Med. 53:320-327.

Cant, S.M., and L.A. Legendre. 1982. Assessment of occupational exposure to arsenic, copper, and lead in a western copper smelter. Am. Ind. Hyg. Assoc. J. 43:223-226.

Chiou H.Y., Y.M. Hsueh, L.L. Hsieh, L.I. Hsu, Y.H. Hsu, F.I. Hsieh, M.L. Wei, H.C. Chen, H.T. Yang, L.C. Leu, T.H. Chu, C. Chen-Wu, M.H. Yang, and C.J. Chen. 1997. Arsenic methylation capacity, body retention, and null genotypes of glutathione S-transferase M1 and T1 among current arsenic-exposed residents in Taiwan. Mutat. Res. 386:197-207.

Concha, G., B. Nermell, and M. Vahter. 1998a. Metabolism of inorganic arsenic in children with chronic high arsenic exposure in northern Argentina. Environ. Health Perspect. 106:355-359.

Concha, G., G. Vogler, D. Lezeano, B. Nermell, and M. Vahter. 1998b. Exposure to inorganic arsenic metabolites during early human development. Toxicol. Sci.44:185-190.

Cornelis, R. 1973. Neutron activation analysis of hair, failure of a mission. J. Radioanal. Chem. 15:305-316.

Curry, A.S., and C.A. Pounds. 1977. Arsenic in hair. J. Forensic. Sci. Soc. 17:37-44.

Das, D., A. Chatterjee, B.K. Mandal, G. Samanta, D. Chakraborti, and B. Chanda. 1995. Arsenic in ground water in six districts of West Bengal, India: The biggest arsenic calamity in the world. Part 2. Arsenic concentration in drinking water, hair, nails, urine, skin-scale and liver tissue (biopsy) of the affected people. Analyst 120:917-924.

Diamond, G.L. 1988. Biological monitoring of urine for exposure to toxic metals. Pp. 515-529 in Biological Monitoring of Toxic Metals. T.W. Clarkson, L. Friberg, G.F. Nordberg, and P.R. Sager. New York: Plenum.

Foà, V., A. Colombi, M. Maroni, M. Buratti, and G. Calzaferri. 1984. The speciation of the chemical forms of arsenic in the biological monitoring of exposure to inorganic arsenic. Sci. Total Environ. 34:241-259.

Gottlieb, K., J.R. Koehler, and J. Tessari. 1993. Non-analytic problems in detecting arsenic and cadmium in children living near a cadmium refinery in Denver, Colorado. J. Exp. Anal. Environ. Epidemiol. 3:139-153.

Grantham, D.A., and J.F. Jones. 1977. Arsenic contamination of water wells in Nova Scotia. J. Am. Water Works Assoc. 69(12):653-657.

Hakala, E., and L. Pyy. 1992. Selective determination of toxicologically important arsenic species in urine by high-performance liquid chromatography–hydride generation atomic absorption spectrometry. J. Anal. At. Spectrom. 7:191-196.

Hakala, E., and L. Pyy. 1995. Assessment of exposure to inorganic arsenic by determining the arsenic species excreted in urine. Toxicol. Lett. 77:249-258.

Hamilton, E.I., E. Sabbioni, and M.T. van der Venne. 1994. Element reference values in tissues from inhabitants of the European community. IV. Review of elements in blood plasma and urine and a critical evaluation of reference values for the United Kingdom population. Sci. Total Environ. 158:165-190.

Harrington, J.M., J.P. Middaugh, D.L. Morse, and J. Housworth. 1978. A survey of a population exposed to high concentrations of arsenic in well water in Fairbanks, Alaska. Am. J. Epidemiol. 108:377-385.

Heydorn, K. 1970. Environmental variation of arsenic levels in human blood determined by neutron activation analysis. Clin. Chim. Acta 28:349-357.

Hopps, H.C. 1977. The biological bases for using hair and nail for analyses of trace elements. Sci. Total Environ. 7:71-89.

Hostýnek, J.J., R.S. Hinz, C.R. Lorence, M. Price, and R.H. Guy. 1993. Metals and the skin. Crit. Rev. Toxicol. 23:171-235.

Jensen G.E., J. M. Christensen, and O.M. Poulsen. 1991. Occupational and environmental exposure to arsenic—Increased urinary arsenic level in children. Sci. Total Environ. 107:169-177.

Johansson, G, A. Åkesson, M. Berglund, B. Nermell, and M. Vahter. 1998. Validation with biological markers for food intake of a dietary assessment method used by Swedish women with three different dietary preferences. Public Health Nutr. 1(3):199-206.

Kagey, B.T., J.E. Bumgarner, and J.P. Creason. 1977. Arsenic levels in maternal-fetal tissue sets. Pp. 252-256 in Trace Substances in Environmental Health—XI, Proceedings of the University of Missouri's 11th Annual Conference on Trace Substances in Environmental Health, D.D. Hemphill, ed. Columbia, Mo.: University of Missouri Press.

Kalman, D.A., J. Hughes, G. van Belle, T. Burbacher, D. Bolgiano, K. Coble, N.K. Mottet, and L. Polissar. 1990. The effect of variable environmental arsenic contamination on urinary concentrations of arsenic species. Environ. Health Perspect. 89:145-152.

Kavanagh, P., M.E. Farago, I. Thornton, W. Goessler, D. Kuehnelt, C. Schlagenhaufen, and K.J.. Irgolic. 1998. Urinary arsenic species in Devon and Cornwall residents, UK. A pilot study. Analyst 123:27-29.

Koons, R.D., and C.A. Peters. 1994. Axial distribution of arsenic in individual human hairs by solid sampling graphite furnace AAS. J. Anal. Toxicol. 18:36-40.

Kristiansen J., J.M. Christensen, B.S. Iversen, and E. Sabbioni. 1997. Toxic trace element reference levels in blood and urine: influence of gender and life-style factors. Sci. Total Environ. 204:147-160.

Kurttio, P., H. Komulainen, E. Hakala, H. Kahelin, and J. Pekkanen. 1998. Urinary excretion of arsenic species after exposure to arsenic present in drinking water. Arch. Environ. Contam. Toxicol. 34:297-305.

Larsen, E.H., G. Pritzl, and S.H. Hansen. 1993. Speciation of eight arsenic compounds in human urine by high-performance liquid chromatography with inductively coupled plasma mass spectrometric detection using antimonate for internal chromatographic standardization. J. Anal. Atomic. Spectr. 8:557-563.

Le, X.C., W.R. Cullen, and K.J. Reimer 1994. Human urinary arsenic excretion after one-time ingestion of seaweed, crab, and shrimp. Clin. Chem. 40:617-624.

Ma, M., and X.C. Le. 1998. Effects of arsenosugar ingestion on urinary arsenic speciation. Clin. Chem. 44:539-550.

Maes, D., and D.B. Pate. 1977. The absorption of arsenic into single human head hairs. J. Forensic Sci. 22:89-94.

Mohri, T., A. Hisanaga, and N. Ishinishi. 1990. Arsenic intake and excretion by Japanese adults: A 7-day duplicate diet study. Food Chem. Toxicol. 28:521-529.

Morse, D.L., J.M. Harrington, J. Housworth, P.J. Landrigan and A. Kelter. 1979. Arsenic exposure in multiple environmental media in children near a smelter. Clin. Toxicol. 14:389-399.

Mürer, A.J.L., A. Abildtrup, O.M. Poulsen, and J.M. Christensen. 1992. Effect of seafood consumption on the urinary level of total hydride-generating arsenic compounds. Instability of arsenobetaine and arsenocholine. Analyst 117:677-680.

Narang, A.P.S., L.S. Chawla, and S.B. Khurana. 1987. Levels of arsenic in Indian opium eaters. Drug Alcohol Depend. 20:149-153.

Norin, H., and M. Vahter. 1981. A rapid method for the selective analysis of total urinary metabolites of inorganic arsenic. Scand. J. Work Environ. Health 7:38-44.

Offergelt, J.A., H. Roels, J.P. Buchet, M. Boeckx, and R. Lauwerys. 1992. Relation between airborne arsenic trioxide and urinary excretion of inorganic arsenic and its methylated metabolites. Br. J. Ind. Med. 49:387-393.

Olguín, A., P. Jauge, M. Cebrián, and A. Albores. 1983. Arsenic levels in blood, urine, hair, and nails from a chronically exposed human population. Proc. West. Pharmacol. Soc. 26:175-177.

Paulsen, F., S. Mai, U. Zellmer, and C. Alsen-Hinrichs. 1996. Blood and hair arsenic, lead and cadmium analysis of adults and correlation analysis with special referene to eating habits and other behavioral influences [in German]. Gesundheitswesen 58:459-464.

Pirl, J.N., G.F. Townsend, A.K. Valaitis, D. Grohlich, and J.J. Spikes. 1983. Death by arsenic: A comparative evaluation of exhumed body tissues in the presence of external contamination. J. Anal. Toxicol. 7:216-219.

Poklis, A., and J.J. Saady. 1990. Arsenic poisoning: Acute or chronic? Suicide or murder? Am. J. Forensic Med. Pathol. 11:226-232.

Pollisar, L., K. Lowry-Coble, D.A. Kalman, J.P. Hughes, G. Van Belle, D.S. Covert, T.M. Burbacher, D. Bolgiano, and N.K. Mottet. 1990. Pathways of human exposure to arsenic in a community surrounding a copper smelter. Environ. Res. 53:29-47.

Pounds, C.A., E.F. Pearson, and T.D. Turner. 1979. Arsenic in fingernails. J. Forensic Sci. Soc. J. 19:165-174.

Raie, R.M. 1996. Regional variation in As, Cu, Hg, and Se and interaction between them. Ecotoxicol. Environ. Safety 35:248-252.

Rogers, C.E., A.V. Tomita, P.R. Trowbridge, J.K. Gone, J. Chen, P. Zeeb, H.F. Hemond, W.G. Thilly, I. Olmez and J.L. Durant. 1997. Hair analysis does not support hypothesized arsenic and chromium exposure from drinking water in Woburn, Massachusetts. Environ. Health Perspect. 105:1090-1097.

Smith, H. 1964. The interpretation of the arsenic content of human hair. J. Forensic Sci. Soc. 240:192-199.

Smith, T.J., E.A. Crecelius, and J.C. Reading. 1977. Airborne arsenic exposure and excretion of methylated arsenic compounds. Environ. Health Perspect. 19:89-93.

Takagi, Y., S. Matsuda, S. Imai, Y. Ohmori, T. Masuda, J.A. Vinson, M.C. Mehra, B.K. Puri, and A. Kaniewski. 1988. Survey of trace elements in human nails: An international comparison. Bull. Environ. Contam. Toxicol. 41:690-695.

Toribara, T.Y., D.A. Jackson, W.R. French, A.C. Thompson, and J.M. Jaklevic. 1982. Nondestructive x-ray fluorescence spectrometry for determination of trace elements along a single strand of hair. Anal. Chem. 54:1844-1849.

Trepka, M.J., J. Heinrich, C. Schulz, C. Krause, M. Popescu, M. Wjst, and H.E. Wichmann. 1996. Arsenic burden among children in industrial areas of eastern Germany. Sci. Total Environ. 180:95-105.

Vahter, M. 1994. Species differences in the metabolism of arsenic compounds. Appl. Organomet. Chem. 8:175-182.

Vahter, M., and B. Lind. 1986. Concentrations of arsenic in urine of the general population in Sweden. Sci. Total Environ. 54:1-12.

Vahter, M., E. Marafante, and L. Dencker. 1983. Metabolism of arsenobetaine in mice, rats and rabbits. Sci. Total Environ. 30:197-211.

Vahter, M., E. Marafante, and L. Dencker. 1984. Tissue distribution and retention of [74]As-dimethylarsinic acid in mice and rats. Arch. Environ. Contam. Toxicol. 13:259-264.

Vahter, M., L. Friberg, B. Rahnster, Å. Nygren, and P. Nolinder. 1986. Airborne arsenic and urinary excretion of metabolites of inorganic arsenic among smelter workers. Int. Arch. Occup. Environ. Health 57:79-91.

Vahter, M., G. Concha, B. Nermell, R. Nilsson, F. Dulout, and A.T. Natarajan. 1995. A unique metabolism of inorganic arsenic in native Andean women. Eur. J. Pharmacol. 293:455-462.

Valentine, J.L., H.K. Kang, and G. Spivey. 1979. ,Arsenic levels in human blood, urine, and hair in response to exposure via drinking water. Environ. Res. 20:24-32.

Valkonen, S., A. Aitio, and J. Jarvisalo. 1983. Urinary arsenic in a Finnish population without occupational exposure to arsenic. Pp. 611-621 in Trace Element Analytical Chemistry in Medicine and Biology, Vol. 2, P. Brätter and P. Schramel, eds. Berlin: de Gruyter.

Van den Berg, A.J., J.J.M. de Goeij, J.P.W. Houtman and M.C. Zegers. 1968. Arsenic content of human hair after washing as determined by activation analysis. Mod. Trends Act. Anal. 1:272-282.

Versieck, J. 1985. Trace elements in human body fluids and tissues. Crit. Rev. Clin. Lab. Sci. 22:97-184.

Versieck, J., and L. Vanballenberghe. 1985. Determination of arsenic and cadmium in human blood serum and packed cells. Pp. 650-652 in Trace Element Metabolism in Man and Animals, TEMA 5, C.F. Mills, I. Bremmer, and J.K. Chesters, eds. Commonwealth Agricultural Bureau, Aberdeen, Australia.

Vienna, A., E. Capucci, M. Wolfsperger, and G. Hauser. 1995. Heavy metals in hair of students in Rome. Anthrop. Anz. 53:27-32.

Wang, C.T., W.T. Chang, C.W. Huang, S.S. Chou, C.T. Lin, S.J. Liau, and R.T. Wang. 1994. Studies on the concentrations of arsenic, selenium, copper, zinc, and iron in the hair of blackfoot disease patients in different clinical stages. Eur. J. Clin. Chem. Clin. Biochem. 32(3):107-111.

Wolfsperger, M., G. Hauser, W. Gössler, and C. Schlagenhaufen. 1994. Heavy metals in human hair samples from Austria and Italy: Influence of sex and smoking habits. Sci. Total Environ. 156:235-242.

Yager, J.W., J.B. Hicks, and E. Fabianova. 1997. Airborne arsenic and urinary excretion of arsenic metabolites during boiler cleaning operations in a Slovak coal-fired power plant. Environ. Health Perspect. 105:836-842.

Yamato, N. 1988. Concentrations and chemical species of arsenic in human urine and hair. Bull. Environ. Contam. Toxicol. 40:633-640.

Yamauchi, H., and Y. Yamamura. 1979. Dynamic change of inorganic arsenic and methylarsenic compounds in human urine after oral intake as arsenic trioxide. Ind. Health 17: 79-83.

Yamauchi, H., and Y. Yamamura. 1983. Concentration and chemical species of arsenic in human tissue. Bull. Environ. Contam. Toxicol. 31:267-270.

Yamauchi, H., K. Takahashi, and Y. Yamamura. 1989. Metabolism and excretion of orally and intraperitoneally administered trimethylarsine oxide in the hamster. Toxicol. Environ. Chem. 22:69-76.

Yamauchi, H., K. Takahashi, M. Mashiko, J. Saitoh, and Y. Yamamura. 1992. Intake of different chemical species of dietary arsenic by Japanese, and their blood and urinary arsenic levels. Appl. Organomet. Chem. 6:383-388.

Zhang, X., R. Cornelis, J. De Kimpe, L. Mees, V. Vanderbiesen, A. De Cubber, and R. Vanholder. 1996. Accumulation of arsenic species in serum of patients with chronic renal disease. Clin. Chem. 42:1231-1237.

7

Mechanisms of Toxicity

IN this chapter, the subcommittee summarizes what is known about the mechanisms of toxicity for arsenic. The chapter is divided into two major sections—cancer and noncancer effects. In the cancer section, the subcommittee summarizes results from in vivo and in vitro bioassays designed to investigate the role of arsenic and metabolites of arsenic, monomethylarsonic acid (MMA) and dimethylarsinic acid (DMA), as tumor promoters and initiators. That summary is followed by a discussion of the data on modes of action for arsenic-induced carcinogenesis and how those data can help delineate the slope of the dose-response curve at low exposure concentrations. In the noncancer section, the subcommittee summarizes what is known about the mechanisms of action leading to noncancer effects. The potential relationships between mechanisms of arsenic-induced cell injury or cell death and carcinogenic processes are discussed with particular attention to the inter-relationships between arsenic-induced formation of reactive oxygen species or oxidative stress and chromosomal damage in target-cell populations. The roles of other documented arsenic-induced cellular responses, such as alterations in the heme biosynthetic pathway, alterations in cellular gene expression, and inhibition of DNA-repair enzyme activities, are discussed as components of the broad spectrum of cellular responses to arsenic exposure.

CANCER EFFECTS

Results from Bioassays

Inorganic Arsenic

In general, long-term studies on the carcinogenicity of arsenic in laboratory animals have yielded negative results. In one of the more extensive studies, which was carried out by the FDA, rats were administered sodium arsenite at concentrations up to 250 ppm or sodium arsenate at concentrations up to 400 ppm in the diet for 2 years. No increases in tumors were observed (Byron et al. 1967). A similar negative finding was noted in beagles maintained on diets containing sodium arsenate or sodium arsenite at 5-125 ppm for 2 years; however, the high dose proved to be lethal (Byron et al. 1967). In another study, rats were administered lead arsenite at concentrations of 463 or 1,850 ppm (arsenic at approximately 400 ppm) or sodium arsenite at a concentration of 416 ppm in the diet (based on body weight and food consumption data, equivalent to approximately 18-20 mg/kg of body weight per day) for 29 months with some indication of toxicity, but no increase in tumorigenicity when compared with controls (Kroes et al. 1974). In a study of 20 *Cynomolgus* monkeys, arsenic was administered by mouth as sodium arsenate at a dose of 0.1 mg/kg per day, 5 days per week, for 15 years. None of the animals developed malignant tumors (Thorgeirsson et al. 1994).

Animal studies on the carcinogenicity of arsenic administered via drinking water have also been conducted. In rats, sodium arsenite administered at a concentration of 5 mg/L for a lifetime did not cause an increase in tumors (Schroeder et al. 1968). The authors calculated that the concentration was equivalent to a dose of 0.38 mg/kg of body weight per day. Although some evidence of arsenic accumulation was found in the animals, it had no effect on survival (Schroeder et al. 1968). In a similar study, rats received sodium arsenate at a concentration of 5 mg/L (approximately 350 μg/kg of body weight per day) for a lifetime and had no indication of tumorigenicity (Kanisawa and Schroeder 1969). In a shorter study examining the effect of arsenic on mammary tumors, Schrauzer and Ishmael (1974) administered sodium arsenite to mice at 10 mg/L in drinking water for 16 weeks. The incidence of mammary tumors was lower in the tested animals (27%) than in the controls (82%). However, they found that arsenic increased the size of spontaneous mammary tumors. In a study, which has not yet been peer reviewed and is available only in abstract form, Ng et al. (1998) reported preliminary results indicating that the administration of sodium arsenate in drinking water (0.500 mg/L) to C57Bl/6J and metallothionein knock-out mice for up to 26 months caused tumors of the gastrointestinal tract, lungs, liver, spleen, bone, skin, reproductive system, and eye. No tumors were observed in the control groups of the study.

Several animal studies have examined the interaction of arsenic with other chemicals to determine if it might be acting as a promoter rather than as an initiator of tumors. Baroni et al. (1963) administered arsenic trioxide as a 0.01% solution in drinking water or sodium arsenate by skin application (two drops of a solution of 15.8 g/L twice weekly) to mice. Each of these treatments was tested in combination with skin application of croton oil (to test for promoting action), and after initiation with a single topical application of 7,12-dimethylbenz[a]anthracene or with administration of ethyl carbamate by intubation (to test for promoting action). There was no indication that either arsenic trioxide or sodium arsenate was acting as an initiator or promoter.

Kroes et al. (1974) found that the administration of arsenic in the diet of rats (lead arsenate at 463 ppm or sodium arsenate at 416 ppm) for 29 months did not enhance the carcinogenicity of diethylnitrosamine (DENA) (5 μg per day administered by intubation 5 days per week). When three strains of mice were administered arsenic trioxide (0.01%) in their drinking water for 8 weeks and then subjected to topical application of methylcholanthrene, arsenic decreased the number of papillomas produced in CxC3H mice (Milner 1969). When arsenic trioxide was administered at 2 ppm in the drinking water of mice for a lifetime with or without selenium at 2 ppm, arsenic alone caused no increase in the incidence of mammary tumors, but some increase occurred in the growth and multiplicity of the tumors (Schrauzer et al. 1978). Selenium was protective in that the incidence of mammary tumors in the group given selenium alone was significantly lower than the control group. However, no protection was observed when selenium was administered with arsenic because the incidence of mammary tumors increased in the co-exposed group compared with the control group.

Shirachi et al. (1983) administered sodium arsenite at a maximum tolerated dose of 160 ppm in drinking water to partially hepatectomized rats with or without a single dose of diethylnitrosamine (30 mg/kg of body weight intraperitoneally). Although 1 of 7 rats administered DENA without arsenic developed kidney tumors at the end of 25 weeks, 7 of 10 administered DENA with arsenic developed kidney tumors, suggesting that arsenic acted as a promoter. In a statistical reanalysis of the data, Smith et al. (1992) concluded that even in rats administered arsenic without DENA, liver and kidney tumors increased for all three forms of arsenic—arsenite, arsenate, and DMA.

Starting with newborn mice, Laib and Moritz (1989) administered sodium arsenite (2 mg/kg per day) or sodium arsenate (20 mg/kg per day) 5 days per week for 3 weeks with or without DENA (2 mg/kg) and found an increase in ATPase-deficient foci in the livers of the mice given arsenite with DENA when compared with the mice given DENA alone or arsenate with DENA, suggesting a cocarcinogenic effect of the arsenite but not the arsenate.

Monomethylarsonic Acid (MMA)

In a study submitted to the EPA Office of Pesticides Program, male and female Sprague-Dawley rats were fed MMA in the diet at concentrations of 0, 25, 50, 100, and 200 ppm for 2 years. There was an increase in thyroid tumors in the males but only at the highest dose (EPA 1981). In another report, when Fischer 344 (F344) rats were fed MMA at concentrations of 0, 50, 400, and 1,300 ppm (equivalent to 0, 3.2, 27, and 93 mg/g per day for the males and 0, 3.8, 33, and 101 mg/kg per day for the females) for 2 years, there was a suggestion of an increased incidence of parathyroid gland adenomas at 400 and 1,300 ppm in the male rats and in the females at 1,300 ppm, but the statistical significance depended upon the test used (EPA 1992a).

Another study showed no evidence of carcinogenicity in male and female B6C3F$_1$ mice fed MMA in the diet at concentrations of 0, 10, 50, 200, and 400 ppm (equivalent to 0, 1.8, 9.3, 38, and 83 mg/kg per day for the males and 0, 2.2, 12, 46, and 104 mg/kg per day for the females) for 2 years (EPA 1992b).

Dimethylarsinic Acid (DMA)

The arsenic metabolite DMA, which is the herbicide cacodylic acid, has been tested for its effects in vivo and in vitro. In studies on the tumorigenicity of DMA, Innes et al. (1969) found no evidence of tumorigenicity after administering DMA orally to two strains of mice at a daily dose of 46.4 mg/kg of body weight (maximum tolerated dose) for 18 months.

In a study for EPA (1992c), male and female F344 rats were fed DMA at concentrations of 0, 2, 10, 40, and 100 ppm in the diet (equivalent to 0, 0.14, 0.73, 2.8, and 7.3 mg/kg per day for the males and 0, 0.16, 0.79, 3.2, and 8.0 mg/kg per day for the females) for 2 years. The results showed a carcinogenic response as evidenced by increases in transitional-cell papillomas and carcinomas at the highest dose in both sexes. In the bladder, urinary transitional-cell hyperplasia and vacuolar degeneration occurred in a dose-related manner at the concentrations of 40 and 100 ppm. The study was judged to be minimally acceptable by EPA (1992c, 1993).

When male and female B6C3F$_1$ mice were fed DMA at concentrations of 0, 8, 40, 200, and 500 ppm for 2 years, vacuolar degeneration of the urinary bladder transitional epithelium increased at 200 and 500 ppm in both sexes. There were no increases in urinary bladder tumors. This submitted study was judged by EPA to be inadequate because it was decided that higher doses of DMA could have been used (EPA 1991, 1992d).

As reported in the Integrated Risk Information System (IRIS) of EPA, cacodylic acid (DMA) is classified as D—not classifiable as to human carcinogenicity. The basis for this classification by the agency is that there are "no human data and inadequate data in animals" (EPA 1998).

In a complex study by Yamamoto et al. (1995), rats were administered DENA, *N*-methyl-*N*-nitrosourea, 1,2-dimethylhydrazine, *N*-butyl-*N*-(4-hydroxybutyl)nitrosamine and *N*-bis(2-hydroxypropyl)nitrosamine and were given DMA in drinking water at concentrations of up to 400 ppm for 30 weeks. DMA alone was without effect, but in the five-carcinogen test group, it significantly enhanced the formation of tumors of the urinary bladder, kidney, liver, and thyroid gland and increased preneoplastic lesions in the liver. In a study by Yamanaka et al. (1996), DMA was administered at concentrations of 200 or 400 ppm in the drinking water of ddY mice for 25 weeks following initiation with 4-nitroquinoline 1-oxide (4NQO). DMA alone was without effect, but DMA at 400 ppm administered with 4NQO increased the number of lung tumors per animal when compared with 4NQO administered alone. In a further study, rats were administered *N*-(4-hydroxybutyl)-nitrosamine for 4 weeks and then given DMA at 0, 2, 10, 25, 50, and 100 ppm in drinking water for 32 weeks (Wanibuchi et al. 1996). Again, no neoplastic lesions were observed in rats administered DMA alone. Urinary bladder tumors increased in rats given *N*-(4-hydroxybutyl)nitrosamine followed by DMA at 10 ppm or higher. The 5-bromo-2'-deoxyuridine labeling index also increased. Collectively, the studies suggest that DMA is not an initiator, but it might be a promoter.

Yamanaka et al. (1989) found that DMA administered orally at 1,500 mg/kg caused DNA strand breaks in mouse lung. That dose is extremely high. In fact, it exceeds the LD_{50} (the lethal dose for 50% of the test animals) of 1,200 mg/kg of body weight in mice reported by other investigators (Kaise et al. 1989). Similarly, incubation of human lung cells (L-132) with 10 mM of DMA for 10 hr caused single-strand breaks (Tezuka et al. 1993). Cross-linking between DMA and nuclear proteins was also observed when L-132 was incubated with 10 mM of DMA (Yamanaka et al. 1993). The investigators have suggested that those effects might be related to the formation of active oxygen species (Yamanaka et al. 1991; Rin et al. 1995). Other investigators have shown that DMA in vitro at concentrations ranging from 62.5 to 250 mg/L induces tetraploids in Chinese hamster cells in a concentration-dependent manner (Endo et al. 1992).

Relevance of Findings of Bioassays to Humans

The findings of the rodent bioassays for inorganic arsenic are generally uniformly negative. Given the unquestionable oncogenic activity of inorganic arsenic in humans, it would at first appear that these studies are of no value in helping to elucidate the carcinogenic mode of action of arsenic. However, in line with the evidence suggested in the sections that follow, such negative data may be supportive of a non-genotoxic mode of action. Certainly if arsenic were a direct and genotoxic carcinogen, one would expect to find positive results in at least one of these assays. The fact that there are species differences with rodents being resistant suggests that understanding the reason for this difference may shed some light on the mode of action.

The very high doses of DMA used in animal bioassays in vivo bring into question whether the low arsenic concentrations in human exposures exert their tumor-promoting effects via the metabolite DMA. At low exposure concentrations, humans would not metabolize arsenic to DMA at the concentrations needed to promote the tumor production observed in the animal studies. Compared with inorganic arsenic, the DMA formed would also be expected to be excreted rapidly (see Chapter 5). In addition, as discussed below (see Mode of Action for Carcinogenicity), in vitro studies suggest that arsenite is orders of magnitude more potent than DMA in the induction of chromatid breaks and gaps in cultured human fibroblasts (Oya-Ohta et al. 1996). Recent studies by M.M. Moore et al. (1997) also compared the relative potentials of sodium arsenite, sodium arsenate, MMA, and DMA for mutagenic and clastogenic activities by using the L5178Y/TK$^{+/-}$ mouse lymphoma assay and found the organic arsenicals to be orders of magnitude less potent in producing genotoxicity.

Mode of Action

For the purposes of cancer risk assessment, it is important to distinguish between genotoxicity and mutagenicity when discussing mechanisms underlying the formation of tumors. Genotoxicity is the broader term that also encompasses cellular effects that are not themselves heritable. Those effects include DNA and protein adducts, sister chromatid exchanges (SCEs) and unscheduled DNA synthesis. In addition, abnormalities in DNA methylation, although not strictly a genotoxic effect, also could be included as a form of potentially reversible DNA modification. Mutagenicity specifically describes the production of changes in DNA that can be transmitted from generation to generation (for organisms and cells). Cancer is a genetic disease that requires the accumulation of mutations in several genes (most notably, oncogenes and tumor-suppressor genes) in a single cell to progress to a tumor. Thus, mutations, either directly or indirectly produced by a chemical, are the most pertinent indicator of the potential for carcinogenicity. The spectrum of mutational classes, their frequencies, and their mechanisms of formation are all important in establishing the nature of the dose response for tumors induced by a particular chemical of interest at exposure concentrations below those for which tumor data can be obtained. These various aspects of mutagenicity for arsenicals are discussed in this section in the context of arsenic-induced carcinogenicity.

To characterize dose-response relationships, it is also appropriate to distinguish between mode of action and mechanism of action. It is much more feasible to establish a mode of action, because the only requirement is identifying the necessary (but not sufficient) steps whereby a particular agent causes tumor development. In contrast, the requirements for understanding the mechanism of action whereby an agent induces a tumor are identifying the necessary steps and characterizing their specific nature (e.g., the specific genes involved). Thus, considerable research efforts are required to move from a mode of action to a mechanism of action for tumor induction. The present state of knowledge for arsenic clearly necessitates that the mode of action be considered.

Genotoxic Effects Induced by Arsenic Compounds

Mutational Spectrum

Genetic alterations induced in cells by chemicals can be of several different types. Broadly these are point mutations that involve alterations of a single base pair in the DNA, chromosomal alterations that include deletions within a chromosome arm, interchanges between two chromosomes and losses or gains of whole chromosomes (aneuploidy).

Arsenic does not induce point mutations in bacterial or mammalian cells (Jacobson-Kram and Montalbano 1985). A recent report by M.M. Moore et al. (1997) showed that sodium arsenite and sodium arsenate induced mutations in L5178Y/TK$^{+/-}$ cells at concentrations of 1-2 μg/mL and 10-14 μg/mL, respectively. In contrast, the methylated metabolites MMA and DMA were mutagenic only at much higher concentrations, 2,500-5,000 μg/mL and almost 10,000 μg/mL, respectively. The organic arsenicals are much less mutagenic than the inorganic arsenicals. Of particular note for the present discussion, all four arsenicals induced deletion mutations and not point mutations at the TK locus.

Hei et al. (1998) showed that arsenic exposure induced deletion mutations of human chromosome 11 in a human–hamster hybrid cell. Analysis at the molecular level showed that all mutants had lost one or more markers and that the frequency of very large deletions increased with exposure concentration. Arsenicals produce a range of chromosomal alterations in mammalian cells in vitro, rodents in vivo, and humans exposed to relatively high concentrations of arsenic in drinking water. A discussion of many of these studies and their relevance to dose-response assessment can be found in Rudel et al. (1996) and in the comprehensive review by Rossman (1998).

In vivo and in vitro studies of rodents and humans have reported chromosomal aberrations, including the induction of micronuclei (Larramendy et al. 1981; IARC 1987; Jha et al. 1992; Warner et al. 1994; Dulout et al. 1996; Gonsebatt et al. 1997; L.E. Moore et al. 1996, 1997).

Arsenic-induced aneuploidy has also been demonstrated in vivo and in vitro in human lymphocytes and in exfoliated bladder cells but not consistently in buccal cells from exposed individuals (Gonsebatt et al. 1997; Warner et al. 1994; Vega et al. 1995; Dulout et al. 1996). SCEs have been induced in vitro, but evidence for their occurrence in exposed humans is equivocal (Nordenson et al. 1978; Larramendy et al. 1981; Lerda 1994; Rasmussen and Menzel 1997). The relative potency of arsenic compounds for clastogenicity in normal human fibroblasts in vitro is the following: (1) arsenite, (2) arsenate, and (3) DMA (Oya-Ohta et al. 1996). For example, more than 7 mM of DMA is required for clastogenicity, whereas only 0.8 μM of arsenite is needed to induce chromosomal alterations.

Comutagenicity

There are reports that arsenic potentiates the mutagenic effects of alkylating agents (Li and Rossman 1989a, 1991; Yang et al. 1992), UV radiation (Rossman 1981; Lee et al. 1985), X-rays and DNA cross-linking agents, 8-methoxypsoralen plus ultraviolet (UV) light and cis-platinum (Lee et al. 1986), and diepoxybutane (Wiencke and Yager 1992).

Plasmid shuttle vector experiments indicated marked potentiation of point mutagenesis by short-wave UV at a concentration of 1 μM of sodium arsenite, an exposure that itself did not affect the cell viability of normal human fibroblasts (Wiencke et al. 1997); arsenic's effects were largely attributed to enhancement of small and large deletions and rearrangements. The enhancement of genotoxicity that has been observed for clastogenic effects and point mutations has not been found for induced SCEs. Arsenite (5 μM) was found to enhance by sixfold the neoplastic transformation of C3H/10T/1/2 cells by bovine papilloma virus (Kowalski et al. 1996).

The role of these reported comutagenic effects on arsenic-induced carcinogenicity are as yet unclear given the somewhat artificial nature of the interactions studied. Further discussion is provided below on the influence of these comutagenic effects on DNA repair.

DNA Methylation

Methylation changes in genes or their control regions could result in altered gene expression and perhaps carcinogenesis (Baylin et al. 1998). Further, nonmutagenic carcinogens, such as arsenic, could be carcinogenic via this mechanism (Costa 1995). In an initial study to test that hypothesis, Mass and Wang (1997) showed that exposure of human lung adenocarcinoma A549 cells to sodium arsenite (0.08-2 μM) or sodium arsenate (30-300 μM) produced dose-responsive hypermethylation within a 341-base-pair fragment of the promoter of p53. In contrast, DMA (2-2,000 μM) did not produce hypermethylation. Some data suggested that such hypermethylation might be a genomic change and not just a region-specific methylation change (Mass and Wang 1997). However, other explanations can be found for the phenomenon described including the possibility of selection of cells that were hypermethylated before arsenic exposure.

Recently, Zhao et al. (1997) showed that chronic exposure to low concentrations of arsenic caused transformation of a rat liver epithelial cell line into one that was capable of causing tumors in nude mice. Hyperexpression of the metallothionein gene was also detected. The authors hypothesized that the methylation of arsenic by methyltransferases could cause a decrease in the S-adenosyl-methionine (SAM) available for methylation of DNA, leading to hypomethylation and a resultant aberrant gene express. They concluded that hypomethylation of DNA is a tenable epigenetic mechanisms for arsenic-induced carcinogenicity.

Given that effects on cellular methylation status could have important consequences for gene expression patterns, levels of methylation donors in the diet could modulate the effects of arsenic on DNA metabolism.

Oxidative Stress

Some evidence supports the concept that arsenite induces oxidative stress in mammalian cells and that the induced oxidative damage can result in genotoxicity. For example, the concept is supported indirectly by the finding that adding superoxide dismutase to the culture medium reduces the frequency of arsenite-induced SCE in human lymphocytes (Nordenson and Beckman 1991). Similarly, vitamin E can protect human fibroblasts from arsenic toxicity (Lee and Ho 1994). Arsenite can also increase the concentrations of a number of proteins that can protect against oxidative stress—e.g., metallo-thionein (Albores et al. 1992) and heme oxygenase (Keyse and Tyrrell 1989). Although those studies and other similar ones suggest that arsenic induces oxidative stress and results in genotoxicity, more direct evidence clearly needs to be provided. Recent studies by Hei et al. (1998) suggest that reactive oxygen species are involved in the formation of deletion mutations of human chromosome 11 in a human-hamster hybrid cell following arsenic treatment. The log-linear shape of the survival curve for these cells is noted to be sup-portive evidence for an effect of arsenic on DNA repair. This conclusion is supported, in part, by the data of Gurr et al. (1998), who showed that arsenic induced micronuclei in cells in vitro at concentrations above 10 μM. The induction of micronuclei was reduced by treatment with NO synthase inhibi-tors and superoxide dismutase, as well as calcium chelators and uric acid.

An alternative explanation for arsenic's possible role in the induction of genotoxicity is that arsenic could affect the repair of endogenously produced oxidative DNA damage. However, without specific studies to address that hypothesis, it remains speculative.

Cell Proliferation

Sodium arsenite can increase the incorporation of 3H-thymidine into the DNA of human keratinocytes in vitro as well as increase cell number at low concentrations (0.001-0.002 μM) indicating increased cell proliferation. At higher concentrations, sodium arsenite was cytotoxic (Germolec et al. 1997). In support of arsenic-inducing cell proliferation, Germolec et al. (1997) showed that sodium arsenite induced increased mRNA transcripts of keratino-cyte growth factors, including granulocyte macrophage–colony-stimulating factor (GM-CSF), transforming growth factor α (TGF-α), and the inflamma-tory cytokine tumor necrosis factor α (TNF-α) in primary human epidermal keratinocytes in vitro. In addition, c-myc expression, as an indicator of proliferation was increased. These effects on transcription were seen at sodium arsenite concentrations of 0.5-4 μM, with an approximately linear response over this range. While these data have the potential for providing input into the mode of action via the cell proliferation pathway, at this time they are observational rather than informative. Arsenicals can also cause cell proliferation in target organs in vivo, most likely as a regenerative response subsequent to induced toxicity.

Oral administration of high concentrations of DMA to rats and mice after exposure to various genotoxic carcinogens caused increases in tumors in lung, bladder, liver, kidney, and thyroid (Yamamoto et al. 1995; Wanibuchi et al. 1996; Yamanaka et al. 1996) (see the previous section Results from Bioassays). With that particular protocol, DMA is presumably acting as a promoting agent that would be supportive of a cell-proliferation effect. However, the specific experimental design can create some difficulties in interpretation.

Arsenic-Induced Carcinogenicity and the Shape of Dose-Response Curve—A Mode-of-Action Approach

The preceding section provides an overview of the various genotoxic effects of arsenicals in vitro and in vivo. The aim of this section is to discuss how some or all of those effects might be involved in arsenic-induced carcinogenicity, and further, how that information can provide information on the shape of the dose-response curve at low exposure concentrations.

As discussed above, cancer is a genetic disease that requires the accumulation of a series of mutations in a single cell during the progression from a normal cell to a cancer cell. Those mutations can be point (gene) mutations, deletion mutations, other structural chromosomal alterations (e.g., inversions or rearrangement), or chromosomal numerical alterations (chromosomal losses or gains). On the basis of the mutagenicity profile for arsenicals discussed above, chromosomal alterations rather than point mutations are more likely to be involved in arsenic carcinogenicity. These chromosomal aberrations could feasibly be induced by direct or indirect interaction of arsenic with the DNA. Although the latter is much more likely to be based on available experimental evidence, direct interaction cannot be ruled out.

Chromosomal structural alterations can arise via one of two basic pathways, direct interaction with DNA and indirect DNA effects. However, on the basis of the published data on mutational spectra for arsenic and the present discussion on other cellular responses to arsenic, arsenic-induced effects on cellular housekeeping processes are more likely to result ultimately in the formation of chromosomal alterations. Such indirect effects are predicted to lead to sublinear dose responses for chromosomal alterations, as supported by the experimental data reviewed by Rudel et al. (1996). Such a sublinear dose response is predicted for the less likely scenario of production of chromosomal aberrations following direct interaction of arsenic with DNA. This conclusion is based on the fact that the majority of structural chromosomal aberrations (with the possible exception of terminal deletions) require at least two independent events at the DNA level for their formation. Chromosomal alterations result from errors of DNA repair at the molecular level, or during DNA replication. The evidence in support of this hypothesis is described in the following paragraph. Chromosomal gains and losses result from failure of chromosomes to separate at anaphase or from failure of chromosomes to move to the poles at anaphase. Either of those processes could result in a threshold dose response.

Chromosomal aberrations are formed by errors in DNA repair of induced or endogenous DNA damage, errors in DNA replication on an altered template, or inhibition of enzymes, such as topoisomerases. Such alterations result in chromosomal damage. For the great majority of chemicals, aberrations result from errors in DNA replication on an adducted template. There is no evidence to support those errors as a mode of action for arsenic other than the possibility that arsenic induces oxidative DNA damage. It is perhaps more likely that the aberrations are produced by errors of DNA repair induced by direct or indirect interference of the process by arsenic. Direct effects could be initiated by oxidative DNA damage, indirect effects by alterations to the repair proteins. The outcome would lead to a sublinear or possibly threshold response whether the effects on repair fidelity were direct or indirect.

Early studies supported the idea that DNA-repair enzymes are the molecular target mediating arsenic's genotoxic and comutagenic effects; studies indicated that relatively high concentrations of sodium arsenite inhibit DNA ligases I and II (Li and Rossman 1989b; Lee-Chen et al. 1994). Evidence supporting an earlier step in DNA repair has also been presented (Okui and Fujimara 1986; Hartwig et al. 1997). Studies indicating that arsenic alters the mutational spectra of UV radiation (Yang et al. 1992; Wiencke et al. 1997) are consistent with interference in either early or late steps in DNA repair. Extension of the concepts of mutational spectra analysis to human tumors in arsenic-exposed populations could provide information on the question of arsenic's mode of action and might be useful in risk assessment (Clewell et al. in press). A study of the pattern of p53 mutations in bladder cancers arising in a blackfoot-disease endemic area in Taiwan suggested that the etiology of the tumors might have involved a mechanism that increased the extent of DNA damage per mutational event (Shibata et al. 1994). The relationship of human tumor data to arsenic's effects on DNA repair requires further study. Recent studies, however, using purified human DNA-repair enzymes indicated that micromolar concentrations of arsenite increase the activities of DNA polymerase beta, O^6-methylguanine-DNA methyltransferase, and DNA ligases I, II, and III (Hu et al. 1998). Inhibition occurred at higher doses (i.e., 1-5 mM of sodium arsenite). Those results cast doubt on the direct inhibition of those components of repair by arsenic. Other enzymatic activities involved in DNA repair have been reported to be inhibited by arsenite; nontoxic concentrations of arsenite inhibit human poly(ADP-ribose)polymerase (PARP) activity (Yager and Wiencke 1997). Although inhibition of PARP might be related to SCE induction, that effect alone is unlikely to account for the magnitude of the synergistic effects of arsenic or the extensive range of agents whose geno-toxicity is augmented by arsenic (i.e., mono- and bi-functional alkylating agents, ionizing radiation, and cross-linking agents).

Biochemical data, however, indicate that preferential binding of arsenic at low micromolar concentrations will target proteins with specific structural features. Although arsenite has long been recognized as highly reactive with protein sulfhydryl groups (Joshi and Hughes 1981; Knowles and Benson 1984; Squibb and Fowler 1983), it can be highly selective in reacting with only a small number of closely spaced (vicinal) dithiol groups in proteins at low concentrations (Wiencke and Yager 1992). For example, the selective inhibi-tion of dexamethasone binding to glucocorticoid receptors by arsenite is thought to be due to the formation of a stable dithioarsenite complex with one vicinal dithiol group within the steroid-binding domain of the glucocorticoid receptor (Lopez et al. 1990). Arsenite also blocks DNA binding by the receptor, presumably through similar interactions with vicinal dithiols present in the DNA-binding domain of the protein (Simons et al. 1990). The number of proteins containing vicinal dithiols is relatively small, but it is important that this structural feature is common among DNA-binding proteins, transcrip-tion factors, and DNA-repair proteins (Berger 1985). Closely spaced thiol groups within the DNA-binding proteins complex with zinc and can form so-called "zinc fingers," which are thought to be positioned into the major groove of the DNA double helix and mediate DNA-protein interactions. Proteins involved in DNA repair that contain putative zinc fingers include the UVRA protein (Husain et al. 1986), PARP (Cherney et al. 1987; Uchida et al. 1987), the RAD-18 protein (Jones et al. 1988), and the XPAC protein (Tanaka et al. 1990).

In support of the concept of preferential binding of arsenic with vicinal dithiols is the inhibition of PARP, which contains two zinc-finger motifs essential to its enzymatic function. Also supportive is the observation that arsenite inhibits the excision of thymine dimers and potentiates the cytotoxicity of 254 nanometers (nm) of UV light in wild-type human fibroblasts but does not affect the cytotoxic effects of UV light in excision-defective xeroderma pigmentosum group A cells (Okui and Fujiwara 1986). The XPAC protein has been shown to contain motifs of both C_4 and C_2H_2 classes of zinc-finger proteins (Tanaka et al. 1990). These studies provide some reasonable support for a role of arsenic in altering the fidelity or kinetics of DNA repair, but clearly further research is needed to address the issue more directly.

With respect to arsenic's mode of action in the induction of aneuploidy, the studies of Ramirez et al. (1997) are pertinent. The researchers examined the aneuploidy-inducing effects of arsenite in cultured human lymphocytes by using a variety of techniques, including fluorescence in situ hybridization (FISH) with DNA probes for chromosomes 1 and 7, immunostaining of the lymphocyte spindle apparatus, and an in vitro assay measuring the polymerization and depolymerization of tubulin. Dose-related increases in hyperdiploidy were seen in lymphocytes treated with arsenite at concentrations ranging from 0.001 to 0.1 μM. Examination of the spindle apparatus using an anti-β-tubulin antibody indicated that arsenite might disrupt spindle formation by interaction with microtubules. In addition, in vitro assays using purified tubulin indicated that arsenite inhibited microtubule assembly and induced tubulin depolymerization. Although these studies are of potential importance, they must be considered in light of the in vivo human data indicating that the predominant effect of arsenic in humans in vivo is clastogenesis and not aberrant chromosomal segregation. As an example, one of the proposed mechanisms for the involvement of alterations in methylation patterns in carcinogenesis involves the induction of chromosomal instability (Gonzalgo and Jones 1997). Hypermethylation of CpG sites within the 5' region of the p16^{INK4a} tumor-suppressor gene (Ahuja et al. 1997) and the DNA mismatch repair gene hMLH1 (Kane et al. 1997) was recently found to be closely associated with microsatellite instability in colorectal cancer cells. It is conceivable that such instability could also be manifested by gross alterations in chromosomal structure, such as those observed in arsenic-exposed cells. However, if arsenic's effects on chromosomal aberrations is mediated by aberrant methylation, a sublinear dose response is likely to result for these effects at low exposure concentrations.

Increased or dysregulated cell proliferation plays a necessary, although not sufficient, role in the development of tumors (Butterworth et al. 1995). Cytotoxicity and regenerative cell proliferation demonstrate sublinear or, most frequently, threshold responses, irrespective of the mechanism by which the cytotoxicity is induced.

In summary, investigations of mode of action for carcinogenicity are conducted to predict the shape of cancer dose-response curves below the level of direct observation of tumors. For arsenic carcinogenicity, the mode of action has not been established, but the several modes of action that are considered plausible (namely, indirect mechanisms of mutagenicity) would lead to a sublinear dose-response curve at some point below the point at which a significant increase in tumors is observed (see EPA (1997) for further discussion). However, because a specific mode (or modes) of action has not yet been identified, it is prudent not to rule out the possibility of a linear response.

NONCANCER EFFECTS

Inhibitory Effects on Cellular Respiration

The mechanisms of arsenical toxicity to individual cell types have historically centered around the inhibitory effects on cellular respiration at the level of the mitochondrion (Fluharty and Sanadi 1960, 1962; Packer 1961). Hepatotoxicity, as evidenced by porphyrinuria, has been seen in arsenic-poisoned humans following acute high-dose exposures and, to a milder extent, following chronic low-dose exposures. That effect is a major health effect related to decreased cellular respiration and mitochondrial toxicity (Fowler 1977). The preferential effects of arsenicals on nicotinamide adenine dinucleotide (NAD)-linked mitochondrial respiration (Fowler et al. 1979) have historically been linked to formation of stable arsenical complexes with the vicinal dithiols of the lipoic acid cofactor for the pyruvate dehydrogenase complex, but alterations in mitochondrial protein synthesis and inner-membrane structural integrity might also play an important role following in vivo exposures (Fowler et al. 1979, 1987). Disruption of oxidative phosphorylation and concomitant decreases in cellular levels of ATP (Chen et al. 1986, Figure 7-1) are thought to be important central events in the onset of cellular injury and cell death, because ultrastructural morphometric alterations in mitochondrial structure, disruption of mitochondrial respiratory function, and hepatic porphyrinuria are closely correlated (Figure 7-2). The hepatic porphyrinuria is dominated by increased amounts of uropophyrins (octa- and hepta-carboxyl isomers have also been observed for arsine gas (Fowler et al. 1989), inorganic arsenic, and indium arsenide (Conner et al. 1995)) with lesser amounts of coproporphyrin III. Those porphyrinurias have also been demonstrated in human populations in Mexico (Garcia-Vargas et al. 1991, 1994; Garcia-Vargas and Hernandez-Zavala 1996) and inner Mongolia (Yamauchi et al. 1998) when proper handling procedures (Woods et al. 1991) for protecting urine samples against photo-oxidation of porphyrins are followed.

Mitochondrial swelling has been reported in human renal proximal tubule cells following acute high-dose poisoning (Frejaville et al. 1972) and in rats following prolonged oral exposure to arsenate in drinking water (Brown et al. 1976). In the latter studies, these ultrastructural effects were associated with inhibition of mitochondrial respiratory function similar to that observed in liver cells. Overt clinical manifestations of nephropathy in humans have not been reported in relation to chronic oral intake of arsenic in drinking water.

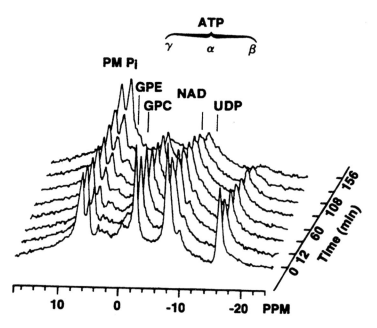

FIGURE 7-1 In vivo ^{31}P nuclear magnetic resonance scans for hepatic ATP showing progressive decreases over time following a single intravenous injection of sodium arsenite to a rat at a concentration of 10 mg/kg. Source: Chen et al. 1986. Reprinted with permission from *Biochemical and Biophysical Research Communications*; copyright 1986, Academic Press.

Alterations in the Heme and Porphyrin Biosynthetic Pathways

Alterations in the heme biosynthetic and degradative pathway also occur (Woods and Fowler 1978; Cebrian et al. 1983; Garcia-Vargas et al. 1991, 1994; Conner et al. 1995; Garcia-Vargas and Hernandez-Zavala 1996; Yamauchi et al. 1998), indicating that this essential pathway is susceptible to arsenical disturbance. The increased urinary excretion of carboxyl uroporphyrins VI, VII, and VIII and carboxyl coproporphyrin IV are the main measurable effects in experimental animal models following subchronic exposure to arsine gas (Fowler et al. 1989) in arsenic or sodium arsenite (Conner et al. 1995). As noted above, proper handling of urine samples is essential to obtain correct porphyrin analyses and avoid co-elution of uroporphyrin peaks under the carboxyl coproporphyrin IV peak.

More recent studies by Garcia-Vargas and Hernandez-Zavala (1996) have confirmed the presence of arsenic uroporphyrinuria-coproporphyrinuria in both human populations following prolonged exposure to arsenic in drinking water. The conditions for appropriate handling of urine samples for high-pressure liquid chromotography are clear and detailed.

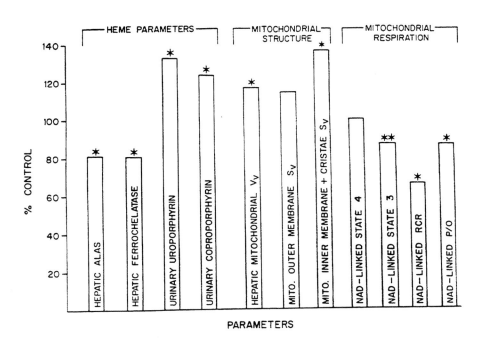

*-DIFFERS FROM CONTROL P<.05
**-DIFFERS FROM CONTROL P<.06

FIGURE 7-2 Summary of statistical correlations between ultrastructural morphometric alterations in mitochondrial substructure, respiratory function, mitochondrial heme pathway enzymes, and increased porphyrin excretion patterns in rats exposed to arsenate at 40 ppm in drinking water for 6 weeks. ALAS, delta-aminoleulinic acid synthetase; V_v, volume density; S_v, surface density; RCR, respiratory control ratio; NAD, linked substrates such as pyruvate and malate; P/O, phosphate-to-oxygen ratio. Source: Fowler et al. 1987. Reprinted with permission from the *Annals of the New York Academy of Sciences*; copyright 1987.

Alterations in Cellular Gene Expression–Stress Protein Induction

Exposure of cells to arsenicals either in vitro (Caltibiano et al. 1986; Taketani et al. 1989; Aoki et al. 1990; Van Delft et al. 1993; Van Wijk et al. 1993) at concentrations ranging from 10^{-6} to 10^{-3} M or in vivo at concentrations of 0.3 mg/kg and 3.0 mg/kg (Conner et al. 1993) has been shown to cause the induction of a number of the major stress proteins including members of the 32, 60, 70, and 90 stress-protein families. Clearly, in vitro exposure of cells to arsenite in a variety of model systems (Chin et al. 1990; Wu and Welsh 1996) results in a broad spectrum stress-protein response. In addition, there is down regulation of a number of constitutively expressed proteins. The increased expression of the major stress proteins suggests the presence of oxidative damage to essential proteins perhaps secondary to uncoupling of mitochondrial oxidative phosphorylation and increased intracellular production of H_2O_2 and subsequent production of reactive oxygen species (ROS). In particular, the increased presence of the 32-kilodalton stress protein known to be heme oxygenase following arsenical exposure (Taketani et al. 1989; Keyse and Tyrrell 1989) provides further support for this concept. Given the capacity of arsenicals to produce oxidative stress, which includes induction of heme oxygenase, it is clear that reactive oxygen species, such as nitrate oxide and hydroxyl radicals, might play important roles in mediating the observed alterations in gene-expression patterns noted in many studies.

Altered cytokine gene expression was recently reported in relation to the development of keratoses and might play a role in the development following chronic arsenical exposure (Germolec et al. 1998).

Arsenic Toxicity and Metallothionein

Tolerance to arsenic toxicity exists, and because metallothionein (MT) is known to be responsible for the tolerance to cadmium toxicity, the interactions of cadmium and MT have been examined.

MT is a low-molecular-weight, cysteine-rich, metal-binding protein. MT has been proposed to play an important role in the homeostasis of essential metals, in the detoxication of heavy metals, and in the scavenging of free radicals (Kägi 1993; Sato and Bremner 1993). Moreover, MT is a small protein easily induced by heavy metals, hormones, acute stress, and a variety of chemicals (Hamer 1986; Kägi 1993). The cysteine contents and the capacity of these MT isoforms to bind metals are similar.

Arsenicals are effective inducers of MT in mice (Maitani et al. 1987; Kreppel et al. 1993) and rats (Albores et al. 1992; Hochadel and Waalkes 1997). The ability of different arsenical forms to induce MT varies markedly: As(III) is a potent MT inducer, as it took approximately 3 times more As(V), 50 times more MMA, and 120 times more DMA to induce MT (Kreppel et al. 1993) (see Figure 7-3). In contrast, MMA is the most effective MT inducer (80-fold), followed by As(III) (30-fold), As(V) (25-fold), and DMA (10-fold)

(Kreppel et al. 1993). The induction of MT is also observed following oral administration. Again, the doses of organic arsenicals (MMA and DMA) required for MT induction are one order higher than those of inorganic arsenicals (As(III) and As(V)) (Maitani et al. 1987). Induction of MT by arsenicals appears to be mediated at the transcription level, because MT-I and MT-II mRNA levels are increased by As(III) and As(V), As(III) being more effective (Albores et al. 1992; Kreppel et al. 1993). However, arsenicals are unable to induce MT in cultured hepatocytes (Bauman et al. 1993; Kreppel et al. 1993), suggesting that induction of MT by arsenicals might occur indirectly. The potency of arsenicals to induce MT (As(III) > As(V) > MMA > DMA) parallels the toxicity of arsenicals (Peoples 1975; Maitani et al. 1987; Klaassen 1995). That implies that MT induction might be, at least in part, due to a toxic event associated with arsenical administration and implies that MT might play a role in the detoxication of arsenicals.

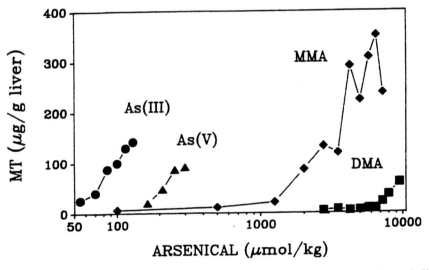

FIGURE 7-3 MT concentration in liver of mice exposed to various doses of arsenic(III), arsenic(V), MMA, and DMA. Mice were exposed subcutaneously with approximately equally toxic doses of the different arsenicals, and liver MT concentration was determined 24 hr after exposure. Data represent the mean of two mice per dose. Source: Kreppel et al. 1993. Reprinted with permission from *Fundamental and Applied Toxicology*, copyright 1993, Society of Toxicology.

MT induction has been proposed as one of the adaptive mechanisms for tolerance to arsenic toxicity (Kreppel et al. 1988; Cherian 1995; Silver and Phung 1996). However, how MT protects against arsenic toxicity is unclear.

The affinity of arsenic for MT in vitro is markedly lower than the affinity of zinc or cadmium for MT (Waalkes et al. 1984). In intact animals, only a small portion of dosed arsenic is found to be associated with the MT fraction (Maitani et al. 1987; Albores et al. 1992; Kreppel et al. 1994; Chen and Whanger 1994). That suggests that, unlike the proposed detoxication mechanism of MT for cadmium (Goering et al. 1995), MT does not protect against arsenic toxicity by "sequestering the metal"; rather, MT might function as an antioxidant against arsenic-induced oxidative injury.

Evidence has been accumulated that oxidative damage is an important mechanism for arsenic toxicity (see above). Because of its high sulfhydryl content, MT has also been suggested to react with free radicals and electrophiles (Klaassen and Cagen 1981; Basu and Lazo 1990). Indeed, MT can serve as a sacrificial scavenger for hydroxyl radicals in vitro (Thornalley and Vasák 1985) and thus protect against free radical-induced DNA damage (Abel and De Ruiter 1989; Chubatsu and Meneghini 1993; Schwarz et al. 1995). MT can also assume the function of superoxide dismutase (zinc and copper SOD) in yeast (Tamai et al. 1993) and protect against lipid peroxidation in erythrocyte ghosts produced by xanthine oxidase-derived superoxide anion, and hydrogen peroxide (Thomas et al. 1986). MT is induced by oxidative stress-producing chemicals (Bauman et al. 1991) and alkylating agents (Kotsonis and Klaassen 1979) and has been shown to protect against oxidative damage (Sato and Bremner 1993) and the toxicity of alkylating anticancer drugs (Lazo and Pitt 1995). Determining whether MT protects against arsenic toxicity via its antioxidant role warrants further investigation.

Thus, in conclusion MT is thought to have a protective effect against arsenic toxicity and to be responsible for at least part of its self-induced tolerance. However, the data supporting that conclusion are indirect, and the availability of genetically engineered mice that lack MT should be examined to determine with greater confidence the role of MT in modifying the toxicity of arsenic.

Arsine Gas Toxicity

The toxicity of arsine gas (AsH_3) is directed primarily toward the red blood cells, producing hemolysis following acute, short-term, or prolonged exposure (Fowler et al. 1989; Blair et al. 1990a,b). Of interest is the apparent involvement of ROS and glutathione depletion in the production of red-cell destruction, providing support for the idea that arsenicals might form radical species in the presence of oxygen by some as yet undefined mechanism within the red cells.

Interactions Between Arsenic and Other Common Toxic Metals

Studies that examined lead, cadmium, and arsenic (Mahaffey and Fowler 1977; Fowler and Mahaffey 1978; Mahaffey et al. 1981) showed a number of interactions between these common toxic trace elements. The interactive effects in rodents are observed to occur in a well-tolerated intermediate-dose range in rodents for each of the elements studied. A number of the interactions involved marked increases in renal concentrations of copper (Mahaffey et al. 1981) in the arsenic exposure groups. Those interactions could be related to arsenic-induced metallothionein. The most dramatic effect was the mixture-specific increases in porphyrins with additive exacerbation of the arsenic-specific porphyrinuria pattern by concomitant lead and cadmium exposures (Mahaffey et al. 1981). (See discussion of selenium and other interactions in Chapters 8 and 9.)

SUMMARY AND CONCLUSIONS

• In vivo studies in rats and mice to determine the ability of inorganic arsenic to act as a cocarcinogen or as a promoter have produced mixed results. Studies on DMA suggest that this metabolite is not an initiator but might act as a promoter. The studies carried out to date, however, used very high doses, making interpretation of the results difficult, especially if DMA is formed in situ following the administration of inorganic arsenic.

• The mode of action for arsenic carcinogenicity has not been established. Inorganic arsenic and its metabolites have been shown to induce deletion mutations and chromosomal alterations (aberrations, aneuploidy, and SCE) but not point mutations. Other genotoxic responses that can be pertinent to the mode of action for arsenic carcinogenicity are comutagenicity, DNA methylation, oxidative stress, and cell proliferation; however, data on those genotoxic responses are insufficient to draw firm conclusions. The most plausible and generalized mode of action for arsenic carcinogenicity is that it induces structural and numerical chromosomal abnormalities without acting directly with DNA.

• Data on the modes of action for carcinogenicity can help to predict the shape of cancer dose-response curves below the level of direct observation of tumors. For arsenic carcinogenicity, the mode of action has not been established, but the several modes of action that are considered most plausible (namely, indirect mechanisms of mutagenicity) lead to a sublinear dose-response at some point below the level at which a significant increase in tumors is observed. However, because a specific mode (or modes) of action has not been identified at this time, it is prudent not to rule out the possibility of a linear response.

- In vitro studies of human and animal cells show that the genotoxic effects occur at submicromolar concentrations of arsenite that are similar to those found in urine of humans consuming drinking water at about the current MCL.

- The inhibitory effects of arsenicals on mitochondrial respiratory function are well known and highly specific to respiration supported by the NAD-linked substrates, such as pyruvate. The mechanism appears to involve inhibition of the pyruvate dehydrogenase complex via arsenic complexation with the vicinal dithiol-dihydrolipoic acid cofactor for that enzyme complex.

- Inhibition of mitochondrial respiration results in decreased cellular production of ATP and increased production of hydrogen peroxide. Those effects could cause formation of ROS, resulting in oxidative stress.

- Oxidative stress produced by ROS formation results in the observed induction of the major stress protein families.

- Intracellular production of ROS results in the inhibition of the heme biosynthetic pathway enzyme uroporphyrinogen decarboxylase. That in turn results in the observed uroporphyrinuria. The observed increases in copro-porphyrin in the urine are secondary to the arsenical inhibition of this mito-chondrial enzyme.

- There is clear quantitative evidence of deleterious ultrastructural morphometric and biochemical alterations in liver mitochondria associated with the observed porphyrinuria in experimental animals, indicating that the porphyrinuria is a good candidate as a putative biomarker of arsenical-induced hepatotoxicity.

- The role of arsenical-induced oxidative stress in mediating DNA damage is not completely clear, but the intracellular production of ROS might play an initiating role in the carcinogenic process by producing DNA damage.

- MT is thought to have a protective effect against arsenic toxicity and to be responsible for at least part of its self-induced tolerance. However, the data supporting that conclusion are indirect.

RECOMMENDATIONS

Identification of proximate markers of arsenic-induced cancers and their application in carefully designed epidemiological studies might better define the cancer dose-response curves at low concentrations. Molecular and cellular characterization of neoplasms from arsenic exposed populations and appropri-ate controls might aid in identifying the mechanism by which arsenic induces tumors. Chronic low-dose studies in a suitable animal model (mouse, hamster, or rabbit) might increase our understanding of the mode of action of arsenic carcinogenicity, particularly the potential role of chromosomal alterations.

There is a pressing need to understand the sequence of cellular arsenic exposure, the methylation processes, inhibition of mitochondrial function, and formation of ROS.

Other studies of less critical importance for characterizing risks but nonetheless needed to fill important data gaps include the following:

— Studies to examine the relationships between ROS formation, oxidative stress, induction of the stress protein response and necrosis or apoptosis.

— Studies to examine the relationships between arsenical-induced oxidative stress, DNA damage, induction of proto-oncogenes, inhibition of DNA mechanisms, and cancer.

— Investigations of the potential role of arsenic as a cocarcinogen, preferably in defined human populations.

— Studies to identify and characterize mechanism-based biomarkers of arsenical effects in human target-organ systems.

— Studies using genetically engineered mice that lack MT to determine with greater confidence the role of MT in modifying the toxicity of arsenic.

REFERENCES

Abel, J., and N. De Ruiter. 1989. Inhibition of hydroxyl-radical-generated DNA degradation by metallothionein. Toxicol. Lett. 47:191-196.

Ahuja, N., A.L. Mohan, Q. Li, J.M. Stolker, J.G. Herman, S.R. Hamilton, S.B. Baylin, and J.P. Issa. 1997. Association between CpG island methylation and microsatellite instability in colorectal cancer. Cancer Res. 57:3370-3374.

Albores, A., J. Koropatnick, M.G. Cherian, and A.J. Zelazowski. 1992. Arsenic induces and enhances rat hepatic metallothionein production in vivo. Chem.-Biol. Interact. 85:127-140.

Aoki, Y., M.M. Lipsky, and B.A. Fowler. 1990. Alteration of protein synthesis in primary cultures of rat kidney proximal tubule epithelial cells by exposure to gallium, indium and arsenite. Toxicol. Appl. Pharmacol. 106:462-468.

Baroni, C., G.J. van Esch, and U. Saffiotti. 1963. Carcinogenesis tests of two inorganic arsenicals. Arch. Environ. Health 7:668-674

Basu, A., and J.S. Lazo. 1990. A hypothesis regarding the protective role of metallothioneins against the toxicity of DNA interactive anticancer drugs. Toxicol. Lett. 50:123-135.

Bauman, J.W. , J. Liu, Y.P. Liu, and C.D. Klaassen. 1991. Increase in metallothionein produced by chemicals that induce oxidative stress. Toxicol. Appl. Pharmacol. 110:347-354.

Bauman, J., J. Liu, and C.D. Klaassen. 1993. Production of metallothionein and heat-shock proteins in response to metals. Fundam. Appl. Toxicol. 21:15-22.

Baylin, S.B., J.G. Herman, J.R. Graff, P.M. Vertino, and J.P. Issa. 1998. Alterations in DNA methylation: A fundamental aspect of neoplasia. Adv. Cancer Res. 72:141-196.

Berger, N.A. 1985. Poly(ADP-ribose) in the cellular response to DNA damage. Radiat. Res. 101:4-15.

Blair, P.C., M.B. Thompson, M. Bechtold, R.E. Wilson, M.P. Moorman, and B.A. Fowler. 1990a. Evidence for oxidative damage to red blood cells in mice induced by arsine gas. Toxicology 63:25-34.

Blair, P.C., M.B. Thompson, R.E. Morrissey, M.P. Moorman, R.A. Sloane, and B.A. Fowler. 1990b. Comparative toxicity of arsine gas in B6C3F1 mice, Fischer 344 rats and Syrian golden hamsters: System organ studies and comparison of clinical indices of exposure. Fundam. Appl. Toxicol. 14:776-787.

·Brown, M.M., B.C. Rhyne, R.A. Goyer, and B.A. Fowler. 1976. The intracellular effects of chronic arsenic exposure on renal proximal tubule cells. J. Toxicol. Environ. Health 1:505-514.

Butterworth, B.E., R.B. Conolly, and K.T. Morgan. 1995. A strategy for establishing mode of action of chemical carcinogens as a guide for approaches to risk assessments. Cancer Lett. 93:129-146.

Byron, W.R., G.W. Bierbower, J.B. Brouwer, and W.H. Hansen. 1967. Pathologic changes in rats and dogs from two-year feeding of sodium arsenite or sodium arsenate. Toxicol. Appl. Pharmacol. 10:132-147.

Caltibiano, M.M., T.P. Koestler, G. Poste, and R.G. Greig. 1986. Induction of the 32- and 34-kDA stress proteins by sodium arsenite, heavy metals and thiol reactive reagents. J. Biol. Chem. 261:13381-13386.

Cebrian, M., A. Albores, M. Aguilar, and E. Blakely. 1983. Chronic arsenic poisoning in the north of Mexico. Hum. Toxicol. 2:121-133.

Chen, C.L., and P.D. Whanger. 1994. Interaction of selenium and arsenic with metallothionein: Effect of vitamin B_{12}. J. Inorg. Biochem. 54:267-276.

Chen, B., C.T. Burt, P.L. Goering, B.A. Fowler, and R.E. London. 1986. In vivo 31-P nuclear magnetic resonance studies of arsenite induced changes in hepatic phosphate levels. Biochem. Biophys. Res. Commun. 139:228-234.

Cherian, M.G. 1995. Metallothionein and its interaction with metals. Handb. Exp. Pharmacol. 115:121-138.

Cherney, B.W., O.W. McBride, D. Chen, H. Alkhatib, K. Bhakia, P. Hensen, and M.E. Smulson. 1987. cDNA sequence, protein structure, and chromosomal location of the human gene for poly(ADP-ribose) polymerase. Proc. Natl. Acad. Sci. USA 84:8370-8374.

Chin, K.V., S. Tanaka, G. Darlington, I. Pastan, and M.M. Gottesman. 1990. Heath shock and arsenite increase expression of the multi-drug resistance (MDR1) gene in human renal carcinoma cells. J. Biol. Chem. 265:221-226.

Chubatsu, L.S., and R. Meneghini. 1993. Metallothionein protects DNA from oxidative damage. Biochem. J. 291:193-198.

Clewell, H.J., P.R. Gentry, H.A. Barton, A.M. Shipp, J.W. Yager, and M.E. Andersen. In press. Requirements for a biologically realistic cancer risk assessment for inorganic arsenic. Int. J. Toxicol.

Conner, E.A., H. Yamauchi, B.A. Fowler, and M. Akkerman. 1993. Biological indicators for monitoring exposure/toxicity to III-V semiconductors. J. Exp. Anal. Epidemiol. 3:431-440.

Conner, E.A., H. Yamauchi, and B.A. Fowler. 1995. Alterations in the heme biosynthetic pathway from the III-V semiconductor metal, indium arsenide (InAs). Chem.-Biol. Interact. 96:273-285.

Costa, M. 1995. Model for the epigenetic mechanism of action of nongenotoxic carcinogens. Am. J. Clin. Nutr. 61(Suppl.):666S-669S.

Dulout, F.N., C.A. Grillo, A.I. Seoane, C.R. Maderna, R. Nilsson, M. Vahter, F. Darroudi, and A.T. Natarajan. 1996. Chromosomal aberrations in peripheral blood lymphocytes from native Andean women and children from northwestern Argentina exposed to arsenic in drinking water. Mutat. Res. 370:151-158.

Endo, G., K. Kuroda, A. Okamoto, and S. Horiguchi. 1992. Dimethylarsenic acid induces tetraploids in Chinese hamster cells. Bull. Environ. Contam. Toxicol. 48:131-137.

EPA (U.S. Environmental Protection Agency). 1981. Methane Arsonic Acid (MAA): 2-Year Chronic/Oncogenic Rat Feeding Study. Memorandum from W. Dykstra, Toxicology Branch, Health Effects Division, to R. Mountfort, Registration Division. May 13. U.S. Environmental Protection Agency, Office of Pesticides and Toxic Substances, Washington, D.C.

EPA (U.S. Environmental Protection Agency). 1991. Cacodylic Acid-Carcinogenicity Study in Mice. Memorandum from L.L. Taylor, Toxicology Branch II, Section II, Health Effects Division, to B. Crompton, Generic Chemical Support Branch, Special Review and

Reregistration Division. Memorandum 008891. Dec. 2. U.S. Environmental Protection Agency, Office of Pesticides and Toxic Substances, Washington, D.C.

EPA (U.S. Environmental Protection Agency). 1992a. Review of Toxicology Studies with Methanearsonic Acid/Methanearsonic Acid, Monosodium to Support Reregistration of the Test Substance. Memorandum from S.L. Malish, Toxicology Branch II, Review Section IV, Health Effects Division, to B. Briscoe, Special Review and Reregistration Division, Health Effects Division. Memorandum 009478. April. U.S. Environmental Protection Agency, Office of Pesticides and Toxic Substances, Washington, D.C.

EPA (U.S. Environmental Protection Agency). 1992b. Review of Toxicology Studies with Methanearsonic Acid to Support Reregistration of the Test Substance. Memorandum from S.L. Malish, Toxicology Branch II, Review Section IV, Health Effects Division, to B. Briscoe, Special Review and Reregistration Division, Health Effects Division. Memorandum 009382. March. U.S. Environmental Protection Agency, Office of Pesticides and Toxic Substances, Washington, D.C.

EPA (U.S. Environmental Protection Agency). 1992c. Review of Toxicology Studies with Cacodylic Acid to Support Registration of Test Substance. Memorandum from S.L. Malish, Toxicology Branch II, Review Section IV, Health Effects Division, to B. Briscoe, Special Review and Reregistration Division, Health Effects Division. Memorandum 009391. March. U.S. Environmental Protection Agency, Office of Pesticides and Toxic Substances, Washington, D.C.

EPA (U.S. Environmental Protection Agency). 1992d. Review of Toxicology Study with Cacodylic Acid to Support Registration of Test Substance. Memorandum from S.L. Malish, Toxicology Branch II, Review Section IV, Health Effects Division, to B. Briscoe, Special Review and Reregistration Division, Health Effects Division. Memorandum 009775. October. U.S. Environmental Protection Agency, Office of Pesticides and Toxic Substances, Washington, D.C.

EPA (U.S. Environmental Protection Agency). 1993. Cacodylic Acid: Registrant's Response to Agency's Review of Toxicology Data. Memorandum from S.L. Malish, Toxicology Branch II, Review Section IV, Health Effects Division, to V. Dietrich, Product Manager, Registration Division. Memorandum 010550. September. U.S. Environmental Protection Agency, Office of Prevention, Pesticides and Toxic Substances, Washington, D.C.

EPA (U.S. Environmental Protection Agency). 1997. Report on the Expert Panel on Arsenic Carcinogenicity: Review and Workshop. Prepared by the Eastern Research Group, Lexington, Mass., for the U.S. Environmental Protection Agency, National Center for Environmental Assessment, Washington, D.C.

EPA (U.S. Environmental Protection Agency). 1998. Cacodylic acid. In Integrated Risk Information System (IRIS). Online. Entry last revised Dec. 1, 1996. Available: http://www.epa.gov/iris/subst/0587.htm#II. U.S. Environmental Protection Agency, National Center for Environmental Assessment, Cincinnati, Ohio.

Fluharty, A., and D.R. Sanadi. 1960. Evidence for a vicinal dithiol in oxidative phosphorylation. Proc. Natl. Acad. Sci. USA 46:608-616.

Fluharty A.L., and D.R. Sanadi. 1962. On the mechanism of oxidative phosphorylation IV. Mitochondrial swelling caused by arsenite in combination with 2,3-dimercaptopropanol and by cadmium ion. Biochemistry 1:276-281.

Fowler, B.A. 1977. Toxicology of environmental arsenic. Pp. 79-122 in Toxicology of Trace Elements. Advances in Modern Toxicology, Vol. 2, R.A. Goyer and M.A. Mehlman, eds. Washington, D.C.: Hemisphere.

Fowler, B.A. and K.R. Mahaffey. 1978. Interactions among lead, cadmium, and arsenic in relation to porphyrin excretion patterns. Environ. Health Perspect. 25:87-90.

Fowler, B.A., J.S. Woods. and C.M. Schiller. 1979. Studies of hepatic mitochondrial structure and function: Morphometric and biochemical evaluation of in vivo perturbation by arsenate. Lab. Invest. 41:313-320.

Fowler, B.A., A. Oskarsson, and J.S. Woods. 1987. Metal- and metalloid-induced porphyrinurias: Relationships to cell injury. Ann. N.Y. Acad. Sci. 514:172-182.

Fowler, B.A., M.P. Moorman, B. Adkins, W.E. Bakewell, P.C. Blair, and M.B. Thompson. 1989. Arsine: Toxicity Data from Acute and Short-term Inhalation Exposures. Pp 85-89 in Hazard Assessment and Control Technology in Semiconductor Manufacturing. American Conference of Governmental Industrial Hygienists. Boca Raton, Fla.: Lewis.

Frejaville, J.P., J. Bescol, J.P. Leclerc, L. Gulliam, P. Crabie, F. Consco, P. Gervais, and M. Gaultier. 1972. Acute poisoning with arsenic derivatives (apropos of 4 personal cases); hemostasis disorders; ultramicroscopic study of the liver and kidney [in French]. Ann. Med. Interne 123:713-722.

Garcia-Vargas, G.G., and A. Hernandez-Zavala. 1996. Urinary porphyrins and heme biosynthetic enzyme activities measured by HPLC in arsenic toxicity. Biomed. Chromatogr. 10(6):278-284.

Garcia-Vargas, G.G., A. Garcia-Rangel, M. Aguilar-Romo, J. Garcia-

Salcedo, L.M. Del Razo, P. Ostrosky-Wegman, C.C. DeNava, and M.E. Cebrian. 1991. A pilot study of the urinary excretion of porphyrins in human populations chronically exposed to arsenic in Mexico. Hum. Exp. Toxicol. 10:189-194.

Garcia-Vargas, G.G., L.M. Del Razo, M.E. Cebrian, A. Albores, P. Ostrosky-Wegman, R. Montero, M.E. Gonsebatt, C.K. Lim, and F. DeMatteis. 1994. Altered urinary porphyrin excretion in a human population chronically exposed to arsenic in Mexico. Hum. Exp. Toxicol. 13:839-847.

Germolec, D.R, J. Spalding, G.A. Boorman, J.L. Wilmer, T. Yoshida, P.P. Simeonova, A. Bruccoleri, F. Kayama, K. Gaido, R. Tennant, F. Burleson, W. Dong, R.W. Lang, and M.I. Luster. 1997. Arsenic can mediate skin neoplasia by chronic stimulation of keratinocyte-derived growth factors. Mutat. Res. 386:209-218.

Germolec, D.R., J. Spalding, H.S. Yu, G.S. Chen, P.P. Simeonova, M.C. Humble, A. Bruccoleri, G.A. Boorman, J.F. Foley, T. Yoshida, and M.I. Luster. 1998. Arsenic enhancement of skin neoplasia by chronic stimulation of growth factors. Am. J. Pathol. 153:1775-1785.

Goering, P.L., M.P. Waalkes, and C.D. Klaassen. 1995. Toxicology of cadmium. Handb. Exp. Pharmacol. 115:189-213.

Gonsebatt, M.E., L. Vega, A.M. Salazar, R. Montero, P. Guzman, J. Blas, L.M. Del Razo, G. Garcia-Vargas, A. Albores, M.E. Cebrian, M. Kelsh, and P. Ostrosky-Wegman. 1997. Cytogenetic effects in human exposure to arsenic. Mutat. Res. 386:219-228.

Gonzalgo, M.L., and P.A. Jones. 1997. Mutagenic and epigenetic effects of DNA methylation. Mutat. Res. 386:107-118.

Gurr, J.R., F. Liu, S. Lynn, and K.Y. Jan. 1998. Calcium-dependent nitric oxide production is involved in arsenite-induced micronuclei. Mutat. Res. 416:137-148.

Hamer, D.H. 1986. Metallothionein. Annu. Rev. Biochem. 55:913-951.

Hartwig, A., U.D. Groblinghoff, D. Beyersmann, A.T. Natarajan, R. Filon, and L.H. Mullenders. 1997. Interaction of arsenic(III) with nucleotide excision repair in UV-irradiated human fibroblasts. Carcinogenesis 18:399-405.

Hei, T.K., S.X. Liu, and C. Waldren. 1998. Mutagenicity of arsenic in mammalian cells: Role of reactive oxygen species. Proc. Natl. Acad. Sci. USA 95:8103-8107.

Hochadel, J.F., and M.P. Waalkes. 1997. Sequence of exposure to cadmium and arsenic determines the extent of toxic effects in male Fischer rats. Toxicology 116:89-98.

Hu, Y., L. Su, and E.T. Snow. 1998. Arsenic toxicity is enzyme specific and its affects on ligation are not caused by the direct inhibition on DNA repair enzymes. Mutat. Res. 408:203-218.

Husain, I., B. van Houten, D.C. Thomas, and A. Sancar. 1986. Sequences of *Escherichia coli* uvrA gene and the protein reveal two potential ATP binding sites. J. Biol. Chem. 261:4895-4901.

IARC (International Agency for Research on Cancer). 1987. Arsenic and arsenic compounds. Pp. 100-206 in IARC Monographs on the Evaluation of Carcinogenic Risks to Humans. Overall Evaluations of Carcinogenicity: An Updating of IARC Monographs 1-42, Suppl. 7. Lyon, France: International Agency for Research on Cancer.

Innes, J.R.M., B.M. Ulland, M.G. Valerio, L. Petrucelli, L. Fishbein, E.R. Hart, A.J. Pallotta, R.R. Bates, H.L. Falk, J.J. Gart, M. Klein, I. Mitchell, and J. Peters. 1969. Bioassay of pesticides and industrial chemicals for tumorigenicity in mice: A preliminary note. J. Natl. Cancer Inst. 42:1101-1114.

Jacobson-Kram, D., and D. Montalbano. 1985. The Reproductive Effects Assessment Group's report on the mutagenicity of inorganic arsenic. Environ. Mutagen. 7:787-804.

Jha, A.N., M. Noditi, R. Nilsson, and A.T. Natarajan. 1992. Genotoxic effects of sodium arsenite on human cells. Mutat. Res. 284:215-221.

Jones, J.S., S. Weber, and L. Prakash. 1988. The *Saccharomyces cerevisiae* RAD18 gene encodes a protein that contains potential zinc finger domains for nucleic acid binding and a putative nucleotide binding sequence. Nucleic Acids Res. 16:7119-7131.

Joshi, S., and J.B. Hughes. 1981. Inhibition of coupling factor B activity by cadmium ion, arsenite-2,3-dimercaptopropanol, and phenylarsine oxide, and preferential reactivation by dithiols. J. Biol. Chem. 256:11112-11116.

Kägi, J. H. R. 1993. Evolution, structure and chemical activity of class I metallothioneins: An overview. Pp 29-56 in Metallothionein III: Biological Roles and Medical Implications, K.T. Suzuki, N. Imura, and M. Kimura, eds. Berlin: Birkhauser Verlag.

Kaise, T., H. Yamauchi, Y. Horiguchi, T. Tani, S. Watanabe, T. Hirayama, and S. Fukui. 1989. A comparative study on acute toxicity of methylarsonic acid, dimethylarsinic acid, and trimethylarsine oxide in mice. Appl. Organomet. Chem. 3:273-277.

Kane, M.F., M. Loda, G.M. Gaida, J. Lipman, R. Mishra, H. Goldman, J.M. Jessup, and R. Kolodner. 1997. Methylation of the hMLH1 promoter correlates with lack of expression of hMLH1 in sporadic colon tumors and mismatch repair-defective human tumor cell lines. Cancer Res. 57:808-811.

Kanisawa, M., and H.A. Schroeder. 1969. Life term studies on the effect of trace elements on spontaneous tumors in mice and rats. Cancer Res. 29:892-895.

Keyse, S.M., and R.M. Tyrrell. 1989. Heme oxygenase is the major 32-Kda stress protein induced in human skin fibroblasts by UVA radiation, hydrogen peroxide, and sodium arsenite. Proc. Natl. Acad. Sci. USA 86:99-103.

Klaassen, C.D. 1995. Heavy Metals and heavy-metal antagonists. Pp. 1649-1672 in Goodman and Gilman's Pharmacological Basis of Therapeutics, 9th Ed., J.G. Hardman, L.E. Limbird, P.M. Molinoff, R.W. Ruddon and A.G. Gilman. eds. New York: McGraw-Hill.

Klaassen, C.D., and S.Z. Cagen. 1981. Metallothionein as a trap for reactive organic intermediates. Adv. Exp. Med. Biol. 136(Pt A):633-646.

Knowles, F.C., and A.A. Benson. 1984. The enzyme inhibitory form of inorganic arsenic. Z. Gesamte. Hyg. 30:625-626.

Kotsonis, F., and C.D. Klaassen. 1979. Increase in hepatic metallothionein in rats treated with alkylating agents. Toxicol. Appl. Pharmacol. 51:19-27.

Kowalski, L.A., S.S. Tsang, and A.J. Davison. 1996. Arsenic and chromium enhance transformation of bovine papillomavirus DNA-transfected C3H/10T1/2 cells. Cancer Lett. 103:65-69.

Kreppel, H., K. Kolb, F.X. Reichl, B. Fichtl, and W. Forth. 1988. Pretreatment with low doses of cadmium or zinc decreases lethality in mice acutely poisoned with arsenic. Pp. 594-600 in Trace Element Analytical Chemistry in Medicine and Biology, Vol. 5, P. Brätter and P. Schramel, eds. Berlin: de Gruyter.

Kreppel, H., J. Bauman, J. Liu, J.M. McKim, Jr., and C.D. Klaassen. 1993. Induction of metallothionein by arsenicals in mice. Fundam. Appl. Toxicol. 20:184-189.

Kreppel, H., J. Liu, Y.P. Liu, F.X. Reichl, and C.D. Klaassen. 1994. Zinc-induced arsenite tolerance in mice. Fundam. Appl. Toxicol. 23:32-37.

Kroes, R., M.J. van Logten, J.M. Berkvens, T. De Vries, and G.J. van Esch. 1974. Study on the carcinogenicity of lead arsenate and sodium arsenate and on the possible synergistic effect of diethylnitrosamine. Food Cosmet. Toxicol. 12:671-679.

Laib, R.J., and H. Moritz. 1989. Investigation of tumor initiating and/or cocarcinogenic properties of arsenite and arsenate with the rat liver foci bioassay. Exp. Pathol. 37:231-233.

Larramendy, M.L., N.C. Popescu, and J.A. DiPaolo. 1981. Induction by inorganic metal salts of sister chromatid exchanges and chromosome aberrations in human and Syrian hamster cell strains. Environ. Mutagen.

3:597-606.

Lazo, J.S., and B.R. Pitt. 1995. Metallothioneins and cell death by anticancer drugs. Annu. Rev. Pharmacol. Toxicol. 35:635-653.

Lee, T.C., and I.C. Ho. 1994. Differential cytotoxic effects of arsenic on human and animal cells. Environ. Health Perspect. 102(Suppl 3):101-105

Lee, T.C., R.Y. Huang, and K.Y. Jan. 1985. Sodium arsenic enhances the cytotoxicity, clastogenicity, and 6-thioguanine-resistant mutagenicity of ultraviolet light in Chinese hamster ovary cells. Mutat. Res. 148:83-89.

Lee, T.C., K.C. Lee, Y.J. Tzeng, R.Y. Huang, and K.Y. Jan. 1986. Sodium arsenite potentiates the clastogenicity and mutagenicity of DNA crosslinking agents. Environ. Mutagen. 8:119-128.

Lee-Chen, S.F., C.T. Yu, D.R. Wu, and K.Y. Jan. 1994. Differential effects of luminol, nickel and arsenite on the rejoining of ultraviolet light and alkylation-induced DNA breaks. Environ. Mol. Mutagen. 23:116-120.

Lerda, D. 1994. Sister-chromatid exchange (SCE) among individuals chronically exposed to arsenic in drinking water. Mutat. Res. 312:111-120.

Li, J.H., and T.G. Rossman. 1989a. Mechanism of co-mutagenesis of sodium arsenite with *N*-methyl-*N*-nitrosourea. Biol. Trace Elem. Res. 21:373-381.

Li, J.H., and T.G. Rossman. 1989b. Inhibition of DNA ligase activity by arsenite: a possible mechanism of its comutagenesis. Mol. Toxicol. 2:1-9.

Li, J.H., and T.G. Rossman. 1991. Comutagenesis of sodium arsenite with ultraviolet radiation in Chinese hamster V79 cells. Biol. Metals 4:197-200.

Lopez, S., Y. Miyashita, and S.S. Simons. 1990. Structurally based selective interaction of arsenite with steroid receptors. J. Biol. Chem. 265:16039-16042.

Mahaffey, K.R., and B.A. Fowler. 1977. Effects of concurrent administration of lead, cadmium, and arsenic in the rat. Environ. Health Perspect. 19:165-171.

Mahaffey, K.R., S.G. Capar, B.C. Gladen, and B.A. Fowler. 1981. Concurrent exposure to lead, cadmium, and arsenic: effects on toxicity and tissue metal concentrations in the rat. J. Lab. Clin. Med. 98:463-481.

Maitani, T., N. Saito, M. Abe, S. Uchiyama, and Y. Saito. 1987. Chemical form-dependent induction of hepatic zinc-thionein by arsenic administration and effect of co-administered selenium in mice. Toxicol. Lett. 39:63-70.

Mass, M.J. and L. Wang. 1997. Arsenic alters cytosine methylation patterns of the promoter of the tumor suppressor gene p53 in human lung cells: A model for a mechanism of carcinogenesis. Mutat. Res. 386:263-277.

Milner, J.E. 1969. The effect of ingested arsenic on methylcholanthrene-induced skin tumors in mice. Arch. Environ. Health 18:7-11.

Moore, L.E., M.L. Warner, A.H. Smith, D. Kalman, and M.T. Smith. 1996. Use of the flourescent micronucleus assay to detect the genotoxic effects of radiation and arsenic exposure in exfoliated human epithelial cells. Environ. Mol. Mutagen. 27:176-184.

Moore, L.E., A.H. Smith, C. Hopenhayn-Rich, M.L. Biggs, D.A. Kalman, and M.T. Smith. 1997. Micronuclei in exfoliated bladder cells among individuals chronically exposed to arsenic in drinking water. Cancer Epidemiol. Biomarkers Prev. 6:31-36.

Moore, M.M., K. Harrington-Brock, and C.L. Doerr. 1997. Relative genotoxic potency of arsenic and its methylated metabolites. Mutat. Res. 386:279-290.

Ng, J.C. A.A. Seawright, L. Qi, C.M. Garnett, M.R. Moore, and B. Chriswell. 1998. Tumors in mice induced by chronic exposure of high arsenic concentration in drinking water [abstract]. P. 28 in Book of Abstracts of the Third International Conference on Arsenic Exposure and Health Effects, July 12–15, San Diego, Calif.

Nordenson, I., and L. Beckman. 1991. Is the genotoxic effects of arsenic mediated by oxygen free radicals? Hum. Hered. 41:71-73.

Nordenson, I., G. Beckman, L. Beckman, and S. Nordstrom. 1978. Occupational and environmental risks in and around a smelter in northern Sweden. II. Chromosomal aberrations in workers exposed to arsenic. Hereditas 88:47-50.

Okui, T., and Y. Fujiwara. 1986. Inhibition of human excision DNA repair by inorganic arsenic and the co-mutagenic effect in V79 Chinese hamster cells. Mutat. Res. 172:69-76.

Oya-Ohta, Y., T. Kaise, and T. Ochi. 1996. Induction of chromosomal aberrations in cultured human fibroblasts by inorganic and organic arsenic compounds and the different roles of glutathione in such induction. Mutat. Res. 357:123-129.

Packer, L. 1961. Metabolic and structural states of mitochondria. II. Regulation by phosphate. J. Biol. Chem. 236:214-220.

Peoples, S.A. 1975. Review of arsenical pesticides. Pp. 1-12 in Arsenical Pesticides, ACS Symp. Ser 7, E.A. Woolson, ed. Washington, D.C.: American Chemical Society.

Ramírez, P., D.A. Eastmond, J.P. Laclette, and P. Ostrosky-Wegman. 1997. Disruption of microtubule assembly and spindle formation as a mechanism for the induction of aneuploid cells by sodium arsenite and vanadium pentoxide. Mutat. Res. 386:291-298.

Rasmussen, R.E., and D.B. Menzel. 1997. Variation in arsenic-induced sister chromatid exchange in human lymphocytes and lymphoblastoid cells lines. Mutat. Res. 386:299-306.

Rin, K., K. Kawaguchi, K. Yamanaka, M. Tezuka, N. Oku, and S. Okada. 1995. DNA-strand breaks induced by dimethylarsinic acid, a metabolite of inorganic arsenics, are strongly enhanced by superoxide anion radicals. Biol. Pharm. Bull. 18:45-48.

Rossman, T.G. 1981. Enhancement of UV-mutagenesis by low concentrations of arsenite in *E. coli*. Mutat. Res. 91:207-211.

Rossman, T.G. 1998. Molecular and genetic toxicology of arsenic. Environ. Toxicol. 17:171-187.

Rudel, R., T.M. Slayton, and B.D. Beck. 1996. Implications of arsenic genotoxicity for dose response of carcinogenic effects. Regul. Toxicol. Pharmacol. 23:87-105.

Sato, M., and I. Bremner. 1993. Oxygen free radicals and metallothionein. Free Radicals Biol. Med. 14:325-337.

Schrauzer, G.N., and D. Ishmael. 1974. Effects of selenium and arsenic on the genesis of spontaneous mammary tumors in inbred C_3H mice. Ann. Clin. Lab. Sci. 4:441-447.

Schrauzer, G.N., D.A. White, J.E. McGinness, C.J. Schneider, and L.J. Bell. 1978. Arsenic and cancer: Effects of joint administration of arsenite and selenite on the genesis of mammary adenocarcinoma in inbred female C_3H/St mice. Bioinorganic Chem. 9:245-253.

Schroeder, H.A., M. Kanisawa, D.V. Frost, and M. Mitchener. 1968. Germanium, tin and arsenic in rats: effects on growth, survival, pathological lesions and life span. J. Nutrition 96:37-45.

Schwarz, M.A., J.S. Lazo, J.C. Yalowich, W.P. Allen, M. Whitmore, H.A. Bergonia, E. Tzeng, T. Billiar, P.D. Robbins, J.R. Lancaster, and B.R. Pitt. 1995. Metallothionein protects against the cytotoxic and DNA-damaging effects of nitric oxide. Proc. Natl. Acad. Sci. USA 92:4452-4456.

Shibata, A., P.F. Ohneseit, Y.C. Tsai, C.H. Spruck, P.W. Nichols, H.S. Chiang, M.K. Lai, and P.A. Jones. 1994. Mutational spectrum in the p53 gene in bladder tumors from the endemic area of blackfoot disease in Taiwan. Carcinogenesis 15:1085-1087.

Shirachi, D.Y., M.G. Johansen, J.P. McGowen, and S.H. Tu. 1983. Tumorigenic effect of sodium arsenite in rat kidney. Proc. West. Pharmacol. Soc. 26:413-415.

Silver, S., and L.T. Phung. 1996. Bacterial heavy metal resistance: New surprises. Annu. Rev. Microbiol. 50:753-789.

Simons, S.S., P.K. Chakraborti, and A.H. Cavanaugh. 1990. Arsenite and cadmium (II) as probes of glucocorticoid receptor structure and function. J. Biol. Chem. 265:1938-1945.

Smith, A.H., C. Hopenhayn-Rich, M.N. Bates, H.M. Goeden, I. Hertz-Picciotto, H.M. Duggan, R. Wood, M.J. Kosnett, and M.T. Smith. 1992. Cancer risks fron arsenic in drinking water. Environ. Health Perspect. 97:259-267.

Squibb, K.S., and B.A. Fowler. 1983. The toxicity of arsenic and its compounds. Pp 233-270 in Biological and Environmental Effects of Arsenic, B.A. Fowler, ed. Amsterdam: Elsevier.

Taketani, S., H. Kohno, T. Yoshinaga, and R. Tokunaga. 1989. The human 32-kDa stress protein induced by exposure to arsenite and cadmium ions is heme oxygenase. FEBS Lett. 245:173-176.

Tamai, K.T., E.B. Gralla, L.M. Ellerby, J.S. Valentine, and D.J. Thiele. 1993. Yeast and mammalian metallothioneins functionally substitute for yeast copper-zinc superoxide dismutase. Proc. Natl. Acad. Sci. USA 90:8013-8017.

Tanaka, K., N. Miura, I. Satokata, I. Miyamoto, M.C. Yoshida, Y. Satoh, S. Kondo, A. Yasui, H. Okayama, and Y. Okada. 1990. Analysis of a human DNA excision repair gene in group A xeroderma pigmentosum and containing a zinc-finger domain. Nature 348:73-76.

Tezuka, M., K. Hanioka, K. Yamanaka, and S. Okada. 1993. Gene damage induced in human alveolar type II (L-132) cells by exposure to dimethylarsinic acid. Biochem. Biophys. Res. Commun. 191:1173-1183.

Thomas, J., G. Bachowski, and A. Girotti. 1986. Inhibition of cell membrane lipid peroxidation by cadmium- and zinc-metallothioneins. Biochim. Biophys. Acta 884:448-461.

Thorgeirsson, U.P., D.W. Dalgard, J. Reeves, and R.H. Adamson. 1994. Tumor incidence in a chemical carcinogenesis study of nonhuman primates. Regul. Toxicol. Pharmacol. 19:130-151.

Thornalley, P.J., and M. Vasäk. 1985. Possible role for metallothionein in protection against radiation-induced oxidative stress: kinetics and mechanism of its reaction with superoxide and hydroxyl radicals. Biochim. Biophys. Acta 27:36-44.

Uchida, K., T. Morita, T. Sato, T. Ogura, S. Yamashita, S. Noguchi, H. Suzuki, H. Nyunoya, M. Miwa, and T. Sugimura. 1987. Nucleotide sequence of a full-length cDNA for human fibroblast poly(ADP-ribose) polymerase. Biochem. Biophys. Res. Commun. 148:617-622.

Van Delft, S., P. Coffer, W. Kruijer, and R. Van Wijk. 1993. c-fos induction by stress can be mediated by the SRE. Biochem. Biophys. Res. Commun. 197:542-548.

Van Wijk, R., M. Welters, J.E. Souren, H. Overlgonne, and F.A. Wiegant. 1993. Serum-stimulated cell cycle progression and stress protein synthesis in C3H1OT1/2 fibroblasts treated with sodium arsenite. J. Cell Physiol. 155:265-272.

Vega, L., M.E. Gonsebatt, and P. Ostrosky-Wegman. 1995. Aneugenic effect of sodium arsenite on human lymphocytes in vitro: An individual susceptibility effect detected. Mutat. Res. 334:365-373.

Waalkes, M.P., M.J. Harvey, and C.D. Klaassen. 1984. Relative in vitro affinity of hepatic metallothionein for metals. Toxicol. Lett. 20:33-39.

Wanibuchi, H., S. Yamamoto, H. Chen, K. Yoshida, G. Endo, T. Hori, and S. Fukushima. 1996. Promoting effects of dimethylarsinic acid on *N*-butyl-*N*-(4-hydroxybutyl)nitrosamine-induced urinary bladder carcinogenesis in rats. Carcinogenesis 17:2435-2439.

Warner, M.L., L.E. Moore, M.T. Smith, D.A. Kalman, E. Fanning, and A.H. Smith. 1994. Increased micronuclei in exfoliated bladder cells of individuals who chronically ingest arsenic-contaminated water in Nevada. Cancer Epidemiol. Biomarkers Prevent. 3:583-590.

Wiencke, J.K., and J.W. Yager. 1992. Specificity of arsenite in potentiating cytogenetic damage induced by the DNA crosslinking agent diepoxybutane. Environ. Mol. Mutagen. 19:195-200.

Wiencke, J.K., J.W. Yager, A. Varkonyi, M. Hultner, and L.H. Lutze. 1997. Study of arsenic mutagenesis using the plasmid shuttle vector pZ189 propagated in DNA-repair proficient human cells. Mutat. Res. 386:335-344.

Woods, J.S. and B.A. Fowler. 1978. Altered regulation of mammalian hepatic heme biosynthesis and urinary porphyrin excretion during prolonged exposure to sodiium arsenite. Toxicol. Appl. Pharmacol. 43:361-371.

Woods, J.S., M.A. Bowers, and H.A. Davis. 1991. Urinary porphyrin profiles as biomarkers of trace metal exposure and toxicity: Studies on urinary porphyrin excretion patterns in rats during prolonged exposure to methyl mercury. Toxicol. Appl. Pharmacol. 110:464-476.

Wu, W., and M.J. Welsh. 1996. Expression of the 25-kDa heat shock protein (HSP27) correlates with resistance to the toxicity of cadmium chloride, mercuric chloride, cis-platinum(II)-diamine dichloride, or sodium arsenite in mouse embryonic stem cells transfected with sense or antisense HSP27 cDNA. Toxicol. Appl. Pharmacol. 141:330-339.

Yager, J.W., and J.K. Wiencke. 1997. Inhibition of poly(ADP-ribose) polymerase by arsenite. Mutat. Res. 386:345-351.

Yamamoto, S., Y. Konishi, T. Matsuda, T. Murai, M.A. Shibata, I. Matsui-Yuasa, S. Otani, K. Kuroda, G. Endo, and S. Fukushima. 1995. Cancer induction by an organic arsenic compound, dimethylarsinic acid (cacodylic acid) in F344/DuCrj rats after pretreatment with five carcinogens. Cancer Res. 55:1271-1276.

Yamanaka, K., A. Hasegawa, R. Sawamura, and S. Okada. 1989. Dimethylated arsenics induce DNA strand breaks in lung via the production of activated oxygen species in mice. Biochem. Biophys. Res. Commun. 165:43-50.

Yamanaka, K., A. Hasegawa, R. Sawamura, and S. Okada. 1991. Cellular response to oxidative damage in lung induced by the administration of dimethylarsinic acid, a major metabolite of inorganic arsenics, in mice. Toxicol. Appl. Pharmacol. 108:205-213.

Yamanaka, K., M. Tezuka, K. Kato, A. Hasegawa, and S. Okada. 1993. Crosslink formation between DNA and nuclear proteins by in vivo and in vitro exposure of cells to dimethylarsinic acid. Biochem. Biophys. Res. Commun. 191:1184-1191.

Yamanaka, K., K. Ohtsubo, A. Hasegawa, H. Hayashi, H. Ohji, M. Kanisawa, and S. Okada. 1996. Exposure to dimethylarsinic acid, a main metabolite of inorganic arsenics, strongly promotes tumorigenesis initiated by 4-nitroquinoline 1-oxide in the lungs of mice. Carcinogenesis 17:767-770.

Yamauchi, H., T. Yoshida, H. Aikawa, F. Kayama, H. Aminaka, K. Yoshida, M. Akkerman, and B.A. Fowler. 1998. Metabolism and biological monitoring of arsenic poisoning following chronic arsenic exposure in Inner Mongolia, China [abstract]. Toxicological Sciences Supplement. Toxicologist 42(1-S):321.

Yang, J.L., M.F. Chen, C.W. Wu, and T.C. Lee. 1992. Post-treatment with sodium arsenite alters the mutational spectrum induced by ultraviolet light irradiation in Chinese hamster ovary cells. Environ. Mol. Mutagen. 20:156-164.

Zhao, C.Q., M.R. Young, B.A. Diwan, T.P. Coogan, and M.P. Waalkes. 1997. Association of arsenic-induced malignant transformation with DNA hypomethylation and aberrant gene expression. Proc. Natl. Acad. Sci. 94:10907-10912.

8

Variation in Human Sensitivity

THERE is a marked variation in susceptibility to arsenic-induced toxic effects among mammalian species (see Chapter 4). A variation in susceptibility between human population groups and individuals has also been suggested. Possible factors influencing the susceptibility are genetic polymorphisms (especially in metabolism), life stage at which exposures occur, sex, nutritional status, and concurrent exposures to other agents or environmental factors that influence the toxicity of the chemical. The problems in understanding human variability in sensitivity to arsenic are compounded by substantial differences in exposure to arsenic among the population groups and individuals. Considerable variation in the quality of analytical data has also made it difficult to compare studies with confidence.

Variability in arsenic metabolism appears to be important in understanding the human response. There is evidence that methylating capacity differs among individuals and population groups. Different capacities would result in variations in tissue concentrations of arsenic. Also, environmental factors, particularly diet, might be important in explaining susceptibility. A diet poor in methionine or protein is likely to decrease the ability to methylate arsenic. Other dietary factors (e.g., selenium and zinc) might play a role in a person's response to arsenic. Those and other factors contributing to variability are discussed in this chapter.

VARIATION IN ARSENIC METABOLISM

This section discusses variations in the metabolism of inorganic arsenic in humans, especially those variations evidenced by the urinary excretion of arsenic metabolites. Factors considered are methodological aspects; genetic polymorphism; age, sex, and recreational habits; effects of dose; and individual variation.

Methodological Aspects

The efficiency of arsenic methylation is often evaluated by the relative distribution of metabolites of inorganic arsenic (inorganic arsenic, monomethylarsonic acid (MMA), and dimethylarsinic acid (DMA)) in the urine. However, the relative amounts of arsenic metabolites in the urine might not reflect the actual methylation efficiency in the body (i.e., the fraction of the absorbed dose that is methylated), because the methylated metabolites are excreted in the urine more quickly than inorganic arsenic (Buchet et al. 1981a). Given that inorganic arsenic, especially As(III), is the main form of arsenic interacting with tissues (Buchet et al. 1981a; Vahter and Marafante 1983; Bogdan et al. 1994), a decrease in tissue methylation would result in more arsenic being retained in the body (Marafante and Vahter 1984; Marafante et al. 1985).

Ideally, the evaluation of the in vivo methylation of arsenic in humans would be based on the assessment of urinary excretion of MMA and DMA in relationship to the absorbed dose. That assessment is not easily done, because the exact amounts of arsenic inhaled or ingested with drinking water and food, as well as the fraction absorbed, are seldom known. However, a few experimental studies on human volunteers have specified the administered dose and form of arsenic. In a study by Tam et al. (1979), six males ingested ^{74}As-labeled arsenate (about 0.01 μg of arsenic, greater than 90% As(V), per person), and the excretion of ^{74}As was followed for 5 days. Results indicate that approximately 58% of the dose was excreted within that time. In another study, two subjects ingesting 200 μg of As(V) (1 L of bottled water each) excreted about 66% of the dose over 7 days following ingestion (Johnson and Farmer 1991). Taken together, the results of these experimental studies indicate that the proportion of DMA in the urine (relative to U-As$_{met}$) is associated with the urinary excretion of DMA (% of ingested dose), as well as the total urinary excretion of metabolites of inorganic arsenic (U-As$_{met}$), in percentage of the given dose. Similar results were reported in studies of human volunteers exposed to arsenite (Crecelius 1977; Buchet et al. 1981a,b), but the variation was considerable. Thus, on a group basis, a low proportion of DMA in urine (relative to U-As$_{met}$) indicates that the rate of methylation is low and that the overall rate of excretion of arsenic metabolites (in percentage of dose) is low. This would lead to more inorganic arsenic being retained in the body which was also indicated in a study of arsenic metabolites in the urine of women and children exposed to arsenic via drinking water in northern Argentina (Concha et al. 1998a). The ratio between the arsenic in blood and urine increased significantly with decreasing proportion of DMA in the urine, indicating that more arsenic was bound to blood, probably also tissues, at low methylation efficiency.

When evaluating the excretion of arsenic metabolites in urine of human subjects and the factors influencing the concentration of metabolites in tissues and urine, it is essential that the analyses are accurate. As for all analytical data, and especially for those concerning trace elements in body tissues and fluids, the accuracy of the reported data should be verified by appropriate quality-control procedures, the results of which should be documented in the published reports (e.g., Friberg 1988). The situation is perhaps even more problematic for arsenic than for most other common metals in the human environment, because very few standard reference materials (SRMs) with certified concentrations of arsenic in biological media, such as blood and urine, are commercially available. In fact, no SRMs are available for arsenic metabolites in urine. The need for quality-control procedures was demonstrated in a recent interlaboratory comparison exercise involving seven experienced laboratories determining arsenic metabolites in human urine samples. The variations among the laboratories were 1.3-2.7 μg/L for inorganic arsenic, 1.3-2.7 μg/L for MMA, and 5.8-11.2 μg/L for DMA in a urine sample with low arsenic concentrations; and 3.2-6.0 μg/L for inorganic arsenic, 3.5-5.5 μg/L for MMA, and 14.9-22.3 μg/L for DMA in a medium concentration sample (Crecelius and Yager 1997). Thus, when comparing the results of different studies, the quality-control data have to be considered. Unfortunately, quality-control data are often not reported or adequate.

Genetic Polymorphism

The average relative distribution of arsenic metabolites in the urine of various population groups seems to be fairly constant, irrespective of the type and extent of exposure. A large number of studies on human subjects exposed to inorganic arsenic occupationally, experimentally, or environmentally have shown that, in general, U-As$_{met}$ consists of 10-30% inorganic arsenic, 10-20% MMA, and 60-80% DMA (for a review, see Hopenhayn-Rich et al. 1993; Vahter 1994). However, some populations seem to have a somewhat different distribution of arsenic metabolites in the urine. Recent studies of urinary excretion of arsenic showed an average of 2-4% MMA in the urine of people (natives and Spanish descendants) exposed to arsenic in drinking water in northern Argentina (Vahter et al. 1995; Concha et al. 1998a). Studies in San Pedro and Toconao in northern Chile showed that about 5% of the study group (220 individuals) had less than 5% MMA in their urine (Hopenhayn-Rich et al. 1996a). The percentage of MMA was significantly lower in Atacameños than in subjects of European descent. On the other hand, a study on drinking-water exposure to arsenic in northeastern Taiwan showed an unusually high percentage of MMA in the urine—on average, 27% (Chiou et al. 1997).

Whether the reported variations in urinary arsenic metabolites are genetically determined or due to environmental factors remains to be investigated. It should be noted that human polymorphism is reported for other methyltransferases—e.g., histamine *N*-methyltransferase, nicotinamide *N*-methyltransferase, thiopurine *S*-methyltransferase, catechol *O*-methyltransferase, O^6-methylguanine-DNA methyltransferase, and guanidinoacetate methyltransferase (Li et al. 1979; Scott et al. 1988; Aksoy et al. 1996; Krynetski et al. 1996; Scheller et al. 1996; Stockler et al. 1996; Ganesan et al. 1997; Yates et al. 1997).

Another example of genetically determined factors possibly influencing arsenic methylation is given in a case report of increased neurotoxicity in a 16-year-old female with 5,10-methylenetetrahydrofolate reductase (MTHFR) deficiency and suspected exposure to arsenic from an open bag, kept in the home, containing the pesticide copper acetate arsenite (Brouwer et al. 1992). MTHFR is necessary for the conversion of 5,10-methylenetetrahydrofolate to 5-methyltetrahydrofolate, the main methyl donor for the remethylation of homocysteine to methionine. The adolescent had high homocysteine concentrations in plasma and urine, and the resulting deficiency in methyl donors might have lowered the methylation of arsenic. Although all family members were exposed to arsenic, only the 16-year-old with MTHFR deficiency showed signs of arsenic poisoning.

Age, Sex, and Recreational Habits

In children exposed to background concentrations of arsenic, sex or age had no influence on the arsenic metabolites found in the urine (Buchet et al. 1980; Kalman et al. 1990). However, children in northern Argentina exposed to arsenic at about 200 μg/L in drinking water had a significantly higher percentage of inorganic arsenic and a lower percentage of DMA in the urine, compared with adults (49% vs. 66% DMA; Concha et al. 1998a). That might indicate that children are more sensitive to arsenic than adults. One recent study from Finland indicates that an increase in the proportion of DMA in urine with an increase in age might occur in adults (Kurttio et al. 1998).

In people exposed to inorganic arsenic via the drinking water in northern Chile, sex, ethnicity, length of exposure, and smoking, but not age, seemed to have a small but significant influence on the relative amounts of urinary arsenic metabolites (Hopenhayn-Rich et al. 1996a). Multiple linear regression ($p = 0.01$) indicated that women had about 3% more DMA and less MMA in the urine than men. Smoking 10 cigarettes a day resulted in an increase of a few points in the percentage of MMA and a corresponding decrease in the percentage of DMA. Also, one study of human exposure to arsenic via drinking water (up to 600 μg/L) in northeastern Taiwan indicates that women had a somewhat higher percentage of DMA and lower percentage of MMA in the urine than men (Hsu et al. 1997). However, the concentrations of arsenic in the urine were not given. In another study from northeastern Taiwan (where U-As$_{met}$ were found to be 173 μg/L), no sex difference was found in the relative amount of the various urinary metabolites of arsenic (Chiou et al. 1997). Neither was sex a determining factor for the relative distribution of urinary arsenic metabolites in the recent study from Finland (Kurttio et al. 1998).

The observed higher relative amount of DMA in urine in women compared with men in some of the above-mentioned studies might be related to hormonal effects. Recently, pregnant women in the third trimester were reported to have more than 90% DMA in plasma and urine, a percentage that was significantly higher than that in nonpregnant women (Concha et al. 1998b). Differences in birth rate result in differences in the number of pregnant women in study populations.

Effect of Dose

As mentioned in Chapter 5, experimental animal studies have shown a decreased methylation at higher doses of arsenic, as well as an inhibition of the second step in the methylation of arsenic in rat-liver cells incubated in vitro with high concentrations of arsenite. In a study using four human volunteers who ingested a daily dose of 125, 250, 500, or 1,000 μg of arsenic as arsenite (one subject per dose) for 5 consecutive days (Buchet et al. 1981b), the excretion of DMA tended to level off at the highest dose (1,000 μg per day). That response has been interpreted by some as saturation of methylation and has provoked considerable discussion in the literature (EPA 1988; Carlson-Lynch et al. 1994; Beck et al. 1995). However, only one individual was tested per dose, and the urinary excretion of arsenic metabolites is known to vary in individuals; therefore, the results should be interpreted with great caution.

In an analysis of data available in studies published up to that time, no major differences were observed in the average relative distribution of urinary metabolites of inorganic arsenic between people exposed to arsenic occupationally, people exposed to high doses of arsenic experimentally or via drinking water, and people exposed to much less arsenic in the general environment (Hopenhayn-Rich et al. 1993).

A number of studies indicate that the methylation of arsenic is fairly insensitive to high doses that are in the range of exposure occuring via drinking water. The average distribution of arsenic metabolites in urine was 10-30% inorganic arsenic, 10-20% MMA, and 60-80% DMA in most studies. A study of people in Nevada with high concentrations of arsenic in their well water (up to 1,300 $\mu g/L$) showed that a group of 18 subjects with an average U-As$_{met}$ of 750 $\mu g/L$ had about 22% MMA and 58% DMA in the urine (Warner et al. 1994). Similar data were reported for a control group of 18 subjects whose drinking water contained arsenic at less than 10 $\mu g/L$, but the speciation data were close to detection limit and not as reliable as those for the exposed group. A few reports have shown that as the exposure to arsenic via drinking water increased, the percentage of urinary DMA (in relationship to total arsenic metabolites in the urine) decreased and that of MMA increased slightly (Hopenhayn-Rich et al. 1996a; Del Razo et al. 1997; Hsu et al. 1997). Although the changes were statistically significant, they were small. For example, speciation of arsenic in urine from people exposed to arsenic via drinking water in northern Chile indicated that a 500-$\mu g/L$ increase in total U-As$_{met}$ corresponded to a 2% increase in urinary MMA and a 3% decrease in DMA (Hopenhayn-Rich et al. 1996a). A temporary (2 months) change in the source of water, involving a decrease in arsenic concentration from 600 to 45 $\mu g/L$, resulted in a small decrease in the average proportion of inorganic arsenic (about 3%) and in the ratio of MMA to DMA in the urine, but those changes were not related to the magnitude of the decrease in concentration of total urinary metabolites (Hopenhayn-Rich et al. 1996b). A further support for arsenic methylation being relatively insensitive to the drinking-water concentration is a case report of a man who developed neuropathy after 4 months of daily consumption of well water containing 25,000 $\mu g/L$ of arsenic (Kosnett and Becker 1988). Urine sampling before the DMSA chelation therapy was initiated showed U-As$_{met}$ at 5,500 $\mu g/L$, out of which 72% was in the form of MMA and DMA (about 36% of each) and 26% inorganic arsenic.

Thus, the observed effects of the arsenic dose on the methylation efficiency seems to be small and mainly affecting the ratio of MMA to DMA. As available data indicate that the rate of excretion of MMA is similar to or slightly higher than that of DMA—about 75% in 4 days (Buchet et al. 1981a) for MMA and DMA compared with about 50% for inorganic arsenic (Tam et al. 1979; Buchet et al. 1981a)—a small change in the MMA-to-DMA ratio is unlikely to have any toxicological significance. However, the formation of reactive As(III) intermediates cannot be excluded (Cullen et al. 1989a,b; Styblo et al. 1997), although they have not been detected in vivo. Furthermore, the increased excretion of MMA at higher doses can indicate that the second methylation step is inhibited by inorganic As(III) in the tissues; that would indicate that As(III) is increasing in the tissues (Thompson 1993).

There are also a few studies indicating an increase in the percentage of DMA in urine at higher exposure concentrations. In children exposed to arsenic via drinking water in northern Argentina, the percentage of urinary DMA increased with increasing U-As$_{met}$ concentration (about a 30% increase in DMA with a 400-μg/L increase in U-As$_{met}$) (Concha et al. 1998a). That response was not observed in adults, who had a significantly higher proportion of DMA in the urine than the children. However, in a study of adults in northeastern Taiwan, the percentage of urinary DMA increased and that of MMA decreased with increasing arsenic concentrations in the drinking water (three groups of people drinking water with 0-50, 51-300, and >300 μg/L, respectively; Chiou et al. 1997).

Interindividual Variation

When studies of arsenic metabolites in human urine are scrutinized, a substantial interindividual variation in the relative amounts of the metabolites is obvious, although group averages seem to be fairly consistent between studies. Some studies on the distribution of arsenic metabolites in the urine of people exposed to arsenic via drinking water are presented in Table 8-1. Obviously, few studies are published, and several of them include few subjects. Thus, although the variation can be assumed to be an integrated result of the various factors influencing the methylation of arsenic (e.g., genetic, physiological, nutrition, recreational, and analytical), little is known about the relative importance of the various factors. In fact, even the day-to-day variation in the urinary arsenic-metabolite pattern in one individual is unknown.

NUTRITIONAL STATUS

This section discusses the modulation of the responses to arsenic toxicity on the basis of the nutritional status of the individual. As mentioned in

Table 8-1 Interindividual Variation in the Relative Amounts (Median or Mean Values and Total Ranges) of Arsenic Metabolites (Inorganic Arsenic, MMA, and DMA) in the Urine of Individuals Exposed to Inorganic Arsenic via Drinking Water

Drinking-Water Exposure to Arsenic	Cases, No.	U-As$_{met}$, μg/L	Urinary Arsenic Metabolites, %			Reference
			Inorganic Arsenic	MMA	DMA	
Argentina, 200 μg/L, women						
S.A. de los Cobres	11	256	25	2.1	74	Vahter et al. 1995
		109-405	6.5-42	0.6-8.3	54-93	
Taco Pozo	12	386	39	2.2	58	Concha et al. 1998a
		90-606	18-52	1.1-3.5	46-80	
Argentina, 200 μg/L, children						
S.A. de los Cobres	22	323	49	3.6	47	Concha et al. 1998a
		125-578	21-76	0.9-12	22-69	
Taco Pozo	12	440	42	3.4	54	Concha et al. 1998a
		337-621	26-54	1.3-7.9	44-68	
Chile, 600 μg/L, adults						
San Pedro	122	482	18	15	67	Hopenhayn-Rich et al. 1996a
		61-1,893	5.6-39	1.7-31	42-93	
Chile, 15 μg/L, adults						
Toconao	98	49	14	9.7	76	Hopenhayn-Rich et al. 1996a
		6-267	3.6-31	3.1-24	51-92	
China, <1 to >300 μg/L, adults						
Taiwan	115	173 ± 19 (SE)	12 ± 1.0 (SE)	27 ± 1.2 (SE)	61 ± 1.4 (SE)	Chiou et al. 1997

Mexico, 415 µg/L, adults

Santa Ana	35	544	31	11	54	Del Razo et al. 1997
		429-689	28-34	9.5-13	50-58	

United States, 300-400 μg/L, adults

California	10	161	24	18	55	Hopenhayn-Rich et al. 1993
		66-299	8-44	13-27	38-77	

Abbreviations: U-As$_{met}$, urinary arsenic metabolites; SE, standard error.

Chapter 5, experimental studies have shown that rabbits fed diets with low amounts of methionine, choline, or proteins had a marked decrease in the urinary excretion of DMA and an increased tissue retention of arsenic (Vahter and Marafante 1987). In addition, the subcellular distribution of arsenic was altered. Whether that is also true for humans is not known. In areas with severe arsenic-related health effects due to ingestion of drinking water with high arsenic concentrations (i.e., southwestern Taiwan and the Antofagasta region in northern Chile), the inhabitants were reported to have a low socioeconomic level and a poor nutritional status (Borgono et al. 1977; Tseng 1977; Zaldivar and Guillier 1977; Hsueh et al. 1995). Several studies have suggested that poor nutrition might increase the health effects of arsenic. In addition to other studies noted in this section, people in and around West Bengal who were below 80% of the standard body weight for their age and sex had a 1.6-fold increase (2.1 in females, 1.5 in males) in the prevalence of keratoses, suggesting that malnutrition might increase susceptibility (Guha Mazumder et al. 1998). Poor nutritional status might indicate an increased susceptibility to arsenic toxicity, leading to reduced methylation of arsenic and therefore increased tissue retention of arsenic. However, the percentage of methylated arsenic metabolites in the urine seems to vary only to a small degree across populations (see Table 8-1 and Hopenhayn-Rich et al. 1993).

No information is available on how responses to arsenic toxicity are modulated by the nutritional status of individuals. For example, there is disagreement among investigators concerning the nutritional status of arsenic-exposed subjects with blackfoot disease, mainly because of the lack of proper studies (Yang and Blackwell 1961; Engel and Receveur 1993; Hsueh et al. 1995).

The remainder of this section discusses (1) the various nutritional factors that influence the toxicity of arsenic (i.e., methyl group donors, selenium, and zinc) and (2) what is known about the nutritional status of the Taiwanese populations on which EPA (1988) based its estimate of the carcinogenic potency of arsenic.

Methyl Group Donors

Sound but sparse data demonstrate that S-adenosyl methionine (SAM) is the main methyl donor in the methylation of inorganic arsenite. Challenger (1945) suggested that arsenic methylation involved reduction and oxidative methylation by the addition of a carbonium ion to arsenic in the +3 oxidation state. In vivo studies on rabbits given periodate-oxidized adenosine (PAD), a potent inhibitor of S-adenosylhomocysteine hydrolase, showed that SAM is an important methyl donor in the formation of MMA and DMA (Marafante and Vahter 1984; Marafante et al. 1985). The use of SAM as a methyl donor was confirmed by Buchet and Lauwerys (1985) and Styblo and Thomas (1997) using in vitro enzyme assays of crude rat-liver cytosol, and by Zakharyan et al. (1995) using a 2,100-fold purified rabbit-liver arsenite and MMA methyltransferases preparation. Because the major source of SAM is the essential amino acid methionine, methylation of inorganic arsenite by SAM is dependent on the nutritional intake of methionine, cysteine, related vitamins, and cofactors. The importance of such nutritional factors for arsenic metabolism was clearly shown by Vahter and Marafante (1987) in a study showing that low amounts of methionine, choline, or protein in the diet decreased the methylation of inorganic arsenite in the rabbit. Cyanocobalamin (vitamin B_{12}) and its coenzymes, 5´-deoxycobalamin and methylcobalamin, have also been implicated (Buchet and Lauwerys 1985), but the involvement of vitamin B_{12} or its coenzymes is far from clear since in vitro methylation of arsenite in the presence of methylcobalamin can occur in the absence of any enzymes (Buchet and Lauwerys 1985). In the case report described earlier of a 16-year-old female with a MTHFR deficiency and a history of exposure to the pesticide copper acetate arsenite, Brouwer et al. (1992) suggested that she had arsenic-related neurotoxicity, which was not seen in the rest of her family, presumably because of the MTHFR inborn error of metabolism. MTHFR is a metabolic source of methyl groups. These observations obviously show that nutritional factors affecting one-carbon and methyl metabolism must be taken into account in any survey of the nutritional status of persons chronically exposed to inorganic arsenic. Although the Brouwer et al. (1992) report is based on only one subject, the importance of the study should not be minimized.

Selenium

A strong interaction between arsenic and selenium was first observed in 1938 (Moxon 1938) and has since been confirmed in many animal experiments. Arsenites and arsenates, whether applied through the diet or by injection, reduce the toxicity of most selenium compounds. Organic arsenic compounds are less active than inorganic forms in modifying selenium toxicity; arsenic sulfides have no effect. In contrast to the protection afforded by arsenic against excessive exposure to most selenium compounds, arsenic increases the toxicity of the metabolic products dimethylselenide and the trimethylselenonium ion through an unknown mechanism. With that exception, the nature of the arsenic-selenium interaction in animals is well known.

While reducing the elimination of dimethylselenide in exhaled air, sodium arsenite (1 mg/kg) strongly increases the concentration and excretion of selenium in bile at the expense of hepatic concentrations. The magnitude of those changes is thought to explain the reduction of toxicity and the formation of a selenoarsenide compound in the liver, proposed as one mechanism responsible for the increased biliary excretion (Levander 1977). That hypothesis is supported by the observation that injected sodium selenite (0.5 mg/kg) increases the biliary excretion of injected arsenite and reduces the hepatic arsenic concentration. Although additional pathways of detoxification might exist, the proposed selenoarsenide compound would explain the well-established bidirectional nature of this interaction: arsenic and selenium reduce each other's toxicity. Enhanced biliary excretion is the common mechanism; however, biliary excretion differs among species and the extent to which that difference applies to humans is unknown.

The health relevance of those interactions has been observed only under laboratory conditions, where selenium reduced the teratogenic, clastogenic, and cytotoxic effects of arsenic, just as arsenic reduced the toxic effects of selenium (ATSDR 1993). Whether such health effects also occur under practical conditions is much less clear. Those interactions could offer some potentially beneficial applications to reduce the toxicity of excessive environmental exposure to arsenic or selenium by raising the exposure to the respective antagonist. A number of arsenicals, approved as feed additives, were tested in South Dakota where the high selenium concentrations in forage proved to be toxic to cattle and sheep, but their use was found to be impractical (Levander 1977). No such plans have been considered for human populations.

There is no evidence of risks to animal and human populations from a toxic synergism between arsenic and methylated forms of selenium, although the possibility has been discussed (Kenyon et al. 1997). Finally, there is no evidence from animal experiments that arsenic, superimposed on a marginal selenium status, would induce selenium deficiency (Levander 1977).

The reports discussed here lead to the conclusion that, despite convincing evidence for a strong arsenic-selenium interaction in experimental animals, there is as yet no direct evidence for its health effect in humans. Such a health effect, however, resulting from the lack of adequate selenium to counteract arsenic excesses would be consistent with the situation in the blackfoot-disease areas of Taiwan. Selenium status there should be considered a moderator of arsenic toxicity and taken into account when the Taiwanese data are applied to populations with adequate selenium intakes.

Zinc

The clinical relevance of the interaction of arsenic and zinc is more tenuous. Injected parenterally, zinc protects mice against acute arsenic toxicity by way of an unknown mechanism (Kreppel et al. 1994), not related to the induction of metallothionein. Long-term protection by dietary zinc, however, has not been demonstrated. Lin and Yang (1988) measured unusually low zinc concentrations in blood and urine of blackfoot-disease patients in Taiwan. Engel and Receveur (1993) estimated the nutritional adequacy of the diet of the Taiwanese population in the blackfoot-disease endemic area and believed that only zinc might be present in inadequate amounts. However, the calculated zinc intake in the blackfoot-disease endemic area of 9 mg per day is above the recent FAO-IAEA-WHO (1996) recommendation of 5.7 and 4.0 mg per day (population minimal requirement for moderate dietary availability for males and females, respectively, 18-60 years of age and older). Early reports of beneficial effects of zinc treatment in patients with peripheral vascular diseases (Henzel et al. 1969, 1971) have not been followed up.

Nutritional Status of Populations in Taiwan

As early as 1961, Yang and Blackwell reported that blackfoot-disease patients had poor nutritional status. Their report appeared before arsenic was implicated as a possible causative agent for blackfoot disease. The study pointed out that the mean protein of the diet made up only 9% of the caloric intake. The mean methionine intake was 1.2 g per day. Blackwell was a member of a highly respected U.S. naval research group who remained in Taiwan for at least 2 years to study blackfoot disease.

In a brief critique of the Yang and Blackwell (1961) study, Engel and Receveur (1993) using the food consumption data of Yang and Blackwell made estimations and stated that "intake of protein and essential amino acids were adequate, and fat intake accounted for only 5.3% of the energy intake. . . . Our results indicate an inadequate zinc intake at 58% of the recommended daily allowance (NRC 1989), which is based on the maintenance of existing zinc status in healthy young adults on a mixed U.S. diet." Engel and Receveur (1993) in their letter speculated that "zinc deficiency may behave synergistically with arsenic in carcinogenesis and atherosclerosis." The most recent recommendation for dietary zinc intake was established in 1996 (FAO-IAEA-WHO). On the basis of the recent data, the dietary zinc intake reported in the Yang and Blackwell (1961) study appears to be adequate.

The malnutrition of persons with blackfoot disease is further supported by Hsueh et al. (1995), who studied 1,571 subjects from the blackfoot-disease endemic area in Taiwan and pointed out that "undernourishment" related to high consumption of dried sweet potato, as indicated from questionnaire data, was associated with the increased prevalence of skin cancer induced by arsenic. Again one must emphasize that these are epidemiological data derived from questionnaires and are not measurements of sweet potato consumption or chemical analysis of sweet potato composition.

There is no question that the nutritional status of persons chronically exposed to arsenic is crucial to understanding the signs and symptoms of arsenic toxicity. Animal studies have shown clearly that methionine, the factors involved in its metabolism, and selenium influence the metabolism and toxicity of arsenate and arsenite. A recent series of studies using biochemical biomarkers and clinical observations indicate a very low selenium status of the population in some areas of Taiwan. A study of selenium, manganese, cobalt, chromium, and zinc concentrations in the urine of 40 patients with blackfoot disease and 40 healthy controls reported concentrations of selenium between 3 and 4 μg/L, regardless of health status (Pan et al. 1996a). That range compares with 3.3 μg/L (26 subjects) in the population of the Keshan area of China, where selenium-responsive cardiomyopathy is endemic (Oster 1992). Both concentrations represent the lowest values in a worldwide comparison; other values are 26 μg/L (173 subjects), 60 μg/L (167 subjects), and 125 μg/L (10 subjects) in populations in China, the United States, and Canada, respectively (Oster 1992).

Urinary excretion accounts for approximately half of the dietary selenium over a wide range of intakes (FAO-IAEA-WHO 1996); thus, assuming a daily urine output of 2 L, the data suggest an average intake of 12-16 μg per day. That selenium intake compares with an average daily intake of 11 μg in the areas of China with endemic Keshan disease and with average daily intakes of 116 μg, 60-159 μg, and 98-224 μg in other areas of China, the United States, and Canada, respectively (Oster 1992). The recommended dietary allowance for selenium in the United States is 55 and 70 μg per day (NRC 1989), the lower limit of the WHO safe ranges for population mean intake are 30 and 40 μg per day for females and males, respectively (FAO-IAEA-WHO 1996).

Consistent with the urinary data, the serum selenium concentrations in areas of Taiwan also ranked lowest in a worldwide comparison. Thirty-two patients with idiopathic dilated cardiomyopathy from central Taiwan presented an average of 27.6 μg/L compared with 42.7 μg/L in 31 age-matched normal volunteers, a significant difference (Chou et al. 1998). The patients' values are only slightly higher than the 21-μg/L value in the blood of 173 subjects from the Keshan disease area of China; healthy control values are 95 μg/L (111 subjects), 109.9 μg/L (1,025 subjects), and 143.9 μg/L (268 subjects) in populations in China, the United States, and Canada, respectively (Oster 1992).

Two additional studies of blackfoot-disease patients and healthy controls from Taiwan reported slightly higher selenium concentrations but still indicated a low selenium status. Wang et al. (1993) in a whole-blood study reported that patient values were 46.7 μg/L (113 subjects) and control values were 62.7 μg/L (49 subjects). In a serum study by Pan et al. (1996b), patient values were 51.2 μg/L (40 subjects) and control values were 56.5 μg/L (40 subjects).

Another report of very high selenium concentrations in the plasma of 36 stroke patients (214 μg/L) and 21 controls (230 μg/L) in Taiwan (Chang et al. 1998) cannot be evaluated because the analyses were not performed by the authors, and no data on analytical methods and quality control were provided.

The sporadic occurrence of idiopathic dilated cardiomyopathy in central Taiwan (Chou et al. 1998), if related to the cardiomyopathy of the Keshan area of China, might be taken as additional, suggestive evidence of marginal selenium deficiency in the population.

SUMMARY AND CONCLUSIONS

Variability in response to arsenic might have its origin in one or a number of intrinsic or extrinsic factors, many of which affect the body's ability to methylate and eliminate arsenic. Other factors, such as nutrition, life stage, pre-existing health conditions, or recreational habits, might play a role in the response to arsenic but have not been studied extensively.

It is plausible but not proved that poor diet substantially exacerbates the toxicity of arsenic. Much more work is needed to draw any definitive conclusions about the role of specific dietary components in the manifestations of arsenic toxicity. Important factors to consider in evaluating diet in this context are methionine, cysteine, vitamin B_{12}, and folic acid, as well as essential trace elements, such as selenium and zinc.

On the basis of its review of the data on the variations in human sensitivity to arsenic exposure, the subcommittee concludes the following:

- Studies on human volunteers show that a low proportion of DMA in urine is associated with a low rate of methylation of ingested inorganic arsenic and a low rate of excretion of arsenic metabolites.
- A few studies indicate a slight decrease in the percentage of DMA and

a corresponding increase in the percentage of MMA with increasing exposure concentrations. However, a few studies indicate an increase in the percentage of DMA with increasing exposure concentrations, particularly in children. At this time, there is no clear relationship between the dose of arsenic ingested and the relative amounts of arsenic metabolites in the urine.

- There is substantial variation among individuals, and among some populations, in the fractions of methylated forms of arsenic in urine. Factors that can contribute to variation are age, sex, nutrition, and genetic polymorphism. Although such factors appear to influence the kinetics and extent of biomethylation, the implications of that for chronic toxicity, including carcinogenesis are uncertain.

- The influence of nutritional factors on arsenic metabolism and toxicity is not clear.

- A wider margin of safety might be needed when conducting risk assessments of arsenic because of variations in metabolism and sensitivity among individuals or groups.

RECOMMENDATIONS

Factors influencing the susceptibility to or expression of arsenic-associated cancer and noncancer effects need to be better characterized. Particular attention should be given to the study of the extent and reasons for interindividual and intraindividual variation in arsenic metabolism, tissue accumulation, and excretion (including total and relative amounts of urinary arsenic metabolites) under various exposure scenarios.

Gene products responsible for metabolism, diet, and other environmental factors that might influence the susceptibility or expression of arsenic-associated toxicity need to be better characterized in comparative studies involving populations and individuals with different susceptibilities and suitable animal models.

Studies of the potential differences in arsenic methylation efficiency between young children and adults need to be validated and considered in the risk assessment of arsenic.

Future studies of arsenic metabolism and toxicity should include quality-control data on the method used to analyze for arsenic species in the urine, because assurance is needed that the variation is not due to the analytical methods or procedures used.

REFERENCES

Aksoy, S., R. Raftogianis, and R. Weinshilboum. 1996. Human histamine

N-methyltransferase gene: structural characterization and chromosomal localization. Biochem. Biophys. Res. Commun. 219:548-554.

ATSDR (Agency for Toxic Substances and Disease Registry). 1993. Toxicological Profile for Arsenic. Rep. TP-92.02. U.S. Department of Health and Human Services, Agency for Toxic Substances and Disease Registry, Atlanta, Ga.

Beck, B.D., P.D. Boardman, G.C. Hook, R.A. Rudel, T.M. Slayton, and H. Carlson-Lynch. 1995. Response to Smith et al. [letter]. Environ. Health Perspect. 103:15-17.

Bogdan, G.M., A. Sampayo-Reyes, and H.V. Aposhian. 1994. Arsenic binding proteins of mammalian systems: I. Isolation of three arsenite-binding proteins of rabbit liver. Toxicology 93:175-193.

Borgono, J.M., P. Vicent, H. Venturino, and A. Infante. 1977. Arsenic in the drinking water of the city of Antofagasta: Epidemiological and clinical study before and after the installation of the treatment plant. Environ. Health Perspect. 19:103-105.

Brouwer, O.F., W. Onkenhout, P.M. Edelbroek, J.F.M. de Kom, F.A. de Wolff, and A.C.B. Peters. 1992. Increased neurotoxicity of arsenic in methylenetetrahydrofolate reductase deficiency. Clin. Neurol. Neurosurgery 94:307-310.

Buchet, J.P., and R. Lauwerys. 1985. Study of inorganic arsenic methylation by rat liver in vitro: Relevance for the interpretation of observations in man. Arch. Toxicol. 57:125-129.

Buchet, J.P., R. Lauwerys, and H. Roels. 1980. Comparison of several methods for the determination of arsenic compounds in water and in urine. Int. Arch. Occup. Environ. Health 46:11-29.

Buchet, J.P., R. Lauwerys, and H. Roels. 1981a. Comparison of the urinary excretion of arsenic metabolites after a single dose of sodium arsenite, monomethylarsonate or dimethylarsinate in man. Int. Arch. Occup. Environ. Health 48:71-79.

Buchet, J.P., R. Lauwerys, and H. Roels. 1981b. Urinary excretion of inorganic arsenic and its metabolites after repeated ingestion of sodium metaarsenite by volunteers. Int. Arch. Occup. Environ. Health 48:111-118.

Carlson-Lynch, H., B.D. Beck, and P.D. Boardman. 1994. Arsenic risk assessment. Environ. Health Perspect. 102:354-356.

Challenger, F. 1945. Biological methylation. Chem. Rev. 36:315-361.

Chang, C.Y., Y.C. Lai, T.J. Cheng, M.T. Lau, and M.L. Hu. 1998. Plasma levels of antioxidant vitamins, selenium, total sulfhydryl groups and oxidative products in ischemic-stroke patients as compared to matched controls in Taiwan. Free Radic Res. 28(1):15-24.

Chiou, H.Y., Y.M. Hsueh, L.L. Hsieh, L.I. Hsu, Y.H. Hsu, F.I. Hsieh, M.L. Wei, H.C. Chen, H.T. Yang, L.C. Leu, T.H. Chu, C. Chen-Wu, M.H. Yang, and C.J. Chen. 1997. Arsenic methylation capacity, body retention, and null genotypes of glutathione S-transferase M1 and T1 among current arsenic-exposed residents in Taiwan. Mutat. Res. 386:197-207.

Chou, H.T., H.L. Yang, S.S. Tsou, R.K. Ho, P.Y. Pai, and H.B. Hsu. 1998. Status of trace elements in patients with idiopathic dilated cardiomyopathy in central Taiwan. Chung Hua I Hsueh Chih (Taipei) 61(4):193-198.

Concha, G., B. Nermell, and M.V. Vahter. 1998a. Metabolism of inorganic arsenic in children with chronic high arsenic exposure in northern Argentina. Environ. Health Perspect. 106:355-359.

Concha, G., G. Vogler, D. Lezcano, B. Nermell, and M. Vahter. 1998b. Exposure to inorganic arsenic metabolites during early human development. Toxicol. Sci.44:185-190.

Crecelius, E.A. 1977. Changes in the chemical speciation of arsenic following ingestion by man. Environ. Health Perspect. 19:147-150.

Crecelius, E., and J. Yager. 1997. Intercomparison of analytical methods for arsenic speciation in human urine. Environ. Health Perspect. 105:650-653.

Cullen, W.R., D. Hettipathirana, and J. Reglinski. 1989a. The effect of arsenicals on cell suspension cultures of the Madagascar periwinkle (Catharanthus roseus). Appl. Organomet. Chem. 3:515-521.

Cullen, W.R., B.C. McBride, H. Manji, A.W. Pickett, and J. Reglinski. 1989b. The matabolism of methylarsine oxide and sulfide. Appl. Organomet. Chem. 3:71-78.

Del Razo, L.M., G.G. Garcia-Vargas, H. Vargas, A. Albores, M.E. Gonsebatt, R. Montero, P. Ostrosky-Wegman, M. Kelsh, and M.E. Cebrián. 1997. Altered profile of urinary arsenic metabolites in adults with chronic arsenicism: A pilot study. Arch. Toxicol. 71:211-217.

Engel, R.R., and O. Receveur. 1993. RE: Arsenic ingestion and internal cancers: A review [letter]. Am. J. Epidemiol. 138:896-897.

EPA (U.S. Environmental Protection Agency). 1988. Special Report on Inorganic Arsenic: Skin Cancer; Nutritional Essentiality. EPA 625/3-87/013. U.S. Environmental Protection Agency, Risk Assessment Forum, Washington, D.C.

FAO-IAEA-WHO (Food and Agriculture Organization of the United Nations–International Atomic Energy Agency–World Health Organization). 1996. Trace Elerments in Human Nutrition and Health. Geneva: World Health Organization. 343 pp.

Friberg, L. 1988. Quality assurance. Pp. 103-126 in Biological Monitoring of Toxic Metals, T.W. Clarkson, L. Friberg, G.F. Nordberg, and P.R. Sager, eds. New York: Plenum.

Ganesan, V., A. Johnson, A. Connelly, S. Eckhardt, and R.A. Surtees. 1997. Guanidinoacetate methyltransferase deficiency: new clinical features. Pediatr. Neurol. 17:155-157.

Guha Mazumder, D.N., R. Haque, N. Ghosh, B.K. De, A. Santra, D. Chakraborty, and A.H. Smith. 1998. Arsenic Levels in drinking water and the prevalence of skin lesions in West Bengal, India. Int. J. Epidemiol. 27:871-877.

Henzel, J.H., B. Holtmann, F.W. Keitzer, M.S. DeWeese, and E. Lichti. 1969. Trace elements in atherosclerosis, efficacy of zinc medication as a therapeutic modality. Pp. 83-99 in Trace Substances in Environmental Health—II, Proceedings of the University of Missouri's Second Annual Conference on Trace Substances in Environmental Health, D.D. Hemphill, ed. Columbia, Mo.: University of Missouri Press.

Henzel, J.H., F.W. Keitzer, E.L. Lichti, and M.S. DeWeese. 1971. Efficacy of zinc medication as a therapeutic modality in atherosclerosis: Followup observations in patients medicated over prolonged periods. Pp.336-341 in Trace Substances in Environmental Health—IV, Proceedings of the University of Missouri's Fourth Annual Conference on Trace Substances in Environmental Health, D.D. Hemphill, ed. Columbia, Mo.: University of Missouri Press.

Hopenhayn-Rich, C., A.H. Smith, and H.M. Goeden. 1993. Human studies do not support the methylation threshold hypothesis for the toxicity of inorganic arsenic. Environ. Res. 60:161-177.

Hopenhayn-Rich, C., M.L. Biggs, A.H. Smith, D.A. Kalman, and L.E. Moore. 1996a. Methylation study of a population environmentally exposed to arsenic in drinking water. Environ. Health Perspect. 104:620-628.

Hopenhayn-Rich, C., M.L. Biggs, D.A. Kalman, L.E. Moore, and A.H. Smith,. 1996b. Arsenic methylation patterns before and after changing from high to lower concentrations of arsenic in drinking water. Environ. Health Perspect. 104:1200-1207

Hsu , K.H., J.R. Froines, and C.J. Chen. 1997. Studies of arsenic ingestion from drinking water in northeastern Taiwan: Chemical speciation and urinary metabolites. Pp. 190-209 in Arsenic: Exposure and Health Effects, C.O. Abernathy, R.L. Calderon, and W.R. Chappell, eds. London: Chapman & Hall.

Hsueh, Y.M., G.S. Cheng, M.M. Wu, T.L. Kuo, and C.J. Chen. 1995. Multiple risk factors associated with arsenic-induced skin cancer: Effects of chronic liver disease and malnutrional status. Br. J. Cancer 71:109-114.

Johnson, L.R., and J.G. Farmer. 1991. Use of human metabolic studies and urinary arsenic speciation in assessing arsenic exposure. Bull. Environ. Contam. Toxicol. 46:53-61.

Kalman, D.A., J. Hughes, G. van Belle, T. Burbacher, D. Bolgiano, K. Coble, N.K. Mottet, and L. Polissar. 1990. The effect of variable environmental arsenic contamination on urinary concentrations of arsenic species. Environ. Health Perspect. 89:145-151.

Kenyon, E.M., M.F. Hughes, and O.A. Levander. 1997. Influence of dietary selenium on the disposition of arsenate in the female B6C3F$_1$ mouse. J. Toxicol. Environ. Health 51:279-299.

Kosnett, M.J., and C.E. Becker. 1988. Dimercaptosuccinic acid: Utility in acute and chronic arsenic poisoning [abstract]. Vet. Hum. Toxicol. 30:369.

Kreppel, H., J. Liu, Y. Liu, F.X. Reichl, and C.D. Klaassen. 1994. Zinc-induced arsenite tolerance in mice. Fundam. Appl. Toxicol. 23:32-37.

Krynetski, E.Y., H.L. Tai, C.R. Yates, M.Y. Fessing, T. Loennechen, J.D. Schuetz, M.V. Relling, and W.E. Evans. 1996. Genetic polymorphism of thiopurine S- methyltransferase: Clinical importance and molecular mechanisms. Pharmacogenetics 6:279-290.

Kurttio, P., H. Komulainen, E. Hakala, H. Kahelin, and J. Pekkanen. 1998. Urinary excretion of arsenic species after exposure to arsenic present in drinking water. Arch. Environ. Contam. Toxicol. 34:297-305.

Levander, O.A. 1977. Metabolic interrelationships between arsenic and selenium. Environ. Health Perspect. 19:159-164.

Li, G.C., W.C. Fei, and Y.P. Yen. 1979. Survey of arsenical residual levels in the rice paddy soil and water samples from different locations in Taiwan. Natl Sci. Council Monthly 7:798-809

Lin, S.M., and M.H. Yang. 1988. Arsenic, selenium, and zinc in patients with blackfoot disease. Biol. Trace Elem. Res. 15:213-221.

Marafante, E., and M. Vahter. 1984. The effect of methyltransferase inhibition on the metabolism of [^{74}As]arsenite in mice and rabbits. Chem.-Biol. Interact. 50:49-57.

Marafante, E., M. Vahter, and J. Envall. 1985. The role of the methylation in the detoxication of arsenate in the rabbit. Chem.-Biol. Interact. 56:225-238.

Moxon, A.L. 1938. The effect of arsenic on the toxicity of seleniferous grains. Science (July 22):81.

NRC (National Research Council). 1989. Recommended Dietary Allowances, 10th Ed. Washington, D.C.: National Academy Press.

Oster, O. 1992. Zum Selenstatus in der Bundersrepublik Deutschland. Universitatsverlag Jena, Germany. 320 pp.

Pan, T.C., Y.L. Chen, W.J. Wu, and C.W. Huang. 1996a. Determination of Se, Mn, Co, Cr, and Zn in urine specimens of patients with blackfoot disease. Jpn. J. Toxicol. Environ. Health 42:437-442.

Pan, T.C., Y.L. Chen, and W.J. Wu. 1996b. Serum trace metals in blackfoot disease patients. Kao Hsiung I Hsueh Ko Hsueh Tsa Chih (J. Med. Sci.) 12:555-560.

Scheller, T., H. Orgacka, C.L. Szumlanski, and R.M. Weinshilboum. 1996. Mouse liver nicotinamide N-methyltransferase pharmacogenetics: Biochemical properties and variation in activity inbred strains. Pharmacogenetics 6:43 -53.

Scott, M.C., J.A. Van Loon, and R.M. Weinshilboum. 1988. Pharmacogenetics of N- methylation: Heritability of human erythrocyte histamine N-methyltransferase activity. Clin. Pharmacol. Ther. 43:256-262.

Stockler, S., D. Isbrandt, F. Hanefeld, B. Schmidt, and K. Figura. 1996. Guanidinoacetate methyltransferase deficiency: The first inborn error of creatine metabolism in man. Am. J. Hum. Genet. 58:914-922.

Styblo, M., and D.J. Thomas. 1997. Factors influencing in vitro methylation of arsenicals in rat liver cytosol. Pp. 283-295 in Arsenic: Exposure and Health Effects, C.O. Abernathy, R.L. Calderon, and W.R. Chappell, eds. London: Chapman & Hall.

Styblo, M., S.V. Serves, W.R. Cullen, and D.J. Thomas. 1997. Comparative inhibition of yeast glutathione reductase by arsenicals and arsenothiols. Chem. Res. Toxicol. 10:27-33.

Tam, G.K., S.M. Charbonneau, F. Bryce, C. Pomroy, and E. Sandi. 1979. Metabolism of inorganic arsenic (^{74}As) in humans following oral ingestion. Toxicol. Appl. Pharmacol. 50:319-322.

Thompson, D.J. 1993. A chemical hypothesis for arsenic methylation in mammals. Chem.-Biol. Interact. 88:89-114.

Tseng, W.P. 1977. Effects and dose-response relationships of skin cancer and blackfoot disease with arsenic. Environ. Health Perspect. 19:109-119.

Vahter, M. 1994. Species differences in the metabolism of arsenic compounds. Appl. Organomet. Chem. 8:175-182.

Vahter, M., and E. Marafante. 1983. Intracellular interaction and metabolic fate of arsenite and arsenate in mice and rabbits. Chem.-Biol. Interact. 47:29-44.

Vahter, M., and E. Marafante. 1987. Effects of low dietary intake of methionine, choline or proteins on the biotransformation of arsenite in the rabbit. Toxicol. Lett. 37:41-46.

Vahter, M., G. Concha, B. Nermell, R. Nilsson, F. Dulout, and A.T. Natarajan. 1995. A unique metabolism of inorganic arsenic in native Andean women. Eur. J. Pharmacol. 293:455-462.

Wang, C.T., C.W. Huang, S.S. Chou, D.T. Lin, S.R. Liau, and R.T. Wang. 1993. Studies on the concentration of arsenic, selenium, copper, zinc, and iron in the blood of blackfoot disease patients in different clinical stages. Eur. J. Clin. Chem. Clin. Biochem. 31:759-763.

Warner, M.L., L.E. Moore, M.T. Smith, D.A. Kalman, E. Fanning, and A.H. Smith. 1994. Increased micronuclei in exfoliated bladder cells of individuals who chronically ingest arsenic-contaminated water in Nevada. Cancer Epidemiol. Biomarkers Prevent. 3:583-590.

Yang, T.H., and R.Q. Blackwell. 1961. Nutritional and environmental condition in the endemic blackfoot area. Formosan Sci. 15:101-129.

Yates, C.R., E.Y. Krynetski, T. Loennechen, M.Y. Fessing, H.L. Tai, C.H. Pui, M.V. Relling, and W.E. Evans. 1997. Molecular diagnosis of thiopurine S-methyltransferase deficiency: Genetic basis for azathioprine and mercaptopurine intolerance. Ann. Intern. Med. 126:608-614.

Zakharyan, R.A., Y. Wu, G.M. Bogdan, and H.V. Aposhian. 1995. Enzymatic methylation of arsenic compounds: I. Assay, partial purification, and properties of arsenite methyltransferase and monomethylarsonic acid methyltransferase of rabbit liver. Chem. Res. Toxicol. 8:1029-1038.

Zaldivar, R., and A. Guillier. 1977. Environmental and clinical investigations on the endemic chronic arsenic poisoning in infants and children. Zbl. Bakt. Hyg. I. Abt. Orig. B 165:226-234.

9

Essentiality and Therapeutic Uses

THIS chapter is organized into four sections. The first section defines essentiality and specifies the criteria that have been used to determine whether a substance is an essential nutrient. The second section summarizes the evidence for or against the hypothesis that arsenic is an essential nutrient. The third section summarizes what is known about the therapeutic uses of arsenic.

DEFINITION OF ESSENTIALITY

There is general agreement about the criteria needed to identify a substance as an essential nutrient (e.g., Cotzias 1967; Mertz 1970; Underwood and Mertz 1987; FAO-IAEA-WHO 1996). The criteria are as follows:

1. The substance is present in all organisms for which it is essential.
2. Reduction of exposure to the substance below a certain limit results consistently and reproducibly in an impairment of physiologically important functions, and restitution of the substance under otherwise identical conditions prevents the impairment.
3. The severity of signs of deficiency increases in proportion to the reduction of exposure to the substance.

An additional criterion was proposed by Cotzias (1967)

4. The abnormalities produced by a substance's deficiency should always be accompanied by specific biochemical changes—that is, the biochemical mechanisms of action should be known.

Of the four criteria, the first two are crucial; if both are met, a substance under investigation is considered essential for that particular animal species. Satisfying the third and fourth criteria requires additional effort and time and is a goal of nutrition research. That goal is consistent with the continuous refinement of knowledge concerning the molecular mechanisms for nutrients that have produced substantial public-health benefits for decades (e.g., selenium and zinc) or even centuries (e.g., ascorbic acid).

EVIDENCE FOR ESSENTIALITY

As stated above, two criteria must be met before a substance under investigation can be considered essential in a particular animal species: (1) that it is present in all organisms for which it is essential, and (2) that reduction of exposure below a certain limit results consistently and reproducibly in a reduction of physiologically important functions. It is universally accepted that arsenic is present in living matter. The remainder of this section, therefore, examines the evidence in support of the second criterion. That discussion is followed by consideration of information of secondary importance pertaining to the hypothesis of essentiality. This includes information on biochemical mechanism of action, similarities with selenium, and dose-response relationships.

Physiological Importance

A function is considered physiologically important when its impairment interferes with the normal development or survival of the individual (or the whole species). Data are presented below that examine the physiological importance of arsenic in goats, minipigs, rats, and chicks and in particular how semisynthetic diets with low arsenic concentrations affect reproduction and growth of young animals.

Essentiality in Humans

Arsenic has not been tested for essentiality in humans nor has it been found to be required for any essential biochemical processes.

Goats and Minipigs

Goats and minipigs fed semisynthetic diets low in arsenic (arsenic at less than 35 ng/g of diet) produced offspring with an average depression of birth weight of 13% compared with the offspring of animals fed diets with arsenic at 350 ng/g of diet ($p < 0.001$ in both species) (Anke et al. 1976; Anke 1986, 1991; see Addendum to Chapter 9 for description of diets). Female goats fed the low-arsenic semisynthetic diet each produced on average 0.96 kids compared with 1.4 kids per arsenic-supplemented goat ($p < 0.0010$). The corresponding reproduction rate in minipigs was 6.3 compared with 12.8 ($p < 0.001$) for sows fed the low-arsenic semisynthetic or the arsenic-supplemented diet, respectively. An average of 0.8 kids delivered per goat fed the low-arsenic diet survived to the end of the suckling period of 91 days, compared with 1.4 kids per arsenic-supplemented goat ($p < 0.05$). The corresponding survival for minipigs was 2.5 compared with 5.9 ($p < 0.01$).

Most of the breeder goats fed the low-arsenic semisynthetic diet were reported to have died suddenly between the 17th and 35th day of their second lactation, and none of the low-arsenic-diet goats survived the second pregnancy. The low-arsenic-diet goats that did not get pregnant survived to more than 6 years of age (Anke 1991). Autopsies of the low-arsenic-diet goats revealed atrophy of cardiac and striated muscle fibers and distinct reduction of oxidative enzyme activity associated with rupture of liver, heart, and muscle mitochondrial membranes (Schmidt et al. 1984).

Rats

Growth retardation in rats fed low-arsenic semisynthetic diets has been reported independently by two groups of investigators. Addition of sodium arsenite at 0.5, 0.75, 1, and 2 μg/g of an amino-acid diet containing arsenic at 50 ng/g stimulated growth rates by 23%, 14%, 17% and 15%, respectively (Schwarz 1977). Those studies were not repeated because of the death of the investigator. Nielsen et al. (1978) reported strong growth depression and premature death in rats fed a milk-powder-based diet containing arsenic at 30 ng/g of diet compared with controls supplemented with arsenic at 4.5 μg/g of diet. Those studies also were not repeated because the supply of the low-arsenic milk powder ran out. Using a casein-based and ground-corn diet containing arsenic at 15 ng/g, Uthus et al. (1983) detected growth depression in a three-generation study; findings were more pronounced in males than in females. In addition, that study and a replicate study detected reduced fertility and litter size in low-arsenic-diet animals. Apparently, however, those results were not consistently obtained with the casein-based diet. In addition to the low-arsenic state, the investigators began imposing various forms of dietary stress, such as deficient or excessive supplies of certain nutrients or metabolites. For example, supplementation with arsenic at 1 μg/g of diet (see Addendum for description of diet) stimulated growth by approximately 40% in methionine-deficient (1 g/kg of diet) rats with reduced growth, but the resulting growth rates were still less than those fed a diet with adequate methionine content. In the latter, arsenic supplements had no effect (Uthus 1992).

Chicks

In two initial experiments, chicks were fed a milk-powder-based diet with arsenic at 20 ng/g supplemented with arginine at 20 g/kg of diet. The addition of arsenic at 1 μg/g of diet produced a significant growth effect, as it did in a third experiment using a milk-powder-based diet containing arsenic at 35 ng/g of diet. A fourth experiment using a diet containing arsenic at 45 ng/g of diet, however, showed no stimulation of growth when arsenic was added (Nielsen 1980) (see Table 9-1). Those studies were not repeated because the supply of low-arsenic milk powder ran out. In subsequent studies using a casein-based diet with arginine and containing arsenic at 5 ng/g of diet, the addition of 2 μg of arsenic produced a significant ($p < 0.004$) growth stimula-tion (894 g compared with 747 g of body weight at 4 weeks; 24 chicks in each group). In a repeat experiment using different concentrations of zinc, arsenic stimulated growth to a lesser degree (Nielsen 1980). In another experiment, compounds that affect methyl-group availability were added to a diet contain-ing arsenic at 15 ng/g of diet (Uthus 1992). The addition of guanidoacetate at 5 g/kg of feed strongly depressed growth rates in chicks. The addition of arsenic at 2 μg/g of diet stimulated growth significantly in the stressed chicks ($p < 0.01$). Arsenic was ineffective in stimulating growth in chicks that were not stressed.

TABLE 9-1 Weight of Chicks After 28 Days on Diet

Arsenic Content (ng/g) (No. of Chicks)	Weight, Basal Diet	Weight, 1,000 ng/g	Percentage Increase
20 (5)	521 ± 9	580 ± 17	11
20 (5)	586 ± 16	674 ± 25	15
35 (10)	699 ± 32	768 ± 15	10
45 (20)	684 ± 20	686 ± 19	0

Source: Adapted from Nielsen 1980.

Data Consistency and Reproducibility

In a series of experiments conducted since 1973, Anke (1991) evaluated the effects of a low-arsenic semisynthetic diet in goats. He repeated the experiments 12 times. The initial concentration of arsenic in the semisynthetic diets fed to goats was approximately 35 ng/g of diet. The concentration was gradually reduced to approximately 10 ng/g of diet. Anke (1991) reported that within the expected fluctuations, the results are considered consistent and reproducible. Confirmation by independent investigators is still lacking. Studies with minipigs, although not as extensive as those with goats, produced similar effects on growth and reproduction and can be considered consistent with the exception that sudden death of lactating animals was not observed in minipigs. Independent confirmation of those results is still lacking.

Two groups of investigators have independently and almost simultaneously observed growth stimulation by arsenic in rats raised in a protected environment and fed low-arsenic diets (Schwarz 1977; Nielsen et al. 1978). Schwarz (1977) used a highly purified synthetic diet based on amino acids (arsenic at 50 ng/g), whereas Nielsen et al. (1978) fed rats a milk-powder-based semisynthetic ration (35 ng/g). Neither experiment was repeated under identical dietary conditions for reasons mentioned above. In subsequent studies with casein-based diets (15 ng/g), Nielsen (1980) found growth stimulation in some experiments, but not consistently so, unless some form of additional nutritional stress was superimposed. With additional stress, such as methionine deficiency or addition of compounds that affect methyl-group availability, consistent effects of arsenic on growth were reported. Providing supplemental arsenic to chicks on low-arsenic diets with superimposed nutritional stresses stimulated growth consistently (Uthus 1992).

Although the studies reviewed here have not been independently confirmed under identical experimental conditions, all replications by the authors have been consistent in goats and minipigs fed semisynthetic diets with low arsenic content, as well as in rats and chicks subjected to additional dietary stresses.

Biochemical Mechanism of Action

Although there is convincing evidence that the symptoms reported for the rats and chicks fed a low-arsenic semisynthetic diet can be modulated by substances that affect methionine metabolism (and perhaps, methyl groups in general), the mechanisms and sequence of events leading to the functional impairments described above are still unknown.

Dose Aspects

On the basis of the review of studies in four animal species, signs of depressed reproductive performance and growth were observed when the animals were raised in a controlled environment (see Addendum to Chapter 9) and fed semisynthetic diets casein-based, containing arsenic at 50 ng/g or less. The experimental diets met the nutritional requirements of the respective species; their protein sources ranged from purified amino acids to milk powder, casein, and urea. Although diets with arsenic as low as 5 and 10 ng/g were administered, a clear relationship between the arsenic content and the severity of the signs in goats, minipigs, and rats was not established. Chicks, on the other hand, fed diets containing arsenic at 20 ng/g exhibited the most marked impairment. Diets with arsenic content at 35 ng/g of diet still produced some impairment; at 45 ng/g, the chicks were no different from their controls (Nielsen 1980). It should be noted that the form of arsenic in the semisynthetic diets is not known. All these observations relate to the total arsenic naturally present in the diets. No speciation of dietary arsenic had been done and therefore the contribution of different arsenic species to the total diet is not known. The investigators also did not monitor concentrations of arsenic in tissues or urine, and thus, it is not known if dietary arsenic was absorbed and present in tissue. In addition, viral infections had not been checked for. In at least one standard experimental diet with a natural arsenic content of only 5 ng/g (Reeves et al. 1993), evidence of functional impairments in rats and mice was not observed.

As shown in Table 9-2, the concentrations of arsenic in the semisynthetic diets overlap with the concentrations of arsenic found in standard experimental diets, which range from 5 to 6,200 ng/g, with substantial variation between different batches of the same formulation (Reeves 1993). Probably, the diets with high concentrations of arsenic contain organic arsenic compounds. One study reported that mouse diets with an arsenic concentration of 500 ng/g contained fish meal, which is likely to contain arsenobetaine, as a source of protein (Vahter and Norin 1980). Also, the concentrations of arsenic in the semisynthetic diets are similar to those found in most human foods, except seafood (i.e., 10-200 ng/g) (see Chapter 3, Table 3-7). Thus, it is not clear whether the above mentioned effects were due to the low arsenic concentrations or to other factors in the prepared semisynthetic diets.

Inorganic arsenic supplements have ranged from 350 to 4,500 ng/g. Although few data establish a dose-response relationship for supplements of inorganic arsenic, a dose of 350 ng/g prevented impairment of reproductive functions and growth in goats and minipigs, as well as sudden cardiac death in lactating goats. Supplements ranging from 500 to 4,500 ng/g were reported to stimulate growth in rats and chicks fed semisynthetic diets, often with additional dietary stress.

Table 9-2 Effects of Dietary Arsenic in Selected Species

Species	Dietary Arsenic[a]	Effects
Humans	10-200 ng/g[b]	—
Goats, minipigs	10-35 ng/g[c]	Reduced growth and reproduction
Rats, chicks	5-50 ng/g[c] often with additional dietary stress	Reduced growth
Goats, minipigs, rats, chicks	350-4,500 ng/g[c] (inorganic arsenic)	Improved growth

[a]Total arsenic.
[b]Range of concentrations (dry weight) in nonmarine foods (see Ch. 3, Table 3-7).
[c]Semisynthetic diets.

The highest supplementation dose (4,500 ng/g) corresponds to a daily dose of several milligrams of inorganic arsenic for an adult human (i.e., in the range of the therapeutic doses of arsenic used for Fowler´s solution) (see the following section). The lowest supplemented dose (350 ng/g) would correspond to more than 100 μg of arsenic per day for an adult human. In the more recent studies on rats and chicks (Uthus 1992), arsenic had a growth-stimulating effect only in animals that were subject to additional dietary stress in the form of methionine deficiency or excess arginine or guanidoacetic acid. The supplemented concentrations (arsenic at 1-2 μg/g of diet) would correspond to 1 mg or more of arsenic per day for an adult human. The foregoing discussion of inorganic arsenic as an essential nutrient in animals should be distinguished from the use of aryl arsenic veterinary medications as additives to animal feed (Adams et al. 1994).

In conclusion, studies to date do not give evidence that arsenic is an essential element in humans or that it is required for any essential biochemical process. At very high doses (concentrations of 350-4,500 ng/g in the diet), arsenic supplementation seems to have a growth-stimulating effect in minipigs, chicks, goats, and rats.

THERAPEUTIC USES OF ARSENIC

The introduction of inorganic arsenic as a therapeutic agent in the modern medical era is generally attributed to Thomas Fowler, a British physician whose treatise "Medical Reports of the Effects of Arsenic in the Cure of

Agues, Remitting Fevers, and Periodic Headaches" was published in 1786. After determining that arsenic was a key ingredient in a locally sold patent medicine, Fowler prepared and used a "mineral solution" containing approximately 1% arsenic trioxide to treat "agues," or malarial fevers. At an oral adult dose equivalent to approximately 11.4 mg of inorganic arsenite per day, Fowler reported therapeutic success in 242 of 247 patients. He did, however, note that "about one-third" of the patients thus treated experienced "operative effects" (side effects) consisting of nausea, vomiting, or abdominal pain. Fowler's mineral solution quickly gained recognition as a therapeutic agent, and under the name Liquor Arsenicalis, it became officially listed in the London Pharmacopoeia beginning in 1809 and the U.S. Pharmacopoeia in 1820 (Langehan 1921). During the first half of the nineteenth century, "Fowler's solution," as Liquor Arsenicalis was commonly known, was advocated by many physicians often at widely variable doses for a broad spectrum of symptoms and illnesses (Haller 1975). By the latter half of the nineteenth century, Fowler's solution was recommended mainly for the treatment of skin diseases (particularly eczema, psoriasis, and pemphigus), asthma, chorea (probably in association with rheumatic fever), periodic fevers (e.g., from malaria), and pain. The noted physician Sir William Osler, writing in the first edition of his textbook *Principles and Practice of Medicine*, recommended inorganic arsenic in the treatment of pernicious anemia, chorea, leukemia, and Hodgkin's disease (Osler 1894). Prescribed doses commonly delivered approximately 5-10 mg of inorganic arsenite orally per day (Farquharson 1880; Stockman 1902; Langehan 1921). The chronic use of inorganic arsenic in this manner was sometimes associated with the development of cutaneous hyperpigmentation or, less commonly, peripheral neuropathy and other multisystemic signs of chronic arsenic poisoning (Osler 1894; Stockman 1902; Pope 1902; Silver and Wainman 1952).

Inorganic arsenic continued to be used as a therapeutic agent through the mid-twentieth century, by which time its recognized uses were confined predominantly to leukemia, psoriasis, and chronic bronchial asthma (Goodman and Gilman 1955). In the 1950s, the chronic, often unsupervised use of Gay's solution containing potassium arsenite, digitalis, potassium iodide, and phenobarbital for asthma created controversy when reports of success were countered by reports of overt arsenic toxicity (Silver and Wainman 1952; Pascher and Wolf 1952; Gay 1954). In 1967, Harvard investigators Harter and Novitch (1967) reported the results of a controlled trial of Gay's solution in patients whose asthma was "intractable" to treatment with either bronchodilators alone or bronchodilators plus corticosteroids. The patients' pre-enrollment regimen was supplemented, in a double-blind manner, with variants of Gay's solution containing or lacking inorganic arsenic. "Definite" clinical improvement was found within 10 days in 7 of 18 patient trials that included arsenic administration (5-6.7 mg of arsenite per day) compared with only 1 of 11 patient trials lacking arsenic ($p = 0.007$). Approximately one-fourth of the patients receiving arsenic manifested gastrointestinal toxicity. Although inorganic arsenic might still occasionally be encountered in non-Western traditional medicines or folk remedies (Kew et al. 1993; Espinoza et al. 1995), its availability in medications listed in official Western formularies ended in the 1970s.

Organic arsenic antibiotics were used extensively in the first half of the twentieth century, principally in the treatment of spirochetal and protozoal diseases (Goodman and Gilman 1955). The first such official agent, Salvarsan, or arsphenamine, was introduced by Ehrlich in 1907 for the treatment of syphilis. Arsphenamine and other trivalent derivatives, such as neoarsphenamine, were widely used as antisyphilitics in the first two decades of the century. They were replaced by more stable trivalent arsenoxides, such as oxophenarsine and dichlorophenarsine, in the 1930s and 1940s. The availability of penicillin in the 1940s and 1950s largely supplanted the use of antisyphilitic arsenicals. Pentavalent arsonic acid derivatives such as tryparsamide, used for trypanosomiasis, and carbarsone, used for amebiasis, were used in the 1930s through the 1960s. By the 1980s, the only remaining organic arsenical was melarsoprol, available through the U.S. Centers for Disease Control and Prevention for treatment of the meningoencephalitic stage of African trypanosomiasis.

The precise mechanisms by which inorganic arsenic exerted salutary effects in treatment have not been elucidated, but it is of interest that its reported benefit in psoriasis, eczema, and bronchial asthma and its antipyretic effect in certain febrile diseases suggest that it might have exerted suppressive effects on immune-mediated inflammation. Recently, intravenous administration of arsenic trioxide (10 mg per day or 0.5 mg/kg per day) was reported to induce remission in acute promyelocytic leukemia (Shen et al. 1997; Soignet et al. 1998). Preliminary investigations suggest that the mechanism might involve induction of apoptosis (Look 1998).

SUMMARY AND CONCLUSIONS

In this chapter, the subcommittee reviewed the evidence for the beneficial effects or essentiality for arsenic from experimental studies. Data on the physiological importance of arsenic in goats, minipigs, rats, and chicks were considered. There are no comparable data for humans. Reported therapeutic effects of arsenic are also reviewed.

On the basis of its review of the data relating to the essentiality and therapeutic effects of arsenic, the subcommittee concludes the following:

- Arsenic has not been tested for essentiality in humans.
- Data from four species indicate that semisynthetic diets with arsenic concentrations in the range of 35 to 50 ng/g or less in combination with dietary or reproductive stress result in functional impairments. Such concentrations might occur naturally in some experimental diets and are similar to those found in most human foods except seafood. The mechanisms and sequence of events leading to functional impairments are not known.
- Studies show that arsenic supplementation of low-arsenic semisynthetic diets prevents the occurrence of abnormal reproductive performance in goats and minipigs (350 ng/g) and reduced growth in chicks, and rats (500 to 4,500 ng/g). Although the studies have had no independent confirmation under identical experimental conditions, replications by the original investigators have been consistent with goats and minipigs fed semisynthetic diets, as well as with rats and chicks subjected to additional dietary stress. Toxic effects of the supplementation have not been studied.
- Studies to date do not provide evidence that arsenic is an essential element in humans or that it is required for any essential biochemical process. Arsenic supplementation seems to have a growth-stimulating effect at very high doses in minipigs, chicks, goats, and rats. This conclusion is consistent with NRC (1989).
- Arsenic might have therapeutic properties for certain disorders.

RECOMMENDATIONS

Validated analytical data on arsenic concentrations in preparations for total parenteral nutrition (TPN) should be obtained and related to the health status of patients on long-term TPN.

Future studies on the beneficial effects of arsenic in experimental animals should carefully monitor the amount and speciation of arsenic in diets and water (as fed), use biomarkers to assess arsenic exposure and bioavailability, and use techniques that assess toxicity to and benefits from arsenic in a more specific manner than is possible through measurement of growth and reproductive success.

REFERENCES

Adams, M.A., P.M. Bolger, and E.L. Gunderson. 1994. Dietary intake and hazards of arsenic. Pp. 41-49 in Arsenic: Exposure and Health, W.R. Chappell, C.O. Abernathy, and C.R. Cothern, eds. Northwood, U.K.: Science and Technology Letters.

Anke, M. 1986. Arsenic. Pp. 347-372 in Trace Elements in Human and Animal Nutrition, Vol. 2, 5th Ed., W. Mertz, ed. Orlando, Fla.: Academic.

Anke, M. 1991. The essentiality of ultra trace elements for reproduction and pre-and postnatal development. Pp. 119-144 in Trace Elements in Nutrition of Children—II, R.K. Chandra, ed. New York: Raven.

Anke, M., M. Grün, and M. Partschefeld. 1976. The essentiality of arsenic for animals. Pp. 403-409 in Trace Substances in Environmental Health—X, Proceedings of the University of Missouri's Tenth Annual Conference on Trace Substances in Environmental Health, D.D. Hemphill, ed. Columbia, Mo.: University of Missouri Press.

Cotzias, G.C. 1967. Importance of trace substances in environmental health as exemplified by manganese. Pp. 5-19 in Proceedings of the University of Missouri's First Annual Conference on Trace Substances in Environmental Health, D.D. Hemphill, ed. Columbia, Mo.: University of Missouri Press.

Espinoza, E.O., M.J. Mann, and B. Bleasdell. 1995. Arsenic and mercury in traditional Chinese herbal balls. N. Engl. J. Med. 333:803-804.

FAO-IAEA-WHO (Food and Agriculture Organization of the United Nations–International Atomic Energy Agency–World Health Organization). 1996. Trace Elerments in Human Nutrition and Health. Geneva: World Health Organization. 343 pp.

Farquharson, R. 1880. On the use of arsenic in skin-diseases. Br. Med. J. (May 29):802-804.

Fowler, T. 1786. Medical Reports of the Effects of Arsenic, in the Cure of Agues, Remitting Fevers, and Periodic Headaches. London: Johnson and Brown.

Gay, E.D. 1954. Asthma and arsenic. JAMA 156 (Dec. 25):1628.

Goodman, L.S., and A. Gilman. 1955. The Pharmacological Basis of Therapeutics. New York: Macmillan.

Haller. J.S. 1975. Therapeutic mule: The use of arsenic in the nineteenth century materia medica. Pharm. History 17(3):87-100.

Harter, J.G., and A.M. Novitch. 1967. An evaluation of Gay's solution in the treatment of asthma. J. Allergy 40:327-336.

Kew, J., C. Morris, A. Aihie, R. Fysh, S. Jones, D. Brooks. 1993. Arsenic and mercury intoxication due to Indian ethnic remedies. Br. Med. J. 306:506-507.

Langehan, H.A. 1921. A Century of the United States Pharmacopoeia: 1820–1920. Liquor Potassii Arsenitis. Bull. Univ. Wisc. Ser. No. 1153,

Gen. Ser. No. 936.

Look, A.T. 1998. Arsenic and aproptosis in the treatment of acute promyelocytic leukemia. J. Natl. Cancer Inst. 90:86-88.

Mertz, W. 1970. Some aspects of nutritional trace element research. Fed. Proc. Fed. Am. Soc. Exp. Biol. 29:1482-1488.

Nielsen, F.H. 1980. Evidence of the essentiality of arsenic, nickel, and vanadium and their possible nutritional significance. Pp. 157-172 in Advances in Nutritional Research, Vol. 3, H.H. Draper, ed. New York: Plenum.

Nielsen, F.H., D.R. Myron, and E. O. Uthus. 1978. Newer trace elements—Vanadium (V) and arsenic (As) deficiency signs and possible metabolic roles. Pp. 244-247 in Trace Element Metabolism in Man and Animals, Vol. 3, M. Kirchgessner, ed. Freising-Weihenstephan, Germany: Technische Universitat Munchen.

NRC (National Research Council). 1989. Recommended Dietary Allowances, 10th Ed. Washington, D.C.: National Academy Press.

Osler, W. 1894. Principles and Practice of Medicine. New York: Appleton.

Pascher, F. and J. Wolf. 1952. Cutaneous sequelae following treatment of bronchial asthma with inorganic arsenic: Report of two cases. JAMA 148:734-736.

Pope, F.M. 1902. Arsenic in the treatment of chorea. Br. Med. J. (Oct.18):1229-1230.

Reeves, P.G., F.H. Nielsen, G.C. Fahey, Jr. 1993. AIN-93 purified diets for laboratory rodents: Final report of the American Institute of Nutrition ad hoc writing committee on the reformulation of the AIN-76A rodent diet. J. Nutr. 123:1939-1951.

Schmidt, A., M. Anke, B. Groppel, and H. Kronemann. 1984. Effects of As deficiency on skeletal muscle, myocardium and liver: A histochemical and ultrastructural study. Exp. Pathol. 25:195-197.

Schwarz, K. 1977. Essentiality versus toxicity of metals. Pp. 3-22 in Clinical Chemistry and Chemical Toxicology of Metals, S.S. Brown, ed. Amsterdam: Elsevier.

Shen, Z.X., G.Q. Chen, J.H. Ni, X.S. Li, S.M. Xiong, Q.Y. Qiu, J. Zhu, W. Tang, G.L. Sun, K.Q. Yang, Y. Chen, L. Zhou, Z.W. Fang, Y.T. Wang, J. Ma, P. Zhang, T.D. Zhang, S.J. Chen, Z. Chen, and Z.Y. Wang. 1997. Use of arsenic trioxide (As_2O_3) in the treatment of acute promyelocytic leukemia (APL): II. Clinical efficacy and pharmaco-kinetics in relapsed patients. Blood 89:3354-3360.

Silver, A.S., and P.L. Wainman. 1952. Chronic arsenic poisoning following use of an asthma remedy. JAMA 150:584-585.

Soignet, S.L., P. Maslak, Z.G. Wang, S. Jhanwar, E. Calleja, L.J. Dardashti, D. Corso, A. DeBlasio, J. Gabrilove, D.A. Scheinberg, P.P. Pandolfi, and R.P. Warrell, Jr. 1998. Complete remission after treatment of acute promyelocytic leukemia with arsenic trioxide. N. Engl. J. Med. 339:1341-1348.

Stockman, R. 1902. The therapeutic value of arsenic and the justification of its continued use in the light of recent observations concerning its toxic action. Br. Med. J. (Oct. 18):1227-1229.

Underwood, E.J. and W. Mertz. 1987. Introduction. Pp. 1-19 in Trace Elements in Human and Animal Nutrition, Vol. 1, 5th Ed., W. Mertz, ed. San Diego, Calif.: Academic.

Uthus, E.O. 1992. Evidence for arsenic essentiality. Environ. Geochem. Health 14:55-58.

Uthus, E.O., W.E. Cornatzer, and F.H. Nielsen. 1983. Consequences of arsenic deprivation in laboratory animals. Pp. 173-189 in Arsenic: Industrial, Biomedical, Environmental Perspectives, W.H. Lederer and R.J. Fensterheim, eds. New York: Van Nostrand Reinhold.

Vahter M., and H. Norin. 1980. Metabolism of [74]As-labeled trivalent and pentavalent inorganic arsenic in mice. Environ. Res. 21:446-457.

10

Statistical Issues

THIS chapter addresses some of the statistical issues related to characterizing the dose-response relationship between cancer incidence and exposure to arsenic in drinking water. The chapter comprises five major sections. The first reviews the broad principles of dose-response modeling and discusses how age effects can be incorporated into the risk-assessment process. The second section briefly summarizes the approach used by the U.S. Environmental Protection Agency (EPA) in its 1988 arsenic risk assessment based on the skin-cancer data reported by Tseng et al. (1968). This section elaborates on some of the sources of uncertainty associated with the 1988 risk assessment, which was reviewed in Chapter 2. Much of the uncertainty comes from the fact that the Tseng study was "ecological": Instead of having individual measurements of arsenic exposure, subjects were assigned exposures according to the village where they lived. The third section presents a description of the problems associated with risk assessment based on ecological data. It also discusses the kind of measurement error that arises in this context and its implication for risk assessment in general, as well as specifically for the analysis of the Tseng data. The fourth section presents some empirical analysis based on cancer mortality data from Taiwan. This analysis should not be interpreted as a formal risk assessment for arsenic in drinking water or as a recommendation on how the risk assessment should be performed. Rather, it is presented only to illustrate points raised earlier in the chapter. The fifth section provides a discussion of some of the different statistical approaches that can be applied to disease mortality data for quantitative risk assessment. In particular, the section discusses some advantages and disadvantages of modeling age effects directly as well as modeling via standardized mortality ratios; the latter requires specification of an external baseline comparison or control group.

A REVIEW OF DOSE-RESPONSE MODELING AND RISK ASSESSMENT

Dose-response modeling refers to the statistical problem of characterizing the probability of the occurrence of an event as a function of exposure. For simplicity, the discussion here will refer to the event of interest as "cancer." In practice, there are always subtleties and complicating factors to consider when performing a specific risk assessment. The purpose here is not to address all these issues but to outline the broad principles of model fitting and quantitative risk assessment. The one issue that the subcommittee does address in some detail is how to incorporate information on age-specific cancer rates into the risk-assessment process.

Suppose we have data from N individuals corresponding to their exposure and cancer status. More precisely, let y_i take the value 1 if person i has cancer and 0 otherwise. Let x_i be the exposure concentration for that same person. Then, if $p_\theta(x)$ represents the assumed dose-response model that characterizes the probability of cancer as a function of exposure through a set of unknown parameters θ, the maximum likelihood estimator (MLE) of θ is the value that maximizes the likelihood

$$\text{Lik} = \prod_{i=1}^{N} p_\theta(x_i)^{Y_i}[1 - p_\theta(x_i)]^{1-Y_i}, \qquad (1)$$

where $\prod$ denotes product. As discussed in Gart et al. (1986, Ch. 5), many dose-response models are available that can be used to describe the relationship between exposure and cancer prevalence. EPA often uses the multistage model (Holland and Sielkin 1993) in the analysis of animal data. That model, which is motivated by the idea that cancer occurs as the last of several irreversible steps, takes the form

$$p_\theta(x) = 1 - \exp[-(Q_0 + Q_1 x + Q_2 x^2 + \ldots + Q_k x^k], \qquad (2)$$

where $Q_0, Q_1, \ldots Q_k$ are elements of the unknown parameter vector θ, which needs to be estimated using maximum likelihood. Usually, the parameters are estimated under the constraint that the $Q's$ are non-negative. Often, K is taken to equal 1 (the 1 hit model) or 2.

In the past, the next step after fitting the dose-response model has been to estimate the exposure concentration that corresponds to an "acceptable" risk above background. The acceptable risk level for cancer risk assessment has historically been 10^{-6}, however, the recent proposed EPA (1996) guidelines have moved away from the idea of extrapolating to such low risks. Instead, the proposed default approach is to estimate a "point of departure," which is the dose corresponding to a risk level within the observable range of data. For animal studies, the 1996 guidelines suggest that the 10% excess risk level will typically provide an appropriate   point of departure that can be estimated without significant extrapolation. For epidemiological studies, however, a lower level (1% or 5%) is usually more appropriate (see EPA 1996, p. 17962). Regardless of whether the goal is low-dose extrapolation or estimation of a point of departure, the statistical methods are the same, namely, solving for the value of x that solves $p(x) - p(0) = r$, where r represents the excess risk level of interest. To allow for statistical variability in estimating unknown model parameters, it is typical to calculate a lower confidence limit on this value. Gart et al. (1986) discussed various methods of calculating confidence intervals for the dose corresponding to a specified excess risk above background. As described in the EPA 1996 guidelines, a popular approach is to calculate an upper 95% confidence limit on the estimated dose-response curve itself, and then to identify the exposure x that corresponds to the desired excess risk on this curve. Standard maximum-likelihood methods can generally be used for this purpose when the assumed dose-response model is differentiable and involves no constraints on the parameter space. Calculating confidence limits becomes more complicated for the multistage model because of the non-negativity constraint on the Q's. Guess and Crump (1978) discussed approaches to obtaining confidence intervals based on the multistage model.

Dose-response modeling becomes more complicated when the data also include information on age. The basic approach depends on whether the end point of interest is presented in the form of incidence or prevalence data. The skin-cancer data used in the 1988 EPA risk assessment were in the form of prevalence (the proportion of subjects with the disease among those alive at each particular age). The data on internal cancers, to be discussed later, are summarized as mortality data (the number of subjects who die from the disease at a certain age, along with the person-years "at risk" at that same age). This section focuses on the analysis of prevalence data. Modeling strategies for incidence data will be discussed later.

From a statistical perspective, it is straightforward to extend dose-response functions to include age and other factors. The multistage Weibull model is such an extension of the multistage model and takes the form

$$p_\theta(x, t) = 1 - \exp[-(Q_0 + Q_1 x + \ldots Q_k x^k) * (t - T_0)^C], \qquad (3)$$

where x represents exposure concentration, t represents age, and $p_\theta(x, t)$ represents the probability of cancer in an individual aged t exposed to concentration x. Note that as above the value $k = 2$ is commonly used. The parameters $Q_0, \ldots Q_k, T_0$, and C represent the elements of the unknown parameter vector θ, which needs to be estimated using maximum likelihood. As above, θ is usually estimated under the constraint that the Q's are positive. Equation 3 implies that the probability of cancer for a fixed age follows a multistage model; for a fixed exposure, the model implies that a person's age at the time of developing skin cancer follows a Weibull distribution.

The step after model fitting is calculating the exposure concentration that corresponds to a specified excess risk above background. This step is more complicated when an age-adjusted model has been used. A typical approach (illustrated in the next section) is to convert to a lifetime risk of cancer by summing the values of $p_\theta(x, t)$ over all values of t, weighted by the proportion of the population alive at each age. Standard methods can then be applied to obtain confidence intervals. Again, the theory becomes more complicated for the multistage Weibull model, because the Q's are constrained to be non-negative, and $p_\theta(t, x)$ is not differentiable everywhere with respect to T_0.

THE EPA 1988 ANALYSIS

As described in Chapter 2, the data used by EPA in its 1988 risk assessment for arsenic in drinking water came from an epidemiological study by Tseng et al. (1968). The study was based on a cross-sectional assessment of the entire population (40,421 people) from 37 villages in a region of Taiwan where artesian wells with high arsenic concentrations had been in use for a long time. For comparison, 7,500 inhabitants from a control region were also studied. Subjects were examined for various skin lesions and skin cancer. Water samples (142 in total) from 114 wells (110 artesian and 4 shallow) were analyzed and found to have arsenic concentrations ranging up to 1.8 ppm. Individuals were assigned to exposure categories according to their village of residence. Villages were divided into three exposure groups: low (less than 0.3 ppm), medium (0.3-0.6 ppm), and high (more than 0.6 ppm) arsenic concentrations. A fourth category of "undetermined" was assigned to villages either where wells had been closed or where the variability was so great that it was impossible to reliably assign the village to an exposure category. Subjects were also classified into four age groups: 0-19, 20-39, 40-59, and 60 and over. Tables 10-1 and 10-2 (EPA 1988) show the data reported in the Tseng study. EPA fitted the multistage Weibull model to the data, omitting the undetermined exposure category and using the value $k = 2$. To use the fitted dose-response model to estimate risk for the U.S. population, several additional calculations were needed. In particular, it was necessary to adjust for differences between the U.S. and Taiwanese populations with respect to (1) age-specific mortality, (2) body weight, and (3) water-consumption rate. To account for mortality differences, the age-specific dose-response curve was translated to a lifetime cancer risk for the U.S. population by multiplying the estimated age-specific probabilities of having developed cancer by the U.S. Life Tables (NCHS 1998) death probabilities:

$$\text{Lifetime risk at exposure } x = \sum_t p_\theta(x, t) q_t,$$

where q_t is the probability of dying at age t in the United States, and $\sum_t$ denotes summation over all age groups. To adjust for differences in weight and drinking rates, EPA assumed that a typical Taiwanese male weighed 55 kg and drank 3.5 L of water per day. A typical Taiwanese women was assumed to weigh 50 kg and drink 3 L per day. A typical U.S. reference person (male or female) was assumed to weigh 70 kg and drink 2 L per day. Assuming that the cancer risk is related to micrograms ingested per kilogram of body weight, it follows that a typical U.S. male drinking water contaminated with arsenic at x μg/L would have the same age-specific cancer risk as a Taiwanese male exposed to $0.45x$ μg/L. Using this approach, EPA estimated the U.S. lifetime skin cancer risk associated with a drinking-water concentration of 50 μg/L as 1×10^{-3} for females and 3×10^{-3} for males.

Sources of Uncertainty in the EPA 1988 Analysis

As discussed in Chapter 2, several complicating factors and sources of uncertainty affect the reliability of the current EPA risk estimate. Some of the issues are generic ones common to any risk assessment. Such issues are suitability of the chosen dose-response model, choice of end point, and whether and how to address biological considerations, such as detoxification and clearance. However, some issues are specific to this particular analysis.

One concern was that the study was ecological in nature, and such studies are often felt to be problematic for the purpose of quantitative risk assessment (NRC 1991). Although arsenic concentrations were measured at the village level, the data were further summarized into low-, medium-, high- and undetermined-exposure groups. Another problem was that only the marginal age distributions were reported, so that the information in Tables 10-1 and 10-2 is based on estimated rather than actual data.

The following section discusses some of the implications, in general and specifically for the Tseng study, of using ecological and grouped data for dose-response modeling and risk assessment.

PROBLEMS WITH RISK ASSESSMENT BASED ON ECOLOGICAL DATA

Many authors have discussed the shortcomings of assessing dose-response relationships based on ecological data (e.g., see Greenland and Morganstern 1989; Greenland and Robins 1994). Among the concerns in such settings is the potential for bias due to unmeasured confounders. Ecological studies are most problematic when the groups being analyzed are very heterogeneous. That would be the case, for example, if one were to measure arsenic concentrations for every county in the United States and then try to correlate those concentrations with county-specific cancer rates. County-to-county variation in income, urbanization, air pollution, and other factors would most likely

TABLE 10-1 Estimated Distribution of the Surveyed Male Population at Risk (Skin-Cancer Cases) by Age Group and Concentration of Arsenic in Well Water in Taiwan[a]

Arsenic Concentration, ppb	Age Group, yr				Total
	0-19	20-39	40-59	≥60	
Low (0-300)	2,714[b] (0)[c]	935 (1)	653 (4)	236 (11)	4,538 (16)
Medium (300-600)	1,542 (0)	531 (2)	371 (18)	134 (22)	2,578 (42)
High (>600)	2,351 (0)	810 (18)	566 (56)	204 (52)	3,931 (126)
Undetermined	4,933 (0)	1,699 (3)	1,188 (61)	429 (64)	8,249 (128)
Total	11,540 (0)	3,975 (24)	2,778 (139)	1,003 (149)	19,296 (312)

[a]For the control group, the number of persons in the age groups 0-19, 30-39, 40-59, and ≥60 are 2,679, 847, 606, and 176, respectively. No skin cancers were observed in the control population.
[b]Estimated number of persons at risk.
[c]Estimated number of skin-cancer cases observed.
Source: Adapted from EPA 1988, Table B-1.

TABLE 10-2 Estimated Distribution of the Surveyed Female Population at Risk (Skin-Cancer Cases) by Age Group and Concentration of Arsenic in Well Water in Taiwan[a]

Arsenic Concentration, ppb	Age Group, yr				
	0-19	20-39	40-59	≥60	Total
Low (0-300)	2,651[b] (0)[c]	1,306 (0)	792 (3)	239 (2)	4,988 (5)
Medium (300-600)	1,507 (0)	742 (1)	450 (9)	136 (8)	2,835 (18)
High (>600)	2,296 (0)	1,131 (4)	686 (33)	207 (22)	4,320 (59)
Undetermined	4,819 (0)	2,373 (2)	1,440 (13)	435 (27)	9,067 (42)
Total	11,273 (0)	5,552 (7)	3,368 (58)	1,017 (59)	21,210 (124)

[a]For the control group, the number of persons in the age groups 0-19, 30-39, 40-59, and ≥60 are 2,036, 708, 347, and 101, respectively. No skin cancer was observed in the control population.
[b]Estimated number of persons at risk.
[c]Estimated number of skin-cancer cases observed.
Source: Adapted from EPA 1988, Table B-2.

cause bias in such an analysis. However, such issues are unlikely to be a serious problem for the Taiwanese analysis. The study region is relatively small, according to Tseng et al. (1968), a "limited area on the southwest coast of Taiwan." The region is also fairly homogeneous in terms of lifestyle: most inhabitants are engaged in farming, fishing, or salt production. Little variation in diet and a low degree of urbanization occur there.

Besides the potential for confounding, a second concern with ecological studies is the lack of individual exposure assessment. Instead of assigning individual-level exposures, an ecological study assigns individuals to exposure categories based on aggregate exposure concentrations measured for the group to which the individuals belong. As a result of assigning exposure in that way, ecological studies are subject to a type of measurement error.

It is well known that measurement error in exposure variables can lead to biased estimates of dose-response parameters and underestimation of the variance of estimated model parameters (Carroll et al. 1995). For the sake of illustrating the ideas, suppose that we are interested in fitting a simple linear model that relates arsenic concentration to a health outcome. Suppose x_i represents the true arsenic exposure for the ith person in the study. The problem is that instead of being able to accurately measure the true x_i for this person, our observed measurement (say, w_i) is contaminated with error. Theory has been developed for two broad classes of measurement-error settings. In the classical measurement-error setting, we can think of the observed value w_i as corresponding to the true exposure x_i plus some independent random error, $w_i = x_i + \epsilon_i$. Such an error structure could occur, for example, in a study design that attempted to assess each subject's average exposure concentration, say, by recording individual drinking patterns over a period of time. The error might arise, for example, through inaccuracies in recording individual drinking patterns or through laboratory and other errors in measuring the arsenic concentrations in the wells from which each person was drinking. The second broad class, the Berkson measurement-error model, occurs in settings where individual exposures are estimated by assigning to individuals the exposure value measured for the group to which the individual belongs. In contrast to the classic setting described above, here one can express the true exposure concentration x_i as the measured average concentration w_i plus random error ($x_i = w_i + \epsilon_i$). An argument can be made that the Berkson model applies in the Tseng study because individuals were assigned an exposure concentration based simply on the average concentrations measured in their villages. The error here would correspond to individual departures from the village mean exposure concentrations, due to variations among wells within a village, individual drinking habits, and so forth. If the Berkson measurement-error model applies and the outcome of interest follows a linear model involving the true exposure concentration, then it is well known that fitting the model naively with x_i replaced by w_i will lead to valid estimates of the regression parameters from this true model, although variances might be incorrectly estimated.

It is tempting to apply the above logic and conclude that one does not need to worry about bias from a dose-response model applied to ecological data, and in certain settings, such an argument is sound (Prentice and Sheppard 1995). There are several reasons why caution is needed, however, in extending that logic to settings such as the one described by Tseng. First, the effect of Berkson measurement error on inference for nonlinear models, such as the multistage Weibull, has not been widely studied. Although one would expect that approximately the same principle would apply, some bias will generally exist (see Carroll and Stefanski (1990) for further discussion). More critical is that fact that validity of regression analysis under the Berkson measurement-error setting requires the strong assumption that the mean exposure concentration for each group has been measured without error. When that assumption is violated, the resulting estimates are likely to be biased, just as in the classical measurement-error setting. In terms of the analysis of the Tseng data, that means that the results will only be reliable if the appropriate representative values are chosen for the low-, medium-, and high-exposure groups. In the case of the arsenic risk assessment, the fact that the well-water concentrations could vary over time and that some villages had more than one well makes it difficult to place much confidence on any one choice for representative concentrations for the low-, medium-, and high-exposure groups. For example, the values used by EPA were 170 ppb, 470 ppb, and 800 ppb. However, other values could also be justified. To assess the impact of choosing different representative values for the concentrations in the three broad exposure groups, the multistage Weibull model was refitted to the data in Tables 10-1 and 10-2 by using some different choices for the representative concentrations in the three exposure groups. The results, summarized in Table 10-3, suggest that varying the assumed representative concentrations has only a moderate effect on the estimated risk of skin cancer associated with exposure to arsenic at 50 ppm of drinking water. However, the estimated risks remain at the same order of magnitude, ranging from 1.5 to 5.1 cancers per 1,000, for the representative values shown in the table. One might also explore the effect of varying the choice of the representative ages chosen to represent each of the four age categories. In Table 10-3, the values used were the same as those used by EPA in its 1988 analysis: 8.45, 30.19, 49.42, and 69.15. As was the case with the representative exposure concentrations, varying those values is likely to have only a moderate effect on estimated risk levels.

The measurement error theory described in this section and the results presented in Table 10-3 suggest a certain robustness of the risk assessment conducted by EPA using the Tseng data. Ideally, however, it would be useful to have access to more detailed exposure data so that the effect of grouping could be addressed more directly. The internal-cancer data discussed in the

TABLE 10-3 A Sensitivity Analysis Obtained by Varying the Assumed Representative Exposure Concentrations of Arsenic in the High, Medium, and Low Groups for the Tseng Data

Arsenic Concentration, ppb[a] (Low, Medium, High)	Estimate of Risk per 1,000[b]	Upper Bound[c]
170, 470, 800	2.5	4.2
128, 466, 700	3.2	5.1
100, 400, 750	5.1	7.1
200, 450, 750	1.5	3.2
100, 500, 800	4.4	6.3

[a]Controls assumed to have zero concentrations of arsenic.
[b]Skin-cancer risk per 1,000 Taiwanese males aged 62.5 years, exposed from birth to drinking water with arsenic concentrations of 22 ppb (U.S. equivalent, 50 µg/L); assumed ages within each group: 8.45, 30.19, 49.42, 69.15 yr.
[c]Based on a 95% upper confidence interval obtained using the program MULTWEIB available from ICF Kaiser.

next section have exposure concentrations reported separately for 42 villages and, hence, are more useful for this purpose. It is important to remember, however, that the discussion here is about the effects of grouping on the robustness of a particular fitted model. The ideal situation is to have reliable individual exposure assessments. Whenever data are grouped, there is the possibility of obscuring the true shape of the dose response curve.

INTERNAL-CANCER DATA FROM TAIWAN

Tseng's 1968 report on skin-cancer data has generated ongoing interest in characterizing the risks associated with arsenic exposure not only in Taiwan but in several other regions of the world (see Chapter 7). This section describes in more detail some mortality data on several internal cancers, including bladder, lung, and liver, for the arsenic endemic region of Taiwan. Although we will also present some dose-response analysis of these data, it is important to emphasize again that the results are not to be interpreted as a formal risk assessment, or as an endorsement of these data for the use of risk assessment for arsenic in drinking water. Rather, we present selected results to illustrate some of the issues that arise in the context of trying to characterize the dose-response relationship of arsenic exposure based on ecological data.

The data are from a study of the population of 42 coastal villages in six southwestern townships including Peimen, Hsuechia, Putai, Ichu, Yensui, and Hsiaying where blackfoot disease is endemic (see Wu et al., 1989, for further discussion). The data were described in a letter by Chen et al. (1988), grouped into three arsenic concentrations (less than 300 ppb, 300-590 ppb, and 600 ppb and over), and weighted by person-years of exposure at each concentration reported by Wu et al. (1989). Two dose-response assessments based on those data appeared about the same time (Chen et al. 1992; Smith et al. 1992), although the data sources were summarized differently. In particular, Chen and colleagues reported data in which arsenic concentration was categorized by four intervals (less than 100 ppb, 100-290 ppb, 300-590 ppb, and more than 600 ppb) and age at time of death by four intervals (less than 30, 30-49, 50-69, and 70 years of age and over). Smith and co-workers used age-standardized data grouped as reported by Chen et al. (1988). The Smith et al. (1992) study used data from an unexposed Taiwanese population as the basis for the age standardization.

The available data (see Addendum to Chapter 10) include the person-years at risk and the number of deaths due to bladder, liver, and lung cancer in 5-

year age increments for each of the 42 villages. The data are summarized in Table 10-4, with villages grouped into the same high-, medium-, and low-exposure categories used in the original Tseng study. The arsenic concentrations in the 42 villages ranged from 10 to 934 ppb. Table 10-5 shows the ordered values. Table 10-5 does not show that, in some cases, arsenic concentrations varied considerably in different wells within the same village (see Addendum). Hence, there is considerable uncertainty in the data.

TABLE 10-4 Internal Cancer Incidence by Age and by Arsenic-Concentration Group[a]

Age Group, yr	Arsenic Concentration, ppb											
	0-300				300-600				>600			
	py[b]	lng[c]	bl[d]	liv[e]	py[b]	lng[c]	bl[d]	liv[e]	py[b]	lng[c]	bl[d]	liv[e]
Male												
20-25	35,521	0	0	0	17,754	0	0	0	10,477	0	0	0
25-30	21,439	0	0	0	9,802	0	0	0	6,132	1	0	0
30-35	13,493	0	0	2	6,356	0	0	2	4,507	0	1	2
35-40	12,432	0	0	4	6,000	1	0	2	3,591	0	0	2
40-45	13,550	2	1	3	6,765	2	2	3	3,852	0	1	3
45-50	13,395	4	0	5	6,423	6	3	5	3,823	3	2	5
50-55	11,293	7	2	6	5,507	5	4	3	3,115	5	3	3
55-60	8,934	7	3	10	4,276	11	4	5	2,482	10	6	5
60-65	7,020	5	3	7	3,431	10	4	4	1,828	4	3	4
65-70	5,229	7	5	9	2,533	4	3	3	1,148	4	3	3
70-75	3,676	15	2	4	1,695	8	5	1	748	3	2	1
75-80	2,005	7	5	3	883	5	4	0	317	3	5	0
80-85	1,190	5	5	1	643	1	3	1	159	0	1	1
Female												
20-25	27,908	1	0	0	13,131	0	0	0	8,442	0	0	0
25-30	15,107	0	0	0	6,799	0	0	0	4,546	0	0	0
30-35	11,600	1	0	0	5,145	0	0	0	3,800	0	0	0
35-40	11,932	0	1	0	5,759	0	0	1	3,612	1	0	1
40-45	13,373	5	0	2	6,774	3	0	1	4,014	1	0	1
45-50	13,109	3	2	2	6,665	3	0	2	4,114	4	0	2
50-55	11,368	7	2	1	5,708	4	3	1	3,512	5	4	1
55-60	9,241	3	4	3	4,616	6	3	1	2,571	11	3	1
60-65	7,753	8	9	5	3,732	4	3	2	1,800	9	10	2
65-70	5,998	10	3	3	2,825	6	10	3	1,201	3	4	3
70-75	4,198	3	5	4	1,907	6	5	1	668	2	3	1
75-80	2,323	5	4	2	1,154	2	2	0	352	1	3	0
80-85	1,860	2	2	5	787	2	4	0	23	1	1	0

[a]Data from Wu et al. 1989; Chen et al. 1992.
[b]Person-years at risk.
[c]Number of deaths from lung cancer.
[d]Number of deaths from bladder cancer.
[e]Number of deaths from liver cancer.

TABLE 10-5 Ordered Median Well Concentrations for Each Village[a]

Arsenic Concentrations, ppb
10, 11, 30, 32, 32, 42, 45, 50, 56, 60, 65, 73, 80, 100, 110, 110, 123, 126, 256, 256, 259, 307, 307, 350, 398, 406, 448, 467, 504, 520, 520, 529, 538,544, 599, 650, 683, 693, 694, 698, 717, 934

[a] Wu et al. 1989; Chen et al. 1992.

As with the skin-cancer data, an ecological study design was used to construct the internal-cancer data. Individual exposures were not assessed; instead, subjects were assigned the exposure concentration corresponding to the median concentration in the water from the village in which they lived. In contrast to the skin-cancer data, however, an advantage is that the data have been kept separately by village, rather than grouping them into low-, medium-, and high-exposure intervals. Although that helps somewhat, it does not alter the fact that the data are still ecological. In fact within some of the villages wide ranges were seen in the measured arsenic concentrations of individual wells (see Addendum to Chapter 10). Of the 42 villages, 20 had only one well tested. In the remaining villages where multiple wells were tested, a wide range of arsenic concentrations were measured. For example, village "0-G" had measurements taken on five wells; concentrations were from 10 to 770 ppb, and the median concentration was 30 ppb. Village "0-E" also had five wells measured. There, the concentrations ranged from 10 to 686 ppb, the median being 110 ppb. The greatest number of wells measured was 47 for village "4-I." The variation highlights the potential for measurement error to affect the reliability of dose-response modeling. It also suggests the potential usefulness of conducting additional analysis to assess the sensitivity of the results to omission of some villages and to other sources of error in the assigned exposures. That will be done presently. First, however, we briefly address the question of how to analyze cancer mortality data of the type presented in Table 10-4.

When the data come in the form of prevalence (the number of subjects alive at various ages and exposure concentrations and the number of those with skin cancer), then a model, such as the multistage Weibull defined in Equation 3, can be fitted by maximizing the likelihood given in Equation 1. When the data are in the form of cancer mortality rates (the number who die of the cancer over a specified period and the number at risk of dying during that same time period), the analysis becomes slightly more complicated. There are basically two possible approaches. One approach is to use a comparison population to construct standardized mortality ratios. That approach will be described in more detail presently. An alternative is to model the cause-specific hazard (see Cox and Oakes 1984) of dying of cancer at age t for someone exposed to arsenic concentration x. The cause-specific hazard function based on the multistage Weibull model is

$$h_\theta(x, t) = \left[\frac{\partial}{\partial t} P_\theta(x, t) \right] / (1 - P_\theta(x, t))$$

$$= C(Q_0 + Q_1 x + Q_2 x^2)(t - T_0)^{C-1}.$$

To simplify calculations, and facilitate use of life tables and death records, age is grouped into 5-year time intervals. The model can be fitted by maximizing the following likelihood:

$$\text{Lik}^{\text{inc}} = \prod_x \prod_t h_\theta(x, t)^{d(x, t)} \exp[-r(x, t)h_\theta(x, t)], \qquad (4)$$

where $d(x, t)$ is the number of people exposed to arsenic concentration x who die with cancer at age t, and $r(x, t)$ is the corresponding person-years at risk at that age and concentration (see Laird and Olivier 1981). The products in Equation 4 are applied over the sets of all concentrations x and age groups t represented in the data set. A nonlinear optimizing routine called *nlminb*, available in the statistical package Splus, was used to find the value of θ that maximizes Equation 4. That routine easily accommodates constraints and does not require differentiability of the function being optimized. Computing an estimate of the variance-covariance matrix of the estimated model parameters, however, is more difficult. Standard maximum-likelihood theory breaks down (i.e., one cannot simply invert the matrix of second derivatives) because of the constraints and nondifferentiability of the log likelihood. Various proposals have been made for constrained optimization settings in general (Self and Liang 1987) as well as specifically in the context of dose-response modeling (Guess and Crump 1978). The approach used here follows Geyer (1991), who suggests the use of the bootstrap for inference in nonstandard maximum-likelihood settings.

The results of fitting the multistage Weibull model to the three internal-cancer data sets for male and females are given in Table 10-6. Both paramet-

TABLE 10-6 Fitted Parameters for Multistage Weibull Model

Organ	Q_0	Q_1	Q_1	T_0	C
Male					
Bladder	1.229862e-11	0.000000	7.339447e-17	1.470252e+01	5.130551
Lung	4.692041e-09	1.467226e-11	0.000000	2.149461e+01	3.919512
Liver	2.270629e-07	3.694680e-14	4.998412e-13	1.689983e+01	2.905370
Female					
Bladder	3.858906e-08	0.000000	2.222528e-13	3.303647e+01	3.473238
Lung	1.612450e-08	0.000000	6.119366e-14	1.709777e+01	3.513685
Liver	3.229792e-07	2.801520e-11	4.939496e-13	2.594200e+01	2.728167

ric and nonparametric bootstrap methods (see Efron and Tibshirani 1993) were applied to estimate the standard errors of the estimated parameters and yielded similar results.

Figure 10-1 shows the predicted age-specific bladder-cancer incidence rates for males from all 42 villages, based on the fitted multistage Weibull model. Each line corresponds to the predicted cancer incidence rate for a specific age group. Notice how for each age group, there is a different dose response curve. Incidence rates increase sharply with age. Once the model has been fitted, the lifetime risk of dying from bladder cancer can be calculated by using the estimated model parameters and the U.S. national census values for the age-specific death rates from all other causes. Some straightforward calculations show that the lifetime risk of dying from bladder cancer can be written as

$$\sum_t p_\theta(x, t)q_t, \quad (5)$$

where $p_\theta(x, t)$ is the estimated probability of developing bladder cancer by age t for someone exposed to concentration x, and q_t is the probability that a U.S. citizen dies at age t, where age is broken into the same 5-year increments used in fitting the multistage Weibull model. The values for q_t were obtained separately for males and females from the Life Tables in *Vital Statistics of the United States, 1994* (NCHS 1998).

The excess lifetime risk of cancer from exposure to concentration x of arsenic in the drinking water can be written as

$$\text{Excess}(x) = \text{Lifetime}(x) - \text{Lifetime }(0), \quad (6)$$

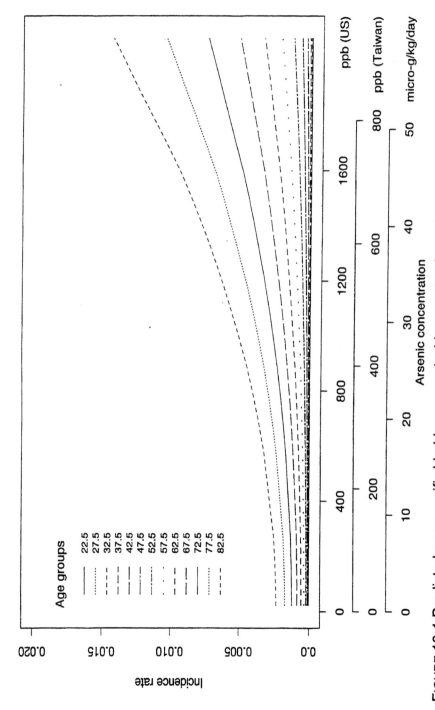

FIGURE 10-1 Predicted age-specific bladder-cancer incidence rates for males based on the multistage Weibull model.

where Lifetime(x) is the lifetime risk of cancer for someone exposed to concentration x. Figure 10-2 shows the estimated excess lifetime risks for males of dying from bladder cancer as a function of arsenic concentration in the drinking water. The solid line shows the fitted curve, and the dotted line shows the upper 95% confidence limit, calculated using the nonparametric bootstrap. To facilitate interpretation, the x axis is labeled in three ways in terms of (1) concentration (in parts per billion) of arsenic found in Taiwan; (2) micrograms of arsenic consumed per kilogram of body weight (assuming that the typical Taiwanese male weighs 55 kg and drinks 3.5 L of water per day and the typical Taiwanese female weighs 50 kg and drinks 2 L of water per day); and (3) equivalent concentration (parts per billion) of arsenic consumed by a U.S. population (assuming that the typical U.S. male or female weighs 70 kg and drinks 2 L of water per day). Figure 10-3 shows the same plot but with the x axis drawn only to 100 ppb (based on equivalent U.S. values). Table 10-7 shows the corresponding estimated excess risks and upper 95% confidence limits for excess lifetime risk for the U.S. population drinking water with arsenic concentrations of 10, 25, and 50 ppb. Once again, confidence limits were calculated using the non-parametric bootstrap.

Examination of the raw data suggests that variability, particularly at older ages, is large. Furthermore, several of the villages at low exposure concentrations appeared to have higher cancer rates than would be predicted from the fitted dose-response model. To assess the impact of this variability on the fitted dose-response curve, a sensitivity analysis was performed by refitting the multistage Weibull model to different subsets of villages and recomputing the estimated excess lifetime risk at 10, 20, and 50 ppb. For example, the numbers on the line labeled "single well" in Table 10-8 correspond to refitting the model excluding all the villages that had only a single well (villages 3-H, 2-I, 3-5, 3-N, 4-7, 6-A, 4-D, 3-P, 6-C, 4-8, 0-0, 4-J, 2-D, O-D, 4-M, 6-6, 3-I, 5-G, 4-P, 3-9). The results of that sensitivity analysis are given in Table 10-8. The results suggest that the risk estimates are fairly sensitive to which villages are included or excluded. For example, depending on which subset is analyzed, the estimated lifetime risk at 50 ppb can range from 0.05 to 1.6 per 1,000. At 10 ppb, the variation in estimated risk is even more marked (ranging from 0.002 to 0.324 per 1,000). Although not shown here, a similar analysis using the alternative models to be discussed in the next section did not show the same sensitivity as the multistage Weibull model.

In addition to the sensitivity of the fitted model to inclusion or exclusion of particular villages, the data provided a good opportunity to assess the effects of various degrees of grouping on the shape of the dose response. The

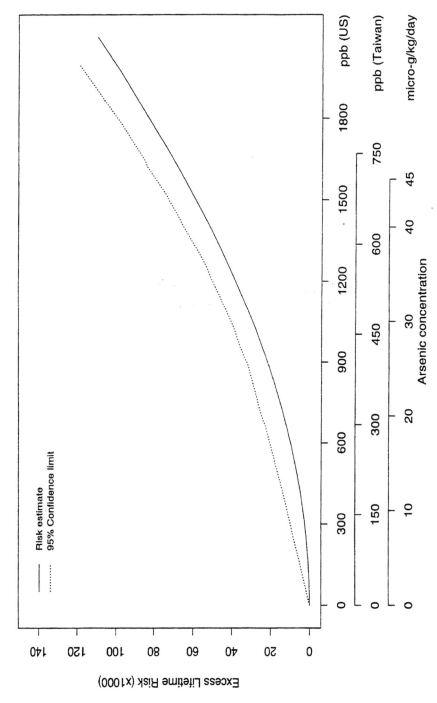

FIGURE 10-2 Male bladder-cancer rates per 1,000 people. Estimated excess lifetime risks, based on 1994 U.S. Life Tables (NCHS 1998) for males and females, along with upper 95% confidence limits.

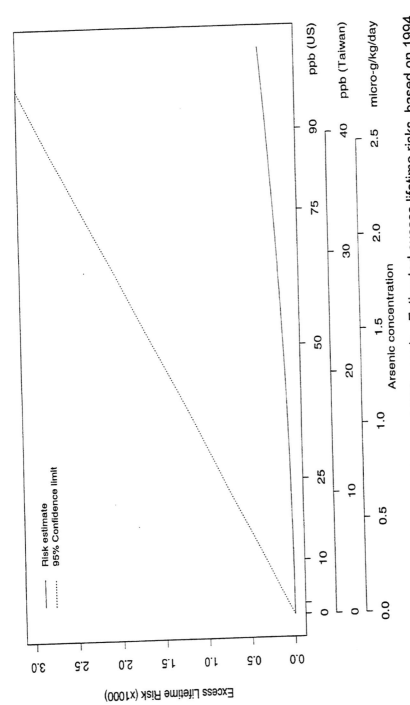

FIGURE 10-3 Male bladder-cancer rates per 1,000 people. Estimated excess lifetime risks, based on 1994 U.S. Life Tables (NCHS 1998) for males and females, along with upper 95% confidence limits; x axis drawn only to 100 ppm (estimated U.S. equivalent for arsenic concentrations).

TABLE 10-7 Excess Lifetime Risk Estimates for Bladder Cancer in U.S. Males and Females

Arsenic Concentration in Water, ppb	Excess Lifetime Risk of Bladder Cancer (per 1,000) (95% Upper Confidence Limit)	
	Males	Females
10	0.0028 (0.314)	0.0086 (0.094)
25	0.0172 (0.787)	0.0540 (0.253)
50	0.0690 (1.580)	0.2161 (0.564)

multistage Weibull model was fitted to the data grouped by exposure intervals of 300 ppb (resulting groups 0-300 ppb, >300-600 ppb, and >600 ppb), 275 ppb (resulting groups 0-275 ppb, >275-550 ppb, and >550 ppb), 250 ppb (resulting groups 0-250 ppb, >250-500 ppb, >500-750 ppb, and >750 ppb), 150 ppb (resulting groups 0-150 ppb, . . . >600-750 ppb, and >750 ppb), 100 ppb (resulting groups 0-100 ppb, . . . >600-700 ppb, and >700 ppb). The results for male bladder cancer are displayed graphically in Figures 10-4 and 10-5. Figure 10-4 shows fitted curves over the entire observable range of concentrations, and Figure 10-5 plots the curves only up to 100 ppb. The figures provide dramatic evidence of the effect that grouping can have on the estimated dose-response curve. The effect is especially noticeable at the lower end of the dose-response curve; that end of course, is of most interest. The figures suggest that the estimated risks at 50 ppb differ 30-fold across groupings. Table 10-9 lists the estimated risks at 10, 25, and 50 ppb under the various groupings displayed in the figures and confirms the impression gained from the figures. It is interesting also to see that there is no particular pattern

TABLE 10-8 Sensitivity Analysis Based on Bladder Cancer in Males (Multistage Weibull Model)

Village Exclusion Criteria	Excess Lifetime Risk of Male Bladder Cancer (per 1,000) by Arsenic Concentration		
	10 ppb	25 ppb	50 ppb
Single well	0.0024	0.0153	0.0612
Multiple wells	0.0037	0.0229	0.0914
Highest five villages	0.0021	0.0130	0.0519
Lowest five villages	0.3244	0.8142	1.6386

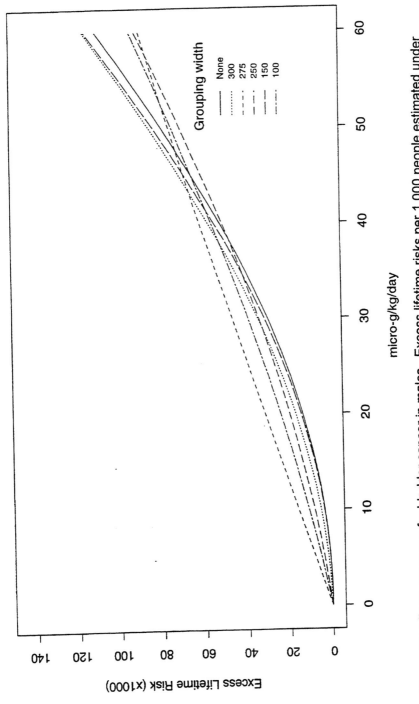

Figure 10-4 Dose response for bladder cancer in males. Excess lifetime risks per 1,000 people estimated under different degrees of grouping of arsenic concentrations.

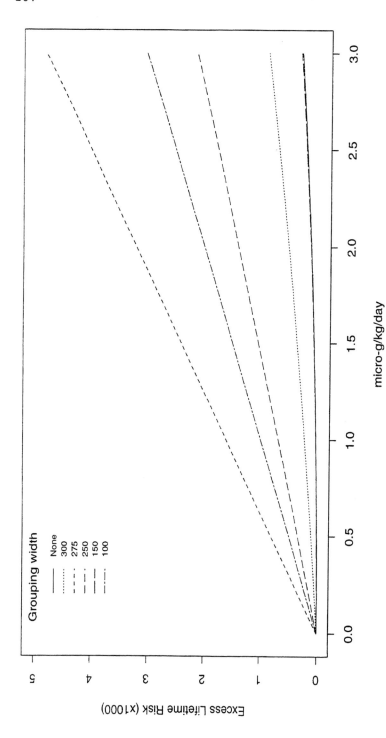

FIGURE 10-5   Dose response for bladder cancer in males.   Excess lifetime risks per 1,000 people estimated under different degrees of grouping of arsenic concentrations; x axis drawn only to 100 ppm (estimated U.S. equivalent for arsenic concentrations).

TABLE 10-9 Excess Lifetime Risk Estimates with Different Groupings of Arsenic Exposure Concentrations

Group	Excess Lifetime Risk of Male Bladder Cancer (per 1,000) by Arsenic Concentration		
	10 ppb	25 ppb	50 ppb
None	0.0028	0.0172	0.0690
300	0.0593	0.1581	0.3494
275	0.4597	1.1485	2.2948
250	0.1928	0.4870	0.9902
150	0.0029	0.0182	0.0727
100	0.2815	0.07072	1.4256

with respect to the degree of grouping. For example, the results under "no grouping" are not particularly close to the results obtained by grouping into the smallest grouping category of 100 ppb. As discussed earlier in the chapter, the Berkson measurement-error theory would predict grouping to have only a relatively minor influence on the fitted curves if the correct mean concentrations were assigned to each group. Thus, the fact that grouping does have a strong effect provides evidence of additional measurement error in the arsenic concentrations being assigned at the village level.

OTHER ISSUES

To address the possibility that some of the model sensitivity to grouping and village deletions might be due to the multistage Weibull model, we explored alternatives based on Poisson regression modeling techniques. Such explorations should be part of any data-analysis exercise and are especially important in the risk-assessment setting where low-dose estimates are well known to be sensitive to model choice. The simplest Poisson modeling approach characterizes the log of the cancer death rate as a linear function of covariates. Nonlinear and interaction effects can easily be explored in the context by considering additional appropriate covariates (Breslow and Day 1988). By modeling on the log scale, such models implicitly assume a multiplicative effect of exposure. Additive models may also be explored, although they are not as easy to fit using standard statistical software. The model assumes that the number of cancer deaths among subjects exposed to a specified concentration in a particular age group follows a Poisson distribution with rate equal to the cancer death rate, multiplied by the person-years at risk in that age group. Several alternatives were considered, including loglinear models that were linear or quadratic in dose and age, along with interactions.

Figure 10-6 shows the excess lifetime risk estimates under the following fitted models: (1) linear in dose and age, (2) quadratic in dose and age, and (3) quadratic in age and linear in dose. The fourth curve, which incorporates background data, will be discussed presently. According to Akaike's information criteria, the best fitting of models 1 -3 was the one with a quadratic age and a linear dose effect, although the improvement in fit over the model that was only linear in dose and age was relatively minor at low doses (see Figure 10-6). Interactions did not improve the model fit. Under the model that was quadratic in age and linear in dose, the estimated lifetime risks per 1,000 people at 10, 25, and 50 ppb were 0.206, 0.518, and 1.049, respectively. The corresponding upper confidence limits were 0.264, 0.665, and 1.347, respectively. Because standard maximum-likelihood theory is straightforward to apply for the Poisson model, confidence limits were based on analytical calculations rather than bootstraps.

Another important issue to address is whether and how to incorporate information about an unexposed population. It could be argued that cancer data from the whole of Taiwan should be used as a comparison unexposed population. The advantage of using such data is that more information is available to estimate the shape of the dose-response curve at low exposure concentrations. Another advantage is that the fitted curves might be slightly more robust to miss-specification of the exposure concentrations in the individual villages. The disadvantage is that data from Taiwan as a whole might not be a suitable comparison group because of differences in lifestyle. Also, the Taiwanese-wide data do not clearly represent a population with zero exposure to arsenic in drinking water. Because good arguments can be made for both sides, the subcommittee felt that it was important to explore the effect of including such baseline data. Table 10-10 shows the data used from Taiwan. There are several approaches to incorporating such baseline data. One approach is to fit exactly the same kinds of models described above but with the data from the whole of Taiwan as additional person-years and cancer data corresponding to zero exposure. Notice in Figure 10-6 that the fitted curves that include the Taiwanese-wide data are somewhat different from those obtained using only data from the endemic region. What seems to happen is that the "zero" point is now estimated with so much precision that the curve changes at low dose, being in fact slightly more sublinear in shape. Table 10-11 summarizes the estimated risks (per 1,000) at 10, 25, and 50 ppb based on Poisson regression models, with and without the baseline data included. Note that, consistent with Figure 10-6, the estimated risks are lower under the model that incorporates baseline data.

Another way to incorporate comparison data, such as those presented in Table 10-10, is through the use of standardized mortality ratios (SMRs), (see

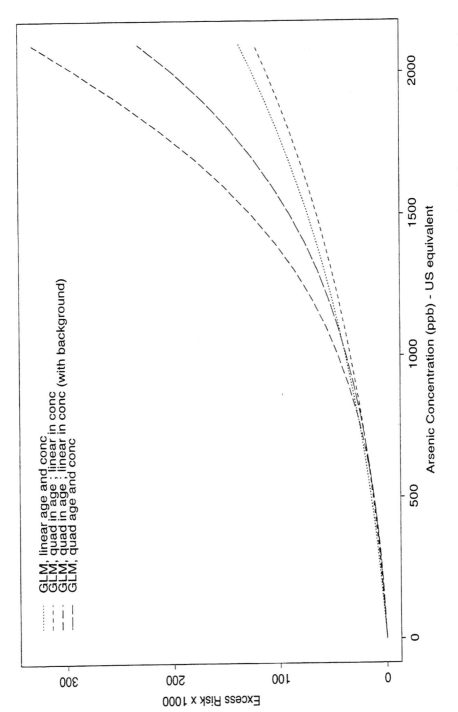

FIGURE 10-6 Estimated excess lifetime risks of bladder-cancer per 1,000 males based on Poisson regression models.

Table 10-10 Taiwanese-Wide Data on Bladder Cancer

Age Group	Population	Bladder Cancers, No.
Male		
20-25	13,271,386	0
25-30	11,054,191	3
30-35	8,628,516	4
35-40	6,793,545	8
40-45	6,375,466	20
45-50	6,384,052	50
50-55	6,062,515	91
55-60	5,018,542	164
60-65	3,666,535	213
65-70	2,443,367	345
70-75	1,480,126	413
75-80	720,375	418
80+	392,714	305
Female		
20-25	13,266,327	0
25-30	11,054,808	0
30-35	8,210,507	2
35-40	6,458,620	2
40-45	5,802,856	5
45-50	5,157,821	20
50-55	4,365,755	41
55-60	3,517,193	76
60-65	2,776,622	124
65-70	2,106,715	153
70-75	1,490,659	173
75-80	888,468	185
80+	650,835	157

Breslow and Day 1988, for an excellent discussion). The basic idea in an SMR analysis is to use a large population based on a comparison group to calculate the expected numbers of cancer deaths within different age categories of the study population. SMRs are widely used by epidemiologists to characterize the excess risk in an exposed population, relative to an appropriate comparison group. Several of the studies reported in Chapter 4 are based on the SMR approach. Smith and Sharp (1985), Wright et al. (1997), and others have also argued that SMRs can be used as the basis for quantitative risk assessment. Indeed, several recent EPA risk assessments (e.g., on butadiene) have been based on this approach.

The subcommittee briefly illustrates how the SMR approach works by considering again the male bladder-cancer data. The first step is to calculate the expected number of cancers within each age group for each village. For example, in village "2-M," there are 1,057 person-years at risk among males aged 40-45. Based on the Taiwanese-wide data in Table 10-10, the expected number of cancers is 1,057*20/6,375,466 = 0.0033, compared with 0 actually observed in that group. Similarly, for 690 person-years at risk among males aged 50-55 in the same village, we expect 690*91/6,062,515 = 0.0104 cancer deaths compared with 2 actually observed. A useful summary statistic for each village can be obtained by summing over all the age groups to get a total expected number. The ratio of observed to expected then gives a village a specific SMR. For village "2-M," for example, these calculations yield an expected number of 0.18 cancer deaths, compared with 9 actually observed. Taking the ratio of those numbers yields an SMR of 50, although the estimates are fairly unstable because of the low expected numbers. As with the analyses described previously, Poisson regression can be again used to characterize the dose response. This time, however, observed numbers of cancer deaths in each age and concentration combination are modeled as following a Poisson distribution with rate parameter $R*\lambda$, where R is the expected number. The parameter λ reflects the relative risk and can be modeled as a function of concentration and any other covariates available. It is also possible to allow age to affect λ as well. For example, it might be that the relative risk is higher among older people (see Breslow and Day 1988, section 4.6). In fact, the best-fitting model was one that had age and concentration as linear terms. Once a model has been fitted in this way, then lifetime risks can be calculated using the formulas given in Equations 5 and 6, except that $p_\theta(x, t)$ is now estimated by using the baseline cancer risks taken from the U.S. population combined with the relative-risk model estimated in the Taiwanese population. For example, that approach yields estimated risks at 10, 25, and 50 ppb of 0.1802, 0.4537 and 0.9181 per 1,000, respectively. The corresponding upper 95% confidence limits are 0.2227, 0.5608, and 1.135428 per 1,000.

Finally, we turn to some discussion of how the new EPA guidelines (EPA 1996) might apply in the present setting. If biological considerations suggest the presence of a nonlinear dose response, then the new guidelines would suggest specifying an appropriate model and using it to estimate low-dose risks. For example, the Poisson model could be used, in which case the model-based estimates in Table 10-11 might be adopted as the estimated risks at 10, 25, and 50 ppb. In the absence of a convincing biological argument for the use of a nonlinear model to predict risks at low doses, EPA generally recommends the use of a point-of-departure approach (EPA 1996). Basically, the idea is to estimate the dose corresponding to a low risk that is still high enough for the corresponding dose to be within the observable range of data. Risks at lower doses can be estimated by linear extrapolation from the point of departure. In the absence of mechanistic data to support linear extrapolation, however, EPA

Table 10-11 Excess Lifetime Risk Estimates for Bladder Cancer in Males[a]

Arsenic Concentration in Water, ppb	Excess Lifetime Risk of Male Bladder Cancer (per 1,000) (95% Upper Confidence Limit)		
	No Baseline Data[a]	With Baseline Data[a]	SMR Approach[b]
10	0.206 (0.264)	0.140 (0.155)	0.179 (0.222)
25	0.518 (0.665)	0.356 (0.393)	0.450 (0.559)
50	1.049 (1.347)	0.731 (0.807)	0.911 (1.132)

[a]Models are quadratic in age and linear in concentration.
[b]Model is linear in age and concentration.

recommends calculating a "margin of exposure," which is the ratio of the dose at the point of departure to doses of environmental concern. The point-of-departure approach is similar in spirit to the benchmark-dose approach (see Crump 1984), which has become popular in noncancer risk assessment. As discussed in the EPA 1996 guidelines, a 10% level of risk is often chosen as the point of departure. (That is about the risk level that can be detected with reasonable power in an animal bioassay.) For risk assessments based on epidemiological data, however, a lower point of departure is often warranted because the observable range of effects can go lower in epidemiological studies than animal studies where the numbers are often small. In the case of the bladder-cancer data, a 10% excess lifetime risk is about the level seen at the very highest concentrations of exposure. Hence, it is more reasonable to select a 5% or a 1% excess risk level as the point of departure. Table 10-12 shows the estimated doses corresponding to a 1% point of departure, along with lower 95% confidence limits. The margin of exposure and the excess risk level at 50 ppb, based on linear extrapolation from the point of departure, are also shown. Three approaches are considered: (1) Poisson modeling without including background data from the whole of Taiwan; (2) Poisson modeling with background data included as part of the data set being modeled; and (3) Poisson modeling using the SMR approach. It is interesting to see from the table that those approaches are fairly consistent at the 1% risk level, although some of them yielded considerably different estimators at very low doses, particularly with respect to the estimated risks at 50 ppb (see Table 10-11). This consistency occurs because the point-of-departure approach does not require extrapolation outside the range where data are directly observable, and it is one of the attractive features of the point-of-departure approach.

DISCUSSION

This chapter has reviewed some of the sources of uncertainty associated with the 1988 EPA arsenic risk assessment, which was based on the skin-cancer

Table 10-12 Estimated Points of Departure at the 1% Excess Risk Level, Correspond-ing Margin of Exposure at 50 ppb, and Corresponding Excess Lifetime Risk Estimates at 50 ppb for Bladder Cancer in Males[a]

Method of Analysis	Point of Departure, ppb	Margin of Exposure at 50 ppb	Risk at 50 ppb (x 1,000)
Poisson model, No background data	404 (323)	8.08 (6.46)	1.237 (1.548)
Poisson model, Background data included	443 (407)	8.86 (8.14)	1.129 (1.229)
Poisson model, SMR approach	450 (372)	9.0 (7.44)	1.111 (1.344)

[a]Figures in parentheses are 95% confidence limits (lower for the point-of-departure estimates, upper for estimated risk at 50 ppb).

data from the Tseng study. One serious problem was the study's ecological design: exposure concentrations were not individually measured; instead, individuals were assigned to one of three broad exposure groups (high, me-dium, and low), according to the mean exposure concentration found in their village. Assigning the average exposure concentration from a group to all individuals within the same group can result in what is known as the Berkson measurement-error model. It is well known that regression models fitted to data subject to the Berkson measurement-error model are unlikely to have serious bias, although variability might be underestimated. However, that result only holds if the exposure concentrations measured at the group level are not themselves subject to measurement error. According to the theory, the exposure concentration assigned to each group should reflect the mean expo-sure concentration of all subjects within the group. In the case of the Tseng data, it is impossible to know whether the representative values assigned to the high-, medium-, and low-exposure categories were appropriate. To assess the possible effects of choosing the wrong representative values for the three exposure categories, the analysis was redone using different values. The estimated excess lifetime risk at 50 ppb was found to range from about 1 to 5 per 1,000 people, with corresponding upper confidence limits of 3.2 to 7.1. Those results suggest that, although problems exist in using the Tseng data, the conclusions to be drawn about estimated exposure effects are not likely to change too drastically, although the level of uncertainty increases quite a lot because of the issues of grouping and measurement error.

This chapter has presented exploratory analyses of some bladder-cancer mortality data from the arsenic endemic region of Taiwan, the focus being primarily on bladder cancer in males. Although these data are ecological, they have some advantages over Tseng's skin-cancer data. First, the age breakdown was more reliable, because the data were extracted from age-specific mortality data. Second, arsenic concentrations were available for each of 42 separate villages and were not simply classified as low, medium, and high. Thus, the new data were perhaps less contaminated by problems of measurement error, although it is still a serious concern and could persist at the village level. In particular, arsenic concentrations detected in multiple wells varied considerably within some of the villages, leading to uncertainty about the exposure concnetrations assigned to each village. Regardless of that uncertainty, the availability of village-specific exposure measurements provided a useful opportunity to assess directly the effects of grouping exposure into high, medium, and low categories, as was done in the Tseng study. Figure 10-5 showed the results of fitting the multistage Weibull model to the bladder-cancer data in males, with various amounts of grouping artificially imposed. The results show that for these data, grouping can have a fairly strong effect on the fitted model.

The chapter has also reported on the issue of model fit. Several approaches were taken to address that concern. First, to see whether individual villages could have a significant impact on the fitted multistage Weibull model, sensitivity analyses were run, refitting the model with certain villages excluded from the analysis. For instance, the 20 villages with only one well measured for arsenic were excluded. Exclusions were also made of the villages with more than one well measured, the five villages with the highest measurements, and the five with the lowest measurements. As seen in Table 10-8, the resulting estimates of the excess lifetime risk of cancer can change fairly substantially by several orders of magnitude.

Those sensitivity analyses were useful and suggested that the fit of the multistage Weibull model was indeed sensitive to the subset of villages chosen for analysis. As an alternative, we explored Poisson regression models, which were found to fit as well as, if not better than, the multistage Weibull model. The basic approach was to include age and exposure terms as possibly linear and quadratic effects on the cancer incidence rate. Although a quadratic effect in age improved the fit, a linear effect for exposure seemed to be adequate. Interactions did not improve the model fit. The Poisson modeling yielded estimated risks that were higher than those based on the multistage Weibull model. For example, the estimated risk at 50 ppb was 1.049 per 1,000, with an upper confidence limit of 1.347 per 1,000, or almost 1 excess cancer per 1,000 population.

Several alternative ways to incorporate external information on age-specific cancer death rates were explored, including methods based on SMRs and Poisson regression models. By providing more information about baseline risks, those approaches can lead to more precise estimates of the dose response (Breslow and Day 1988, p. 151). A disadvantage, however, is the potential for bias if the comparison population is not well chosen. Also, it is difficult to determine whether the comparison population can be considered to have zero exposure. The analyses presented in this chapter used age-specific cancer rates reported for the whole of Taiwan. Bias could be a potential problem, because the Taiwanese-wide data might not form an appropriate comparison group for the arsenic endemic region, which is a poor, rural area. Thus, the choice to use external information on baseline cancer rates represents a tradeoff that to some extent can be explored using sensitivity analysis.

This chapter has focused primarily on issues related to the analysis and dose-response modeling of the data from Taiwan. In addition to the modeling issues already discussed, extrapolating the results to the U.S. population raises some additional sources of uncertainty. For example, differences between the United States and Taiwan with respect to the amount of arsenic in food could affect the relevance of the results.

It should be noted that ecological studies in Chile (Smith et al. 1998) and Argentina (Hopenhayn-Rich et al. 1996, 1998) have observed risks of lung and bladder cancer of the same magnitude as those reported in the studies in Taiwan at comparable levels of exposure. As presented in Chapter 4, in both the high-exposure regions in Chile and Argentina, the excess numbers of male lung-cancer deaths was in a range of 4 to 5 times that of the excess number of bladder-cancer deaths. Risk estimates for Taiwan have also been reported to be greater for lung cancer than bladder cancer (Smith et al. 1992). Among males, the contribution to risk from lung cancer based on Taiwan data (5.3 per 1,000) (see Table 4-5) was well over twice the bladder-cancer risk (2.3 per 1,000) for estimates for consumption of water with a concentration of 50 µg/L. In view of the analyses discussed in this chapter indicating that the risk for bladder cancer in males at the current maximum contaminant level (MCL) might be 1.0 to 1.5 per 1,000, a similar approach for all cancers in both sexes could easily result in a combined cancer risk on the order of 1 in 100.

The analyses presented in this chapter are based primarily on what is sometimes called a statistical approach to risk assessment. An argument can be made that the multistage Weibull model is derived for biological considerations; however, the philosophy behind statistical modeling is simply to describe the data using a flexible class of dose-response models that can accommodate a wide variety of shapes. In recent years, there has been a lot of interest in the development and application of more biologically based models that account for intake, metabolic pathways, and mode of action; in practice, the approach is rarely used because usually not enough is known about the mode of action for the compound in question. Arsenic certainly falls into that category. Use of biomarkers in the construction of dose-response models is a related idea that has generated a lot of interest in recent years. In practice, however, the data are generally not available to use that approach. Furthermore, statistical methods to incorporate biomarkers into dose-response models have not been developed. Research to develop such approaches would be extremely valuable.

SUMMARY AND CONCLUSIONS

The statistical issues surrounding risk assessment for arsenic in drinking water are challenging. The lack of reliable animal data means that risk assessment needs to be based solely on epidemiological data. However, the best available data are from ecological studies, which are not ideal for risk-assessment purposes (NRC 1991). Thus, even though issues of interspecies extrapolation are avoided through the use of human data, issues of confounding and measurement error have the potential to bias the results. This chapter has reviewed a number of issues:

1. The limitations of risk assessment based on ecological data.
2. The effects of measurement error induced by the use of ecological data, grouping of exposure concentrations, or both.
3. The impact of model choice; in particular, comparison of estimates based on the multistage Weibull model and other classes of dose-response models.
4. The appropriate ways to adjust for age in risk assessments based on epidemiological data and to incorporate baseline data on expected cancer rates among unexposed subjects.

Based on the subcommittee's findings, a number of general comments can be made. First, there is no question that the ideal basis for risk assessment is a well-conducted epidemiological study involving accurate assessment of individual exposures. In the absence of such data, however, ecological data might be the only choice. Such analyses must be conducted with caution, keeping in mind the potential for measurement error and confounding to bias the results. It is important to remember that any risk assessment based on ecological data must be cautiously interpreted because of the inherent uncertainty in the exposure-assessment methods used for such studies. In the case of the Taiwanese data, the fact that it came from a culturally homogeneous area provides some reassurance that confounding might not be too serious a concern. Our findings also suggest that additional caution might be needed when exposure concentrations are grouped into broad exposure categories. It is important to keep in mind that the considerable variability in the arsenic concentrations detected in multiple wells within some of the villages leads to considerable uncertainty about exposure concentrations in the Taiwanese data.

The subcommittee's explorations suggest that model choice can have a major impact on estimated low-dose risks when the analysis is based on epidemiological data. The impact of model choice is amplified in that setting, because the model must also account for the effect of age. We began by considering the multistage Weibull model, because it was used by EPA in its 1988 evaluation of the skin-cancer data. As an alternative, we considered Poisson regression models, with age and exposure allowed to enter the model with linear and quadratic terms as well as interaction terms. We found that a Poisson model with a quadratic term in age and a linear term in exposure fitted the data well (using likelihood-based criteria) and yielded estimated low-dose risks that were substantially higher than those based on the multistage Weibull model. It is important to note that "exposure" in our models referred to concentration of arsenic in the drinking water. A good argument could also be made for using cumulative exposure instead. Although interaction terms did not improve our model (suggesting that concentration in the drinking water might be an appropriate basis for modeling), further exploration of this issue is needed.

The subcommittee also explored analyses that incorporated data on Taiwanese-wide cancer rates. One approach simply included the Taiwanese-wide data as additional data for the Poisson regression analysis. A second approach was based on SMRs, which can also be analyzed using Poisson regression but replacing person-years at risk with the expected numbers of cancer deaths, estimated using the baseline comparison population. Because there are advantages and disadvantages of all the approaches discussed here, the subcommittee repeated the analysis using several feasible assumptions before drawing conclusions. In the case of bladder cancer in males, the Poisson regression analyses yielded fairly consistent results, regardless of whether baseline data were incorporated into the analysis.

As an alternative to model-based estimates of risk at low doses, the subcommittee explored methods based on point-of-departure methods discussed in the 1996 draft EPA guidelines for carcinogen risk assessment. As expected, we found that using this method gave much more consistent low-dose risk estimates across a wide range of dose-response models. Indeed, the estimated points of departure for male bladder cancer were all around 400 ppb (±50 ppb), which yields a margin of exposure of only 8 with respect to the current MCL.

Finally, some factors should be noted that might affect assessment of risk in Taiwan or extrapolation to the United States but could not be taken into account quantitatively in this chapter. These factors include poor nutrition and low selenium concentrations in Taiwan, genetic and cultural characteristics, and arsenic intake from food.

RECOMMENDATIONS

Ideally, risk assessment for arsenic in drinking water would be based on a well-designed and well-executed epidemiological study involving individual exposure assessment. In the absence of such a study, however, ecological data might be the only choice. Although such data can provide a basis for risk assessment, it is important to keep in mind the potential for bias due to confounding and measurement error. Therefore, the subcommittee recommends that several analyses be conducted to assess the sensitivity of the results to model choice, particular subsets of data, and the way that exposure concentrations are grouped together.

Although the subcommittee has not tried to perform a definitive risk assessment, it has used data on bladder-cancer rates for the 42 villages in the arsenic endemic region of Taiwan to illustrate statistical issues that arise in this context. For the actual risk assessment, the subcommittee recommends conducting analyses based on bladder, lung, and other internal cancers. Specifically, separate analyses should be conducted for each of those cancers, as well as for the combined end point corresponding to those three cancer types.

Model selection can be particularly important in settings where one needs to account for both age and dose effects. The subcommittee found that the multistage Weibull model was sensitive to omitting various subsets of villages, as well as to the way that exposure was grouped. Although not presented in this chapter, limited sensitivity analyses suggest that generalized linear models (GLMs) might be more robust. In particular, the male bladder-cancer data seemed to be well described by a GLM that included a linear dose and quadratic age effect, although we did not explore additive models. Models based on SMRs could also be used and might be advantageous in the context of being less sensitive to how age is characterized in the modeling process. The SMR approach can also provide added precision by incorporating external information on baseline cancer death rates. However, care is needed in choosing an appropriate comparison population. Regardless of the data set that is ultimately used for the arsenic risk assessment, the subcommittee recommends that a range of feasible modeling approaches be explored. The final calculated risk should be supported by a range of analyses over a fairly broad feasible range of assumptions. Performing a sensitivity analysis ensures that the conclusions do not rely heavily on any one particular assumption.

REFERENCES

Breslow N.E., and N.E. Day. 1988. Statistical Methods in Cancer Research:

The Design and Analysis of Cohort Studies, Vol. 2. Oxford, U.K.: Oxford University Press.

Brown, K.G., H.R. Guo, T.L. Kuo, and H.L. Greene. 1997. Skin cancer and inorganic arsenic: Uncertainty status of risk. Risk Anal. 17:37-42.

Carroll, R.J., and L.A. Stefanski. 1990. Approximate quasi-likelihood estimation in models with surrogate predictors. J. Am. Stat. Assoc. 85:652-663.

Carroll R.J., D. Rappert, and L.A. Stefanski. 1995. Measurement Error in Nonlinear Models. New York: Chapman & Hall. 336 pp.

Chen, C.J., T.L. Kuo, and M.M. Wu. 1988. Arsenic and cancers [letter]. Lancet i:414-415.

Chen, C.J., C.W. Chen, M.M. Wu, and T.L. Kuo. 1992. Cancer potential in liver, lung, bladder and kidney due to ingested inorganic arsenic in drinking water. Br. J. Cancer 66:888-892.

Cox, D.R., and D. Oakes. 1984. Analysis of Survival Data. New York: Chapman & Hall.

Crump, K.S. 1984. A new method for determining allowable daily intakes. Fundam. Appl. Toxicol. 4:854-871.

Efron, B., and R.J. Tibshirani. 1993. An Introduction to the Bootstrap. New York: Chapman & Hall.

EPA (U.S. Environmental Protection Agency). 1988. Special Report on Inorganic Arsenic: Skin Cancer; Nutritional Essentiality. EPA 625/3-87/013. U.S. Environmental Protection Agency, Risk Assessment Forum, Washington, D.C.

EPA (U.S. Environmental Protection Agency). 1996. Proposed guidelines for carcinogen risk assessment. Notice. Fed. Regist. 61(79):17959-18011.

Gart, J.J., D. Krewski, P.N. Lee, R.E. Tarone, and J. Wahrendorf. 1986. Statistical Methods in Cancer Research. Vol. 3: The Design and Analysis of Long-Term Animal Experiments, J. Wahrendorf, ed. Oxford, U.K.: Oxford University Press.

Geyer, C.J. 1991. Constrained maximum likelihood exemplified by isotonic convex logistic regression. J. Am. Stat. Assoc. 86:717-724.

Greenland, S., and H. Morgenstern. 1989. Ecological bias, confounding and effect modification. Int. J. Epidemiol. 18:269-274.

Greenland, S. and J. Robins. 1994. Invited commentary: Ecologic studies-biases, misconceptions, and counter-examples. Am. J. Epidemiol. 139:747-760.

Guess, H. A., and K.S. Crump. 1978. Maximum likelihood estimation of dose-response functions subject to absolutely monotonic constraints. Ann. Stat. 6:101-111.

Holland, C.D., and R.L. Sielken, Jr. 1993. Quantitative Cancer Modeling and Risk Assessment. Englewood Cliffs, N.J.: Prentice-Hall.

Hopenhayn-Rich, C., M.L. Biggs, A. Fuchs, R. Bergoglio, E.E. Tello, H. Nicolli, and A.H. Smith. 1996. Bladder cancer mortality associated with arsenic in drinking water in Argentina. Epidemiology 7:117-124.

Hopenhayn-Rich C., M.L. Biggs, and A.H. Smith. 1998. Lung and kidney cancer mortality associated with arsenic in drinking water in Córdoba, Argentina. Int. J. Epidemiol. 27:561-569.

Laird, N., and D. Olivier. 1981. Covariance analysis of censored survival data using log-linear analysis techniques. J. Am. Stat. Assoc. 76:231-240.

NCHS (National Center for Health Statistics). 1998. Vital Statistics of the United States, 1994, Preprint, Vol. 2, Mortality, Pt. A, Sec. 6 Life Tables. National Center for Health Statistics, Hyattsville, Md.

NRC (National Research Council). 1991. Environmental Epidemiology. Washington, D.C.: National Academy Press.

Prentice, R.L., and L. Sheppard. 1995. Aggregate data studies of disease risk factors. Biometrika 82:113-125.

Self, S.G., and K.Y. Liang. 1987. Asymptotic properties of maximum likelihood estimators and likelihood ratio tests under nonstandard conditions. J. Am. Stat. Assoc. 82:605-610.

Smith, A.H., and D.S. Sharp. 1985. A standardized benchmark approach to the use of cancer epidemiology data for risk assessment. Toxicol. Ind. Health 1:205-212.

Smith, A.H., C. Hopenhayn-Rich, M.N. Bates, H.M. Goeden, I. Hertz-Picciotto, H. Duggan, R. Wood, M. Kosnett, and M.T. Smith. 1992. Cancer risks from arsenic in drinking water. Environ. Health Perspect. 97:259-67.

Smith, A.H., M. Goycolea, R. Haque, and M.L. Biggs. 1998. Marked increase in bladder and lung cancer mortality in a region of northern Chile due to arsenic in drinking water. Am. J. Epidemiol. 147:660-669.

Tseng, W.P., H.M. Chu, and S.W. How. 1968. Prevalence of skin cancer in an endemic area of chronic arsenicism in Taiwan. J. Natl. Cancer Inst. 40:453-463.

Wright, C., P. Lopipero, and A.H. Smith. 1997. Meta analysis and risk assessment. Pp. 28-63 in Topics in Environmental Epidemiology, K. Steenland and D.A. Savitz, eds. New York: Oxford University Press.

Wu, M.M., T.L. Kuo, Y.H. Hwang, and C.J. Chen. 1989. Dose-response relation between arsenic concentration in well water and mortality from cancers and vascular diseases. Am. J. Epidemiol. 130:1123-1232.

11

Risk Characterization

IN its Statement of Task to the subcommittee, EPA requested guidance regarding "the adequacy of the current EPA maximum contaminant levels (MCLs) and ambient-water-quality-criteria (AWQC) values for protecting human health in the context of stated EPA policy. . . ." EPA's stated policy in setting MCLs for known human carcinogens has the "goal of ensuring that the maximum risk at the MCL falls within the 10^{-4} to 10^{-6} range that the agency considers protective of the public health, therefore achieving the overall purpose of the SDWA (Safe Drinking Water Act)" (EPA 1992). EPA has not requested, nor has the subcommittee endeavored to provide, a formal risk assessment for arsenic in drinking water. However, the subcommittee believes it can provide EPA with an up-to-date summary appraisal of two key elements of the risk-assessment process—hazard identification and dose response—that qualitatively, if not quantitatively, address the protective nature of the current MCL.

As the subcommittee discussed in detail elsewhere in this report, there is sufficient evidence from human epidemiological studies in Taiwan, Chile, and Argentina to conclude that ingestion of arsenic in drinking water poses a hazard of cancer of the lung and bladder, in addition to cancer of the skin. Overt noncancer effects of chronic arsenic ingestion have been detected at arsenic doses on the order of 0.01 mg/kg per day and higher. Of the noncancer effects, cutaneous manifestations of exposure have been studied most widely. No human studies of sufficient statistical power or scope have examined whether consumption of arsenic in drinking water at the current MCL (approximately 0.001 mg/kg per day) results in an increased incidence of cancer or noncancer effects. Therefore, a characterization of the risk that exists at the current MCL must rely on extrapolation by using observed epidemiological findings, experimental data on mode-of-action-related end points, and available information regarding the anticipated variability in human susceptibility.

At present, studies from the arsenic endemic area of Taiwan continue to provide the best available empirical human data for use in assessing the dose-response relationship for arsenic-induced cancer. The current state of knowledge is insufficient to reliably apply a biologically based model to those data. In accordance with EPA's "Proposed Guidelines for Carcinogen Risk Assessment" (EPA 1996), the subcommittee reviewed modes of action based on markers of tumor response and on available data that can determine the shape of the dose-response curve in the range of extrapolation. As discussed in Chapter 7, the several modes of action that are considered most plausible would lead to a dose-response curve that exhibits sublinear characteristics at some undetermined region in the low-dose range. Nonetheless, in the context of its task, the subcommittee considered the magnitude of the likely cancer risks within the range of human exposure at approximately the current MCL.

In vitro studies of the genotoxic effect of submicromolar concentrations of arsenite on human and animal cells and one study of bladder-cell micronuclei in humans with arsenic concentrations of 57 to 137 μg/L in urine indicate that perturbations in cellular function related to plausible modes of carcinogenesis might be operating at arsenic exposure concentrations associated with the current MCL. The subcommittee believes that those data and the confidence with which they can be linked to arsenic-induced neoplasia are insufficient to determine the shape of the dose-response curve between the point of departure and the current MCL. The subcommittee also finds that existing scientific knowledge regarding the pattern of arsenic metabolism and disposition across this dose range does not establish mechanisms that mitigate neoplastic effects. In light of all the uncertainties on mode of action, the current evidence does not meet EPA's stated criteria (EPA 1996) for departure from the default assumption of linearity in this range of extrapolation.

In Chapters 2 and 10, the subcommittee reviewed the strengths and limitations of the Taiwanese data. Chapter 10 also discussed the implications of applying different statistical models to the Taiwanese internal-cancer data for the purpose of characterizing cancer risk at the current MCL in the United States. With respect to EPA's 1988 risk assessment for arsenic-induced skin cancer in which the multistage Weibull model was used, a sensitivity analysis, within the limits of the available data, suggests that misclassification arising from the ecological-study design and the grouping of exposures would likely have only a modest impact on EPA's risk estimates. Sensitivity analyses applied to male bladder-cancer risk estimated by the multistage Weibull model had a greater impact on results. However, a more stable and reliable fit was provided by Poisson regression models that characterized the log relative risk as a linear function of exposure and a quadratic function of age. For male bladder cancer, a straight-line extrapolation from the 1% point of departure (LED$_1$) yielded a risk at the MCL of 1 to 1.5 per 1,000. Considering the data on bladder and lung cancer in both sexes noted in the studies in Chapter 4, a similar approach for all cancers could easily result in a combined cancer risk on the order of 1 in 100. It is also instructive to note that daily arsenic ingestion at the MCL, approximately 100 μg in adults, provides a margin of exposure less than 10.

As discussed in Chapter 8, the subcommittee recognizes that human susceptibility to the adverse effects of chronic arsenic exposure is likely to vary based on genetics, sex, and other possible factors. Some factors, such as poor nutrition and arsenic intake from food, might affect assessment of risk in Taiwan or extrapolation of results in the United States.

Upon assessing the available evidence, it is the subcommittee's consensus that the current EPA MCL for arsenic in drinking water of 50 μg/L does not achieve EPA's goal for public health protection and therefore requires downward revision as promptly as possible.

REFERENCES

EPA (U.S. Environmental Protection Agency). 1988. Special Report on Ingested Inorganic Arsenic: Skin Cancer; Nutritional Essentiality. EPA 625/3-87/013. U.S. Environmental Protection Agency, Risk Assessment Forum, Washington, D.C.

EPA (U.S. Environmental Protection Agency). 1992. Drinking water; national primary drinking water regulations—synthetic organic chemicals and inorganic chemicals; national primary drinking water regulations implementation. Fed. Regist. 57(138):31797.

EPA (U.S. Environmental Protection Agency). 1996. Proposed guidelines for carcinogen risk assessment. Notice. Fed. Regist. 61(79):17959-18011.

Addendum to Chapter 9

Experimental Conditions for Nutritional Studies with Arsenic

EXPERIMENTS designed to induce deficiencies of trace elements in animals with very low requirements depend on strict control of contamination from diet, water, air, and caging (Smith and Schwarz 1967). Proteins and salts furnishing macrominerals are the major sources of dietary contaminants. Careful selection, backed by analysis, is routinely applied to the ingredients; the latter might have to be further purified by recrystallization or other means. Drinking water is of the highest attainable purity and is constantly monitored with resistance measurements. Animals are housed in plastic cages that are often isolated in laminar-flow hoods. These conditions of an "ultraclean environment" make it necessary to supply all essential micronutrients as supplements in an acceptable balance. Such complex diets have their own problems of contamination. Contamination from protein sources can be avoided by acid washing, by substituting chemically pure amino acid mixtures or by using ruminant animal species that can synthesize much of their protein needs from chemically pure urea.

RATS AND CHICKS

The animals are raised in plastic cages. In the earlier experiments, the cages were kept in laminar-flow hoods, but the extra protection was later found to be unnecessary when the arsenic content of the diets was consistently less than 20 ng/g. All ingredients are of the highest obtainable purity, but some sources of minerals, especially of potassium, calcium, and phosphate, require additional purification. The composition of representative diets, fed ad libitum, is given in Table A9-1.

TABLE A9-1 Composition of Representative Diets for Rats and Chicks[a]

Ingredient	Rat Diet (g/kg)	Chick Diet (g/kg)
Milk powder		250
Casein, high protein	200	150
Ground corn, acid washed	673	230
Non-nutritive fiber		50
Dextrose, anhydrous		142.5
Corn oil		100
Soybean oil	70	
CaCo$_3$	15	14
KH$_2$PO$_4$	10	4
Choline bitartrate	2.5	

A vitamin mix in cornstarch and a mineral mix in dextrose was added to the rat diet to furnish all known miconutrient requirements. The chick diet was slightly different to meet requirements of that species.

Vitamins added to diet: (mg/kg): Niacin (30); d-pantothenic acid calcium (16); pyridoxin HCl (7); thiamin HCl (6); riboflavin (6); folic acid (2); d-biotin (0.2); vitamin B$_{12}$ (0.02); d,l-α-tocopherol acetate (120); retinyl palmitate (16); vitamin D$_3$ (2.5); vitamin K$_1$ (0.75).

Trace elements added to diet: (mg/kg): CaHPO$_4$ (1,265); K$_2$SO$_4$ (1,632); CaCl$_2$.2H$_2$O (1,000); Na$_2$CO$_3$ (1,500); Mg(C$_2$H$_3$O$_2$)$_2$.4H$_2$O (3,600); NaSiO$_3$.9H$_2$O (254); ferric citrate (220); zinc carbonate (58); manganese carbonate (22); copper acetate (11); KIO$_3$ (0.35); Na$_2$SeO$_4$ (0.36 mg/kg); NH$_4$MO$_7$O$_{24}$.4H$_2$O (0.37); CrK(SO$_4$)$_2$.12 H$_2$O (9.6); H$_3$BO$_3$ (2.9); NaF (2.2); NiCO$_3$ (2.2); SnO (0.25); NH$_4$VO$_3$ (0.46).

[a]Data from Nielsen et al. 1978; Nielsen 1980; Uthus et al. 1983; Uthus 1992.

GOATS AND MINIPIGS

The animals are kept in plastic-lined wooden cages with cellulose as bedding material. An estimated 100 g per day of cellulose (arsenic at less than 15 ng/g) is eaten by goats. Cellulose contributes to their energy intake and dilutes the arsenic content from less than 35 ng/g in the semisynthetic diet to less than 20 ng/g in the total. Table A9-2 gives the composition of the rations fed ad libitum to both species.

TABLE A9-2 Composition of Representative Diets for Goats and Minipigs[a]

Ingredient	Goat Diet (g/kg)	Minipig Diet (g/kg)
Potato starch	483	570
Beet sugar	320	147
Casein	100	200
Urea	30	
Sunflower oil	30	20
$CaCO_3$	10	10
KH_2PO_4	13.4	22

Micronutrients added to goat diet: NaCl (3.5 g); $Al_2(SO_4)_3$ (2 g); MgO (2.2 g); K_2SO_4 (3.5 g); $ZnSO_4.7H_2O$ (0.5g); $FeSO_4.7H_2O$ (0.45 g); $MnSO_4.7H_2O$ (0.4 g); S (0.35 g); $LiCO_3$ (106 mg); $CuSO_4.5H_2O$ (40 mg); KBr (30 mg); $Ni_2SO_4.7H_2O$ (34 mg); $Cr_2(SO_4)_3.18H_2O$ (6 mg); $(NH_4)VO_3$ (4.6 mg); NaF (2.2 mg); $NaWO_4.H_2O$ (1.8 mg); KJ (1.0 mg); $(NH_4)_6Mo_7O_{24}.4H_2O$ (0.92 mg); SeO_2 (0.8 mg); $CoSO_4.7H_2O$ (0.8 mg); $CdCl_2.H_2O$ (0.36 mg); vitamin A (20 mg); vitamin D_3 (4 mg); vitamin E (200 mg).

Micronutrients added to minipig diet: $MgSO_4.7H_2O$ (5.0 g); NaCl (5.2 g); K_2SO_4 (12.4 g); $FeSO_4.7H_2O$ (0.5 g); $MnSO_4.4H_2O$ (0.25 g); $ZnSO_4.7H_2O$ (50 mg); $CuSO_4.5H_2O$ (40 mg); $Ni_2SO_4.7H_2O$ (48 mg); $NaHSO_3$ (1.6 mg); $Ni_2SO_4.7H_2O$ (34 mg); $Cr_2(SO_4)_3.18H_2O$ (6 mg); KI (0.6 mg); $CoSO_4.7H_2O$ (0.5 mg); $NaWO_4.2H_2O$ (1.8 mg); NaF (2.2 mg); KBr (30 mg); $(NH_4)_6Mo_7O_{24}.4H_2O$ (0.92 mg); choline (2 g); vitamin C (80 mg); vitamin E (100 mg); Ca pantothenate (80 mg); Niacin (80 mg); vitamin E (20 mg); vitamin D (40 mg); vitamin B_1 (4 mg); vitamin B_2 (6 mg); vitamin B_6 (4 mg); vitamin B_{12} (0.05 mg); folic acid (2 mg); ethoxyquinolin (200 mg).

[a]Data from Anke 1986, 1991; Anke et al. 1976.

REFERENCES

Anke, M. 1986. Arsenic. Pp. 347-372 in Trace Elements in Human and Animal Nutrition, Vol. 2, 5th Ed., W. Mertz, ed. Orlando, Fla.: Academic.

Anke, M. 1991. The essentiality of ultra trace elements for reproduction and pre-and postnatal development. Pp. 119-144 in Trace Elements in Nutrition of Children—II, R.K. Chandra, ed. New York: Raven.

Anke, M., M. Grün, and M. Partschefeld. 1976. The essentiality of arsenic for animals. Pp. 403-409 in Trace Substances in Environmental Health—X, Proceedings of the University of Missouri's Tenth Annual Conference on Trace Substances in Environmental Health, D.D. Hemphill, ed. Columbia, Mo.: University of Missouri Press.

Nielsen, F.H. 1980. Evidence of the essentiality of arsenic, nickel, and vanadium and their possible nutritional significance. Pp. 157-172 in Advances in Nutritional Research, Vol. 9, H.H. Draper, ed. New York: Plenum.

Nielsen, F.H., D.R. Myron, and E.O. Uthus. 1978. Newer trace elements—Vanadium (V) and arsenic (As) deficiency signs and possible metabolic roles. Pp. 244-247 in Trace Element Metabolism in Man and Animals, Vol. 3, M. Kirchgessner, ed. Freising-Weihenstephan, Germany: Technische Universitat Munchen

Uthus, E.O. 1992. Evidence for arsenic essentiality. Environ. Geochem. Health 14:55-58.

Uthus, E.O., W.E. Cornatzer, and F.H. Nielsen. 1983. Consequences of arsenic deprivation in laboratory animals. Pp. 173-189 in Arsenic: Industrial, Biomedical, Environmental Perspectives, W.H. Lederer and R.J. Fensterheim, eds. New York: Van Nostrand Reinhold.

Smith, J.C., and K. Schwarz. 1967. A controlled environment system for new trace element deficiencies. J. Nutr. 93:182-188.

Addendum to Chapter 10

TABLE A10-1 Internal Cancer Data from Arsenic-Exposure Studies Conducted in Taiwan Region Endemic to Blackfoot Disease

TABLE A10-1 Internal Cancer Data from Arsenic-Exposure Studies Conducted in Taiwan Region Endemic to Blackfoot Disease[a]

Village	No. of Wells	Arsenic Concentration, ppm	Median	Person-Years		Bladder		Lung		Liver	
				M	F	M	F	M	F	M	F
3-H	1	0.010	0.010	4,159	4,043	1	6	3	1	3	5
2-I	1	0.011	0.011	3,529	3,194	0	0	0	0	0	1
0-G	5	0.010, 0.010, 0.030, 0.259, 0.770	0.030	5,388	4,861	3	2	3	3	4	5
3-5	1	0.032	0.032	7,851	7,033	3	3	5	2	6	2
3-N	1	0.032	0.032	2,689	2,392	4	3	1	1	3	1
4-7	1	0.042	0.042	10,629	10,227	0	0	4	0	0	0
6-A	1	0.045	0.045	7,716	6,820	0	0	1	1	0	0
0-J	2	0.020, 0.080	0.050	6,501	5,888	1	0	2	2	0	0
3-L	2	0.053, 0.058	0.056	6,238	5,094	3	4	3	0	5	7
4-D	1	0.060	0.060	10,107	9,227	1	2	1	1	1	2
3-P	1	0.065	0.065	6,574	5,927	0	0	3	0	2	5
6-C	1	0.073	0.073	12,767	11,937	0	1	2	0	2	0
4-8	1	0.080	0.080	11,307	10,332	1	0	3	1	2	2
0-O	1	0.100	0.100	6,895	6,392	0	0	2	2	3	1
0-E	5	0.010, 0.085, 0.110, 0.288, 0.686	0.110	5,753	5,310	6	3	3	1	4	5
0-I	7	0.020, 0.050, 0.110, 0.110, 0.190, 0.580, 0.590	0.110	4,249	3,833	0	2	1	3	3	2
4-N	2	0.073, 0.172	0.123	4,709	4,291	0	0	3	1	1	2
4-J	1	0.126	0.126	6,508	6,026	0	1	6	1	2	2
2-D	1	0.256	0.256	9,702	8,869	0	2	2	1	7	1
0-D	1	0.256	0.256	3,872	3,412	1	3	2	3	5	2
3-Q	6	0.148, 0.198, 0.242, 0.276, 0.291, 0.458	0.259	5,580	5,079	2	0	4	2	5	4
4-M	1	0.307	0.307	2,953	2,758	1	0	0	0	2	3
6-6	1	0.307	0.307	5,364	4,505	3	0	3	1	4	1
4-E	2	0.340, 0.360	0.350	3,942	3,586	0	0	1	0	0	0
4-L	2	0.310, 0.485	0.398	3,069	2,723	1	1	1	1	0	1

Village	No. of Wells	Arsenic Concentration, ppm	Median	Person-Years M	Person-Years F	Bladder M	Bladder F	Lung M	Lung F	Liver M	Liver F
4-F	11	0.120, 0.170, 0.229, 0.260, 0.260, 0.406, 0.469, 0.485, 0.595, 0.779, 0.819	0.406	4,482	3,886	2	3	1	0	5	1
3-I	1	0.448	0.448	4,551	4,259	2	3	5	1	4	3
5-G	1	0.467	0.467	3,179	5,298	7	5	2	3	7	1
4-P	1	0.504	0.504	5,843	5,397	1	0	1	1	1	1
0-H	5	0.050, 0.394, 0.520, 0.610, 1.752	0.520	4,390	4,313	3	2	4	0	4	5
4-I	47	0.020, 0.020, 0.030, 0.090, 0.100, 0.110, 0.120, 0.120, 0.160, 0.190, 0.230, 0.240, 0.250, 0.270, 0.270, 0.290, 0.290, 0.350, 0.370, 0.410, 0.430, 0.450, 0.510, 0.520, 0.540, 0.560, 0.660, 0.700, 0.730, 0.740, 0.760, 0.760, 0.780, 0.810, 0.810, 0.840, 0.840, 0.850, 0.850, 0.850, 0.870, 0.880, 0.900, 0.930, 0.940, 0.970	0.520	4,870	4,432	2	2	1	0	3	5
3-J	2	0.529, 0.529	0.529	8,454	8,689	4	8	3	1	6	5
3-S	2	0.480, 0.595	0.538	4,287	3,667	4	3	7	0	8	4
3-9	1	0.544	0.544	3,655	3,413	0	1	1	1	1	0
2-2	10	0.560, 0.580, 0.580, 0.590, 0.597, 0.600, 0.618, 0.620, 0.650, 0.704	0.599	9,059	7,977	2	2	9	5	8	5
4-G	2	0.620, 0.680	0.650	2,425	2,108	2	0	0	0	2	2
5-4	2	0.630, 0.735	0.683	3,155	2,983	1	1	2	1	5	2
2-M	2	0.435, 0.950	0.693	11,123	11,263	9	9	6	4	14	4
0-F	5	0.415, 0.660, 0.694, 0.720, 0.749	0.694	7,010	5,720	5	1	8	3	2	9
3-R	5	0.397, 0.440, 0.698, 0.750, 1.010	0.698	4,310	3,576	3	6	3	2	6	7
3-M	4	0.221, 0.329, 1.105, 1.411	0.717	5,815	4,877	0	1	2	0	0	0
2-N	3	0.560, 0.934, 0.960	0.934	8,341	8,342	7	10	8	2	4	4

[a]Data from Wu et al. 1989; Chen et al. 1992.

REFERENCES

Chen, C.J., C.W. Chen, M.M. Wu, and T.L. Kuo. 1992. Cancer potential in liver, lung, bladder and kidney due to ingested inorganic arsenic in drinking water. Br. J. Cancer 66:888-892.

Wu, M.M., T.L. Kuo, Y.H. Hwang, and C.J. Chen. 1989. Dose-response relation between arsenic concentration in well water and mortality from cancers and vascular diseases. Am. J. Epidemiol. 130:1123-1232.